The Spread of the Modern Central Bank and Global Cooperation

Central banks were not always as ubiquitous as they are today. Their functions were circumscribed, their mandates ambiguous, and their allegiances once divided. The interwar period saw the establishment of twenty-eight new central banks – most in what are now called emerging markets and developing economies. *The Spread of the Modern Central Bank and Global Cooperation: 1919–1939* provides a new account of their experience, explaining how these new institutions were established and how doctrinal knowledge was transferred. Combining synthetic analysis with national case studies, this book shows how institutional design and monetary practice were shaped by international organizations and leading central banks, which attached conditions to stabilization loans and dispatched "money doctors." It highlights how many of these arrangements fell through when central bank independence and the gold standard collapsed.

Barry Eichengreen is George C. Pardee and Helen N. Pardee Chair and Distinguished Professor of Economics and Political Science, University of California, Berkeley and Research Associate of the National Bureau of Economic Research and Research Fellow of the Centre for Economic Policy Research.

Andreas Kakridis is Assistant Professor of Economic History at Panteion University, Athens, Greece. He is also academic adviser to the Historical Archives of the Bank of Greece and a member of the Academic Council of the European Association for Banking and Financial History (*eabh*).

STUDIES IN MACROECONOMIC HISTORY

Series Editor: Michael D. Bordo, Rutgers University

Editors

Owen F. Humpage, *Federal Reserve Bank of Cleveland*
Christopher M. Meissner, *University of California, Davis*
Kris James Mitchener, *Santa Clara University*
David C. Wheelock, *Federal Reserve Bank of St. Louis*

The titles in this series investigate themes of interest to economists and economic historians in the rapidly developing field of macroeconomic history. The four areas covered include the application of monetary and finance theory, international economics, and quantitative methods to historical problems; the historical application of growth and development theory and theories of business fluctuations; the history of domestic and international monetary, financial, and other macroeconomic institutions; and the history of international monetary and financial systems. The series amalgamates the former Cambridge University Press series Studies in Monetary and Financial History and Studies in Quantitative Economic History.

Books in the Series

William A. Allen, *The Bank of England and the Government Debt: Operations in the Gilt-Edged Market, 1928–1972* (2019)

Eric Monnet, *Controlling Credit: Central Banking and the Planned Economy in Postwar France, 1948–1973* (2018)

Laurence M. Ball, *The Fed and Lehman Brothers: Setting the Record Straight on a Financial Disaster* (2018)

Rodney Edvinsson, Tor Jacobson, and Daniel Waldenström, Editors, *Sveriges Riksbank and the History of Central Banking* (2018)

Peter L. Rousseau and Paul Wachtel, Editors, *Financial Systems and Economic Growth: Credit, Crises, and the Regulation from the 19th Century to the Present* (2017)

Ernst Baltensperger and Peter Kugler, *Swiss Monetary History since the Early 19th Century* (2017)

Øyvind Eitrheim, Jan Tore Klovland, and Lars Fredrik Øksendal, *A Monetary History of Norway, 1816–2016* (2016)

Jan Fredrik Qvigstad, *On Central Banking* (2016)

Michael D. Bordo, Øyvind Eitrheim, Marc Flandreau, and Jan F. Qvigstad, Editors, *Central Banks at a Crossroads: What Can We Learn from History?* (2016)

Michael D. Bordo and Mark A. Wynne, Editors, *The Federal Reserve's Role in the Global Economy: A Historical Perspective* (2016)

Owen F. Humpage, Editor, *Current Federal Reserve Policy Under the Lens of Economic History: Essays to Commemorate the Federal Reserve System's Centennial* (2015)

Michael D. Bordo and William Roberds, Editors, *The Origins, History, and Future of the Federal Reserve: A Return to Jekyll Island* (2013)

Michael D. Bordo and Ronald MacDonald, Editors, *Credibility and the International Monetary Regime: A Historical Perspective* (2012)

Robert L. Hetzel, *The Great Recession: Market Failure or Policy Failure?* (2012)

Tobias Straumann, *Fixed Ideas of Money: Small States and Exchange Rate Regimes in Twentieth-Century Europe* (2010)

Forrest Capie, *The Bank of England: 1950s to 1979* (2010)

Aldo Musacchio, *Experiments in Financial Democracy: Corporate Governance and Financial Development in Brazil, 1882–1950* (2009)

Claudio Borio, Gianni Toniolo, and Piet Clement, Editors, *The Past and Future of Central Bank Cooperation* (2008)

Robert L. Hetzel, *The Monetary Policy of the Federal Reserve: A History* (2008)

Aurel Schubert, *The Credit-Anstalt Crisis of 1931* (1992)

Trevor J. O. Dick and John E. Floyd, *Canada and the Gold Standard: Balance of Payments Adjustment under Fixed Exchange Rates, 1871–1913* (1992)

Kenneth Mouré, *Managing the Franc Poincaré: Economic Understanding and Political Constraint in French Monetary Policy, 1928–1936* (1991)

David C. Wheelock, *The Strategy and Consistency of Federal Reserve Monetary Policy, 1924–1933* (1991)

The Spread of the Modern Central Bank and Global Cooperation

1919–1939

Edited by

BARRY EICHENGREEN
University of California, Berkeley

ANDREAS KAKRIDIS
Bank of Greece and Panteion University, Athens

CAMBRIDGE
UNIVERSITY PRESS

Shaftesbury Road, Cambridge CB2 8EA, United Kingdom

One Liberty Plaza, 20th Floor, New York, NY 10006, USA

477 Williamstown Road, Port Melbourne, VIC 3207, Australia

314–321, 3rd Floor, Plot 3, Splendor Forum, Jasola District Centre, New Delhi – 110025, India

103 Penang Road, #05–06/07, Visioncrest Commercial, Singapore 238467

Cambridge University Press is part of Cambridge University Press & Assessment, a department of the University of Cambridge.

We share the University's mission to contribute to society through the pursuit of education, learning and research at the highest international levels of excellence.

www.cambridge.org
Information on this title: www.cambridge.org/9781009367547

DOI: 10.1017/9781009367578

First published 2023

A catalogue record for this publication is available from the British Library.

A Cataloging-in-Publication data record for this book is available from the Library of Congress

ISBN 978-1-009-36754-7 Hardback
ISBN 978-1-009-36755-4 Paperback

Contents

ix

Figures

Tables

Editors and Contributors

Roumen Avramov is member of the Academic Advisory Council of the Centre for Advanced Studies Sofia (CAS) and served as member of the Board of Governors of the Bulgarian National Bank (BNB) (1997–2002). His publications are in the fields of economic history, history of economic ideas, monetary economics, business cycles, and economics of interethnic conflicts. He is the author of *Communal Capitalism: Reflections on the Bulgarian Economic Past* (vols. 1–3) (2007, in Bulgarian) and editor of eight volumes (1999–2009) with documents about the history of the BNB.

G. Balachandran is Professor of International History and Politics and Co-Director of the Albert Hirschman Centre on Democracy at the Graduate Institute of International and Development Studies, Geneva. He is currently researching money, sovereignty, and statehood in the Indian Ocean world. His books include *John Bullion's Empire: British Gold Problems and India between the Wars* (1996, 2013, 2015); *Globalizing Labour? Indian Seafarers and World Shipping, c. 1870–1945* (2012); and the *Reserve Bank of India, 1951–1967* (1998). He has also edited *India and the World Economy, c. 1850–1950* (2002), and is Managing Editor of the *Indian Economic and Social History Review.*

Patricia Clavin is Professor of Modern History at Oxford University and Fellow of History at Worcester College. Her book *Securing the World Economy: The Reinvention of the League of Nations* (2013) won the British Academy medal in 2015, and she recently coedited *Internationalisms. A Twentieth-Century History* (2017) with Glenda

Sluga. She is currently working on the ideas and practices of human security in the twentieth century, and is a project director of the Oxford Martin School program, Changing Global Orders.

Piet Clement holds a PhD in History from Leuven University, Belgium, and has been the archivist and historian of the Bank for International Settlements in Basel, Switzerland since 1995. He recently contributed to *Promoting Global Monetary and Financial Stability: The Bank for International Settlements after Bretton Woods, 1973–2020* (2020).

Barry Eichengreen is George C. Pardee and Helen N. Pardee Chair and Distinguished Professor of Economics and Professor of Political Science at the University of California, Berkeley. He is a research associate of the National Bureau of Economic Research and research fellow of the Centre for Economic Policy Research. In 1997–1998 he was senior policy advisor at the International Monetary Fund. He is a fellow of the American Academy of Arts and Sciences, distinguished fellow of the American Economic Association, corresponding fellow of the British Academy, and a life fellow of the Cliometric Society. He is a regular monthly columnist for Project Syndicate.

Juan Flores Zendejas is Head of the Paul Bairoch Institute of Economic History and Associate Professor at the Department of History, Economics, and Society of the University of Geneva. His research focuses on the history of financial crises and sovereign defaults, the history of international financial organizations, and the history of international monetary cooperation. He has extensively published in journals such as *International Organization*, the *European Review of Economic History*, the *Journal of Economic History*, and the *Economic History Review*. He coedited (with Pierre Pénet), *Sovereign Debt Diplomacies: Rethinking Sovereign Debt from Colonial Empires to Hegemony* (2021).

Harold James is Claude and Lore Kelly Professor in European Studies at Princeton University and official historian of the International Monetary Fund. Before moving to Princeton in 1986, he was a fellow of Peterhouse, Cambridge, for eight years. His books include *The German Slump* (1986), *The End of Globalization* (2001), *Family Capitalism* (2006), and *The War of Words: A Glossary of Globalization (2021)*.

Andreas Kakridis is Assistant Professor of Economic History at Panteion University, Athens, Greece and academic adviser to the Historical Archives of the Bank of Greece. He specializes in the economic history and history of economics in modern Greece, particularly with regard to money and banking, public finance, and economic development. His most recent book is the biography of a prominent Greek central banker and statesman, *Kyriakos Varvaressos: Biography as Economic History* (2017).

Hans Kernbauer studied business management and economics in Vienna. After serving as an assistant professor at the Institute for Advanced Studies, in Vienna, he worked for the central bank of Austria on the history of Austrian monetary policy. Later, he held various jobs in financial institutions before he became research associate at the Institute for Economic and Social History of the Vienna University of Economics and Business, where he taught economic history (2014–2019). He is the author (with Clemens Jobst) of *The Quest for Stable Money: Central Banking in Austria 1816–2016* (2016).

Jakub Kunert studied history and archival science in the Faculty of Philosophy and Arts of Charles University, Prague. He joined the Archive of the Czech National Bank in 2004 as senior archivist and has been chief archivist since 2009. He is a member of the Academic Council of the European Association for Banking and Financial History (*eabh*). He is also the representative of the Czech National Bank in the European System of Central Banks (ESCB) Information Management Network and ESCB Museum Network. His research focuses mainly on the history of central banking in Czechoslovakia.

Cecylia Leszczyńska is an assistant professor of economic history at the Faculty of Economic Sciences, University of Warsaw. She was advisor to the president of the Central Statistical Office (2008–2011) and served on the editorial board of *The History of Poland in Numbers*. She has published articles and books on the economic history of Poland, Polish central banking, and historical statistics. Among her major publications are *History of Poland in Numbers. Poland in Europe* (2014); *An Outline History of Polish Central Banking* (2011); and 'Urbanization and GDP Per Capita: New Data and Results for the Polish Lands, 1790–1910', *Historical Methods*, no. 4, 2019.

Gianandrea Nodari is a research associate at the Paul Bairoch Institute of Economic History, University of Geneva. He holds a PhD in History from El Colegio de México and was a postdoctoral fellow at the Library of Congress of Washington DC (2019–2020). He is the author of *'Putting Mexico on its Feet Again': The Kemmerer Mission in Mexico,*

1917–1931 (2019). His current research interests include the early evolution of central banks in Latin America and central bank cooperation during the interwar years.

Şevket Pamuk is retired Professor of Economics and Economic History at Bogaziçi (Bosporus) University, Istanbul. He is a leading economic historian and the author of many books and articles on Ottoman, Middle Eastern, and European economic history; in 2018, he published *Uneven Centuries: Economic History of Turkey since 1820*. Pamuk was president of the European Historical Economics Society (2003–2005), president of the Asian Historical Economics Society (2012–2014), and editor of *European Economic History Review* (2011–2014).

György Péteri is Professor Emeritus at the Department of History and Classical Studies, Norwegian University of Science and Technology, Trondheim. His publications include *Revolutionary Twenties: Essays on International Monetary and Financial Relations After World War I* (1995). He has researched and published widely on the twentieth-century European and Hungarian economy, science, and culture. He is currently finishing a book titled *Greed and Creed. The Everyday and Private Life of Communist Ruling Class*.

John Singleton is Emeritus Professor of Economic and Business History at Sheffield Hallam University, UK. He is the author of *Central Banking in the Twentieth Century* (2011) and is principal author of a commissioned history of the Reserve Bank of New Zealand. He has written extensively on trade, financial, and policy networks within the British Empire/Commonwealth in the twentieth century, especially those between New Zealand, Australia, and the United Kingdom.

Preface

Central banks are among the most prominent agents on the contemporary monetary and financial landscape. Their presence is taken for granted. It is, therefore, striking that as recently as a century ago they were absent from two-thirds of the world's countries. Where they existed, their functions were circumscribed, their mandates ambiguous, their allegiances divided.

In the 1920s and 1930s an unprecedented number of new central banks were established, most in what are now called emerging markets and developing economies. Some were founded in the wake of and response to the experience of wartime inflation. Others sprang up along with the creation of new states. All of them pledged allegiance to monetary cooperation and the international gold standard, with the goal of fostering credibility and confidence, and thereby gaining access to global financial flows.

This book provides a new account of their experience. It explains how these new institutions were established and how doctrinal knowledge, emphasizing the virtues of central bank independence and the gold standard, was transferred from countries with a longer history of central banking, while also highlighting the unforeseen and sometimes unfortunate consequences. It shows how institutional design and monetary practice were shaped by international organizations and leading central banks that attached conditions to their stabilization loans and dispatched 'money doctors' to treat monetary disfunction and gain disciples, not to mention financial business. It highlights how these arrangements came to grief in the 1930s, with the collapse of both central bank independence and the gold standard. It tracks the implications of the subsequent reaction, which rendered central banks less independent but also, paradoxically, more powerful.

For help in completing this volume, we are most grateful to the governor of the Bank of Greece, Professor Yannis Stournaras, who gave us an early opportunity to discuss the emergence of interwar central banks at a conference he hosted in Athens. Governor Stournaras and Panagiotis Panagakis, director of the Bank's cultural department, have been steadfast supporters of this project from the outset. We would also like to thank Christina Linardaki for her assistance in the preparation of the book's index, as well as our authors, for their contributions and for enduring several rounds of editing to arrive at what we hope is a volume that is more than just the sum of its parts.

PART I

GENERAL

1

Interwar Central Banks

A Tour d' Horizon

Barry Eichengreen and Andreas Kakridis

1.1 INTRODUCTION

Central banks are ubiquitous. Of the 195 sovereign states in the world today, 185 have delegated money issuance, monetary policy, oversight of the payment system, and lender-of-last-resort functions to specialized institutions known as central banks.[1] Their pronouncements make headlines. These send tremors through money and asset markets, whose reaction central banks seek to channel using forward guidance and other communication. Ever-growing lists of their functions have entered college textbooks, as have tales of their exploits in helping countries navigate global financial shoals.

Such has not always been the case. A century ago, nearly two-thirds of the world's sovereign states lacked a central bank (Figure 1.1). Central banking institutions then in existence commanded less authority. Their functions were circumscribed, their mandates ambiguous, their allegiances divided between multiple roles as commercial banks and appendages to the Treasury.

The key period of transition was the 1920s and 1930s. Between 1919 and 1939, twenty-eight new central banks were set up, most in what are now called emerging markets and developing economies. The studies collected in this volume examine the origins and early operation of these banks.[2]

---

[1] The definition implicit in this formulation is functional and cannot be applied uniformly or historically; many of today's central banks started with a subset of these functions. Capie et al. (1994: 5) bypass this hurdle by arguing that 'in one sense, we recognise [central banking] when we see it'.

[2] Of twenty-eight central banks established between 1919 and 1939, twenty-two are covered by the various country-specific case studies and comparative chapters in this volume.

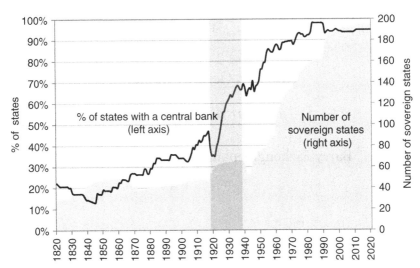

FIGURE 1.1 Sovereign states and central banks, 1820–2020
Source: See Appendix.

While an extensive literature documents the historical development of central banking in the now-advanced economies, the historical literature on central banking in emerging and developing countries, then and now, is more limited.[3] This imbalance deserves correction. Creating a central bank was seen as a key step in the process of modernization in late-developing economies. It was a step toward putting economic policy on a sound and stable footing and integrating emerging economies into the global system.

The list includes the Reserve Bank of India, even though India did not become a free nation until 1947 or adopt a constitution until 1950 (and thus is excluded from the inter-war data underlying Figure 1.1). Countries not considered in this volume are Estonia, Yugoslavia, Latvia, Lithuania, Albania, and Ethiopia; for recent literature in English, see Troitiño et al. (2019) on Estonia, Jeftic (2021) for Yugoslavia, Puriņš (2012) on Latvia, Ahmetaj (2017) on Albania, and Mauri (2011) on Ethiopia.

[3] Limited should not be misunderstood to mean non-existent. Holtfrerich et al. (1999) offer two chapters on central banks in emerging and developing countries. Contributions to Cottrell (1997) focus on Central and Eastern Europe. Maxfield (1998) covers the post-Second World War period, when central banks were set up differently in newly independent countries (also evident in our Figure 1.1). Earlier work includes Kirsch and Elkin (1932) and de Kock (1954), while very recent contributions include Jacome (2015) and Caldentey and Vernengo (2019). Distinct but related is scholarship on monetary management before the emergence of central banks (de Cecco, 1975; della Paolera and Taylor, 2001), and on so-called money doctors advising on the design of monetary institutions (Drake, 1989; Flandreau, 2003).

No sooner had the ink of newly drafted central bank statutes dried than the Great Depression swept across economies and political systems, putting new institutions to the test. Few interwar central banks successfully met the challenge. As a result of the political reaction to this failure, central banks became key agents in the Polanyian transition from the unfettered market system of the nineteenth century to the managed economy of the twentieth. In 1944, Karl Polanyi argued that the nineteenth-century combination of laissez-faire capitalism, unregulated labour markets, and the gold standard contained within it the seeds of this reaction, as popular opinion turned against the instability and inhumanity of market mechanisms (Polanyi, 1944). New central banks had been established in the 1920s in an effort to temper the operation of this system. When they fell short (Schenk and Straumann, 2016), the economic and political crisis of the 1930s brought a Polanyian reaction. Private banks of issue were nationalized. Central banks were enlisted in managing the economy in cooperation with other branches of government. This set the stage for their role in supporting import substitution in Latin America and central planning in Eastern Europe during and after the Second World War. The newly established central banks of the 1920s and 1930s thus were integrally involved in the pivotal economic developments of the mid-twentieth century.

The ideas underpinning both the spread of central banking and the subsequent reaction are introduced in Chapter 2. Chapters 3 and 4 then focus on the role of the League of Nations and the Bank of International Settlements. These two organizations promulgated international standards for the structure and conduct of central banking (best practice, if you will) and sought to foster international cooperation amongst these newly created monetary institutions. Part II of the volume turns to eight country studies and two chapters of greater geographical ambition, one on Latin America and one on the British Dominions. All chapters nevertheless provide readers with the necessary political and economic background before tackling the key questions that run through the entire volume. Under what circumstances was each new bank established? What was the role of domestic and international players and how did they impact the structure, mandate, and powers of the resulting institutions? The authors are careful to distinguish de facto and de jure independence, as well as compliance (or otherwise) with the so-called rules of the game, which extended beyond the rules and regulations associated with the operation of the gold standard. All country studies discuss the impact of the Great Depression: the specific challenges to each economy, the monetary policy response, the extent to which policy was conditioned by each bank's recent past, but also how it affected its future, not least by influencing the speed of economic recovery.

I.2 THE INTERWAR WAVE OF NEW CENTRAL BANKS

If not the father of *all* things, war was certainly the father of many of the new central banks of the 1920s. This was true of new states that emerged from the dissolution of the Habsburg, Ottoman, and Russian empires. It was equally true elsewhere, however, as old monetary arrangements were swept away and new banks were established.[4]

Table 1.1 lists, in chronological order, the twenty-eight new central banks established between 1919 and 1939. Most of these institutions received statutory independence and a mandate to defend the value of the currency in terms of gold or gold-convertible foreign exchange.[5] As Harold James explains in Chapter 2, with extensive references to German experience, independence was designed to mitigate risks of fiscal and financial dominance that had become apparent with wartime and post-war inflation.[6] This, in a nutshell, was the argument behind the interwar drive to establish new central banks, and why most were established with the primary objective of averting inflation and maintaining the gold standard.

This mantra gained broad international currency, not least through the efforts of a network of central bankers, financiers, civil servants, and

---

[4] Other well-known aspects of the war's financial legacy, such as the structural imbalances emanating from wartime shifts in producers, markets, and borders, the complications arising from reparations and inter-allied debt, the 1920–1 recession and countries' diverse roads to stabilization are not discussed in this introduction, which has a narrower focus. Needless to say, these developments influenced the new institutions. Feinstein et al. (1995) offer a succinct summary.

[5] This was the gold-exchange standard, which was meant to economize on scarce gold supplies; limits on the purchase of gold bullion to large quantities and the withdrawal of all gold coin from circulation were other aspects of the post-war gold standard (Eichengreen, 2019: 59).

[6] Insulated from political interference and operating at arm's length from business, central banks were designed to resist pressures to finance budget deficits and provide inflationary credits to the private sector. In modern parlance, central bank independence was expected to solve the problem of time-inconsistency by requiring commitment to monetary rules (Kydland and Prescott, 1977; Barro and Gordon, 1983). Despite its 'rediscovery' in the context of rational expectations, the underlying idea was hardly new, especially in post-war years. Historical parallels date back at least as far as the central banks of Norway, Denmark, and Austria-Hungary, which were established after the end of the Napoleonic wars (Capie et al. 1994: 5). For a discussion of the German experience with central bank independence since the nineteenth century, see Holtfrerich (1988).

TABLE 1.1 *Central banks established in the interwar years (in chronological order), 1919–1939*

	Country	Central bank	Year[1]	Interwar money doctors/foreign missions[2]
1	Yugoslavia	National Bank of the Kingdom of Serbs, Croats, and Slovenes	1920 [1884]	Harry Arthur Siepmann, 1927 Banque de France, 1931
2	South Africa	South African Reserve Bank	1920	Henry Strakosch, 1920* Edwin Kemmerer and Gerhard Vissering, 1924–5
3	Latvia	Bank of Latvia	1922	–
4	Lithuania	Bank of Lithuania	1922	–
5	Peru	Central Reserve Bank of Peru	1922 [1913]	W. W. Cumberland (gov't financial adviser, 1921–4*) Edwin Kemmerer, 1931
6	Austria	Austrian National Bank	1923 [1816]	LoN/Drummond Fraser, 1921; LoN/Arthur Salter, 1922*; LoN/Albert Janssen, 1923*; Francis Rodd (BIS) and Peter Bark (BoE), 1931; LoN/Carel Eliza ter Meulen and Otto Niemeyer, 1931. Advisers: Charles Schnyder von Wartensee (1923); Anton von Gijn (1924–6); Robert Ch. Kay (1926–9); Gijsbert W. J. Bruins (1931–2), and Maurice P. Frère (1932–6).
7	Colombia	Central Bank of Colombia	1923 [1905]	Edwin Kemmerer, 1923* and 1930
8	Australia	Commonwealth Bank	1924 [1920]	Ernest Harvey (BoE), 1927 Otto Niemeyer (BoE) and T. E. Gregory, 1930
9	Hungary	Hungarian National Bank	1924 [1878]	LoN/Arthur Salter and Joseph Avenol, 1923* LoN/Henry Strakosch, 1924* Advisers: Harry Arthur Siepmann (1924–6) and Henry J. Bruce (1931–6)

(continued)

TABLE 1.1 (continued)

	Country	Central bank	Year[1]	Interwar money doctors/foreign missions[2]
10	Poland	Bank of Poland	1924 [1918]	Edward Hilton Young, 1923–4* Edwin Kemmerer, 1925 and 1926 Adviser: Charles Dewey (1927–30)
11	Albania	National Bank of Albania	1925	LoN/Albert Calmès, 1922 LoN (indirectly)/ Mario Alberti, 1924–5* Adviser: Jan Doekes Hunger, 1923–4*
12	Chile	Central Bank of Chile	1925	Edwin Kemmerer, 1922, 1925,* and 1927 Adviser: Walter M. Van Deusen (1926–33)
13	Mexico	Bank of Mexico	1925	Edwin Kemmerer, 1917*
14	Estonia	Bank of Estonia	1926 [1919]	LoN/Joseph Avenol and Alexander Loveday, 1925* LoN/Albert-Édouard Janssen, 1926* Adviser: Walter James Franklin Williamson
15	Czechoslovakia	National Bank of Czechoslovakia	1926	–
16	Guatemala	Bank of Guatemala	1926	Edwin Kemmerer, 1919 and 1924
17	Ecuador	Central Bank of Ecuador	1927	John Hord (gov't financial adviser, 1922–6) Edwin Kemmerer, 1926–7* Adviser: Earl B. Schwulst (1927–8)
18	Bulgaria	Bulgarian National Bank	1928 [1885]	LoN/René Charron, 1926* LoN/Otto Niemeyer, 1927* Advisers: René Charron (1928–31), Jean Watteau (1931–2), Nicholas Koestner (1932–40)
19	Greece	Bank of Greece	1928 [1920]	LoN/Joseph Avenol, 1927* Adviser: Horace G. F. Finlayson (1928–37)

	Country	Central bank	Year[1]	Interwar money doctors/foreign missions[2]
20	Bolivia	Central Bank of Bolivia	1929 [1924]	Edwin Kemmerer, 1927* Adviser: Abraham F. Lindberg (1929–31)
21	Turkey	Central Bank of the Republic of Turkey	1930	Mr. Friedleb, 1927; Gerard Vissering, 1928*; Karl Mueller, 1929; Hjalmar Schacht, 1929*; Count Giuseppe Volpi, 1929*; Edwin Kemmerer, 1934
22	Ethiopia	Bank of Ethiopia	1931 [1906]	Everett Colson (adviser to H. Selassie, 1930–5)*
23	New Zealand	Reserve Bank of New Zealand	1933	Otto Niemeyer (BoE), 1930
24	Canada	Bank of Canada	1934	Lord Macmillan and Charles Addis (BoE), 1933*
25	El Salvador	Central Reserve Bank of El Salvador	1934	Frederick Francis Joseph Powell (BoE), 1934*
26	Argentina	Central Bank of Argentina	1935	Otto Niemeyer (BoE), 1934
27	India	Reserve Bank of India	1935	Hilton Young Commission/Henry Strakosch, 1926*
28	Venezuela	Central Bank of Venezuela	1939	Hermann Max (Central Bank of Chile), 1939*

1. Years in [brackets] refer to the year a predecessor bank acquired de jure monopoly of issue in the country; when no such [year] appears, the new central bank was the first one to exercise such monopoly.

2. Missions comprising several experts are identified solely by the official who headed them, with additional details provided in corresponding chapters or notes; institutional affiliations are also noted, when relevant. LoN stands for League of Nations, BoE is Bank of England, and BIS is the Bank of International Settlements. Missions with an * are considered important for the establishment of the central bank.

Sources and notes on individual countries in the Appendix.

academics (Meyer, 1970; Schuker, 2003; Marcussen, 2005). With missionary zeal the Bank of England encouraged the establishment of overseas clones of itself (Sayers, 1976: 201). Otto Niemeyer, senior Treasury official turned Bank adviser, was dispatched as money doctor to administer the appropriate medicine. Eager to check this British imperialism, the Banque de France launched missions to Romania and Poland.[7] The governor of the Federal Reserve Bank of New York, Benjamin Strong, shared Norman's suspicion of politicians and his vision of a global network of cooperating central banks (Chandler, 1958: 281–285) and for his part encouraged American money doctors to spread the gospel. The most prominent American money doctor, Edwin Kemmerer, advanced this vision of central banking in Latin America and elsewhere on behalf of New York financial circles (Seidel, 1972; Drake, 1989; Eichengreen, 1989; Helleiner, 2009).

Multilateral institutions such as the League of Nations also helped to disseminate new monetary ideology. Patricia Clavin (Chapter 3) explains how new ideas about central banking dovetailed with the League's desire to limit state agency and relegate policy decisions to an international, rules-based depoliticized sphere. Intergovernmental conferences in Brussels in 1920 (under the League's auspices) and Genoa in 1922 called on governments to return to the gold standard and establish central banks free of political control and open to cooperation. An Economic and Financial Organization (EFO) was set up within the League to gather intelligence and provide advice on economic and financial matters, including those related to central banking. Its representatives emphasized fiscal prudence, currency reform, and central bank independence, where the latter would be guaranteed by a statutory commitment to gold convertibility, limits on lending to the public sector, and a cap on state ownership.[8]

Although the EFO projected itself as impartial and multilateral, it was close to London and the Bank of England in practice (Péteri, 1992). Its head, Arthur Salter, was British and had a collegial relationship with Norman. The US decision not to join the League tilted its scales toward London – much to the chagrin of the French, who remained suspicious of the League's activities. These political tensions pushed central bankers away from the League and towards the Bank for International

---

[7] Pierre Quesnay and Charles Rist played important roles in the stabilization of the leu, while the latter also became an adviser to the Bank of Romania. Romania is excluded from Table 1.1 because the National Bank of Romania had been established in 1880, and the reforms carried out in 1929 did not produce a stark discontinuity – see Cottrell (2003), Mouré (2003), and Chiappini et al. (2019).

[8] New institutions would be set up as private joint stock companies.

Settlements (BIS), which opened its doors in 1930 as a discreet venue for central bank cooperation away from meddlesome politicians (Toniolo, 2005). As Piet Clement shows in Chapter 4, the vision behind the new organization extended far beyond the management of German reparations to functions previously performed by the League and that would later be entrusted to the Bretton Woods institutions.

1.3 STABILIZATION AND CONDITIONALITY

New central banks were often set up in the effort to attract foreign capital. Bankers preferred lending to countries with a central bank on the gold standard. Hence developing countries eager to attract foreign capital could not afford to ignore their doctors' prescriptions. Surveying Latin America for this volume (Chapter 12), Flores Zendejas and Nodari find no causal relationship between past macroeconomic performance and the establishment of new central banks; what mattered instead was the desire to attract foreign capital, which setting up a central bank promised to fulfil.

Similar considerations informed policy in Europe's war-ravaged economies. With a trade surplus and no hyperinflation, policymakers in Czechoslovakia felt little pressure to tie their hands. But faced with the prospect of being excluded from international financial markets, they were coaxed into setting up a central bank, as Jakub Kunert explains in Chapter 8. In Chapter 11, Şevket Pamuk similarly describes how Turkish officials seeking to attract foreign investment invited foreign advisers, who paved the way for a new central bank in 1930.

Conditionality was strongest in supervised stabilizations. The League of Nations organized a string of programmes in the 1920s, four of which are covered by Hans Kernbauer (Austria, Chapter 5), Györgi Péteri (Hungary, Chapter 6), Andreas Kakridis (Greece, Chapter 9), and Roumen Avramov (Bulgaria, Chapter 10).[9] Austria was the first country to accept League assistance and submit to foreign control; this took the form of the appointment of a foreign commissioner in charge of fiscal policy and a foreign adviser to the new Austrian National Bank. The Austrian model was then exported to Hungary and Estonia. While Czechoslovakia and Poland also negotiated with Geneva, both ultimately rejected the League's terms. Bulgaria and Greece were last to stabilize with the League's assistance, their reforms tied to loans for refugee resettlement.

---

[9] See League of Nations (1945); the only two cases not covered in this volume are Estonia and Danzig.

But conditionality was not unique to the League. As Cecylia Leszczyńska shows in Chapter 7, similar conditions underpinned Poland's second stabilization in 1927, which was backed by the Federal Bank of New York and Banque de France and came on the heels of a Kemmerer mission. The abortive attempt by the BIS to stabilize the Spanish peseta in 1930, described by Clement, was taken from the same playbook.

Stabilization programmes, whether bilateral or multilateral, combined conditionality with external supervision. If independent central banks were meant to lend credibility to monetary policy, foreign enforcement was designed to enhance the credibility of stabilization and encourage fiscal and monetary rectitude.[10] Stabilization programmes could be painful and controversial. Political reaction was strong in Austria, for example, where stringent financial terms combined with heavy-handed intervention in the country's relations with Germany; further, the role of international banks in the process fuelled antisemitism. In Hungary, the peg to sterling precipitated a painful *Sanierungskrise* in 1924–5; by 1926 an exasperated senior economist at the Hungarian National Bank complained to the League's appointee, Harry Siepmann, that it might have been easier 'to just gas Hungary with cyanide' (see Péteri, Section 6.4). In Greece, controversies around stabilization toppled the coalition government, and calls for the abolition of the Bank of Greece persisted into the 1930s. In many ways, interwar adjustment programmes anticipated the post-1945 activities of the International Monetary Fund (IMF), in both their allegedly apolitical design and the political reaction they provoked.

A problem was the 'one size fits all' approach to stabilization and central bank design. Plans for new institutions derived from the experience of advanced countries were often 'impracticable or even irrelevant' to the problems of emerging markets.[11] As several chapters explain, shallow markets, combined with prohibitions on open-market operations aimed at preventing the indirect financing of public expenditure, limited the

---

[10] Santaella (1993) sees League stabilizations as attempts to overcome commitment problems à la Barro and Gordon (1983); in a similar vein, but with a modern focus, Reinsberg et al. (2021) discuss the IMF's rationale and record of prescribing structural loan conditions to increase central bank independence. Whether conditionality is bilateral or multilateral may affect credibility and thus impact financial outcomes and access to credit; Flores Zendejas and Decorzant (2016) make this argument explicitly for the interwar years and League stabilizations.

[11] Triffin (1944: 101); Triffin was writing about central banks in Latin America, but his point could easily be extended to the other countries examined in this volume. Plumptre (1940) makes the same argument about central banks in the Dominions; In Chapter 13 John Singleton reviews several of the interwar textbooks on central banking.

ability of central banks to control the money supply. The problem could be exacerbated by conflicts between the bank of issue and commercial banks (for example in New Zealand, Australia, and Argentina, among others) that previously possessed limited central banking powers. Such conflicts were acute when the new institution was not the sole treasurer to the state (as in Greece, Hungary, or Czechoslovakia). John Singleton calls central banks in this position 'banks in waiting'. He attributes their weakness to money doctors who, eager to bind emerging markets to the gold standard, paid inadequate attention to the capacity of new central banks to provide services to their host governments and economies.[12]

Did countries seeking to tap international capital markets have no choice but to adopt the model forced upon them? 'Beggars cannot be choosers' was Siepmann's reaction to questions about the design of Hungary's stabilization programme (Péteri, Section 6.3). His colleague in Greece, Horace Finlayson, noticed locals' negative reaction to externally guided banking reform – how this reform was received with a mixture of suspicion and hostility. The new central bank was 'nobody's child', an orphan placed on the country's doorstep by foreign advisers. Questions of parenthood, or lack of programme 'ownership', as this problem is known in the literature on IMF adjustment programmes (James, 2003), arose in several countries covered in this volume.

At the same time, external enforcement could be welcomed as a way of deflecting political fallout from reforms that domestic elites recognized as necessary but unpopular. This argument, made by Kernbauer (Chapter 5) for Austria, is implicit in a number of other instances described in these pages.[13] Foreigners, in addition to serving as convenient scapegoats, were instruments for settling domestic distributional conflicts. Domestic interest groups and foreign advisers, finding themselves in the same trenches, formed alliances. In Greece, for example, commercial banks were keen to use League of Nations advisers in support of their campaign to rid themselves of unprofitable state debt.

Sometimes, domestic resistance could be effective in checking foreign interference. Although Santaella (1993) cites the absence of a single

[12] Flores Zendejas and Nodari counter that banks designed by Kemmerer missions were less rigid than those influenced by British money doctors, but neither were able to use conventional tools such as discounts and open-market operations to control their markets.

[13] Similarly, several countries invited foreign intervention for reasons of foreign policy: Hungary sought British assistance to offset the pressure of the Little Entente; Poland turned to the United States and France to deflect territorial revisionism by Russia and Germany. But inasmuch as these examples substitute one form of leverage (financial) for another (foreign policy support), they are less revealing of ownership.

occasion when League of Nations' advisers used their veto power as evidence of tough external enforcement (knowing that ambitious fiscal initiatives would be vetoed, no government dared implement them), this could equally be taken as evidence of the opposite. The correspondence between Niemeyer and Horace Finlayson, the British consultant charged with monitoring the Greek agreement, reveals a constant tug of war between Athens, London, and Geneva, sometimes resulting in the Bank of England and League of Nations having to agree to uncomfortable concessions. The 'sneaking nationalization' of Hungarian monetary management, over the objections of foreign advisers, is another example of how those responsible for the operation of these new institutions were sometimes able to deviate from their operational guidelines. In Bulgaria, domestic political opposition to privatizing the central bank, as advocated by foreign advisers, led to its indefinite postponement. Similarly, the Austrian National Bank systematically ignored its foreign advisers when providing liquidity to struggling banks.

1.4 INSTITUTIONAL CONVERGENCE?

By the late 1930s, central banks were operating in two-thirds of sovereign states, up from one-third in 1920 (Figure 1.1). Still, this appearance of institutional convergence masked the persistence of very different visions of central banking (Singleton, 2011: 58). If the League of Nations and leading central bankers envisioned an international network of cooperating banks tied to a liberal economic order, many new institutions were set up with nationalist and statist objectives (Helleiner, 2003: 152).[14] Publics and politicians saw their central banks as symbols of national sovereignty. This was true of European successor states but also, for example, of Turkey, where money issue was wrested from the foreign-owned Imperial Ottoman Bank, marking the Republic's break with the Ottoman past.[15] Inasmuch as new central banks were meant to attract

---

[14] To be fair, Norman and Strong also hoped that the new institutions would bolster their own *national* currencies, not least by keeping their foreign exchange reserves with the Fed or the Bank of England, while using London and New York to raise new capital. Norman's messianic zeal was thus also 'for the good of sterling' (see Péteri, Section 6.3). The Polish decision to base the złoty on the Latin Monetary Union franc, discussed by Leszczyńska, probably reflects similar motives.

[15] Note how greater central bank independence, formally understood as autonomy from the state's financial needs, thus took on several additional meanings: independence from other countries, independence from foreign capital, and so on.

foreign capital and investment, policymakers saw them as instruments of activist intervention rather than as constraints on government.

The tension between these visions is evident, for example, in the case of Britain and its empire. As Singleton explains in Chapter 13, by encouraging new banks of issue, London hoped to insulate monetary management from local political control and keep it within sterling's orbit. The Dominions, by contrast, saw their new banks as a first step towards financial autonomy and active policy. Given this conflict over the meaning of independence, both sides risked disappointment.

But the struggle was not just between the metropolitan centre and colony but also within the metropolitan bureaucracy itself. G. Balachandran (Chapter 14) describes how early controversies surrounding the establishment of an Indian central bank reflected a power struggle between the Bank of England and the India Office. Both agreed on the importance of keeping Indians out of monetary affairs. But whereas the India Office insisted on direct control, Norman wanted policy in the hands of an institution free from the India Office's political interference, but allied with the Bank of England. Decisions were postponed until the deflationary crisis of the 1930s made further delay untenable. India then became the first colony with its own central bank. But any illusions as to the true power of the new institution were dispelled when the India Office replaced the governor with a civil servant and in 1938 overruled a decision to devalue the rupee.

Colonialism distinguishes India's case but also invites us, more generally, to think differently about central banks. One way or another, the new institutions were designed to remove management of monetary affairs from the domestic political arena at the very time when the latter was becoming more representative. Extension of the franchise, the rise of labour politics, and the growth of social spending after the First World War rendered governments more likely to prioritize employment over gold convertibility. As one money doctor put it: 'the trend of political evolution the world over [...] is in a direction which makes it less safe to entrust governments with the management of currencies than it may have been in pre-war days.'[16]

If delegation to a technocratic body was meant to contain this problem, the results could be disappointing. The hope that political problems

---

[16] Henry Strakosch to Basil Blackett, 17.10.1925; Treasury: Papers Otto Niemeyer, National Archives, T176/25B; see also Eichengreen (1992: 31) and de Cecco (1994: 3).

could be bypassed by institutional fiat proved an illusion. As several chapters reveal, the very process of de-politicization was political, not only in its motives, but also in its distributional consequences.

1.5 THE GREAT DEPRESSION IN DEVELOPING ECONOMIES – A POLICY DILEMMA

Many emerging markets and developing countries ran current account deficits in the 1920s, financing them with foreign – mainly US – capital.[17] After 1928, when stock market volatility and a shift in monetary policy brought US capital exports to a halt, debtors were forced to retrench. Countries reliant on US capital, such as Germany and Poland, slipped into recession even before the United States. Next came the collapse in commodity prices, precipitated by shrinking demand and dumping of supplies. Countries like Hungary, Poland, Bulgaria, Argentina, Australia, and Brazil, who specialized in agricultural exports, faced deteriorating terms of trade, falling incomes, and balance of payments difficulties. By 1931, most developing countries – including those that stabilized under League of Nations tutelage – were having trouble keeping current on their foreign debts. As capital- and commodity-market shocks compounded one another, the recession deepened and spread.

Deflation especially strained debtors, whose liabilities increased in real terms.[18] The pressure shifted to banks, and countries with weak financial systems experienced banking crises (Bernanke and James, 1991). Emerging markets were vulnerable to these disturbances, especially in countries where banks financed long-term assets (for example loans and equity) with short-term foreign liabilities. When foreign capital fled, depositors followed, and banking crises morphed into currency crises.

In Europe's successor states, the banks never fully recovered from hyperinflation or adjusted their business to new national borders. Austria's

---

[17] This was part of the rebalancing of international payments that had occurred after the war, which undermined the stability of the gold standard. The United States became the largest international creditor. France and the United Kingdom remained net lenders, but their position was significantly diminished, while the rest of Europe became a net debtor, Germany absorbing more than half the capital inflows. Inasmuch as they recycled the dollars necessary to cover Europe's current account deficit with the United States, US loans were crucial in maintaining interwar monetary stability – until they came to a sudden stop (Feinstein and Watson, 1995; Accominotti and Eichengreen, 2016).

[18] Czechoslovakia stands out among our case studies as a net creditor spared the initial impact of the 'sudden stop' in capital flows. But it was not spared from the debilitating

crisis in May 1931 is the best known example, not least because it spread to Hungary and – once compounded by trouble in Germany – helped to push sterling off gold. The Creditanstalt debacle reveals how efforts to paper over bank troubles turned Austria into the weak link in Europe's financial chain. But while domestic authorities may have been too soft on Austrian banks, Hans Kernbauer reminds us that foreign advisers were also too narrowly focused on fiscal and monetary discipline, to the neglect of financial fragilities. Back in 1924, they had vetoed an ambitious plan to re-capitalize Austria's financial system on grounds of expense. With more radical measures off the table, mergers were instead used to paper over banking-sector weaknesses. This precarious financial edifice came crashing down in 1931.

More broadly, central banks designed to fight deficit-fuelled inflation were ill prepared to address financial fragility. Like the earlier institutions after which they were modelled, they did not consider prudential supervision as part of their mandate.[19] Nor did they have the expertise, information, and instruments needed to regulate the financial system. The Bank of Greece, for example, lobbied tirelessly for legislation requiring commercial banks to disclose detailed financial information and hold mandatory reserves, in a futile effort to control a market dominated by its predecessor, the National Bank.[20]

Not that all new institutions were keen to police their banks. With more power came more responsibility, and a central bank responsible for commercial banks might be expected to act as a lender of last resort at times of crisis. Given a mandate to uphold the exchange rate at any cost, interwar central banks were at best ambivalent about this role. Intervention on behalf of the banking system invited speculation against

---

effects of protracted deflation. In 1931, the country's trade surplus turned to deficit. By the following year, industrial production was down 40% from its 1929 level.

[19] De Cecco (1994) also points out that the US Federal Reserve, tasked with bank supervision, was a partial exception to this rule; this suggests another reason to distinguish between central banks set up by European and American money doctors (see Chapter 12, this volume).

[20] A minimum reserve requirement had been inserted by Henry Strakosch in the original drafts of the 1927 stabilization plan negotiated in Geneva, but it was subsequently removed at the request of the Greek government, acting under the advice from the National Bank. When the proposal resurfaced in 1931, commercial banks resisted bitterly, going so far as to appeal to J. M. Keynes, who – clearly oblivious to Greek realities – suggested an agreement reached amicably between all parties, rather than through legislative fiat; the proposal was watered down in subsequent parliamentary debate.

the exchange rate; if investors feared devaluation, capital flight would undermine both the liquidity of the financial system and the central bank's foreign exchange reserves. Thus, lender-of-last resort interventions were not only ineffective but could be counterproductive.

With the onset of the Depression, policymakers thus found themselves on the horns of a dilemma. The orthodox response was to stay on gold, raise taxes and discount rates, cut spending and credits, and thus preserve the foreign exchange necessary to maintain convertibility and service the country's external obligations. This is what most countries did initially, while struggling to secure additional loans and re-negotiate existing liabilities, including war debts and reparations.

The alternative was to abandon the gold standard and reflate, prioritizing output and employment over the currency peg. But this was unappealing for countries that had struggled to return to international markets in the 1920s. Inasmuch as the gold standard inspired investor confidence, devaluation threatened access to foreign capital. Moreover, debtors with substantial foreign-currency liabilities would be hard pressed to avoid default if that debt was revalued, and default could trigger commercial retaliation if creditor nations imposed sanctions or raised tariffs.

There was also a third option, but it required international cooperation. Monetary expansion in surplus countries (as per the rules of the game), coordinated central bank intervention to support the exchange rate in countries facing financial distress, a general moratorium on debt and reparations payments, and even simultaneous devaluations could have mitigated adjustment pressures and deflation. But cooperation was hindered by divergent interpretations of the challenge at hand and divided opinions on such matters as war debts and reparations. Moreover, the very asymmetry inherent in the gold standard – that deficit countries felt pressure to adjust while surplus countries did not – undermined the symmetry of the international reaction.

Multilateral organizations, for their part, were little help. In Chapter 3, on the League of Nations, Clavin singles out the Gold Delegation's inquiry into the operation of the gold standard, launched in 1928, as a turning point in the relationship between central banks and the League. Portrayed as technical, the inquiry inevitably acquired political overtones: any discussion of global monetary conditions raised questions about French and American gold accumulation that neither country wished to entertain. The Bank of England was not willing to jeopardize relations with the Federal Reserve, whose officials disapproved of the League's proceedings and advocated moving the Delegation's work to the BIS, newly created as a venue of central bank cooperation.

In the event, the BIS proved no more able than the League to muster a concerted response. An attempt in 1930 to provide credit facilities for investment faltered when the BIS's Directors discovered that the Bank's own liquidity was limited. A plan to finance a corporation to issue bonds and provide long-term credits was stymied by French concerns that it would drain capital from the Paris market. And the emergency loan to the Austrian central bank during the Creditanstalt crisis was only half what Austria requested and failed to stem the tide. Piet Clement asks whether these failures reflected difficult economic conditions or strained political circumstances. Without minimizing economic difficulties, he emphasizes the role of political conflict. Reparations were still outstanding, and the United States opposed any revision that might compromise its war debt claims. Opposed to the recently announced Austro–German customs union, France angrily scuttled proposals for a more ambitious Austrian rescue.

Left to fend for themselves, emerging markets could either defend the exchange rate at the expense of economic activity; or accommodate their economy and financial system at the cost of abandoning the gold standard. Most took the orthodox route at first, hoping to secure a trickle of foreign capital. But as the trickle dried up entirely, their position became increasingly untenable, and they began leaving gold. After sterling's devaluation in September 1931, these departures became a stampede. By the summer of 1933, when US President Franklin D. Roosevelt decried the 'old fetishes of so-called international bankers', Poland was one of the last developing countries still on the gold standard, not least because of its political and financial ties with Paris.[21]

Departures from gold took different forms (Table 1.2). Devaluation was most common. But in countries where inflation had been steep, devaluation evoked memories of hyperinflation. Such countries therefore chose to combine capital controls with protectionism in order to ration foreign exchange and/or alter the de facto exchange rate while maintaining the de jure price of currency in terms of gold. Both Bulgaria and Hungary resisted altering their official exchange rates but were drawn into elaborate clearing arrangements with Germany. The Turkish lira also spent most of the 1930s officially pegged to gold, enjoying nominal

---

[21] On Roosevelt's bombshell message and its effect on the World Economic Conference in London, see Clavin (1992) and Eichengreen and Uzan (1993).

TABLE 1.2 *The Great Depression and interwar central banks*
(in alphabetical order)

			Dates of:	
Country	Currency	Official gold standard suspension	Exchange control enforcement	First devaluation/ depreciation from par
1 Albania	Alb. frank	–	4/39	–
2 Argentina	Paper peso	16/12/29	13/10/31	11/29
3 Australia	Aust. £	17/12/29	–	3/30
4 Austria	Schilling	5/4/33	9/10/31	9/31; 4/34
5 Bolivia	Boliviano	25/9/31	3/10/31	3/30
6 Bulgaria	Lev	–	15/10/31	–
7 Canada	Canadian $	19/10/31	–	9/31
8 Chile	Peso	19/4/32	30/7/31	4/32
9 Colombia	Peso	24/9/31	24/9/31	1/32
10 Czechoslovakia	Koruna	–	2/10/31	11/34; 10/36
11 Ecuador	Sucre	8/2/32	2/5/32–7/10/32; 31/7/36–31/7/37	6/32
12 El Salvador	Colon	7/10/31	8/33–10/33	10/31
13 Estonia	Kroon	28/6/33	18/11/31	6/33
14 Ethiopia	Birr	–	–	–
15 Greece	Drachma	26/4/32	28/9/31	4/32
16 Guatemala	Quetzal	–	–	4/33
17 Hungary	Pengö	–	17/7/31	–
18 India	Rupee	–	–	10/31
19 Latvia	Lat	28/9/36	8/10/31	9/36
20 Lithuania	Litas	–	1/10/35	–
21 Mexico	Peso	25/7/31	–	8/31
22 New Zealand	NZ £	21/9/31	5/12/38	4/30
23 Peru	Sol	14/5/32	–	5/32
24 Poland	Zloty	–	26/4/36	–
25 South Africa	SA £	28/12/32	–	1/33
26 Turkey	Turkish lira	–	20/11/30	–
27 Venezuela	Bolivar	–	1/12/36	9/30
28 Yugoslavia	Dinar	–	7/10/31	7/32

Sources: See Appendix.

stability behind stringent controls. Developing countries choosing to devalue were in any case reluctant to let their exchange rate float, so they sought to join one of the emerging currency blocs into which the post-1931 world was fragmented (Urban, 2009). Most British Dominions, with the exception of Canada, quickly joined the sterling area. Greece let the drachma float for a few months before re-pegging to gold and following the Gold Bloc from a distance. Chile and Colombia imposed exchange controls in 1931 and devalued in 1932, after which their currencies followed the dollar.

At this point, the choice between outright devaluation and the pretence of a gold peg, propped up by protectionism and exchange controls, became secondary. What mattered now was whether governments and central banks, having regained a modicum of monetary autonomy, opted to use it. Since many exchange-control countries had histories of high inflation, policymakers were often reluctant to reflate aggressively. Eichengreen (1992) compares countries that devalued with those maintaining the façade of the gold standard behind exchange controls. He confirms that exchange control countries were more reluctant to increase money supplies.

Timing also mattered. Countries that unshackled themselves sooner recovered faster (Eichengreen and Sachs, 1985; Campa, 1990). The depth of recessions in Poland and Czechoslovakia, to mention the most obvious examples from this volume, illustrate the costs of waiting too long before abandoning gold.

1.6 CENTRAL BANK FETTERS

Were central banks uniformly part of the problem that was the Great Depression? After all, these institutions had been designed to uphold the gold standard, whose failings contributed to the depth of the Depression. Indeed, Simmons (1996) argues that greater central bank independence perversely increased the system's deflationary bias: zealous to stave off inflation, central banks in surplus countries were reluctant to increase their money supplies. By sterilizing gold inflows they deviated from the 'rules of the game' and shifted the entire adjustment burden onto deficit countries.

This line of criticism, developed in the earlier literature, focused on leading central banks in industrialized nations, specifically France and the United States, rather than on newly established banks in emerging markets. We have already mentioned how many central banks in emerging markets often had little leverage over domestic credit conditions. In the early stages of the Depression this handicap was a blessing, insofar as they lacked the policy tools to engineer an even more powerful monetary contraction. Moreover, the handful of tools at their disposal was frequently used to mitigate, rather than exacerbate, deflation. This is apparent in their lender-of-last-resort interventions, which – as the Austrian example reveals – led to further drains of foreign reserves, as well as in a reluctance to let foreign exchange losses affect domestic circulation (see the cases of Hungary and Greece). Unlike France and the United States, most emerging markets were deficit countries, where breaches of the rules of the game were countercyclical and reflationary rather than deflationary.

Ultimately, of course, such interventions were futile: they could neither offset deflation nor continue indefinitely so long as gold convertibility was maintained. Eventually reserves would run out and the policy trilemma would bind, at which point exiting the gold-standard system might become irresistible (Obstfeld et al., 2004). Did new central banks affect the timing of these exits? The evidence doesn't speak clearly. Flores Zendejas and Nodari point out that Latin American countries still without a central bank were actually first to devalue. Focusing exclusively on eight European countries with central banks, Wolf (2008) finds that those with more independent institutions abandoned the gold standard earlier.[22] Wandschneider (2008) expands the sample to twenty-four countries but finds no correlation between central bank independence and the decision to leave gold.

Different conclusions reflect different country samples, but they are also indicative of the difficulty of quantifying central bank independence.[23] Interwar money doctors, like modern quantitative economic historians, focused on bank statutes as their measure of independence.[24] Statutory

[22] Wolf (2008) claims this was presumably because countries with more independent central banks were *less* worried about the potential loss of credibility from devaluation. But since a credible reputation is established by being hard-nosed, one could easily have expected the opposite to be the case – especially in the case of new central banks.

[23] Not least because independence itself is open to different definitions; for a critique, see Hartwell (2018).

[24] An important aspect of those statutes, in the eyes of British money doctors and the League of Nations, was setting up central banks as joint stock companies with private investors. Other measures included ceilings and prohibitions on state lending, long tenures for senior bank management (whose appointment was subject to government approval), and statutory mandates to maintain convertibility (Ulrich, 1931; de Cecco, 1994; Capie et al. 1994).

provisions alone, however, cannot shield central banks from interference, any more than they can depoliticize an inherently political process.[25] This is especially true of newly established institutions, which have little time to build reputations or forge domestic political alliances.

Foreign allies, when present, failed to make up for this shortfall. This is not surprising: where statutory independence had been a symbolic gesture designed to placate foreign creditors, it was disregarded once international lending collapsed after 1929. In Czechoslovakia, for example, Jakub Kunert points out that the Banking Office, legally a department of the Ministry of Finance, was arguably more independent than its successor, the central bank, which was overruled by the government on exchange rate policy. In Poland, the regime of Józef Piłsudski eagerly awaited the term of the American central bank adviser to end so that it could 'stage a war to subjugate the Bank of Poland to the government' (Leszczyńska, Section 7.6). In Greece, the decision to stay on gold after sterling's devaluation was taken by the prime minister, who dismissed the central bank governor.[26]

Although distinguishing de facto from de jure independence is useful, doing so still doesn't provide an unambiguous guide to 1930s gold-standard policy. Some independent central banks resisted political pressures to devalue, but others faced the opposite challenge of resisting pressure from the government to stay on gold. By 1929, Poland's Piłsudski had effectively subjugated the central bank; its foreign adviser was gone, and a new governor, Władysław Wróblewski, had replaced his less compliant predecessor. As the recession deepened, the Bank of Poland recommended leaving the gold standard, only to be overruled by the government, Piłsudski insisting that a strong currency was needed to avoid inflation.[27] Similarly, Pamuk explains how the Turkish monetary authorities remained conservative in the 1930s despite autonomy from the government. Recalling high inflation during the First World War, they were unwilling to experiment with the lira.

This brings us to a central theme of this volume. Central banks are embedded within a broader network of institutions, political and societal relations, shared experiences, and ideas that shape their actions and effects (McNamara, 2002: 55). In this context, establishment of a new, independent central bank and subsequent pursuit of monetary orthodoxy, rather

---

[25] For critiques of the modern central bank independence literature in this vein, see Forder (1998 and 2005) and, more recently, Hartwell (2018); the case of the US Federal Reserve is examined by Conti-Brown (2017), as well as by Binder and Spindel (2017).

[26] Nor did bank ownership matter. Australia's state-owned bank was better at resisting political pressure than its privately owned counterpart in South Africa.

[27] Polish monetary policy did not change until after Piłsudski's death in 1935.

than one determining the other, may both reflect a deeper common cause. Harold James hints at this when he reaches back to Adam Posen's (1993) seminal paper on the role of financial interests and history in creating a broader 'culture of stability' that explains *both* low inflation and central bank independence.[28] Memories of past inflation discouraged developing countries from leaving the gold standard in the 1930s, just as they had encouraged the establishment of independent central banks in the 1920s. Even where new banks were associated with more orthodox policy, the effect was not necessarily causal.

If the advent of new central banks does not explain subsequent policy choices, then what does? Why did some countries take longer to leave the gold standard than others? The possibility that they might be able to continue borrowing made some countries more patient, as we have seen. So did concerns over foreign retaliation in the event of a debt default. The association of the return to gold with national prestige discouraged politicians from sacrificing the political capital invested in stabilization. Interest groups standing to lose from devaluation defended orthodox policy, while those hurt by deflation pushed back (Frieden, 2014). Less democratic regimes were able to ignore such pressures for longest. In emerging markets, fear of inflation was compounded fear of floating (Calvo and Reinhart, 2002), which is why governments opted for capital controls and re-pegged after devaluing. It is why none of the countries discussed in this volume used their new-found freedom to pursue aggressive monetary expansion (cf. Mitchener and Wandschneider, 2015). The experience of the 1920s made policymakers err on the side of caution. The tragedy in the deflationary circumstances of the 1930s was that caution was the last thing required.

1.7 THE LEGACY

Surveying the landscape of interwar central banks, the Canadian economist Wynne Plumptre noted that 'one of the primary tenets of accepted central banking thought has been the importance of keeping central banks politically independent' (Plumptre, 1940: 23). By the time this sentence was written at the end of the 1930s, it was already out of date. In the wake of the Great Depression, an event widely interpreted as signifying the failure of market liberalism, governments reclaimed the powers delegated to central banks.

---

[28] The fact that many interwar central banks were established *after* inflation had been brought down suggests that both monetary stability and central bank independence were caused by some deeper, structural effect.

Often, radical measures had to await a new government. Following sterling's devaluation in 1931 and the shift from Labour to the new Conservative-led National Government, Norman noticed an 'immediate redistribution of authority and responsibility' from the Bank to the Treasury (cited in Clay, 1957: 437; see also Kynaston 1995). In the United States, the Roosevelt administration pushed the central bank aside; a series of legislative reforms, starting with the Thomas Amendment granting the President the power to alter the dollar price in gold, curtailed the independence of the Federal Reserve.[29] Similar steps were taken by Leon Blum's government in France shortly before the Gold Bloc unravelled in 1936 (Mouré, 2002: 221–226).

Central banks in emerging markets followed suit, as their recently acquired powers were returned to national governments. Governors were replaced; statutes were revised. In New Zealand, the Reserve Bank built at Niemeyer's behest was barely two years old when the new Labour government nationalized it.[30] Most banks surveyed in this volume experienced a shift in the locus of power. Those that did not either had little power to begin with (as in India) or faced a divided government too weak to impose its will (for example Australia).[31]

Signalling the 'triumph of discretion over automaticity', the departure from gold gave policymakers leeway to experiment (Cairncross and Eichengreen 1983: 4). In Latin America, central banks engaged in re-discounting and open-market operations in an effort to encourage reflation. These policies have been heralded as a reaction against money-doctor orthodoxy and a mark of monetary emancipation. But Flores Zendejas and Nodari argue that the reality was more complex, at least when it comes to Edwin Kemmerer, who himself became a champion of counter-cyclical monetary policy in the 1930s and nudged Latin American central bankers toward greater activism.

Simultaneously, the rise in state activism involved central banks in additional facets of economic policy. From the 1930s, they were called

---

[29] A more radical economist, Marriner Eccles, was installed as Chairman in 1934 (Meltzer, 2003: 415–486).

[30] This was an extreme case: however widespread after the Second World War, central bank nationalizations were rare in the late 1930s, although the subordination of monetary policy to the Ministry of Finance was not. Denmark and Canada are the only other cases (Capie et al. 1994: 23), though some other statutory changes were equivalent to de facto nationalizations (Mouré 2002: 222).

[31] Mexico's reforms in the early 1930s, which sought to enhance central bank autonomy, are less an exception to the rule than a reminder that statutory provisions cannot guarantee de facto independence.

on to manage clearing balances and exchange stabilization funds, provide liquidity to the state and banking sectors, and refinance specialized credit institutions' lending to farmers and industry. Tasked with administering exchange controls and clearing arrangements, they became agents of regulation and dirigisme. Their organizational charts and employee rosters expanded accordingly. The Bank of Greece, having started with a spartan staff of 400 in 1928, employed almost 2,200 people in 1940. Bulgaria's Finance Minister noted in 1933 how the country's 'entire economic life [was now] concentrated' in the hands of the central bank, a transformation that paved the way for its future role as the communist monobank (Avramov, Section 10.6). In the aftermath of banking crises, and now freed from the gold standard, central banks embraced their role of lenders of last resort. In some cases, that role extended to prudential supervision and bank regulation. Central banks took advantage of their new relationship to the state and of the swing of opinion against financial liberalism to consolidate their authority and tilt the balance of power away from commercial banks.[32]

These late 1930s trends then were reinforced by the exigencies of the Second World War. Now fiscal dominance was expected, not abhorred. Following the war, acute dollar shortages threatened post-war reconstruction. Borders again were redrawn, while Britain and France became embroiled in a reluctant retreat from empire not unlike that experienced earlier by the Austrians and Ottomans. Interwar history seemed destined to repeat itself.

But this time was different. Thanks to memories of interwar experience, reparations and war debts were minimized. With the advent of the Cold War, the United States financed Europe's trade deficit with Marshall Plan funds. The international monetary system was redesigned following Anglo-American blueprints negotiated at Bretton Woods. Exchange rates were again pegged, but now they were made more adjustable. Capital controls were authorized to shield countries from destabilizing hot money flows, and the IMF was charged with monitoring economic policies and helping countries with balance of payments difficulties. Much like its interwar predecessors, the Fund fashioned itself as an apolitical, rule-based agent of international cooperation. Continuity extended to personnel: Per Jacobson, an early member of

---

[32] An interesting example from the developed world comes from Eccles' initiatives and the passing of the 1935 Banking Act, which helped the Federal Reserve consolidate its power (Meltzer 2003: 484–486); for a survey of bank supervision laws around the world, see Zahn (1937); in most cases, supervision was shared with another public agency.

the EFO staff transferred to the BIS in 1931, became IMF managing director in the 1950s.

For central banks, the end of the Second World War did not signal a return to earlier concerns over independence and financial liberalism. To the contrary, central banks coordinated closely with governments and continued to expand their range of responsibilities and interventions (Singleton, 2011: 128ff). Policy implementation now relied on direct controls (lending caps, reserve requirements, restrictions on bank asset holdings, and so on), while exchange controls provided leeway to pursue domestic policy objectives without sparking immediate balance of payments problems (Eichengreen, 2019). Policy outcomes were favourable, though whether this was a cause or consequence of the post-war golden age of economic prosperity is debatable.

In this new post-war environment, central banks possessed less independence but more power. Under Soviet-style central planning, the extreme case, they were fully integrated into the state-owned banking apparatus. But even elsewhere, emphasis on state intervention and modernization meant that central banks established in the 1920s and 1930s now became instruments of development policy, allowing the authorities to allocate credit and target industries in pursuit of economic growth. Before long, they were joined by another post-colonial wave of new central banks. The gold standard was gone, but the call at the 1920 Brussels Conference for all nations to establish their own central banks echoed down the years.

The coda then came in the 1980s and 1990s, as additional reforms were put in place in response to the failures (as well as the successes) of these credit-allocation and targeting policies, and specifically in response to the problem of accelerating inflation. This entailed renewed emphasis on the virtues of central bank independence (Bade and Parkin 1982; Alesina and Summers 1993). That emphasis manifested itself in steps to enhance the independence of established central banking institutions (the Bank of England, for example) and in the creation of new ones (the European Central Bank, arguably the most independent central bank of all). The reforms of the 1920s anticipated this contemporary paradigm. A look back at that history, through the lens of the studies that follow, sheds light on the circuitous route by which we got here.

APPENDIX: NOTE ON DATA SOURCES

The dates of establishment of each central bank were compiled on the basis of the most recent *Central Banking Directory* (Mitchell 2021) and

the list of banks covered by Capie et al. (1994, Appendix B). Where
necessary, this was combined with additional information from both
primary and secondary sources, including the chapters in this volume.
Doing so was particularly important when tracking down the money
doctors and foreign advisers identified in Table 1.1. The UN archives in
Geneva, which comprise the League of Nations' archives, proved invalu-
able in determining details of League missions and personnel. Additional
sources used for countries not considered elsewhere in this volume, are
mentioned in the notes to Table 1. Archival references are suppressed to
save space.

The number of sovereign states per year was derived from the database
constructed by Dedinger and Girard (2021), who identify 250 historically distinct sovereign 'political entities' from 1816–2020. These entities
were then matched with data on central banks to arrive at the calculations underpinning Figure 1.1. The data in Table 1.2 were compiled from
'Table 101: Exchange Rates' in the *Statistical Year-book of the League of
Nations, 1939–40* (League of Nations, 1940: 193–204).

Country notes and sources to Table 1.1

---

1   Renamed National Bank of the Kingdom of **Yugoslavia** in 1929, the bank
     was established in 1920 to extend the powers of the Privileged National
     Bank of the Kingdom of Serbia, which had been founded in 1884, to the
     (broader) Yugoslavian territory. Yugoslavian authorities negotiated with
     the Bank of England and the Banque de France from 1926, with a view
     to a obtaining a new loan. Harry Arthur Siepmann, allegedly in a private
     capacity, helped prepare a stabilization plan, and Britain attempted to
     organize a League mission in 1928, to no avail. Stabilization was postponed
     till 1931, and carried out with the aid of a French stabilization loan and
     Banque de France support; the 1931 reforms included an increase in central
     bank independence, as the dinar was pegged to gold. See Meyer (1970: 117)
     and Jevtic (2021).
2   Foreign experts were invited by the government of **South Africa**. See Chapter
     13 in this volume.
3   After an abortive attempt to establish a Latvian rouble in 1919 and 18 months
     of high inflation, a stabilization program – known by the name of the coun-
     try's Finance Minister, R. Kalning – was implemented in the spring of 1921.
     This brought public finance under control and led to the introduction of a
     new currency, the lat; de jure stabilization came in August 1922, followed by
     the establishment of the Bank of **Latvia**. Banknotes continued to circulate in
     parallel with a considerable volume of Treasury notes. See RIIA (1938: 131)
     and Puriņš (2012).

(*cont.*)

4　During the war, both Russian roubles and German Reichsmarks were circulating in **Lithuania**; after 1916, the latter were mainly exchanged for special 'Oberost' notes; these continued to be issued by Lithuanian authorities after the war (known as 'Auksinas'). Their link to the German mark brought rapid depreciation in 1922, leading to the introduction of the Lithuanian litas, set at one-tenth of the US gold dollar. Simultaneously, the Bank of Lithuania was established with a monopoly of issue and an obligation to maintain a gold cover of one-third. See RIIA (1938: 132) and Simutis (1942: 104).

5　The Reserve Bank of **Peru** was founded in 1922 at the behest of William Wilson Cumberland, a former student of Kemmerer's who served as senior customs collector and financial adviser to the government. Prior to its establishment, inconvertible bills (cheques circulares) were issued by a committee of bankers and businessmen (Junta de Vigilacia), who answered to the government. Cumberland modelled the Reserve Bank after the Federal Reserve and joined its board of directors, until his resignation in 1924. The Bank was overhauled after a Kemmerer mission in 1931. See McQueen (1926: 30), Seidel (1972: 536), Flores Zendejas (2021: 440) and Chapter 12 in this volume.

6　The **Austrian** National Bank's predecessors were the Chartered Austrian National Bank (est. 1816) and the Austro-Hungarian Bank (est. 1878), both of which had enjoyed monopoly of note issue within the respective borders of the Habsburg monarchy. The advisers listed concern the central bank, and should not be confused with the Commissioners-General appointed by the League, Zimmermann (1922–6) and van Tonningen (1931–6). See League of Nations (1945) and Chapter 5 in this volume.

7　**Colombia**'s first central bank had been created in 1905 but only lasted until 1909 (Ibañez Najar, 1990). After several years of monetary instability, **Colombia**'s central bank was ultimately established in 1923, shortly after Edwin Kemmerer's first visit to the country. Thomas Russell Lill, an accountant who had participated in the Kemmerer mission, stayed behind as financial adviser to the government, while a German national was hired as superintendent of banks. A second Kemmerer mission followed in 1930. See Seidel (1972), Drake (1989: 38, 69) and Chapter 12 in this volume.

8　Originally established in 1911, the Commonwealth Bank assumed (limited) central banking functions after its re-organization in 1924; the Reserve Bank Act of 1959, separated the central bank, henceforth called the Reserve Bank of **Australia** (RBA), from the rest of the Commonwealth Bank which carried on as a commercial and savings bank. The monopoly over the issue of bank notes belonged to the (federal) Commonwealth Treasury since 1910. The monopoly was taken over by an independent Note Issue Board (on which the Commonwealth Bank governor had the casting vote) in 1920, before being fully absorbed into the Commonwealth Bank in 1924. Harvey was invited by the Commonwealth Bank, while Niemeyer and Gregory were officially invited by the Australian government. See Chapter 13 in this volume.

(cont.)

9   After the First World War, **Hungary** and Austria had to liquidate the
    Austro-Hungarian Bank (est. 1878), which had been the sole note issu-
    ing authority of the dual monarchy. Hungary thus created the Note Insti-
    tute of the Royal Hungarian State on 1 August 1921, which maintained
    the monopoly of note issue until the Hungarian National Bank started its
    operations on 24 June 1924. The advisers listed concern the central bank,
    and should not be confused with the Commissioners-General appointed by
    the League, Jeremiah Smith, Jr. (1924–6) and Royall Tyler (1931–6). See
    League of Nations (1945) and Chapter 6 in this volume.

10 The Bank of **Poland** was preceded by the Polish National Loan Bank,
    which had been established by the Germans in 1916; in 1918, the Polish
    National Loan Bank became the interim bank of issue (with a monopoly
    on the issue of Polish marks, as crowns and German marks were with-
    drawn between 1918 and 1920), until the establishment of the new
    Bank of Poland and the introduction of the zloty. See Chapter 7 in this
    volume.

11 In 1922, responding to an official request for financial assistance, the
    LoN dispatched Luxembourgian professor Albert Clamès to investigate
    the financial situation in **Albania** and submit a report. Subsequently,
    J. D. Hunger was appointed financial adviser to the Albanian gov-
    ernment. His proposals for a new bank of issue led to the Financial
    Committee's draft statutes for the new institution being approved in
    September 1923. Subsequent negotiations to secure the bank's capital
    were headed by Mario Alberti, who represented Italy on the Financial
    Committee in 1923, and eventually signed an agreement between the
    Albanian government and an international bank syndicate to establish
    the National Bank of Albania in March 1925. The syndicate comprised
    mainly Italian banks (COMIT, Credit, and Banco di Roma), as well as
    institutions from Switzerland, Belgium, and Yugoslavia; the bank was
    founded in Rome and Alberti became the first Governor. See Ahmetaj
    (2017).

12 In **Chile**, a conversion office was established as early as 1907 and several
    proposals to transform it into a proper central bank had been discussed.
    After 1913, the office engaged in additional banking activities (includ-
    ing re-discounting), and could thus be considered a predecessor to the
    Central Bank of Chile, which was established after a Kemmerer mission
    in 1925, and opened its doors in January 1926. At Kemmerer's behest,
    the US banker Walter M. Van Deusen, who had worked for several US
    banks in Latin America, became its technical adviser; Van Deusen also
    participated in Kemmerer's 1931 mission to Peru. Kemmerer had been to
    Chile back in 1922 and returned briefly in 1927, though neither visit led
    to central banking reform. See Seidel (1972), Drake (1989: 89), Carrasco
    (2009), and Chapter 12 in this volume.

(*cont.*)

13 After the civil war, **Mexico**'s regional banks of issue were liquidated and
   circulation of gold and silver coins was gradually restored in 1916–17, when
   a Kemmerer mission was also organized. Of the two commercial banks that
   enjoyed note-issuing privileges across the entire country, some policy makers
   favoured the transformation of the Banco Nacional de México – the largest
   commercial bank and banker to the government – into a central bank. Kemmerer, however, recommended the establishment of a new institution. His
   proposal was eventually implemented in 1925, although with some discern-
   ible differences. See Nodari (2019) and Chapter 12 in this volume.
14 Established in 1919, the Bank of **Estonia** was a state bank that combined
   commercial banking with monopoly note issue (Estonian marks). A crisis in
   1924 led to a request for League assistance, which in turn led to the 1925
   and 1926 missions, recommending bank and currency reform; at the same
   time, Norman was approached to recommend a financial adviser. The Bank
   was reformed in 1926 (with BoE staff members Siepmann and Osborne
   helping redraft the statutes) and Walter J. F. Williamson became the Bank's
   financial adviser. The League helped Estonia issue a new loan in 1927; a
   portion of the proceeds helped move long-term assets from the Bank of
   Estonia to a new Mortgage Institute. A new currency, the Estonian kroon,
   was introduced and linked to the gold standard; the kroon was put into
   circulation in 1928. See RIIA (1938: 133) and Sayers (1976: 304).
15 The National Bank of **Czechoslovakia** replaced the Banking Office of the
   Ministry of Finance, which had had sole control of the koruna ever since
   its separation from the Austro-Hungarian crown, in 1919. The country
   eschewed League stabilization but the Bank of England was consulted regularly. See Chapter 8 in this volume.
16 Ever since 1899, when the government suspended convertibility for the
   banknotes issued by six banks, Guatemala had experienced considerable
   exchange rate fluctuations, while the US dollar was widely used in transactions. In 1923, efforts were made to stabilize the exchange rate. In 1924, the
   government invited Kemmerer to visit; a new monetary unit, the quetzal,
   was introduced and, in 1926, the Central Bank of **Guatemala** was established, but it differed significantly from Kemmerer's original proposals, so
   he did not recognize it as his own creation. See McQueen (1926), Calderón
   (2018) and Chapter 12 in this volume.
17 Projects to establish a central bank in **Ecuador** date back to 1890; however,
   until the establishment of the Central Bank of Ecuador, in 1927, six banks
   shared note issue privileges. At Kemmerer's behest, five North American
   experts were appointed, including Earl B. Schwulst (from the Federal Reserve
   Bank of Dallas) who became bank 'assessor'; he soon clashed with the Bank
   president and his contract was repudiated; Harry L. Tompkins, employed as
   the 'superintendent of banks' was removed in 1929. See Drake (1989), Naranjo Navas (2017), and Chapter 12 in this volume.

(cont.)

18 Transformed into a fully fledged central bank in 1928, the Bulgarian National Bank had enjoyed the de jure monopoly of note issue in **Bulgaria** since 1885. The advisers listed concern the central bank, and should not be confused with the Commissioners appointed by the League, although both Charron and Watteau also served in that capacity. See Chapter 10 in this volume.

19 The Bank of **Greece** took over the monopoly of issue of the National Bank of Greece, which had been established in 1842, but only became the country's sole note-issuing authority in 1920. Prior to 1920, its monopoly had been regional. After the Avenol mission, negotiations on the new bank statutes continued in London, where Bank of England staff and Henry Strakosch played key roles. See Chapter 9 in this volume.

20 Established in 1911, the quasi-governmental Bank of the Bolivian Nation enjoyed a monopoly of note issue since 1914, though private banks had until 1924 to withdraw their issue; Kemmerer's mission in 1927, however, felt the need to establish a new institution and drew up the blueprints for the Central Bank of **Bolivia**, which was established by law in 1928 and opened its doors in 1929. At Kemmerer's behest, Abraham F. Lindberg was appointed 'technical assessor' for three years. Lindberg had previously been appointed chairman of the Permanent Fiscal Commission, a US-controlled supervisory body that had been a product of a 1922 loan to Bolivia. E. O. Detlefsen was appointed superintendent of banks for 1929–30. See McQueen (1926: 35), Drake (1989), Flores Zendejas (2021) and Chapter 12 in this volume.

21 Several experts were invited to advise the government of the Republic of **Turkey**. See Chapter 11 in this volume.

22 The Bank of **Ethiopia** was preceded by the Bank of Abyssinia, which had been established in 1906 and was controlled by the British-owned National Bank of Egypt. Soon after his coronation, Emperor Selassie arranged for the transfer of ownership and note-issuing privileges to a new, Ethiopian-owned institution, which thus became one of the first indigenous central banks in Africa. Monetary reform owed much to the work of Selassie's American financial adviser and staunch defender of the gold standard, Everett Colson. Colson had been recommended to Selassie by the State Department and was one of a 'trinity' of foreign advisers to the emperor (the other two being his military adviser, Eric Virgin (Sweden), and his legal adviser, Jacques Auberson (Switzerland)). The Canadian banker, C. S. Collier, formerly of the Bank of Abyssinia, became the Bank's Governor, until it was liquidated in 1936, shortly after the Italian occupation of Addis Ababa. See Pankhurst (1963: 115) and Mauri (2011).

23 Established through the 1933 Reserve Bank of **New Zealand** Act, the Bank began business on 1 August 1934 and was nationalized in 1936. Otto Niemeyer's visit came at the invitation of the New Zealand government, but is not related to the establishment of the RBNZ. See Chapter 13 in this volume.

(*cont.*)

24 The establishment of the **Bank of Canada** was influenced by the Royal Commission of 1933. Macmillan had been a judge and was approached directly by the Canadian Prime Minister to chair the commission. Canada had also contacted Norman to request Sir E. Harvey, but Norman nominated Addis to the Commission instead. Besides Macmillan and Addis, the Royal Commission also had several Canadian members. See Chapter 13 in this volume.

25 In **El Salvador**, issuing rights were shared by three major commercial banks until the Bank of England dispatched F. F. J. Powell, who had previously assisted Niemeyer in his missions to Argentina and Brazil. The Powell mission proposed the conversion of one of the 'big three' (the Commercial Agricultural Bank) into a central bank and the reform was carried out in 1934, establishing the Central Reserve Bank of El Salvador. See Sayers (1976: 524), Sato (2012), and Chapter 12 in this volume.

26 In **Argentina**, prior to the establishment of the Central Bank of Argentina in 1935, paper money was issued in exchange for specie at a fixed rate at the Conversion Office (est. 1899), while the Bank of the Argentine Nation (est. 1891) managed gold reserves and provided credit to the state and other commercial banks. While the new institution was established after a Niemeyer mission, the final outcome differed significantly from orthodox prescriptions, not least due to the influence of Raúl Prebisch. See Sato (2012), Sember (2018) and Chapter 12 in this volume.

27 **India** is the only country included in the table that was not sovereign at the time. The 1861 Paper Currency Act vested the monopoly power of issue in the government, which set up a Currency Department. The three Presidency banks of Calcutta, Bombay, and Madras acted as its agents of issue and redemption in their respective areas of operation, but elsewhere the Currency Department operated through its own offices. In 1913 the Currency Department was replaced by the Office of the Controller of Currency, which was replaced by the RBI's Issue Department in 1935. Despite London's strong interest in Indian monetary affairs, the Hilton Young Commission was the first expert mission to visit India per se; Henry Strakosch was its leading member and a major influence on its majority report. See Chapter 14 in this volume.

28 Until the establishment of the Central Bank of **Venezuela**, banknotes were issued by four multiple banks, while government relied mostly on the largest one, the Bank of Venezuela. Plans to establish a central bank were first aired in 1936, as part of the February Program of reforms. Experts were dispatched to other central banks in the Americas and Hermann Max, of the Central Bank of Chile, was invited to contribute to the final draft. The bank was created in 1939, but opened its doors in 1940. See Delfino (2020) and Chapter 12 in this volume.

REFERENCES

Accominotti, Olivier and Eichengreen, Barry (2016). 'The Mother of All Sudden Stops: Capital Flows and Reversals in Europe, 1919–32'. *Economic History Review*, 69(2): 469–492.

Ahmetaj, Lavdosh (2017). 'Establishment of the National Bank of Albania and the Society for Economic Development of Albania (SVEA)', in Anamali, Armela, Muka, Majlinda, and Myftraj, Ervin (eds.), *Proceedings of 13th ASECU Conference on Social and Economic Challenges in Europe, 2016–2020*, organized by Aleksander Moisiu University, 19–20 May. Durres, Albania: Aleksander Moisiu University, 510–519.

Alesina, Alberto and Summers, Lawrence (1993). 'Central Bank Independence and Macroeconomic Performance: Some Comparative Evidence'. *Journal of Money, Credit and Banking*, 25(2): 151–162.

Barro, Robert J. and Gordon, David B. (1983). 'Rules, Discretion and Reputation in a Model of Monetary Policy'. *Journal of Monetary Economics*, 12(1): 101–121.

Bernanke, Ben and James, Harold (1991). 'The Gold Standard, Deflation and Financial Crisis in the Great Depression: An International Comparison', in Hubbard, Glenn R. (ed.), *Financial Markets and Financial Crises*. Chicago: National Bureau of Economic Research, 33–68.

Binder, Sarah and Spindel, Mark (2017). *The Myth of Independence: How Congress Governs the Federal Reserve*. Princeton: Princeton University Press.

Cairncross, Alec and Eichengreen, Barry (1983). *Sterling in Decline – the Devaluations of 1931, 1949 and 1967*. Oxford: Basil Blackwell.

Caldentey, Esteban and Vernengo, Matias (2019). 'The Historical Evolution of Monetary Policy in Latin America', in Battilossi, Stefano, Cassis, Youssef, and Yago, Kazuhiko (eds.), *Handbook of the History of Money and Credit*. Singapore: Springer Nature, 953–980.

Calderón, José Molina (2018). *El Banco Central de Guatemala, 1926–1946: Antecesor del Banco de Guatemala*. Guatemala City: Banco de Guatemala, Seminario de Investigadores Económicos de Guatemala.

Calvo, Guillermo A. and Reinhart, Carmen M. (2002). 'Fear of Floating', *Quarterly Journal of Economics*, 117(2): 379–408.

Campa, José Manuel (1990). 'Exchange Rates and Economic Recovery in the 1930s: An Extension to Latin America'. *Journal of Economic History*, 50(3): 677–682.

Capie, Forrest, Goodhart, Charles, Fischer, Stanley, and Schnadt, Norbert (1994). *The Future of Central Banking: The Tercentenary Symposium of the Bank of England*. Cambridge: Cambridge University Press.

Carrasco, Camilo (2009). *Banco Central de Chile, 1925–1964: Una historia institucional*. Santiago: Banco Central de Chile.

Chandler, Lester V. (1958). *Benjamin Strong, Central Banker*. Washington, DC: The Brookings Institution.

Chiappini, Raphaël, Torre, Dominique, and Tosi, Elise (2019). 'Romania's Unsustainable Stabilization: 1929–1933'. GREDEG Working Papers 2019–43, Université Côte d'Azur, France.

Clavin, Patricia (1992). '"The Fetishes of So-called International Bankers"': Central Bank Co-operation for the World Economic Conference, 1932–3'. *Contemporary European History*, 1(3): 281–311.

Clay, Henry (1957). *Lord Norman*. London: Macmillan/New York: St Martin's Press.

Conti-Brown, Peter (2017). *The Power and Independence of the Federal Reserve*. Princeton: Princeton University Press.

Cottrell, Philip (ed.) (1997). *Rebuilding the Financial System in Central and Eastern Europe, 1918–1994*. London: Routledge.

Cottrell, Philip (2003). 'Central Bank Co-operation and Romanian stabilisation, 1926–1929', in Gourvish, Terry (ed.), *Business and Politics in Europe, 1900–1970: Essays in Honour of Alice Teichova*. Cambridge: Cambridge University Press, 106–144.

de Cecco, Marcello (1975). *Money and Empire: The International Gold Standard, 1890–1914*. Oxford: Blackwell.

de Cecco, Marcello (1994). 'Central Banking in Central and Eastern Europe: Lessons from the Interwar Years' Experience'. IMF Working Paper, October, WP/94/127, Washington, DC: International Monetary Fund.

de Kock, Gerhard (1954). *A History of the South African Reserve Bank, 1920–52*. Pretoria: J. L. Van Schaik.

Dedinger, Béatrice and Girard, Paul (2021). 'How Many Countries in the World? The Geopolitical Entities of the World and Their Political Status from 1816 to the Present'. *Historical Methods: A Journal of Quantitative and Interdisciplinary History*, 54(4): 208–227.

Delfino, Carlos Hernández (2020). 'La creación del Banco Central de Venezuela'. *Tiempo y Espacio*, 38(74): 61–119.

Della Paolera, Gerardo and Taylor, Alan (2001). *Straining at the Anchor: The Argentine Currency Board and the Search for Macroeconomic Stability, 1880–1935*. Chicago: University of Chicago Press.

Drake, Paul W. (1989). *The Money Doctor in the Andes*. Durham, NC: Duke University Press.

Eichengreen, Barry (1994 [1989]). 'House Calls of the Money Doctor: the Kemmerer Missions to Latin America, 1917–1931', in Calvo, Guillermo A., Findlay, Ronald, Kouri, Pentti J.K., and de Macedo, Jorge Braga (eds.), *Debt, Stabilization and Development: Essays in Memory of Carlos Díaz-Alejandro*. Oxford: Blackwell; reprinted in Drake, Paul W. (ed.) (1994). *Money Doctors, Foreign Debts, and Economic Reforms in Latin America from the 1980s to the Present*. Wilmington, DE: Scholarly Resources, 110–132.

Eichengreen, Barry (1992). *Golden Fetters: The Gold Standard and the Great Depression, 1919–1939*. New York: Oxford University Press.

Eichengreen, Barry (2019). *Globalizing Capital: A History of the International Monetary System*. Princeton: Princeton University Press (third edition).

Eichengreen, Barry and Sachs, Jeffrey (1985). 'Exchange Rates and Economic Recovery in the 1930s'. *Journal of Economic History*, 45(4): 925–946.

Eichengreen, Barry and Uzan, Marc (1993). 'The 1933 World Economic Conference as an Instance of Failed International Cooperation', in Evans, Peter B., Jacobson, Harold K., and Putnam, Robert D. (eds.), *Double-Edged*

Diplomacy: International Bargaining and Domestic Politics, Studies in International Political Economy, Vol. 25. Berkeley: University of California Press, 171–206.

Feinstein, Charles H., Temin, Peter, and Toniolo, Gianni (1995). 'International Economic Organization: Banking, Finance, and Trade in Europe between the Wars', in Feinstein, Charles H. (ed.), *Banking, Currency, and Finance in Europe between the Wars*. Oxford: Clarendon Press, 9–75.

Flandreau, Marc (ed.) (2003). *Money Doctors: The Experience of Financial Advising, 1850–2000*. London: Routledge.

Flores Zendejas, Juan H. (2021). 'Money Doctors and Latin American Central Banks at the Onset of the Great Depression'. *Journal of Latin American Studies*, 53(3): 429–463.

Flores Zendejas, Juan H. and Decorzant, Yann (2016). 'Going Multilateral? Financial Markets' Access and the League of Nations Loans, 1923–8'. *Economic History Review*, 69(2): 653–678.

Forder, James (1998). 'Central Bank Independence: Conceptual Clarifications and Interim Assessment'. *Oxford Economic Papers*, 50(3): 307–334.

Forder, James (2005). 'Why Is Central Bank Independence so Widely Approved?' *Journal of Economic Issues*, 49(4): 843–865.

Frieden, Jeffry (2014). *Currency Politics: The Political Economy of Exchange Rate Policy*. Princeton, NJ: Princeton University Press.

Hartwell, Christopher A. (2018). 'On the Impossibility of Central Bank Independence: Four Decades of Time- (and Intellectual) Inconsistency'. *Cambridge Journal of Economics*, 43(1): 61–84.

Helleiner, Eric (2003). *The Making of National Money: Territorial Currencies in Historical Perspective*. Ithaca, NY: Cornell University Press.

Helleiner, Eric (2009). 'Central Bankers as Good Neighbours: US Money Doctors in Latin America during the 1930s'. *Financial History Review*, 16(1): 5–25.

Holtfrerich, Karl L. (1988). 'Relations between Monetary Authorities and Governmental Institutions: The Case of Germany from the 19th Century to the Present', in Toniolo, Gianni (ed.), *Central Banks' Independence in Historical Perspective*. Berlin, Boston: De Gruyter, 105–159.

Holtfrerich, Karl L., Reis, Aaime, and Toniolo, Gianni (eds.), (1999). *The Emergence of Modern Central Banking from 1918 to the Present*. London: Ashgate.

Ibañez Najar, Jorge Enrique (1990). 'Antecedentes legales de la creación del Banco de la República', in Banco de la República (Colombia), *El Banco de la República: Antecedentes, evolución y estructura*. Bogotá: Banco de la República, 194–237.

Jacome, Luis (2015). 'Central banking in Latin America: from the gold standard to the golden years'. IMF Working Paper no. 15/60.

James, Harold (2003). 'Who Owns "Ownership"? The IMF and Policy Advice', in Flandreau, Marc (ed.), *Money Doctors: The Experience of International Financial Advising 1850–2000*. London and New York: Routledge, 78–102.

Jevtic, Aleksandar R. (2021). 'Gold Rush: The Political Economy of the Yugoslavian Gold Exchange Standard'. *Financial History Review*, 29(1): 52–71.

Kirsch, Cecil and Elkin, Winifred (1932). *Central Banks*, London: Macmillan.

Kydland, Finn E. and Prescott, Edward S. (1977). 'Rules rather than Discretion: The Inconsistency of Optimal Plans'. *Journal of Political Economy*, 85(3): 473–492.

Kynaston, David (1995). 'The Bank of England and the Government', in Roberts, Richard and Kynaston, David (eds.), *The Bank of England: Money, Power and Influence, 1694–1994.* Oxford: Clarendon Press, 19–55.

League of Nations (1940). *Statistical Year-Book of the League of Nations.* Geneva: League of Nations Economic Intelligence Service.

League of Nations (1945). *The League of Nations Reconstruction Schemes in the Inter-war Period.* Geneva: Publications Department of the League of Nations.

Marcussen, Martin (2005). 'Central Banks on the Move'. *Journal of European Public Policy*, 12(5): 903–923.

Mauri, Arnaldo (2011). 'A Nationalization of a Bank of Issue Carried Out in a Soft Way: The Case of the Establishment of the Bank of Ethiopia'. Working Paper No. 2011-01, Università Degli Studi di Milano Dipartimento di Scienze Economiche Aziendali e Statistiche, http://dx.doi.org/10.2139/ssrn.1740565.

Maxfield, Sylvia (1998). *Gatekeepers of Growth: The International Political Economy of Central Banking in Developing Countries.* Princeton: Princeton University Press.

McNamara, Kathleen R. (2002). 'Rational Fictions: Central Bank Independence and the Social Logic of Delegation'. *West European Politics*, 25(1): 47–76.

McQueen, Charles Alfred (1926). *Latin American Monetary and Exchange Conditions.* Washington, DC: Government Printing Office.

Meltzer, Alan H. (2003). *A History of the Federal Reserve, Vol. I, 1913–1951.* Chicago and London: University of Chicago Press.

Meyer, Richard Hemmig (1970). *Banker's Diplomacy: Monetary Stabilization in the Twenties.* New York and London: Columbia University Press.

Mitchell, Jade (ed.) (2021). *Central Bank Directory 2022.* Riskbooks – Infopro digital.

Mitchener, Kris James and Wandschneider, Kirsten (2015). 'Capital Controls and Recovery from the Financial Crisis of the 1930s'. *Journal of International Economics*, 95(2): 188–201.

Mouré, Kenneth (2002). *The Gold Standard Illusion: France, the Bank of France, and the International Gold Standard, 1914–1939.* New York: Oxford University Press.

Mouré, Kenneth (2003). French Money Doctors, Central Banks, and Politics in the 1920s," in Flandreau, Marc (ed.), *Money Doctors: The Experience of International Financial Advising 1850–2000.* London and New York: Routledge: 138–165.

Naranjo Navas, Cristian Paúl (2017). 'Fundación del Banco Central del Ecuador', in Marichal, Carlos and Gambi, Thiago (eds.), *Histoira bancaria y monetaria de América Latina (siglos XIX y XX): Nuevas perspectivas.* Santander: Editorial de la Universidad Cantabria; Alfenas (Brasil): Universidade Federal de Alfenas, 397–428.

Nodari, Gianandrea (2019). '"Putting Mexico on Its Feet Again": The Kemmerer Mission in Mexico, 1917–1931'. *Financial History Review*, 26(2):223–246.

Obstfeld, Maurice, Shambaugh, Jay, and Taylor, Alan M. (2004). 'Monetary Sovereignty, Exchange Rates, and Capital Controls: the Trilemma in the Interwar Period'. *Staff Papers – International Monetary Fund*, 51(Special Issue): 75–108.

Pankhurst, Richard (1963). 'Ethiopian Monetary and Banking Innovations in the Nineteenth and early twentieth centuries'. *Journal of Ethiopian Studies*, 1(2): 64–120.

Péteri, György (1992). 'Central Bank Diplomacy: Montagu Norman and Central Europe's Monetary Reconstruction after World War I'. *Contemporary European History*, 1(3): 233–258.

Plumptre, Arthur F. W. (1940). *Central Banking in the British Dominions*. Toronto: University of Toronto Press.

Polanyi, Karl (1944). *The Great Transformation*. New York: Farrar & Reinhart.

Posen, Adam S. (1993). 'Why Central Bank Independence Does Not Cause Low Inflation: There Is No Institutional Fix for Politics', in O'Brien, Richard (ed.), *Finance and the International Economy*, Vol. 7. Oxford: Oxford University Press, 40–65.

Puriņš, Āris (2012). 'The Bank of Latvia, 1922–1940', in *The Bank of Latvia XC*. Riga: Latvijas Banka, 48–86, www.bank.lv/en/news-and-events/other-publications/bank-of-latvia-xc.

Reinsberg, Bernhard, Kern, Andreas, and Rau-Göhring, Matthias (2021). 'The Political Economy of IMF Conditionality and Central Bank Independence'. *European Journal of Political Economy*, 68(2), 101987.

RIIA (1938). *The Baltic States: Estonia, Latvia, Lithuania*. Prepared by the Information Department of the Royal Institute of International Affairs. London, New York, Toronto: Oxford University Press.

Santaella, Julio A. (1993). 'Stabilization Programs and External Enforcement'. *Staff Papers – International Monetary Fund*, 40(3): 584–621.

Sato, Jun (2012). 'The Bank of England Financial Advisory Missions to Latin America during the Great Depression: From the Perspective of the Periphery', in *Asia-Pacific Economic and Business History Conference*. Canberra: Australian National University.

Sayers, Richard S. (1976). *The Bank of England, 1891–1944*. Cambridge: Cambridge University Press.

Schenk, Catherine R. and Straumann, Tobias (2016) 'Central Banks and the Stability of the International Monetary Regime', in Bordo, Michael D., Eitrheim, Øyvind, Flandreau, Marc, and Qvigstad, Jan F. (eds.), *Central Banks at a Crossroads: What Can We Learn from History?* Cambridge: Cambridge University Press, 319–355.

Schuker, Stephen A. (2003). 'Money Doctors between the Wars: The Competition between Central Banks, Private Financial Advisers, and Multilateral Agencies, 1919–39', in Flandreau, Marc (ed.), *Money Doctors: The Experience of International Financial Advising 1850–2000*. London and New York: Routledge, 49–77.

Seidel, Robert N. (1972). 'American Reformers Abroad: The Kemmerer Missions in South America'. *Journal of Economic History*, 32(1): 520–545.

Sember, Florencia (2018). 'Challenging a Money Doctor: Raúl Prebisch vs Sir Otto Niemeyer on the Creation of the Argentine Central Bank'. *Research in the History of Economic Thought and Methodology*, 36: 55–79.

Simmons, Beth A. (1996). 'Rulers of the Game: Central Bank Independence during the Interwar Years'. *International Organization*, 50(3): 407–443.

Simutis, Anicetas (1942). *The Economic Reconstruction of Lithuania after 1918*. New York: Columbia University Press.

Singleton, John (2011). *Central Banking in the Twentieth Century*. Cambridge: Cambridge University Press.

Toniolo, Gianni (2005). *Central Bank Cooperation at the Bank for International Settlements, 1930–1973*. Studies in Macroeconomic History. Cambridge: Cambridge University Press.

Triffin, Robert (1944). 'Central Banking and Monetary Management in Latin America', in Harris, Seymour E. (ed.), *Economic Problems of Latin America*, New York and London: McGraw-Hill Book Co, 93–116.

Troitiño, David R., Kerkmäae, Tanel, and Hamulák, Ondrej (2019). 'The League of Nations: Legal, Political and Social Impact on Estonia'. *Slovak Journal of Political Sciences*, 19(2): 75–93.

Ulrich, Edmond (1931). *Les principes de la réorganisation des banques centrales en Europe après la guerre*. Paris: Librairie du Recueil Sirey.

Urban, Scott (2009). 'The Name of the Rose: Classifying 1930s Exchange-rate Regimes'. Oxford University Economic and Social History Working Paper, No.76 (April).

Wandschneider, Kirsten (2008). 'The Stability of the Interwar Gold Exchange Standard: Did Politics Matter?' *Journal of Economic History*, 68(1): 151–181.

Wolf, Nikolaus (2008). 'Scylla and Charybdis: Explaining Europe's Exit from Gold, January 1928–December 1936'. *Explorations in Economic History*, 45(4): 383–401.

Zahn, Johannes C. D. (1937). *Die Bankaufsichtsgesetze der Welt: in deutscher Sprache*. Berlin: de Gruyter.

2

The Ideology of Central Banking in the Interwar Years and Beyond

Harold James

2.1 INTRODUCTION

Why have a central bank? These institutions evolved historically in a regime of metallic money, but their story raises a curious question that deserves more serious investigation than it has largely received either from economists or historians. The particular institution of a central bank is not needed under a pure gold-standard regime, with an automaticity of operation; all that is legally required is a currency law. However, in practice, the institution was used in some cases to facilitate admission to the gold-standard club. The central bank was designed to deal with particular instances of poor coordination or market failure. But by whom, and in furtherance of whose interests? Was the central bank a link to the international order, or a protection against the slings and arrows of international fortune?

Before the First World War, central banks sprang from a domestic debate about what sort of institution might protect against the forces of international finance, and the shifting tides of global capital. By contrast, in the interwar period, central banks were often the result of external missions that advised on reform and frequently directed that reform in a direction specific to the interests of a central core. That was the case with the League of Nations mission to Greece, headed by the League's Deputy Secretary General, Joseph Avenol, which produced the Geneva Protocol of September 15, 1927, or of the Banque de France Deputy Governor Charles Rist's mission to Romania in 1929, or of the Bank of England adviser Sir Otto Niemeyer's visit to Argentina. In this context, the central bank was designed to maintain its independence from the government and exercise a kind of control.

The literature often points to the establishment of central banks coming in two waves (Capie et al., 1994). The first wave followed the creation of the Bank of England and was based on that model. The fundamental insight has been famously presented in a celebrated article by Douglass North and Barry Weingast as creating a contractual framework within which a private entity could take over a substantial portion of the government debt and at the same time secure commitments that guaranteed a fiscal revenue stream making the commitment to service this debt credible (North and Weingast, 1989). The key to the original exercise was that the shareholders of the Bank of England, who subscribed the money used to buy government debt, were also well represented in the House of Commons, meaning that the granting of tax revenue to the Crown was secure. The English example became an attractive model for Alexander Hamilton, Napoleon, and many other reformers.

The second generation of central banks that followed in the late nineteenth century comprised a rather different set of desired functions. They were frequently responses to financial crises that followed from internationalization or globalization. The iconic – and much imitated case – was the German central bank, the Deutsche Reichsbank or Imperial Bank, established after the transition of the German Empire to a gold-based currency in 1873, and in response to the stock market crash of that same year. What emerged was a system that would underwrite or guarantee banks and the banking system as a whole. The system was indeed designed by private bankers – the critical voice as rapporteur for the parliament (Reichstag) on the Reichsbank law being Ludwig Bamberger. Bamberger was a former 1848 liberal revolutionary exile, who returned to Germany after a banking career in London, during which he had looked at the operation of the British system, to found what soon became Germany's most important joint stock bank, Deutsche Bank. The establishment of the Reichsbank was a double operation: gold tied Germany to the international system, and a state bank provided it with additional margin for maneuver. Bamberger explained that "we chose gold, not because gold is gold, but because England is England" (Thiemeyer, 2013). But then he also told parliament that Germany needed "an institution which operates under the supervision and influence of the Reich, and which in turn supervises and influences the entire monetary and currency conditions of the Reich." On the other hand, the more radical parliamentarians explained that they feared influences from the Reich Chancellor and the Reichstag on the Reichsbank, "which are not commercial but political in nature" (James, 1997:14–15).

The case of the United States was in some ways related to the German experience. Critical inspiration was given by Paul Warburg, also in response to a devastating financial crisis. Warburg was the younger brother of the Kaiser's principal financial adviser, the Hamburg banker Max Warburg. His first contribution to the debate appeared well before the panic of October 1907 demonstrated the terrible vulnerability of New York as a financial center and was a response to the market weakness of late 1906. That initial contribution, "Defects and Needs of Our Banking System" came out in the *New York Times Annual Financial Review* on January 6, 1907; its main message was about the need to learn from continental Europe. Warburg started his article with a complaint that:

> The United States is in fact at about the same point that had been reached by Europe at the time of the Medicis, and by Asia, in all likelihood, at the time of Hammurabi. [...] Our immense National resources have enabled us to live and prosper in spite of our present system, but so long as it is not reformed it will prevent us from ever becoming the financial center of the world. As it is, our wealth makes us an important but dangerous factor in the world's financial community. (Warburg, 1914: 7)

The Cassandra warning about the danger posed by the American financial system would make Warburg look like a true prophet after the renewed period of tension that followed October 1907. The panic itself, the response coordinated by J. P. Morgan, and the debate about whether Morgan had profited unduly from his role as lender of last resort comprise one of the most celebrated incidents in US financial history (Strouse, 1999: 589–593). By 1910, Warburg had firmly established himself as the preeminent banking expert on monetary system reform.

In Warburg's eyes, the problem of the American system was that it relied on single signature promissory notes: when confidence evaporated during a crisis, the value of these became questionable and banks refused to deal with them. Warburg proposed to emulate the trade finance mechanism of the City of London, where the merchant banks (acceptance houses) had established a third signature or endorsement on bills of exchange, a guarantee that they would stand behind the payment; the addition of this guarantee provided a basis on which a particular bank, enjoying a legally conferred banking privilege – the Bank of England – would rediscount bills, that is, pay out cash, thus functioning as a lender of last resort. The second element of the Warburg plan was fundamentally a state bank, an innovation that recalled the early experimentation of Alexander Hamilton but also the controversies about the charter renewals of the First and the Second Bank of the United States.

In both cases, the central bank, closely modeled on the Bank of England, had been attacked by Jeffersonians, who argued that farmers and local communities would be drained of credit by the centralization of financial resources in big money centers (Cunningham, 2000).

The language of Warburg's public appeals made analogies to armies and defense: "Under present conditions in the United States ... instead of sending an army, we send each soldier to fight alone." His proposed reform would "create a new and most powerful medium of international exchange – a new defense against gold shipments" (Warburg, 1914: 9–10). During both the 1893 and 1907 financial crises, the United States had depended on gold shipments from Europe; this experience had indicated a profound fragility. Building up a domestic pool of credit that could be used as the basis for issuing money was a way to obviate this dependence. The reform project involved the search for a safe asset, independent from the vagaries and political interference surrounding the international gold market. The term "reserves" became fashionable in the 1900s, as both its narrow financial usage and its general meaning made frequent appearances on the printed page, in part thanks to an increasingly fragile international political stage. In the tense debates about the design of the new institution, Warburg consistently presented the issue in terms of a need to increase American security in the face of substantial vulnerability. As Warburg presented it, the term chosen in the original Aldrich Plan, as well as the eventual name of the new central bank, brought a clear analogy with military or naval reserves.

The word "reserve" has been embodied in all these varying names, and this is significant because the adoption of the principle of co-operative reserves is the characteristic feature of each of these plans. There are all kinds of reserves. There are military and naval reserves. We speak of reserves in dealing with water supply, with food, raw materials, rolling stock, electric power, and what not. In each case its meaning depends upon the requirements of the organization maintaining the reserve. (Warburg, 1916: 8)

Other countries had similar debates. Even in a monetary and political union, Hungarian politicians pressed for a separate central bank. The second volume of the Transylvanian trilogy written by the Hungarian politician Miklós Bánffy, published in Hungarian between 1934 and 1940, is a striking indictment of the failure of a ruling class. That volume, *They Were Found Wanting*, opens with a 1906 debate in Hungary about the need for a separate National Bank and about the customs union in the Hungarian half of the Dual Monarchy (Bánffy, 2013).

The central banks were seen as defense mechanisms that created wiggle room for politics and special interests. They could bend the rules. A purely automatic mechanism – such as the one embodied in the operation of the gold standard – might lead to intolerable pressures. The central bank could buffer such pressures by providing additional lending, favoring particular economic sectors and even by interfering in the currency and gold flows. The Reichsbank, for instance, liked to intervene to stop trains with gold shipments from Berlin to the port of Hamburg so that they missed the weekly transatlantic steamer – and thus increased the cost of arbitrage. There were political interventions, most famously in 1887 when the Reichsbank refused to accept Russian paper as security (the *Lombardverbot*). In financial crises, they were the bastion of a domestic market, largely thanks to their lender-of-last-resort operations. The Reichsbank's commemorative volume for its twenty-fifth anniversary in 1901 proudly boasted, that the Reichsbank had become "the last support of the German home market" (Deutsche Reichsbank, 1901: 19).

Before the First World War, the central bank was conceived as a bold instrument of national defense, a "can do" institution; after that it was reconceptualized, destructively, in a "can't do" framework that narrowed down its options and tied up politics. Before the war, the system was highly credible, and the institutional framework that surrounded it complemented rather than constituted the system. The institutions of central banking could make the currency more "elastic," in the terminology used to justify the creation of the Federal Reserve system, and hence more resilient to shocks. After the war, the system was much less credible, and central banking institutions were supposed to ensure that the rules were kept (rather than find ways of getting round the rules). The burden of these expectations politically overburdened the new generation of central banks, and the rules themselves became the target of criticism and controversy – were they really necessary?

The interwar wave of central banking differed from the previous cycles of innovation in that the new vision of central banking was dominated by an awareness of the double risk that all central banks that had grown up in the gold standard world but survived into an age of fiat currency, would be liable to. The first, and most obvious, was fiscal dominance, that is, a response to high levels of government debt, when central banks would use monetary policy to support the prices of government securities, maintaining low interest rates in order to hold down the costs of servicing sovereign debt (Reinhart and Belen Sbrancia, 2015: 291–333).

2.2 FISCAL DOMINANCE

The risk had been recognized a long time before it was realized during and after the First World War. In 1903, the German economist Karl Helfferich wrote in *Das Geld*:

In the hand of the state, the unlimited possibility of making money out of nothing is so tempting that an abuse for fiscal purposes cannot be ruled out. In addition, especially in our age of ruthless special interest advocacy, the regulation of the value of money would cause considerable conflicts of interest, that – in the absence of an objective criterion – would not be settled beforehand by reason or justice, but only through the application of brute force. [...] More than any other conflict of economic interests, the struggle for the value of money would lead to the demoralization of economic and social life. (Helfferich, 1903: 530)

The argument is rich in irony, in that it was Helfferich who, as Treasury Secretary in the First World War, was responsible – more than any other individual – for the Great Inflation that caused such long-lasting trauma in Germany's collective memory.

The immediate purpose of the adoption of the gold-exchange standard and the strengthening of central banks was control of fiscal policy. It was an ambitious effort, because the whole foundation of nineteenth-century prudent public finance had been destroyed by the First World War. No country could finance a total twentieth-century war through taxation (see Table 2.1). In every state, the major source of war finance had been borrowing – either through bond issues or, as governments became increasingly desperate, through short-term issuing of treasury bills. As a consequence, every state emerged with a high public debt: the Russian empire's increased by a factor of four, Italy's and France's by five, Germany's by eight, Britain's by eleven, and that of the United States (where there had been only a very small public debt before the war) by nineteen. In addition to the cost of servicing this debt, the legacy of war inevitably brought new expenditures. The most obvious were the pensions for war widows and for those crippled in battle.

After the war there appeared to be a stark choice – either revert to fiscal rigor or wipe out the national debt with inflation. The first required a conviction that sacrifice could be imposed without provoking revolution. Measures such as the British "Geddes Axe," the report of 1922 by a committee on public expenditure under Sir Eric Geddes, recommended military cuts, reductions in educational spending, and the abolition of five government departments. Continental Europe, with stronger left-wing and revolutionary movements, largely felt unable or unwilling to take

TABLE 2.1 *Government budget deficits in select countries (% of total expenditures)*

	1913	1918
United Kingdom	61.3	69.2
France	54.8	80.0
Germany	73.5	93.8
Italy	6.1	70.2
United States	0.1	71.2

Source: Eichengreen (1992: 75).

such action, and opted for inflation instead (see Figure 2.1). But this too had immense – and rising – social and political costs.

The German central bank, the Reichsbank, played a starring role not only in war finance during the World War, directly monetizing government debt, but also in the Great Inflation that started in the war but then shaped the first years of the Weimar Republic. The German inflation and hyper-inflation is one of the most notorious, and most studied, monetary catastrophes in human history. By November 1923, the Mark had sunk to $1/10^{12}$ of its pre-war value against the dollar. In the last months of the German inflation the central bank believed that it needed to respond to the real fall in the value of currency by producing more currency at faster rates. The Reichsbank even boasted of the efficiency of its 30 paper factories and 29 plate factories producing 400,000 printing plates to be employed by the 7,500 workers in the Reichsbank's own printing works, as well as by 132 other printing firms temporarily working to satisfy the need for currency (James, 1999: 99).

Germany's inflation experience is best described in modern terms as fiscal dominance. In 1920, 12 percent of central government expenditure went to finance deficits in the post and railroad systems, where employment was judged a social and political necessity. The deficits rose in subsequent years, as the government in effect adopted a full employment program. Similar political considerations guided tax policy, with weak coalition governments finding tax rises impossible in the face of militant opposition from business interests. The political constellation was similar throughout Central Europe: in the Habsburg successor states, only Czechoslovakia tried a costly fiscal stabilization immediately after the war. In Austria and Hungary the stabilization came later, and as in Germany, was conducted under the auspices of foreign supervision.

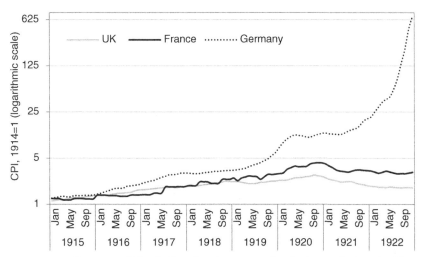

FIGURE 2.1 Consumer Price Indices in select countries during and after the First World War
Source: Global Financial Data.

The critical reconstruction of the German financial system in 1923–4 required a new central bank law, which in its most critical aspects was designed by foreign central bankers, above all by Montagu Norman, governor of the Bank of England. Norman blocked the appointment of Helfferich as the new president of the central bank after President Rudolf Havenstein succumbed to a heart attack at the height of the hyperinflation. Helfferich, he said, was "an official, a publicist and a politician, of great abilities, representing more or less the same official and antique view as was represented by von Havenstein" (James, 1987: 66). Instead, he supported and secured the appointment of a left-wing democrat, Hjalmar Schacht, who was regarded with deep suspicion by the German political and business elite – and who had been accused of illegitimate transactions in occupied wartime Belgium.

The new central bank would be required to remain separate from politics. As Norman put it:

It is quite certain that the world is not going now to be reconstructed, politically, so far as I can see; it remains therefore to try and first do something economically. In the case of Germany, the conditions and need of credit are not such as to justify an appeal to the publics of foreign countries, or indeed to the Bankers. But it is essentially a position in which Central Bankers ought to take the burden if anyone is to do so. They would not only be helping the World and Europe, but also their own Bankers and publics, and they can divorce economics from politics to an extent which is usually impossible in the case of Germany. It would have a limit on the amount of Treasury debt that it could take onto its books: and that position would be locked in by the composition of a new General Council, half of whom would be foreigners. (James, 1987: 69)

As Norman explained:

The permanent independence of such Establishment can only be assured, however, if satisfactory understanding of enduring character were reached between Britain and France so as to enable latter to endorse and support programme. [...] The budget difficulty will be menace to the functioning of such an Establishment until remedied and consequently assurance of a balanced Budget which would involve consideration of the Reparations question would then seem to be a necessary preliminary to this proposal. (James, 1987: 69)

Norman built this view up as a doctrine. As he put it, this kind of central banking was a completely new sort of activity. He was quite wrong in this interpretation: after all, the Bank of England had famously been set up as a constraint to ensure that government debt was handled responsibly (North and Weingast, 1989). But in the circumstances of high postwar debt levels, Norman wanted to set aside the legacy of the central bank as national savior that had been characteristic of antebellum Europe:

Central Banking is young and experimental and has no tradition: it may last and may develop, or its usefulness, to fill a short post-war need and no more, may soon come to an end. On the one hand its sphere is limited by the qualification that no Central Bank can be greater than its own State – the creature greater than the creator. On the other hand, a Central Bank should acquire by external help (as in some ex-enemy countries) or by internal recognition (as in France) a certain freedom or independence within, and perhaps without, its own State. By such means alone can real co-operation be made possible. I cannot define the position thus acquired but it should surely permit a Bank to "nag" its own Government even in public and to decide on questions on other than political grounds.[1]

Central banks were to be established before a country stabilized on gold in order to prepare the institutional ground. The Brussels Conference made Norman's point when it concluded in 1920, "Banks and especially Banks of Issue should be free from political pressure and should be conducted only on lines of prudent finance" (Sayers, 1976: 159). The constitutions of the new banks were thus framed with clear political objectives. Norman made the point quite explicit: "It seems evident that the limitations imposed on new or reorganized [Central] banks during the last few

---

[1] Bank of England Archive (henceforth BOEA). G1/307, Montagu Norman letter to J. P. Morgan, November 19, 1927.

years arise more from the fear and mistrust of political interference than from the needs of Central Banking as such."[2]

Schacht lived up to Norman's billing in resisting and publicly criticizing government fiscal and debt policy. The tone of Schacht's interventions became increasingly strident until he unleashed a memorandum in December 1929 which aimed at bringing down the government. This may have led to Schacht's resignation, but the government itself fell a few months later. Schacht's "nagging" had produced the end of the last democratically supported government in Germany. After that, Germany was ruled by emergency decrees imposed by minority governments, until Adolf Hitler established the Nazi dictatorship in 1933.

In many countries, as some of the contributions to this volume suggest, central banks were designed to facilitate foreign borrowing and foreign investment. But there was always an ambiguity in the position of the central bank: a "can't do" institution was supposed to make lending more credible because it would block and prevent financial excess, not only by the government, but also by the private sector.

2.3 FINANCIAL DOMINANCE

The second and equally dangerous risk that central banks in a non-commodity currency world would be exposed to may be termed "financial dominance." It was not just vis-a-vis their governments that central banks needed independence: they were also threatened by the claims of their commercial banking systems.

During the Great Inflation the Reichsbank did not only lend to the government and monetize government debt; it also continued to discount private commercial bills, at negative real interest rates. The policy rate (discount rate) was held at an amazingly low 5 percent until July 1922. This policy was highly controversial at the time and has remained so subsequently. Contemporary critics, including the Italian economist Costantino Bresciani-Turroni (a member of the Allied Reparation Commission who wrote the first major study of the German inflation) thought that the discount policy represented an illegitimate subsidy to that part of the business community having access to the Reichsbank (Bresciani-Turroni, 1937). That point is borne out fully by detailed archive-based studies of banks and industry during the German inflation. Above all, the extensive account by Gerald Feldman details how the

---

[2] Montagu Norman, preface to Kisch and Elkin (1928: vi).

issue was at the centre of German controversies. In the corporatist Reich Economic Council (*Reichswirtschaftsrat*) socialists, notably the economist (and medical doctor) Rudolf Hilferding, attacked the central bank for failing to pursue an "energetic restriction" of capital. The left liberal (and former socialist) newspaper editor Georg Bernhard used examples from the Berlin clothing industry to show how the credit policies were encouraging businesses to hoard raw material, foreign exchange, and finished materials, and claimed that credit banks were springing up like mushrooms. The industrialists replied that the alternative was to close down, and that the result would be a politically dangerous rise in unemployment. And the central bank representative simply noted that the action of the Reichsbank was "not to be prevented and one has to accept it at the present moment." At the same time, the Reichsbank knew perfectly well that it was charging a highly negative real rate, and that it produced an "extraordinary advantage" for the debtor (Feldman, 1993: 649–650). Banks thought that they could gain high profits from the difference between the discount rate they charged, and the rate at which they could draw funds from the Reichsbank. They pushed commercial bills on their industrial clients (Feldman, 1995: 194).

As inflation accelerated, the Allies insisted on legislation making the Reichsbank independent in 1922, but that did not really affect the central bank's thinking or policy in any way. Indeed, the Reichsbank consistently argued that it had taken treasury bills by choice, to discharge its "duty" to the German economy, and not because it had been instructed to do so by the Reich Chancellor. As continental central banks fueled inflation by cheap rediscounting of bills (the German Reichsbank raised its rate only in 1922, long after the inflation had turned into hyperinflation). Norman quite appropriately declared: "A Central Bank should protect its own traders from the rapacity of other banks in his own country."[3]

That was indeed the course that Schacht followed after his appointment. The critical measures were: a rationing of credit in 1924 that Schacht believed had nipped renewed inflation in the bud; guidance on bank lending to stop a stock market boom in 1927, which indeed produced a downturn on the stock market; and most decisively (and catastrophically) a restriction of bank lending in the run up to the 1931 financial crisis. Indeed, in 1931, the Reichsbank was pressed by the Bank of England and the Federal Reserve Bank of New York to take "more drastic credit control" (James, 2001: 61). A key element in the German

---

[3] BOEA, OV50/8, Compendium, Principles of Central Banking, quoting Norman in 1921.

banking crisis, which provided the critical link in the contagion that transferred financial collapse from the small case of Austria to the big economies of Britain and the United States, was the fear of the western central banks' renewed financial dominance.

The western central banks operated in an altogether different business environment. In the British model of banking, financial institutions were narrowly specialized, and a range of intermediate institutions, notably the discount houses, stood between the central bank and the commercial banks (Hotson, 2017). It was through the discount houses, rather than directly by asserting regulatory powers in banking, that the Bank of England "exercised that control over the quality of credit which it regarded as one of its essential duties" (Sayers, 1976: 273). In that way, the accusation of some analysts (de Cecco, 1994) that interwar central banks were so focused on fiscal issues that they forgot about financial stability, misses the point: In Great Britain, financial stability was a product of the structure of markets, and in other countries the Bank tried to push new central banks to observe rules of prudence. The tragedy was that in the course of the deflation of the Great Depression, rules of prudence were exactly what were not required.

2.4 THE LEGACY

The central bank as a constraint imposed by the outside was a dramatic failure. It made for bad policy and bad outcomes and contributed greatly to the inability to stem contagion in the 1931 financial crisis. Faced with capital flight, central banks in indebted countries were barred from acting as lenders of last resort: Creditor central banks told them that such action would exclude them from emergency support from the outside. The German Reichsbank was in that position, but so was the Bank of England in 1931. The revived gold exchange standard was not able to cope with high levels of debt.

The actions of central banks in the Depression also set up a political blame game. Central banks were widely blamed for the severity of the Depression, as governments complained that their hands had been tied by what were then still mostly privately owned institutions. The German central bank, reestablished in 1924 with statutes designed at the London conference, was seen as an international imposition, and German nationalists wanted to "take back control."

The 1930s produced in almost every country a dramatic pushback against the idea of central bank independence, and the Banque de France was nationalized by the Popular Front in 1936, and the Bank of England by the Labour party ten years later. Central banks after the Depression and the Second World War were largely integrated into a framework of government policy-making. In the United Kingdom, the Bank of England now saw itself as part of a "macro-economic executive" (James, 2020: 54). When the makers of the postwar order reflected on lessons from the interwar depression, at the 1944 Bretton Woods Conference of the United Nations, they firmly believed that coordination had to be controlled by politically responsible governments, and not by autonomous central banks.

It may be worth asking whether there was a better route: how the monetary mechanism that connects national economies to the wider world can be more stabilizing economically and less polarizing politically. In the 1990s, when a new debate about the status and role of independent central banks occurred internationally, and central bank independence became widely recognized as a legitimate and beneficial institutional reform, Adam Posen pointed out that, as a matter of fact, a better predictor of stability enhancement lay less in a particular institutional design than in the internalization of a stability culture. "Central bank independence levels reflect national differences in effective financial opposition to inflation" (Posen, 1995). Once again, the prime case was Germany – this time after the Second World War. The Bank Deutscher Länder and its successor institution, the Deutsche Bundesbank, were designed very much on the model of the Federal Reserve and were also – like the 1922 and 1924 Reichsbank – supposed to be insulated against political pressure. But that origin in a foreign diktat was soon forgotten, and the Bundesbank mobilized a kind of historical memory to explain to itself, and more importantly to German citizens and voters, what it was doing.

Hyperinflation had destroyed the German capital market and weakened German banks to the extent that they operated on a very narrow capital basis; these effects made the country much more vulnerable to the shocks that led to the Great Depression. Foreign observers often wonder why Germans should historically be so obsessed by the inflation experience, while it was the Depression that finally destroyed democracy and prepared the way for the Nazi dictatorship. There is an economic argument about the link between inflation, financial instability, and depression (and political disorder); but that is probably too sophisticated for most people.

There is a much deeper, social-psychological argument. The most perceptive and near-contemporary overall analysis of the inflation was that of the writer Elias Canetti, who vividly documented how the inflation focused people's attention on monetary transactions, to the exclusion of other values; and how the sharp fluctuations in monetary worth produced a growing sense of unreality, and at the same time a search for who was to blame (Canetti, 1978: 187–188). With the First World War, price controls, inflation, and the evolution of a black market, large numbers of people were obliged to take up speculative, illegal or semi-legal activities simply in order to survive. Such actions conflicted with traditional ideas of what kinds of business conduct were legitimate. One powerful argument as to why anti-Semitism flared up so poisonously during and after the First World War is that Germans widely took up activities previously defined as Jewish, hated themselves for this breach of traditional values, and reacted by transferring their hatred to the members of the ethnic group associated with the stereotype of bad behavior. An important example of such a transition, in someone who played a crucial role in the development of the Nazi state's anti-Semitic policy is Joseph Goebbels who seems to have learnt Jew-hating as a bank clerk (with Dresdner Bank) during the Great Inflation of the early 1920s. Canetti actually concluded that the inflation and the hyperinflation laid the mental foundation for the Nazi holocaust: that people became used to figures in which money was expressed with large numbers of meaningless zeroes, and then applied the same logic of meaninglessness to human life.

Countries are always learning from the experiences of others. The German view of inflation spilled over into French debates, and France also had a particularly severe bout of inflation after the First World War (albeit not a hyperinflation): the value of the currency fell by four-fifths. In Britain, in the Great Depression, Prime Minister Ramsay MacDonald campaigned for an austerity budget by waving Weimar bank notes in his election addresses.

As for the German view itself, this may have been inspired from an observation of French currency abuses in the early 1700s, when John Law introduced a paper currency that quickly lost its value, and in the French Revolution, when assignats based on confiscated land produced renewed inflation. Accounts of the process by French émigrés influenced Goethe: one, Ignace de Wendel, settled in Weimar and tried to recover a lost secret process of smelting iron. His fiery experiments made him look diabolical or Mephistophelean. In Part II of *Faust*, he presents a story of how money manipulation – inflation – follows from a diabolical agenda. Mephisto presents his proposal as a job-creating measure that will put the Emperor's subjects to productive employment. But the proposal also represents a call on their imagination. The state has infinite power to create money: "But grasping Spirits, worthy to look deeply, / Trust in things without limit, limitlessly. / Such paper's convenient, for rather than a lot / Of gold and silver, you know what you've got. / You've no need of bartering and exchanging / Just drown your needs in wine and love-making."[4]

Once a stability culture is entrenched, it leads to a political economy equilibrium in which large numbers of people have a high proportion of their assets in nominally denominated assets (bank savings accounts) and are consequently frightened by measures that would lead to a depreciation. By contrast, it is possible to imagine another equilibrium, in which nominal depreciation leads to a flight into non-monetary assets (*Sachwerte*) and often to real estate. Many people (and voters) are thus insulated against the immediate effects of inflation and come to think of it as not so bad. Higher levels of inflation in the United Kingdom and the United States made home ownership a national obsessions, and a substantial part of the electorate began to judge policies in terms of whether they were good for house prices, rather than good for monetary stability.

The argument about why modern inflation preferences follow from a historical lesson is thus rather complex. It relies on different policy orientations in the 1970s that may well be traced back to experiences of the interwar era. Lower inflation then created a political constituency for lower inflation later – and in today's world as well. Helfferich's claims about the operation of *Interessenkonflikte* are as relevant as they were before the First World War – in part because the effects of his own policies would live on long after Germans had forgotten his name.

Looking at this long historical trajectory of how central banks and their institutional role may be viewed, the movement from "can do" to "can't do" was fatal. The critical measure that allowed a new vision of central banking was the elaboration of a social consensus that brings back something of the "can do" environment.

REFERENCES

Unpublished (Archival) Sources

Bank of England Archive (BOEA), Bank of England, London (United Kingdom).
  OV50 Overseas Department: Central Banking
  G1 Governor's Files

---

[4] Johann Wolfgang von Goethe (2015), *Faust II*, lines 6117–6122 (translated in English by A.S. Kline).

Published Sources

Bánffy, M. trans. Patrick Thursfield (2013). *The Transylvanian Trilogy: They Were Found Wanting / They Were Divided*. New York: Everyman's Library.

Bresciani-Turroni, C. (1937). *The Economics of Inflation: A Study of Currency Depreciation in Post War Germany*. London: Allen & Unwin.

Canetti, E. trans. Carol Stewart (1978). *Crowds and Power*. New York: Seabury.

Capie, F., Goodhart, C., and Schnadt, N. (1994). *The Development of Central Banking: The Tercentenary Symposium of the Bank of England*. Cambridge, UK: Cambridge University Press.

Cunningham, N. E. Jr. (ed.) (2000 [1914]). *Jefferson vs. Hamilton: Confrontations That Shaped a Nation*. Boston & Bedford: St. Martin's Press.

de Cecco, M. (1994). 'Central Banking in Central and Eastern Europe Lessons from the Interwar Years' Experience.' IMF Working Paper No. 94/127, https://ssrn.com/abstract=883403.

Deutsche Reichsbank (1901). *Die Reichsbank. 1876–1900*. Berlin; Jena: Reichsdruckerei; Gustav Fischer.

Eichengreen, B. (1992). *Golden Fetters: The Gold Standard and the Great Depression, 1919–1939*. New York: Oxford University Press.

Feldman, G. D. (1993). *The Great Disorder: Politics, Economics and Society in the German Inflation 1914–1924*. New York: Oxford University Press.

Feldman, G. D. (1995). 'The Deutsche Bank 1914–1933', in Lothar Gall et al. (eds.), *The Deutsche Bank 1870–1995*. London: Weidenfeld, 130–276.

von Goethe, J. trans. A. S. Kline (2015 [1832]). *Faust II*. Scotts Valley, CA: CreateSpace Independent Publishing Platform.

Helfferich, K. (1903). *Das Geld*. Leipzig: Hirschfeld.

Hotson, A. (2017). *Respectable Banking: The Search for Stability in London's Money and Credit Markets since 1695*. Cambridge, UK: Cambridge University Press.

James, H. (1987). 'Die Währungs- und Wirtschaftsstabilisierung 1923/24 in internationaler perspektive', in Werner Abelshauser (ed.), *Die Weimarer Republik als Wohlfahrtsstaat*, Vierteljahrschrift für Sozial- und Wirtschaftsgeschichte, Beiheft 81. Stuttgart: Franz Steiner Verlag, 63–79.

James, H. (1997). *Monetary and Fiscal Unification in Nineteenth Century Germany; What Can Kohl Learn from Bismarck?* Princeton, NJ: Princeton University Press.

James, H. (1999). 'The Reichsbank, 1876–1945', in Deutsche Bundesbank (ed.), *Fifty Years of the Deutsche Mark: Central Bank and the Currency in Germany since 1948*. Oxford: Oxford University Press, 3–54.

James, H. (2001). *The End of Globalization: Lessons from the Great Depression*. Cambridge, MA: Harvard University Press.

James, H. (2020). *Making a Modern Central Bank: The Bank of England 1979–2003*. Cambridge, UK: Cambridge University Press.

Kisch, C. H. and Elkin, W. A. (1928). *Central Banks: A Study of the Constitutions of Banks of Issue*. London: Macmillan.

North, D. and Weingast, B. (1989). 'Constitutions and Commitment: The Evolution of Institutions Governing Public Choice in Seventeenth-Century England'. *Journal of Economic History*, 49(4): 803–832.

Posen, A. (1995). 'Declarations Are Not Enough: Financial Sector Sources of Central Bank Independence', in Ben S. Bernanke and Julio J. Rotemberg (eds.), *NBER Macroeconomics Annual 1995*, Vol.10. Cambridge, MA: MIT Press, 253–274.

Reinhart, C. M. and Belen Sbrancia, M. (2015). 'The Liquidation of Government Debt'. *Economic Policy*, 30(82): 291–333.

Sayers, R. S. (1976). *The Bank of England 1891–1944*, Vol. 1. Cambridge, UK: Cambridge University Press.

Strouse, J. (1999). *Morgan: American Financier*. New York: Random House.

Thiemeyer, Guido (2013). 'Internationalismus als Vorläufer Wirtschaftlicher Integration? Otto von Bismarck, das Phänomen der Supranationalität und die Internationalisierung der Wirtschaft im 19. Jahrhundert', in Ulrich Lappenküper and Guido Thiemeyer (eds.), *Europäische Einigung im 19. und 20. Jahrhundert. Akteure und Antriebskräfte*, Wissenschaftliches Reihe der Otto-von-Bismarck-Stiftung, Vol. 19. Paderborn: Schöningh, 69–93.

Warburg, Paul M. (1914). 'Defects and Needs of Our Banking System'. *Proceedings of the Academy of Political Science in the City of New York*, 4(4): 7–22.

Warburg, Paul M. (1916). 'The Reserve Problem and the Future of the Federal Reserve System. Address of Hon. Paul M. Warburg before the Convention of the American Bankers Association, Kansas City, Mo.,' September 29, 1916. https://fraser.stlouisfed.org/files/docs/historical/federal%20reserve%20history/bog_members_statements/Warburg_19160929.pdf

3

Habit Not Heredity

Central Banks and Global Order

Patricia Clavin

3.1 INTRODUCTION

This chapter shows how central banks' efforts to stabilize the international system gave them a pivotal role in the global order established after the First World War. Section 3.2 explores the emergence of new ideas and practices for global governance during and after the First World War. Section 3.3 asks why in 1919 bankers stood at a distance from the peace negotiations and the creation of the League of Nations, the world's first inter-governmental organization. This apparent absence merits explanation because of the crucial role financial networks played in orientating US neutrality towards the Allied powers and in determining the outcome of the war. Section 3.4 shows how, by the time of Brussels Conference of 1920, financial concerns and the disorderly, war-like character of the peace prompted central bankers to turn to the League of Nations in order to stabilize and facilitate financial markets. Section 3.5 explores how, thereafter, the League's new Economic and Financial Organization (EFO) became a valuable source of financial and economic intelligence. Overtime, the EFO's increased determination to offer a steer on policy, notably with regard to the operations of the gold standard, put it on a collision course with central bankers. The chapter concludes by reflecting on how the foundation of the Bank of International Settlements (BIS) in 1930 signalled an irrevocable break of relations between central bankers and the League. The outcome also marked a shift in the global ordering of capital markets, states, and civil society with long-term consequences for their institutional relations until the Second World War and its aftermath, which signalled a new phase of global disorder, and re-ordering.

3.2 IDEAS AND PRACTICES OF GLOBAL GOVERNANCE

With the end of the First World War in November 1918, the victorious Allied powers, led by Britain and France, alongside the Associated Power of the United States of America sought to establish procedural rules on which stable and legitimate international cooperation would depend. These rules, they argued, would safeguard the prospects for peace, and global stability. In US and British political circles, legal ideas about global order were especially influential, and these states took a prominent role in orchestrating the move from war to peace through the Armistice declared in November 1918.

US President Woodrow Wilson, lawyer and statesman Elihu Root, and Hamilton Holt, educator and journalist, argued that competition between nations would be positive and benign if protected and tamed by the rule of international law.[1] Taken together, their ideas were foundational to the ideology of Wilsonianism. In Root's words: 'American democracy stands for ... something that cannot be measured by the rate of exchange and does not rise or fall with the balance of trade ... The American people stand for a government of laws and not of men' (Root 2014 [1916]: 440–441). These ideas helped to frame the Paris Peace Treaties concluded with the new representatives of the defeated Central powers, and establish a new international organization, the League of Nations. They shaped élite and popular expectations of the peace around the world, and US leadership. Many of these aspirations were to be frustrated as early as 1919, notably when it came to the application of self-determination promised in the Fourteen Points, and when the United States rejected the Covenant of the League of Nations (Manela, 2007).

A great deal of comment at the time, and subsequently, focused on the role of the United States in global order. Some of it related to the impact of Wilson's ideas. It was also the result of the United States' move from being a debtor to creditor, and its emergence as the world's banker. The change was foundational to narratives of the American Century informed by a view of the nineteenth century that cast imperial Britain as the world's policeman. In 1919, Pax Americana replaced Pax Britannica (Kindleberger, 1973; Tooze, 2014).

Latterly this picture has begun to shift. It is now clear the United States was never an all-powerful hegemon even after 1945. Its commitment to international cooperation was often ambivalent, as it was

[1] On Wilson, see Notter (1937) and Skowronek (2006); for Root, see the compilation Root (2014 [1916]); and for Holt, see Holt (1917: 65–69).

in 1919. Moreover, this single-minded focus on the United States in history-writing obscured two equally significant developments for global order in the longer term that emerged in 1919. The first was the importance of multilateral coordination and cooperation (Eichengreen, 1992; Clavin, 1996). The second was the decline of European power in the rest of the world (Hurrell, 2018). This was not self-evident despite the disintegration of the Russian, German, and Austro-Hungarian Empires. The expansion of British and French imperial power, and the effect this had on global geopolitics, masked these trends for some time. Under the auspices of the new Mandates system administered by the League of Nations, Britain and France took charge of territories such as Palestine, Iraq, and Syria (Pedersen, 2015). Moreover, the continued importance of Empire in British and French politics enabled Germany, Japan, and Italy to question the quality of Anglo-French imperial governance on the one hand, and demand the realization of their own claims to empire on the other. The demands of what ultimately became the Axis powers set the world on course for a second world war within a generation of the first.

In 1919, the United States did not yet equate its national security with the security of the world. US naval power was ascendant, but it commanded neither the military nor global strategic assets at Britain's behest (McKercher, 1991). The United States' power was material. What heralded the United States' arrival on the global stage was its emergence as the world's banker in the war, the superior productivity of the US worker, the variety of its exports, and its abundant supplies of commodities (Nolan, 2012: 11–76).

The Norwegian-speaking American-born economist Thorstein Veblen identified the display power of US capital. For a short time, he was a member of The Inquiry, the think-tank established by Wilson in 1917. The President charged it with preparing any future peace settlement after US entry into the war (Gelfand, 1963). By the time Veblen became involved, he was on the way to establishing his reputation as an outlander, an iconoclast … more than a little mad.[2] He soon parted company with The Inquiry, and published part of his contribution to these debates as an *Inquiry into the Nature of Peace* (Veblen, 1964 [1917]; Herman, 1969). In it, Veblen – in contrast to Wilson, Root, and Holt – was pessimistic regarding the prospects of a stable international order based on the primacy of law and state sovereignty. He was sceptical of easy slogans regarding the innate superiority of

---

[2] Chase, Foreword to Veblen (1934 [1899]: xii).

democratic governments, arguing that even at the widest democratic departure from that ancient pattern of masterful tutelage they still bore features
of the old-fashioned patrimonial state (Veblen, 1964 [1917]: 11). He rightly
anticipated that the imperial impulse underlying the operations of major
states, notably democratic ones such as Britain, France, and Italy, threatened the future prospects of a pacific league of nations.[3]

Veblen was an important, non-Marxist critic of capitalism. For him,
the circulation of money that fuelled the processes of globalization, and
the unprecedented expansion of the international economy was not based
on reason alone. It was also as an expression of power. In *The Theory
of the Leisure Class* published in 1899, Veblen outlined how capital had
display-value in a global context, with archaic, barbaric qualities, as well
as progressive ones. For Veblen the processes of globalization were neither uniformly progressive, nor ones that could be readily overthrown
(Diggins, 1999: 41–57, 111–135).[4]

Veblen's focus on the operations and character of global capital implicitly criticized the state-centric view of Wilson, Root, and Holt. The latter
had much less to say about how states related to – or were affected by –
global exchanges of capital, goods, or communicable disease. These were
all phenomena that exploited (or disregarded) state borders. Veblen's
stress on states' limitations recognized the challenges these transnational
currents posed. For all state leaders the realm of foreign relations was
where they had least control, and where power was mutable. His sober
ruminations on new world order led Veblen to conclude, 'powers answer
to an acquired bias, not to an underlying trait ... a matter of habit, not of
heredity' (Veblen, 1964 [1917]: 11).

Veblen's stress on the habitus of government offers us a useful way
of thinking about the relations between the state, markets, and people –
the constituent elements of global order (Hurrell, 2007). These evolved
during the First World War and had important consequences for global
governance. The economy was the decisive weapon of the First World
War. States had developed ever-more sophisticated bureaucratic practices intended to manage the movement of people and goods. Britain led
this transformation by orchestrating the Allied blockade of the central

---

[3] Veblen was prescient on the pressure exerted by the continuity of empire, arguing without the definitive collapse of the Imperial power no pacific league of nations can come to
anything much more than armistice. Veblen (1964 [1917]: 239).

[4] Capital behaved rationally for both Marx and Weber, although it had negative outcomes
for society.

powers. The blockade was a wholesale intervention into international trade with lasting effects. It comprised a series of political, bureaucratic, military, and naval manoeuvres, administered and guided by the British Foreign Office, to convince Allied and neutral countries to cease trading with the Central Powers.

During the war, the belligerent powers suspended membership of the gold standard. Nevertheless, financial cooperation with the United States underpinned the Allied war effort. In 1915, the British and French governments asked J. P. Morgan in New York to float a loan in the United States to facilitate the Allied war effort (Burk, 1985; Horn, 1995). The move helped orientate the neutral United States towards the Allied powers. Subsequently, Morgan Grenfell in London facilitated British credit operations, and by the end of the war, the New York and London firms together constituted the most important merchant bank in the world (Burk, 1989: 133–134; Pak, 2013). In 1920, governments, central bankers, and the League of Nations would call on them to take a lead in the reconstruction of Europe too.

More broadly, prosecuting the war led to the deepening of multilateral ties between the lead Allied powers of Britain and France, and key neutral states, notably the United States, Belgium, the Netherlands, Sweden, Norway, Denmark, Portugal, and Spain. The operations of the Allied blockade, in particular, marked a graduated departure from traditional state-to-state diplomacy to include bureaucratic relationships. The shift towards administration was significant for the future of global order (Clavin, 2020). The work of the Allied Maritime Transport Council (AMTC) was foundational. Managed by a British civil servant and a French businessman – James Arthur Salter and Jean Monnet – the AMTC secretariat set up in 1917 coordinated twenty separate inter-allied committees to organizing shipping and supply lines between the allied powers of Britain, France, Italy, and the United States.

The experience of the AMTC had important consequences for the evolution of global order in the decades that followed. Salter, and others, used the AMTC to make the case for some sort of international administration in the new League of Nations. The League of Nations appointed both Salter and Monnet to leading administrative roles in its secretariat, a significant innovation in the practice of international administration (Decorzant, 2011: 111–141).

Ordinarily, scholars exclude central bankers and their financial networks from the making of a new global order in 1919. This chapter, by contrast, sets out to explore how central bankers sought to build good national habits by promoting key aspects of global governance. Currently, the history of international relations after the First World War is related through three, linked narratives. The first focuses on the failings of US leadership and the 1919 Paris Peace treaties (Steiner, 2005; Ikenberry, 2019). The second, on national comparative histories, recounts governments' decisions to move from economic management and social engagement and allow markets to self-right after a period of greater state intervention during the First World War.[5] The third narrative covers financial histories of the 1920s and focuses on financial reconstruction after hyperinflation, and on the shortcomings of the re-established gold-standard regime (Eichengreen, 1992). Alongside, is a new body of work on the history of internationalism. It explores the formulation and contestation of communal rights for ethnic groups, women, children, and colonial subjects. It also looks at the creation and operations of the League of Nations, and associated institutions such as the International Labour Organization, written from the hitherto largely neglected archive of the institutions themselves.[6]

3.3 CENTRAL BANKS AND THE LEAGUE OF NATIONS

The recovery of the League's institutional archives revealed the wide-ranging international networks that engaged with the new institution. These help expose how central banks and central bankers were a core constituent of the post-1918 global order. The focus on Wilson in general, and his Fourteen Points in particular, hid this from view. The Fourteen Points famously said little about economics and finance, aside from a general commitment to equality of trade conditions expressed in Point III. Even on this, ideas were comparatively underdeveloped. For Wilson, free trade related primarily to two important desiderata: open diplomacy and freedom of the seas (Clavin and Dungy, 2020). It was Wilson's Point XIV that announced a general association of nations. Its purpose was to afford mutual guarantees of political independence and territorial integrity, thereby stressing the traditional aspects of international security: the protection of borders and territorial sovereignty in his programme of world peace.[7] For the Big Three in Paris – US President Woodrow Wilson, Britain's Prime Minister David Lloyd George, and

---

[5] For example, Soutou (1989).
[6] For example, Miller (1994), Pedersen (2015), and Maul (2019).
[7] See https://avalon.law.yale.edu/20th_century/wilson14.asp

the French Premier Georges Clemenceau – the League's focus should be the mediation of geopolitical conflict, as and when it arose (Macmillan, 2003; Yearwood, 2009).

The absence of central banking engagement with the new organization was not, as Rosenberg has suggested, the result of disinterest, or indeed hostility to the League of Nations per se (Rosenberg, 1999: 99). The correspondence of Benjamin Strong, Governor of the Federal Reserve Bank of New York, and Montagu Norman, Governor of the Bank of England, reveals their close interest in the Paris Peace Conference and the League.[8] Norman became Governor in 1920, having been an active and internationally prominent Director of the Bank through the war. The central bankers monitored developments regarding the peace settlement and the new institution closely.[9] The new body would incorporate and be responsible for upholding the new body of international law generated by the peace treaties, managed by individuals in the secretariat, such as Salter, Monnet, and its General Secretary, Eric Drummond, who had also held an important administrative role during the war. Central bankers were closely connected to the networks institutionalized in the League. The body came to serve as a platform to facilitate introductions, as well as connections, and the exchange of information and practices.

The bonds between the bankers and the League of Nations were not purely social and practical. They were ideological. Central bankers may not have seemed like natural bedfellows with humanitarian activists or rights campaigners who also looked to the League to advance their own agendas, but all of them wanted to challenge and, where necessary, limit the agency of the imperial or nation state in relation to their own concerns. The League of Nations, the world's first inter-governmental organization, was founded in 1920. The first few years after the end of the First World War witnessed a great flowering of new international institutions, of differing scale and ambition.[10] Many still exist today. They include the International Union

---

[8] Memorandum by Strong, 30 July 1919, Archives of the Federal Reserve Bank of New York (hereafter FRBNY), FRBNY, 1000.3 2 Foreign Countries – Trips to Europe, 1919, July 20, 1919. The document stresses the importance of leadership both to realize the project of the League of Nations, and the institution's importance to the prospects of peace. See, also Strong to Leffingwell, 21 Aug. 1919, and 30 Aug. 1919, FRBNY, Papers of Benjamin Strong Jr. 1111.1.

[9] See, for instance, the League reports on the Austria situation sent via Arthur Sweetser to Strong, 31 May 1921, FRBNY, Papers of Benjamin Strong Jr. 1111.1.

[10] See the scores of organizations recorded in the League of Nations Search Engine (LON-SEA) database, accessible on www.lonsea.de/.

Against Tuberculosis and Lung Disease, which was instrumental in creating the League's Epidemic Commission, and the International Chamber of Commerce – today the self-styled world business organization boasting over six million members in more than 100 countries.

Despite these initiatives, central bankers and financiers remained aloof from efforts to institutionalize their networks immediately after the war. In key respects financial questions had become more, not less politicized after the war in ways that repelled central bankers and leading private banks, notably J. P. Morgan and Morgan Grenfell. In 1919, war debts due between the Allies and to the associated power of the United States became caught up in Anglo-French determination to impose reparations on the vanquished. The United States opposed this step. Wilson, Lloyd George, and Clemenceau disagreed about the relationship between war debts and reparations; the new nation states that emerged from the former empires, notably Germany, Hungary and Austria, disputed whether they were liable for reparations and whether they would pay them. The peacemakers decided to keep the League of Nations out of these deeply divisive and intensely political discussions.

Indeed, debates about how to pay for war debts and reparations burdened financial relations after the war. The problem had not been of the bankers' making. They had no say in the decision to go to war, yet became responsible for the financial consequences of the conflict because belligerent states resolved the question of how to pay for the war by kicking the problem into the international. Rather than increase taxes nationally during the war, the Allied governments borrowed from one another, and from the Associated Power, the United States. Once the war was over, the victorious European governments sought reparations in the aspiration that these would tame German power, help pay off the costs of reconstruction, and some of the attendant political-social consequences of the war (including widows pensions that were promised to keep conscripted men in the field of battle), and the debts owed to US bondholders (Kent, 1991).

There was the risk that bankers' involvement in the League would politicize financial relations yet further. As Strong put it to Arthur Salter, '[he] was not at all convinced that [in] a … common organisation of central banks the policies of certain banks would not be dictated by the interest of their respective banks rather than by purely monetary considerations'.[11]

---

[11] Record of conversation between Strong and Arthur Salter in Paris, 25 May 1928,4, Papers of Benjamin Strong Jr., FRBNY, 1000.9, Foreign Countries – Trip to Europe, (May 21–July 8, 1928).

Central bank operations in the war offered some prominent examples. The raison d'être of the Bank of England and the Norges Bank may have been to support the fiscal policy of the state or to refinance sovereign debt in ways that were alien to the Banque of France until the First World War. As Bignon and Flandreau have reminded us, the First World War effectively created a dual mandate for the Bank of France: it had to hold huge amounts of sovereign debt while sustaining its commitment to support private agents hit by liquidity shocks. The tensions in this obligation took time to work out, and at some cost to the banks' authority and power (Bignon and Flandreau, 2018: 19–24). This is one example of the way in which the war triggered a recalibration of long-established central-bank obligations within states that would also shape their international behaviour.

In November 1919, after a lengthy tussle with Wilson, the US Congress rejected the Treaty of Versailles with Germany, and with it the covenant of the League of Nations. The development marked a rapid evolution in US foreign policy, further cemented under the subsequent Presidencies of Warren G. Harding and Calvin Coolidge. The year 1920 signalled a new phase in the alignment of the relationships between states, civil society, and markets that would give central-bank relations a renewed prominence.

3.4 THE BRUSSELS CONFERENCE 1920 AND FINANCE ORGANIZED

Like the backward step in a waltz, the retreat of the US state from the international stage created the space for US financiers to step forwards, to recover and redesign their late-nineteenth-century role as financial missionaries to the world (Costigliola, 1984; Rosenberg, 1999). Under Republican Presidents Harding and Coolidge, the White House and State Department denounced foreign entanglements. With stakes in the global markets for capital and goods, financial and business operations stepped into the breach. Financial and business actors also offered connections to, and a window on, the world for successive Republican administrations.

The notion of saving souls associated with missionary work took on a new meaning in the warlike context of the post-war world. The spectacle of communist revolution gripping Russia and threatening Hungary and Germany, was obviously unsettling to capitalists. Strident nationalism was on the rise in central Europe, while Italy succumbed to a new Fascist movement. More directly in the purview of central bankers was the danger posed by the spectacle of hyperinflation licking at the feet of the new republican states of Austria, Germany, Hungary, and Poland.

The situation in Austria was especially acute. As the Austrian Krone slid into hyperinflation, communist revolution in Red Vienna threatened to engulf the republic in civil war, as the politics of the surrounding countryside were resolutely nationalist and catholic. Hunger and disease reached such endemic, life-threatening proportions it triggered a huge international programme of humanitarian aid (Bane and Lutz, 1943). The Swiss government was a close and acute observer. Like other bordering states, it was conscious of the implications of the risk an Austrian implosion posed for its own security. As the Head of the Swiss Army, Major General Emil Sonderegger put it: 'some sort of Putsch would lead to a form of civil war … it would disrupt economic exchanges; forcing us to significantly increase border controls for an extended period, and then there was risk of Swiss volunteers getting mixed up triggering greater, and unwelcome, involvement from the Swiss government'.[12]

Governor Strong had extensive knowledge of the desperate conditions of central Europe, including Austria. He travelled to Europe in the late summer of 1919. His diary recounted his admiration for the work of the American Relief Administration led by Herbert Hoover: 'a magnificent piece of work which could only be conducted successfully by a bold and adventurous spirit with limitless courage'. Strong's arrival in Europe in July coincided with Wilson's failure to win support for article X of the Treaty of Versailles, which pertained to the covenant of the League of Nations. It meant US state actors withdrew from Paris as well as from the Supreme Economic Council of Supply and Relief. This short-lived body had been set up in February 1919 by the governments of Britain, France, Belgium, Italy, and the United States to advise on economic measures pending the peace negotiations. In June 1919, Hoover argued for a discrete continuing 'economic body … in connection with the granting of private and public credits and in the supplying of raw material and food to various countries in Europe'.[13] Hoover's stress on practical cooperation appealed to Strong. The Fed Chairman contrasted it with Wilson, who 'became subject to the influence of a lot of college professors and theorists and idealists who were lacking in practical ideas'.[14]

---

[12] Emil Sonderegger to Head of the Military Department, K. Scheurer, Bern 21 January 1921, Records of the Swiss Foreign Ministry, E 2001 (B)3/10, Diplomatic Documents of Switzerland.

[13] Hoover to Wilson, June 27, 1919, Hoover Institution, Stanford, CA., Supreme Economic Council and American Relief Administration Documents Project, Box 9.

[14] Journal, July 21 to September 20, 1919, 22, Papers of Benjamin Strong Jr, FRBNY, 1000.3.

Over the next few months over a hundred other bankers, economists, and humanitarians joined Hoover's call for more effective economic and financial cooperation. It resulted in a financial conference to be held under the auspices of the new League of Nations (Clavin, 2013). They included representatives from J. P. Morgan, Morgan Grenfell, and Lloyds banks, who were joined by Gerard Vissering, the President of the Bank of the Netherlands, economists Gustav Cassel and John Maynard Keynes and Arthur Pigou, and Gustave Ador, the Swiss President of the International Committee of the Red Cross. Held in Brussels in 1920, it became the world's first ever international financial conference, setting the template for many more such conferences spanning the twentieth and twenty-first centuries. The first resolution passed by delegates at the conference determined 'the first step is to bring public opinion in every country to realise the need for re-establishing public finances on a sound basis as a preliminary to the execution of those social reforms which the world demands.' (League of Nations, 1922: 7)

The reconstruction of the gold standard was at the heart of this programme. Although Britain would not re-join the gold exchange standard until 1925, and France until 1926 (formally 1928), the British and French governments championed the international gold standard as a tool of global order much earlier. Their dominance in the League of Nations was a key part the strategy. They were the leading powers in the institution. The League's machinery for public engagement, established to promote publicly accountable foreign policy in 1920, also put its weight behind sound money. As part of the Brussels conference preparations, League members agreed to the creation of a new Economic and Financial Section in the Secretariat, under Arthur Salter's direction. This body was an evolution of the League's Economic Intelligence Service. Now the League was not just empowered to gather intelligence, but also to take practical steps to facilitate communication and cooperation regarding world markets (Clavin, 2013: 15–33).

The shape of the League's practical steps emerged in the context of central and eastern Europe's continued turbulence, and the faltering global economy (Ansell et al., 2016). What happened on the ground contradicted talk of reconstruction – what was underway was construction. It also contradicted the expressed aspiration to recover the transnational flows of capital and goods independent of the types of state intervention that had characterized the Allied war economy. It soon became clear that new states in central Europe would not be able to secure the capital they needed by a simple approach to the international capital markets, via J. P Morgan, for example. There followed the attempts by the Dutch banker, K. E. Ter Meulen to market Austrian state-guaranteed bonds in London through an office opened by the League of Nations. This, too, failed. In the meantime, during 1921 into 1922 Austrian inflation began to slip into hyperinflation as levels of economic and social distress went up. Studies by Marcus, and Flores Zendejas and Decorzant, stress market conditions as the reasons why financiers at first held back (Marcus, 2018: 78–111; Flores Zendejas and Decorzant, 2016).

Politics also explains why tinkering with established practices of financial diplomacy was not enough in the Austrian case. In a series of moves coordinated via Geneva between Vienna, London, Paris, and New York, in the summer and autumn of 1922, Prime Minister Ignaz Seipel approached the Council of the League of Nations asking for its assistance to bring financial stability to the country. The resultant Geneva Protocol, negotiated through the League Council in October 1922, established an independent central bank in Austria. The new republic became the first former belligerent to return to the gold standard. Throughout, the Bank of England and the Federal Reserve Bank of New York were regularly briefed on the progress of the League's intervention directly from Geneva.[15]

Politics also helps to explain the move to the League of Nations. It is often forgotten that one outcome of the Geneva process was that Austria was spared financial reparations, although it still had to pay reparations in kind, notably commodity supplies to Italy. While reparations were unresolved, it was impossible to determine which national assets could serve as security for the international loan. The Geneva protocol also reinforced the prohibition of *Anschluss* (union) with Germany. The agreement reinforced the boundaries around (and the unequal international treatment of) Austria and Germany. Austria, like Hungary, was admitted as a full League member in 1920; Germany, and for that matter Russia, were not. The financial security afforded to foreign investors was also delivered by political action: a series of extraordinary political guarantees that handed financial oversight of a nation state to an intergovernmental organization. State expenditure, notably in relation to pensions and food subsidies was slashed; and exports, notably in tobacco, were offered as collateral. The League appointed a Commissioner General, Alfred Rudolf Zimmerman. As Marcus has underlined, international control of Austria was 'a measure

---

[15] See, for example, Arthur Sweetser to Benjamin Strong Jr., 31 May 1921; Benjamin Strong to Arthur Sweetser 19 June 1921, and Basil Blackett to Benjamin Strong Jr., 29 June 1921, and FRBNY 1111.1.

that all sides came to see as necessary and even beneficial after alternative routes to raise money had repeatedly proven ineffective'. (Marcus, 2018: 80) Based in Vienna, Zimmerman soon took on the appearance of an effective Governor-General of an occupying colonial power. In the context of the time, when anti-colonial arguments were rooted in debates about poor colonial governance (rather than the immorality of colonialism in absolute terms) the description was not necessarily negative.

League officials took great pride in the way it helped facilitate Austria's stabilization, using the scheme as the basis for similar stabilization and loan programmes extended to Hungary, Greece, and Bulgaria (Clavin, 2013: 11–48; Peterecz, 2013). The process informed the stabilization of Germany (Fraser, 1924) too. The stabilization initiative became the means to show the League could deliver tangible achievements to sceptical member states (Walré de Bordes, 1924: ix). Financial markets developed a positive view of the League's role as an external, multilateral agent, solving the credibility problem of borrowing countries and facilitating a process of domestic reform (Fraser, 1924). Crucially, history would show that this multilateral solution performed better than the bilateral arrangements adopted by other countries in central and eastern Europe, such as Poland. It offered lower borrowing and transaction costs (Flores Zendejas and Decorzant, 2016). The organization readily translated the narrative of Austria's successful stabilization into an account of success for the great experiment in Geneva. Subsequently, this experience would be foundational for the work of the International Monetary Fund after 1945 (Pauly, 1997).

Austrians remembered this early history of their republic's encounter with the new global order very differently. Social Democrats and communists in Vienna were vociferous opponents of the budget cuts (Ausch, 1968). German nationalists and Catholics, who dominated the politics in rural areas, complained about Austria's loss of sovereignty, and insults to its nationhood (Berger, 2000). The Geneva Protocol doubled down on the peacemakers' 1919 prohibition of union with Germany. An increase in antisemitism throughout the region was an overt result. Salter came to understand the risks to the League, and Liberal internationalism, if not to central Europe's Jewish populations. Already by the time of the League efforts to stabilize Hungary in 1923, he worried about more intense national feeling, with a sterner and less pliant population.[16] By the time he advised China on how to tackle its own inflationary challenges, in

---

[16] The Reconstruction of Hungary, address by Salter to Chatham House, 22 May 1924 in League of Nations (1924) 2–5.

1931, Salter no longer regarded the Austria case as a model. Its political effects had been too severe.[17] In the case of Austria, the republic was never able to heal the wounds of defeat, nor overcome the local perceptions of a marked deterioration of its people's living standards or prospects after the end of Empire. Over time, the responsibility for the region's decline was transferred from Austria-Hungary's failed imperial leadership to the treaties drafted by the victorious powers at the Paris Peace Conference and to the institution of the League of Nations (Bischof et al., 2010). *Anschluss* with National-Socialist led Germany – in violation of international law – was the outcome.

What endured unquestioned in the 1920s, 1930s, and 1940s was the League's growing and unparalleled global role in gathering information and exchanging knowledge. This had begun with the advertisement of Austrian conditions on the international capital markets, and had snowballed. In the 1920s alone, the League investigated the causes and remedies of international protectionism; the operations of commodity markets and cartels; double taxation and fiscal evasion. In 1927 and 1933, the League hosted two major World Economic Conferences – templates for the Bretton Woods Conference of 1944. States that formally never joined, such as the United States, or left in umbrage, including Germany and Japan, consulted and referenced this League-generated data (Burkman, 2008; Herren, 2009: 74–79). Today, it continues to be the primary historical data source of the operation of the global economy in the period from 1914 to 1946 – the year the League was dissolved officially.

Mining and curating this information continued throughout the organization's lifetime, even during the Second World War. In 1940, safeguarding the economic and financial intelligence garnered by the League, and defining the lessons of twenty years of institutional experience, informed the League's Mission to Princeton. Based at the Institute of Advanced Study in Princeton, the mission acted as an international focal point for the exchange of ideas and practices for post-war planning and reconstruction. Even E. H. Carr, one of the most forceful and vociferous critics of the League's operations in its lifetime, acknowledged and praised the quality of this work (Carr, 1939: 102).

---

[17] Mission to China, January–April 1931, draft report by Arthur Salter, Papers of Arthur Salter, SALT 1/10, Churchill Archives Centre, Cambridge. I am indebted to C. H. Lucas Tse for this comparative connection.

3.5 THE BREAK WITH THE LEAGUE OF NATIONS

None of these activities was value neutral. The League inquiry into the operation of the gold standard launched in 1928 set leading central bankers on a collision course with one another, and with the League. The League's special Sub-committee on the Purchasing Power of Gold – which became known as the Gold Delegation – brought together more than twenty-five monetary experts from around the world in a series of meetings. Together, they published three substantial reports, a variety of supplementary commentaries, and wealth of statistical information (Clavin and Wessels, 2004).

The inquiry was focused on two tightly drawn, technical concerns that emerged from debates between the League's inter-governmental Financial Committee and bureaucrats of the Economic and Financial Section. The first was the uneven distribution of gold reserves around the world. The war and post-war inflation had caused a massive outflow of gold to the United States, and after 1926 to France, following its return to the gold standard at a markedly undervalued rate. The second issue was that, for various reasons, the price of gold was falling, making it less profitable to mine, which reduced the overall level of supply. All this at a time when the League of Nations was actively encouraging states to become responsible members of the gold standard club. It increased the demand for monetary gold, notably US dollars, in ways that increased global deflationary pressures.

Publicly, the League Council, made up of leading member states, linked the investigation to its long-standing commitment to the financial stability of Austria and Hungary (League of Nations, 1928: 1031). Privately the inquiry had a much bigger remit, which enabled some members to question the effects of the gold standard on the operation of the global economy, and ultimately its viability.

The history of life behind the scenes of the Gold Delegation revealed that Strong and Norman were happy to hitch their star to the League when it came to promoting the gold standard as part of the move to a rules-based global order in 1919. But they changed their mind when the League officials and some state representatives began to ask questions about how well the system was working in general, and examining the operations of the Federal Reserve Bank and the Banque de France, in particular. In May 1928, Salter sought Strong's support for the Gold Delegation, describing it as 'the second phase of post-war monetary reconstruction … to determine whether or not there was likely to be an insufficient supply of gold to meet the post-war world, and if so to find out what were the best means of meeting the situation.' Strong was forceful in his rebuttal, making clear his long-held and deep-seated animosity of the League's incursion into this policy-space.[18] Strong's successor in 1928, George L. Harrison, was only moderately less hostile. He would tolerate the inquiry, he told League officials visiting him in New York, only if 'the most responsible people' served on the Sub-committee; proceedings were slow; there was no publicity; and no reports or interim reports 'as to substance'. Even then, Harrison refused to supply a delegate from the Fed. Choosing his words carefully, Salter did not agree but promised to 'make the study as unobjectionable as possible to the banks of issue'.[19] The central banks of France and Germany made similar protests.[20]

From the League's vantage point imbalances and risks to the global economy, and the stabilization project which it sought to support, were becoming readily apparent. The Wall Street crash in October 1929 underscored that the world economy faced major problems. The challenge was agreeing what these were and how to tackle them. League data pointed to the increasing divergence between US and French monetary and economic fortunes, and British and German performance. British dominance in the League, and Salter and Lovedays close ties to Whitehall, where they had worked in the past, to the City of London and to British academic circles meant they were all too aware of mounting pressures on sterling. Behind the scenes, the Bank of England was prepared to use the League as an alternative forum to central bankers' meetings to discuss challenges facing the international gold exchange standard.

At the start, Norman was a covert but interested supporter of the Gold Delegation's work. He was in close contact with key players in it. They included Sir Otto Niemeyer, the British representative to the Financial Committee, and Sir Henry Strakosch, an important confident of Norman's who was then serving as chairman of the Union Corporation, a South African mining company. Norman told Strong and Moreau he did not approve of the League looking into the operation of the gold standard while at the same time encouraging the secretariat to pursue the

---

[18] Strong Conversation with Arthur Salter, Paris, 25 May 1928, 4–5, Papers of Benjamin Strong Jr., FRBNY, 1000.9, Foreign Countries – Trip to Europe, (May 21–July 8, 1928).

[19] Memorandum by Harrison, 26 February 1929, and conversation with Avenol, 26 April 1929, Papers of George L. Harrison, FRBNY, C798/1st File/1927-Dec 1929 – League of Nations.

[20] Summary of a letter by Siepman, 20 November 1928, Bank of England Archives (hereafter BOEA), OV48/2; Norman to Schacht, 13 December 1928, and Schacht to Norman, 21 December 1928, and Moreau to Norman, 28 December 1928, BOEA, G1.

enquiry (Clavin and Wessels, 2004). It was a risky strategy for Norman, for the central bankers of Belgium, the Netherlands, Poland, and Czechoslovakia, lined up to take part. It also carried reputational dangers for the League given its fledgling authority in the field of economic and financial affairs. It was now moving more overtly in the direction of offering policy advice, which risked alienating powerful private financial interests, and incurring hostility from leading member states, notably France, which was strongly committed to the gold standard order.

The real intellectual heft of the committee came from its expert members, notably the Swedish economist Gustav Cassel and Strakosch. While in April 1929, Harrison warned that the delegation's work could endanger future American cooperation with European central banks, Strakosch urged the group to move quickly: 'an all-round contraction of credit, with an all-round tendency for falling prices' looked inevitable. For Cassel, too, grave economic danger lay ahead.[21] Both men were right. They identified the problem in the delegation's private meetings, and in its published materials.

The League proved a useful vehicle to exchange data and to disseminate and exchange expert interpretations (League of Nations, 1930a–d; 1931; 1932). But it was the wrong institution to facilitate central banking cooperation. The organization also attempted to rise to the challenge of coordinating national responses to the global challenge posed by the Great Depression with preparations for a World Economic Conference after 1931. It met in London in the summer of 1933 and failed because of the lack of political will to cooperate by all the key players (Clavin, 1991).

When it came to facilitating central banking cooperation, the Fed's opposition to the gold inquiry on political grounds was an insuperable obstacle. Fed officials disliked the implicit criticism by the League of American monetary policy, however obliquely Geneva expressed it. The Fed also pointed to domestic hazards. The League's activities drew attention to the Fed's international activities, risking increased domestic opposition to its international activities as a whole; not least because the United States was not formally a member of the League.[22] Although a comparatively obscure, technical investigation, the Gold Delegation nevertheless drew unwelcome public attention to the international operations of US finance broadly conceived.

---

[21] First Session, Minutes of the Sixth Meeting of the Gold Delegation held in Geneva, 29 August 1929, 16, Archives of the League of Nations, LON R2964, 10E/14089/5196.

[22] Norman to Harrison, 29 August 1930, BOEA, G 1/30. For the French reaction to the Interim Report see Mouré (2002: 191–193).

Britain was the League's main backer. But in 1929, with pressure mounting on sterling, the Bank of England placed greater weight on preserving its gold standard membership, however problematic it was proving to be. Relations with the Fed and the Banque and France came first; supporting the wider operations of the League's economic and financial agenda came second. Norman fell in behind Harrison's call to transfer some of the delegation's work to a less public forum, the newly established BIS. Central bankers could do nothing to supress the Gold Delegation reports entering the public domain. Technically and politically they were a landmark. It was the first time an international organization had asked trenchant questions about financial policy and demanded answers from the world's leading monetary authorities. On a practical level, the Gold Delegation's work was less successful. The League's hands were tied by its official commitment to present a scientific, impartial, and collective view. Its final report contained a huge and varied amount of statistical material; its Covenant prevented it from offering clear policy prescriptions. Individual, expert reports, notably the one by Strakosch, condemning the 'excessive accumulation of gold' by the United States and France, and shortcomings in central bank coordination were closer to the mark. They were useful discussion points, but no roadmap to action.

Strakosch identified the problem, but tellingly when Britain came off the gold standard a year later, the British government and the Bank of England largely abandoned the League of Nations as a site for inter-governmental coordination and cooperation on monetary questions. For contemporaries, the change was made visible by the failure of British leadership at the World Economic Conference of 1933. This League-sponsored conference was held in London, because the League of Nations hosted the long-anticipated International Disarmament Conference at the same time. In Geneva, planning for the event had begun in 1930. By the time it convened in the summer of 1933, Britain and the United States had left the gold standard, and the 'fetishes of so-called international bankers' were roundly denounced by US President Franklin D. Roosevelt. The break between central bankers and the League was now complete and irrevocable (Clavin, 1991; 1992).

3.6 CONCLUSION

This history of the central bankers' engagement and subsequent disenchantment with the League of Nations demonstrated their interest in institutionalised cooperation. It underscored their commitment to what they described as 'technical' aspects of financial cooperation, although the history of central bankers' early engagement with the League and the case of Austria's stabilization revealed a clear ideological component. As the financial world of the League took shape, and bankers turned away from it, they did not turn away from efforts to institutionalize global order.

In 1930, at the point when central bankers' relations with the League ruptured thanks to the work of the Gold Delegation, along came the BIS. Established as part of the Young Plan loans to Germany, the BIS was charged with responsibilities hitherto carried by the Agent General for Reparations in Berlin. The BIS name derived from this role. But reparations payments stalled within a year, and the BIS instead developed some of the same functions of financial coordination and intelligence gathering pioneered by the League. Indeed, early BIS members greatly admired the data-collection aspects of the League's gold inquiry and hired some of the Economic and Financial Sections former staff members. They included a future and highly regarded director of the IMF, Per Jacobsson. Only a scenic train-ride away from Geneva, with offices in Basel, the BIS underscored its difference from the technical work of the League. It described itself as a 'club for central bankers'. In contrast to the League's stress on open diplomacy, and its wide-ranging brief, the BIS's contribution to the emerging architecture of institutionalized governance stressed the importance of exclusivity and confidentiality (Toniolo, 2005).

The habits of institutionalized financial cooperation that developed during and after the First World War left deep tracks. Central bankers consistently stressed the primacy of sound money, and the importance of rules to manage monetary exchange. The rules-based habits of the gold exchange standard matched the wider move to establish a rules-based order in 1919. Throughout the twentieth-century, social networks and institutionalized cooperation remained vital as central banks became a core pillar of new, nation-states set up in a post-colonial world. Here, habits set by the creation and stabilization of the first Austrian Republic helped create the template. As then, after 1945 international recognition of a new central bank was a key condition for new states seeking access to the global capital market.

In 1919, the Paris peacemakers and the League of Nations sought primarily to bring order to European affairs. Capitalism, imperialism, and 'rights talk' shaped the League's global reach. During the course of the twentieth century, this Western system of governance assumed global dominance. One hundred years later, relations between states are changing with the emergence of 'Superpower China' and 'Rising India'. It seems likely, however, that the history of the twenty-first century will not be determined solely by China any more than the twentieth century was determined by the United States. With the structures of global capitalism in flux and new forms of communication creating a disruptive, open diplomacy of their own, the need to imagine and realize a new future for global order is more pressing than ever. The history of global order after 1919 shows us that the challenges the world faces are common ones that lie beyond the boundaries and sole control of states. And it reminds us of the key role played by central banks and institutionalized cooperation.

REFERENCES

Unpublished (Archival) Sources

Archive of the League of Nations (LON), Geneva (Switzerland).
Archives of the Federal Reserve Bank of New York (FRBNY), New York (United States).
Bank of England Archive (BOEA), Bank of England, London (United Kingdom).
 OV48 Overseas Department: Gold
 G1 Governor's Files
Churchill Archives Centre, Cambridge (United Kingdom).
Supreme Economic Council & American Relief Administration Documents Project, Hoover Institution, Stanford, California (United States).

Published Sources

Ansell, Christopher, Levi-Faur, David, and Trondal, Jarle (2016). 'An Organizational–Institutional Approach to Governance', in Christopher Ansell, Jarle Trondal, and Morten Øgård (eds.), *Governance in Turbulent Times*. Oxford: Oxford University Press, 1–24.
Ausch, Karl (1968). *Als die Banken fielen: Zur Soziologie der politischen Korruption*. Vienna: Europa.
Bane, Suda Lorena and Lutz, Ralph Haswell (1943). *Organization of American Relief in Europe, 1918–1919, including Negotiations Leading up to the Establishment of the Office of Director General of Relief at Paris by the Allied and Associated Powers*. Hoover Institution Publication No. 20. Stanford, CA: Stanford University Press.
Berger, Peter (2000). *Im Schatten der Diktatur. Die Finanzdiplomatie des Verters des Völkerbundes in Österreich, Meinoud Marius Rost van Tonnigen, 1931–1936*. Vienna: Böhlau Verlag.
Bignon, Vincent and Flandreau, Marc (2018). 'The Other Way: A Narrative History of the Bank of France'. Discussion Paper (Centre for Economic Policy Research [Great Britain]); No. 13138. London.
Bischof, Günter, Plasser, Fritz, and Berger, Peter (2010). *From Empire to Republic: Post-World War I Austria*. Contemporary Austrian Studies, Vol. 19. New Orleans, LA; Innsbruck: UNO Press; Innsbruck University Press.

Burk, Kathleen (1985). *Britain, America and the Sinews of War, 1914–1918.* Boston and London: G. Allen & Unwin.

Burk, Kathleen (1989). *Morgan Grenfell 1838–1988: The Biography of a Merchant Bank.* Oxford: Oxford University Press.

Burkman, Thomas W. (2008). *Japan and the League of Nations: Empire and World Order, 1914–1938.* Honolulu: University of Hawai'i Press.

Carr, Edward Hallett (1939). *The Twenty Years Crisis, 1919–1939: An Introduction to the Study of International Relations.* London: Macmillan.

Clavin, Patricia (1991). 'The World Economic Conference 1933: The Failure of British Internationalism'. *Journal of European Economic History*, 20(3): 489–527.

Clavin, Patricia (1992). 'The Fetishes of So-Called International Bankers: Central Bank Co-operation for the World Economic Conference, 1932–3'. *Contemporary European History*, 1(3): 281–311.

Clavin, Patricia (1996). *The Failure of Economic Diplomacy: Britain, Germany, France and the United States, 1931–36.* Basingstoke and New York: Macmillan; St. Martin's Press.

Clavin, Patricia (2013). *Securing the World Economy: The Reinvention of the League of Nations, 1920–1946.* Oxford: Oxford University Press.

Clavin, Patricia (2020). 'The Ben Pimlott Memorial Lecture 2019: Britain and the Making of Global Order after 1919'. *Twentieth Century British History*, 31(3): 340–359.

Clavin, Patricia and Dungy, M. (2020). 'Trade, Law and the Global Order of 1919'. *Diplomatic History*, 44: 554–579.

Clavin, Patricia and Wessels, J. W. (2004). 'Another Golden Idol? The League of Nations Gold Delegation and the Great Depression, 1929–1932'. *International History Review*, 26(4): 765–795.

Costigliola, Frank (1984). *Awkward Dominion: American Political, Economic, and Cultural Relations with Europe, 1919–1933.* Ithaca and London: Cornell University Press.

Decorzant, Yann (2011). *La Société des Nations et la naissance d' une conception de la régulation économique internationale.* Brussels: Peter Lang.

Diggins, John P. (1999). *Thorstein Veblen: Theorist of the Leisure Class.* Princeton, NJ: Princeton University Press.

Eichengreen, Barry (1992). *Golden Fetters: The Gold Standard and the Great Depression, 1919–1939.* Oxford: Oxford University Press.

Flores Zendejas, Juan H. and Decorzant, Yann (2016). 'Going Multilateral? Financial Markets Access and the League of Nations Loans, 1923–8'. *Economic History Review*, 69(2): 653–678.

Fraser, Drummond (1924). 'A Return to the Gold Standard'. *Barrons* (1921–1942), 21 July 1924.

Gelfand, Lawrence E. (1963). *The Inquiry: American Preparations for Peace, 1917–1919.* New Haven: Yale University Press.

Herman, Sondra R. (1969). *Eleven against War: Studies in American Internationalist Thought, 1898–1921.* Stanford, CA: Hoover Institution Press, Stanford University.

Herren, Madeleine (2009). *Internationale Organisationen seit 1865. Eine Globalgeschichte der Internationalen Ordnung.* Darmstadt: Wissenschaftliche Buchgesellschaft.

Holt, Hamilton (1917). 'The League to Enforce Peace'. *Proceedings of the Academy of Political Science in the City of New York*, 7(2): 65–69.

Horn, Martin (1995). 'External Finance in Anglo-French Relations in the First World War, 1914–1917'. *The International History Review*, 17(1): 51–77.

Hurrell, Andrew (2007). *On Global Order: Power, Values, and the Constitution of International Society*. Oxford: Oxford University Press.

Hurrell, Andrew (2018). 'Beyond the BRICS: Power, Pluralism, and the Future of Global Order'. *Ethics and International Affairs*, 32(1): 89–101.

Ikenberry, G. John (2019). *After Victory: Institutions, Strategic Restraint, and the Rebuilding of Order after Major Wars*. New edition. Princeton Studies in International History and Politics 161. Princeton, NJ: Princeton University Press.

Kent, Bruce (1991). *The Spoils of War: The Politics, Economics and Diplomacy of Reparations 1918–1932*. Reprinted with Corrections edition. Oxford: Clarendon Press.

Kindleberger, Charles P. (1973). *The World in Depression, 1929–1939*. History of the World Economy in the Twentieth Century, Vol. 4. Berkeley: University of California Press.

League of Nations (1922). *Brussels Financial Conference, 1920. The Recommendations and their Application. A Review after Two Years*, Vol. II. Geneva: League of Nations.

League of Nations (1924). *Financial Reconstruction of Hungary: Agreements Drawn up by the League of Nations and Signed at Geneva on March 14th, 1924 Together with the Documents and Public Declaration Relating Thereto*. Geneva: League of Nations.

League of Nations (1928). 'Meeting of 31st Session of the Gold Delegation'. *Official Journal*. Geneva: League of Nations.

League of Nations (1930a). *Legislation on Gold*. Geneva: League of Nations.

League of Nations (1930b). *Interim Report of the Gold Delegation of the Financial Committee*. Geneva: League of Nations.

League of Nations (1930c). *Principles and Methods of Financial Reconstruction Work Undertaken Under the Auspices of the League of Nations*. Geneva: League of Nations.

League of Nations (1930d). *Selected Documents Submitted to the Gold Delegation of the Financial Committee*. Geneva: League of Nations.

League of Nations (1931). *Interim Report of the Gold Delegation of the Financial Committee*. Geneva: League of Nations.

League of Nations (1932). *Final Report of the Gold Delegation of the Financial Committee*. Geneva: League of Nations.

MacMillan, Margaret (2003). *Peacemakers: The Paris Peace Conference of 1919 and Its Attempt to End War*. London: John Murray.

Manela, Erez (2007). *The Wilsonian Moment: Self-determination and the International Origins of Anticolonial Nationalism*. New York: Oxford University Press.

Marcus, Nathan (2018). *Austrian Reconstruction and the Collapse of Global Finance, 1921–1931*. Cambridge, MA: Harvard University Press.

Maul, Daniel (2019). *International Labour Organization: 100 Years of Global Social Policy*. Berlin: De Gruyter.

McKercher, B. J. C. (1991). *Anglo-American Relations in the 1920s: The Struggle for Supremacy*. Basingstoke: Macmillan.

Miller, Carol (1994). '"Geneva – the Key to Equality": Inter-war Feminists and the League of Nations'. *Women's History Review*, 3(2): 219–245.

Mouré, Kenneth (2002). *The Gold Standard Illusion: France, the Bank of France, and the International Gold Standard, 1914–1939*. Oxford: Oxford University Press.

Nolan, Mary (2012). *The Transatlantic Century: Europe and the United States, 1890–2010*. New Approaches to European History; 46. Cambridge and New York: Cambridge University Press.

Notter, Harley A. (1937). *The Origins of the Foreign Policy of Woodrow Wilson*. Baltimore, MD: Johns Hopkins Press.

Pak, Susie (2013). *Gentlemen Bankers: The World of J. P. Morgan*. Cambridge, MA: Harvard University Press.

Pauly, Louis W. (1997). *Who Elected the Bankers? Surveillance and Control in the World Economy*. Cornell Studies in Political Economy. Ithaca and London: Cornell University Press.

Pedersen, Susan (2015). *The Guardians: The League of Nations and the Crisis of Empire*. New York: Oxford University Press.

Peterecz, Zoltán (2013). *Jeremiah Smith, Jr. and Hungary, 1924–1926: The United States, the League of Nations, and the Financial Reconstruction of Hungary*. Budapest: Versita.

Root, Elihu (2014). *Addresses on International Subjects, compiled and edited by Robert Bacon and James Brown Scott*. Cambridge, MA: Harvard University Press, originally published in 1916.

Rosenberg, Emily S. (1999). *Financial Missionaries to the World: The Politics and Culture of Dollar Diplomacy, 1900–1930*. Cambridge, MA and London: Harvard University Press.

Skowronek, Stephen (2006). 'The Reassociation of Ideas and Purposes: Racism, Liberalism, and the American Political Tradition'. *American Political Science Review*, 100(3): 385–401.

Soutou, Georges-Henri (1989). *L'or et le Sang: Les Buts de Guerre Économiques de la Première Guerre Mondiale*. Paris: Fayard.

Steiner, Zara (2005). *The Lights That Failed: European International History, 1919–1933*. Oxford: Oxford University Press.

Toniolo, Gianni (2005). *Central Bank Cooperation at the Bank for International Settlements, 1930–1973*. Studies in Macroeconomic History. Cambridge: Cambridge University Press.

Tooze, J. Adam (2014). *The Deluge: The Great War, America and the Remaking of Global Order, 1916–1931*. New York: Penguin.

Veblen, Thorstein (1934). *The Theory of the Leisure Class: An Economic Study of Institutions*. New York: Modern Library, originally published in 1899.

Veblen, Thorstein (1964). *An Inquiry into the Nature of Peace and the Terms of Its Perpetuation*. Reprints of economic classics. New York: A.M. Kelley, originally published in 1917.

Walré de Bordes, J. Van (1924). *The Austrian Crown, Its Depreciation and Stabilization*. London: P. S. King.

Yearwood, Peter J. (2009). *Guarantee of Peace: The League of Nations in British Policy, 1914–1925*. New York & Oxford: Oxford University Press.

4

Institutionalizing Central Bank Cooperation

The Norman–Schacht Vision and Early Experience of the Bank for International Settlements, 1929–1933

Piet Clement

In July 1927, four central bankers spent a long weekend at the summerhouse of US Under-Secretary of the Treasury Ogden Mills on Long Island, New York.[1] They were Montagu Norman, Governor of the Bank of England, Hjalmar Schacht, the President of the German Reichsbank, Charles Rist, Vice-Governor of the Bank of France, and, finally, Benjamin Strong, President of the Federal Reserve Bank of New York – who had organized the gathering. The meeting has gone down in history as the occasion when the Europeans – Norman in particular – persuaded Strong to lower US interest rates and thereby reduce market pressures on sterling and on the recently restored gold standard. This would turn out to be a momentous decision; it has been directly linked to the ensuing stock market boom, and hence to the eventual Wall Street crash of October 1929, that marked the start of the Great Depression (Clarke, 1967: 123–124; Ahamed, 2009: 291–344).

The Long Island meeting may be seen as the high point of the bilateral diplomacy that bound the world's leading central banks together during the turbulent 1920s. It developed from the strong professional and personal relationship between Strong and Norman that had developed subsequent to their initial meeting in 1916. From 1924 they were joined by Schacht, who had been instrumental in ending German hyperinflation and stabilizing the Reichsmark. And from 1927, the Bank of France joined in, once the French franc had been restored to the

---

[1] The views expressed in this chapter are those of the author and do not necessarily reflect those of the Bank for International Settlements.

gold standard and the ensuing boom propelled France to a position of economic and monetary strength. Gathering in a secluded villa on Long Island the four most powerful central bankers of the day must have had different objectives in mind. If Norman was set on protecting sterling's wafer-thin gold base, Schacht had Germany's crippling reparations burden foremost on his mind. Nevertheless, all were united in their view that only their close cooperation could safeguard the gold exchange standard, and thus transatlantic monetary and financial stability and economic prosperity.

To be sure, cooperation among central banks was not a novelty. Even under the classical gold standard (1870s–1914) the main central banks had cooperated sporadically – for instance during the 1890 Baring crisis, and at the time of the financial crisis of 1907. However, the historian Marc Flandreau has forcefully argued that such cooperation 'had been exceptional, never reciprocal, and always failed to institutionalize'.[2] Yet, mindful of the monetary chaos caused by the First World War, many central bankers – and notably Montagu Norman – held the view that the world's leading central banks ought to cooperate more closely and within an established institutional setting. Such a setting, Norman argued, would remove one of the main obstacles to ad hoc cooperation, as it would dispel undue expectations and press interest on each occasion when a central bank Governor left his capital to seek out his counterparts abroad.[3] Within a decade the Bank for International Settlements (BIS) would be established, and Norman's vision became a reality. Both he, and Hjalmar Schacht to an even greater degree, would claim that the BIS was their creation. It is therefore worth exploring what kind of an international, cooperative organization they had in mind, and whether the BIS eventually lived up to their expectations.

---

[2] Flandreau (1997: 737). Other scholars have taken a more positive view of central bank cooperation during the classical Gold Standard era. See: Eichengreen (1992) and Borio and Toniolo (2008: 16–75).

[3] In 1930, in his testimony to the UK Government Macmillan Committee, Norman explained that he had been unsuccessful in summoning a formal conference of central bankers during the 1920s, for the simple reason that: 'people would not come (...), not because they were unwilling to cooperate, but because they were unwilling to face the publicity and the questionings in their own countries which would arise if they attended any such conference' (Einzig 1932: 242). The idea of a regular gathering or conference of central bank governors had been given impetus by the League of Nations economic and financial conferences of Brussels (1920) and Genoa (1922).

4.1 NORMAN, SCHACHT, AND CENTRAL BANK COOPERATION IN THE 1920S

It is hard to pin down what exactly Norman and Schacht had in mind when they spoke of the need to institutionalize central bank cooperation. Neither was in the habit of explaining their actions or spelling out their vision in public. Both were comfortable with – and may even have relished – the aura of mystery and mystique that defined their public image; not unlike the Chairman of the Federal Reserve Board more than sixty years later. Nevertheless, some insight can be gained from archival sources, memoirs, and later scholarly work.

In the 1920s, the primary objective of international central bank cooperation was to guarantee the restoration and smooth functioning of the gold standard, which was regarded as the linchpin that would enable a return to the monetary and financial stability that had prevailed before 1914. Yet, everyone recognized that the restoration of the pre-war gold standard was far from easy. The war had caused massive destruction, economic dislocation, and run-away inflation in many European countries. Restoring economic prosperity and trade while at the same time lowering prices required a massive domestic and international effort. In fact, most European countries, with the notable exception of the United Kingdom, did not succeed in restoring their currencies at pre-war gold parity. Instead, they opted for stabilization at a new parity, based on the gold and foreign exchange holdings of their central banks. Yet it was clear that operating this reformed gold exchange standard by just relying on the kind of automaticity that had been characteristic of the pre-war, pure gold standard, was not a realistic option for many reasons – not least the increased political constraints to domestic monetary policy in the era of democracy, and the uneven distribution of gold reserves between the main central banks. In short, it was felt that enhanced international cooperation was required not just to help countries restore the gold standard but also to make it run smoothly.

During the 1920s, the primary locus for this international cooperation was the Financial Committee of the newly founded League of Nations in Geneva. Montagu Norman played a leading role in promoting the restoration of the gold exchange standard and, through this, the cooperation of central banks. On more than one occasion this meant not just giving advice, but also arranging financial assistance contingent on the implementation of monetary, financial, and budgetary reforms in the recipient countries.

The League of Nations, as an inter-governmental organization, was essentially a political body. Central banks may have tried to assert control through the Finance Committee, but ultimately they remained dependent on political power-brokering and decision making. Montagu Norman was himself a political operator, who was keen to restore sterling's pre-war pre-eminence as a global reserve currency by doing everything in his power to extend the Bank of England's influence over the newly founded and smaller central banks in Europe (Schuker, 2003: 60–63). He fiercely believed that international monetary and financial arrangements and cooperation should be left to the central banks, not to the politicians. Therefore, he insisted that central banks ought to be as independent as possible from government. In a rare memorandum, which he circulated to an inner circle of central bankers in March 1921, Norman spelled out his vision of the constitution and remit of the modern central bank. Independence from national government, separation from, and supervision of, commercial banking, and international cooperation among central banks were the key strategic points he described (Clay, 1957: 282–285 and Toniolo, 2005: 19).

Hjalmar Schacht had an even more comprehensive vision of what central bank cooperation might achieve. Naturally, his views were shaped by his experience of overcoming German hyperinflation and then having to defend the Reichsmark's fragile stability in the face of exaggerated reparation demands and foreign exchange pressures. Even during the Long Island meeting in July 1927, Schacht made a case for renegotiating the 1924 reparations arrangement – the Dawes Plan. The need to fund reparation payments and to restore the German economy after the war had increased Germany's reliance on external funding (through government and commercial loans) to breaking point. Furthermore, Schacht argued, Germany's capacity to generate income from investments abroad and from international trade had been seriously curtailed as the result of territorial changes, reduced market access, and the loss of German colonies imposed by the Treaty of Versailles. If the other countries – and by this he meant primarily France, the United Kingdom, and the United States – wanted to help Germany meet its reparation obligations, they needed to provide loans to less developed countries, which would enable those to purchase investment goods and equipment from Germany (Schacht, 1953: 311–313). What Schacht apparently had in mind was the creation of some sort of international consortium that would float loans for global economic development, thereby stimulating industrial exports from Europe, and from Germany in particular. He would return to this idea again in early 1929, in discussions with Owen Young. In the late 1920s, Schacht became increasingly worried about the inflow of short-term credits into Germany. He repeatedly pleaded for some sort of international mechanism to foster medium- and long-term lending and world economic development as a more viable alternative. What role central banks were to play in such a scheme was less clear, but if they could be leveraged for this purpose, all the better.

Both Norman and Schacht understood that for international monetary cooperation to be successful it was essential to keep the US Federal Reserve on board. The United States had granted significant war loans to the Allies, which the European countries were hoping to redeem thanks to the reparation payments transferred to them by Germany. Moreover, US banks had funded investments in Europe on a massive scale during the 1920s boom. For all these reasons, transatlantic monetary cooperation was deemed to be essential. However, the spirit of Long Island failed to endure. Benjamin Strong, Norman's strongest ally, died suddenly in October 1928. His successor at the helm of the New York Fed, George Harrison, shared Strong's international outlook but not his strong personal bond with Norman or the other European central bankers. Moreover, the independence of the New York Fed was being increasingly challenged by the other Federal Reserve Banks as well by the Federal Reserve Board in Washington, forcing Harrison to proceed with greater caution. These developments would prove to be a serious obstacle to institutionalizing international central bank cooperation. Considering that both Norman and Schacht claimed the BIS was their idea, the question arises how much of their vision on central bank cooperation inspired the negotiations leading up to the creation of the Bank, and how much of it materialized in practice once the BIS had first opened its doors in Basel in May 1930.

4.2 THE CREATION OF THE BANK FOR INTERNATIONAL SETTLEMENTS, 1929–1930

The Bank for International Settlements (BIS) was set up through an intergovernmental treaty (The Hague Conference, August 1929–January 1930), but it was very much the brainchild of the directors of the founder central banks. The immediate cause for the creation of the BIS was the so-called final settlement of the issue of First World War reparations that had blighted international relations following the war. In June 1929, a committee of experts, chaired by the American banker Owen D. Young, proposed a revised payments scheme for the reparations due by Germany to the creditor nations (Belgium, France, Italy, and the United Kingdom), which would allow them to be commercialized through an international bank specifically created for this purpose. This would enable the abolition of the Office of the Agent General for Reparations in Berlin, and the lifting of military and political controls imposed on Germany in the wake of the 1919 Treaty of Versailles.

The Young Plan was agreed to in principle at the first Hague Conference in August 1929, where a number of expert committees were tasked with working out the technical details for final approval at the second Hague Conference (January 1930). One of these committees, the Organisation Committee for the Bank for International Settlements, met in October-November 1929 in the German spa resort of Baden-Baden.[4] It was almost entirely composed of central bankers. Hjalmar Schacht represented the German Reichsbank, and Clément Moret the Bank of France. Somewhat surprisingly, the Bank of England was not represented by Montagu Norman, but by one of its directors, Charles Addis.

The deliberations at Baden-Baden focused on the scope and objectives of the Bank for International Settlements, and on how these should be reflected in the Bank's statutes. All participants agreed that the BIS should be more than a mere 'reparations bank'. To be sure, guaranteeing the smooth handling – or settlement – of reparations was the prime objective of the BIS, but it was not to be its sole objective. The Young Plan had already vaguely alluded to a possible role for the BIS in 'opening new fields of commerce' and in 'providing additional facilities for the international movement of funds' (Toniolo, 2005: 42). In Baden-Baden, Schacht sought to interpret the BIS's mandate as broadly as possible, arguing that the newly created Bank should be allowed to engage in short-term lending and trade financing in order to promote economic development, particularly in under-developed countries. His colleagues were less enthusiastic, fearing that an overly active BIS might compete with commercial banks and contribute to credit inflation. A compromise formula was found. The explicit objective for the BIS to 'provide additional facilities for international financial operations' was retained

---

[4] Minutes and supporting documentation of the Baden-Baden committee meetings are preserved in: Bank for International Settlements Archives (BISA), 1.1.13 – *Minutes of the meetings of the Organisation Committee for the Bank for International Settlements*, Baden-Baden, 3 October to 13 November 1929. Also: Baffi (2002).

in the Bank's statutes.[5] At the same time, the member central banks were granted the right to veto any operations carried out by the BIS on their own markets.

Another important outcome of the Baden-Baden conference was that the BIS emerged as the institutionalized forum for central bank cooperation that Montagu Norman had envisaged for so long. The statutes drafted at Baden-Baden reflect this very clearly (art. 3: 'The object of the Bank is to promote the cooperation of central banks'). In the minds of Norman and his colleagues, such cooperation was needed to support the smooth functioning – and indeed further expansion – of the restored gold exchange standard. To meet this overarching objective it was envisaged that central bank cooperation might range from: low-key, purposeful information exchange; to technical cooperation such as the mutual extension of gold custody or foreign exchange facilities; and, if required, extending to high-profile cooperation, joint policy decisions and their implementation.[6] The case for low-key and technical cooperation under the gold exchange standard regime was uncontested. The expectation was that an international institution like the BIS would be able to facilitate this with consistency and discretion, a marked improvement to the ad-hoc and largely bilateral cooperation of the 1920s. The case for potentially high-profile cooperation was much more controversial. Most central banks – not least the Bank of France and the Bank of England – were resolved to maintain full autonomy rather than having their hands tied by the need to support a common position. This would become more significant in the 1930s when the position and policy stance of the main central banks began to diverge considerably.

All in all, the central bankers gathered in Baden-Baden in the autumn of 1929 managed to create an innovative international organization largely suited to their own preferences (Simmons, 1993). They set out the remit of an institution that would be controlled by central banks (they were the only shareholders with voting rights at the annual general meetings), which would work exclusively for them, and which, being largely insulated from political interference, would be devoted to promoting central bank cooperation so as to maintain and perfect the gold exchange standard. But these were extraordinary circumstances: the Wall Street Crash occurred midway into the proceedings at Baden-Baden.

---

[5] The Hague Agreement of January 1930, *Statutes of the Bank for International Settlements*, art. 3.

[6] For an insightful discussion of the different forms of central bank cooperation and their evolution throughout recent history, see: Borio and Toniolo (2008).

4.3 THE BIS IN ACTION, 1930–1933

Expectations were high when the BIS opened its doors in Basel, Switzerland, on 17 May 1930. Public attention was naturally focused on the BIS's primary role as a reparations bank. It was hoped that the commercialization of Germany's reparations debt via the BIS would at long last bring an end to the acrimonious disputes and political stand-off of the 1920s. For the central bankers there was even more at stake. In March 1930, in a testimony before the Macmillan Committee, set up by the UK government to look into the root causes of the economic depression, Montagu Norman expressed ambitious expectations of the newly founded BIS, describing it as 'the climax of our efforts in bringing about cooperation among the central banks of Europe and the world' (Einzig, 1932: 181). Hjalmar Schacht, who had finally turned against the Young Plan because it had failed to bring about a substantial reduction of Germany's reparations burden and who had resigned as president of the Reichsbank as a result, nevertheless continued to refer proudly to the BIS as 'meine Bank für Internationalen Zahlungsausgleich' [my Bank for International Settlements] (Schacht, 1953: 315).

Soon, however, the international monetary and financial system became embroiled in the turmoil of the Great Depression. With it, the high hopes and expectations placed in the BIS quickly unravelled. The first blow, and a sign of things to come, was the disengagement of the Americans. In the summer of 1929, the United States had decided not to be party of The Hague Agreement, or the Young Plan. The Great Depression reinforced isolationist tendencies in the United States in general, and in Congress in particular. The Federal Reserve was not allowed to participate directly in the BIS for fear that official membership of the 'Reparations Bank' would expose the United States to the risk that, if German reparation payments were reduced, the Europeans would leverage the Federal Reserve's participation in the BIS to reduce the war debt payments they owed to the United States. The BIS shares offered to the Federal Reserve were eventually subscribed by a consortium of US commercial banks, led by J. P. Morgan.

A case can be made that under more propitious circumstances the BIS might have developed into something resembling the International Monetary Fund (IMF) or the World Bank (International Bank for Reconstruction and Development or IBRD) that were established after the Second World War – or even a combination of both. The key objectives and functions of the Bretton Woods institutions were laid down in

July 1944, when the war was still raging. They reflected the universal disenchantment with the pre-war gold exchange standard. The dominant view was that the gold exchange standard had been badly mismanaged by the central banks, leading directly to the Great Depression and to the breakdown of the international financial system. The Bretton Woods institutions were designed to prevent this from happening again. To promote more balanced economic growth on a global level, the IBRD was given the mandate to provide development loans to its member countries, and particularly to the low-income ones that found it difficult to raise commercial loans. The IMF was tasked with restoring a multilateral payments system and facilitating the expansion of international trade, based on stable and orderly exchange-rate arrangements. To this end, the IMF was supposed to facilitate international monetary cooperation through regular consultation (a role Norman had hoped the BIS would perform more successfully). The IMF was also endowed with ample resources (member quotas) that, in case of need, could be used to help countries deal with temporary balance-of-payments or exchange rate difficulties. The Bretton Woods institutional framework, the binding arrangements and the promise of financial support for economic development and any balance of payments disequilibria that might accompany this, were all meant to contribute to a more orderly and stable international monetary and financial system. Prima facie, nothing in the BIS statutes, as elaborated in Baden-Baden, would have prevented the BIS from developing its field of activities into these areas earlier in the 1930s. Indeed, the early history of the BIS demonstrates the initial impetus to give the BIS a more active and prominent role, in many ways akin to that taken on by the Bretton Woods institutions after 1945. How and why these attempts were ultimately unsuccessful, pushing the BIS into relative oblivion by the late 1930s, deserves closer scrutiny.

4.3.1 Towards a Development Bank?

Could the BIS have developed into an IBRD *avant la lettre*? As we have seen, this had been Schacht's initial ambition. In a scheme he proposed to Owen Young at the beginning of the Paris reparation talks in February 1929, Schacht had envisaged an International Clearing House that would be authorized to grant credits to promote trade and economic development, not just to central banks but also to governments, public authorities, and any other borrower benefitting from a government guarantee (Lüke, 1985). The idea did not find favour with Schacht's counterparties. In particular, the Bank of France and the Bank of Italy feared that the creation of an international bank with broad lending powers would have inflationary consequences (Toniolo, 2005: 37–43). Moreover, the French were adamant that the focus of the envisaged BIS should remain firmly on handling reparation payments (from which France stood to gain the most). The Bank of England, while not entirely hostile to the idea, worried that the scheme as proposed by Schacht would promote unfair competition with commercial banks. Nevertheless, the inclusion in the BIS statutes of 'the provision of additional facilities for international financial operations' as one of the key objectives of the new Bank should be seen as a concession to Schacht's insistence on a broader role for the BIS.

After the BIS began operating in May 1930, several initiatives were launched to make the 'provision of additional facilities for international financial operations' more concrete. In October 1930, while the BIS's investment policy was being defined, a small committee of central bankers was asked to look into the possibility of financing medium-term credit. In its report to the BIS Board of Directors the study committee concluded that the BIS's room for action in this field was limited.[7] Given the circumstances, the Bank had to maintain a high level of liquidity and was bound to operate in national credit markets only through the central banks or via authorized domestic credit institutions. The committee recommended that the BIS should set aside up to 150 million Swiss francs to stimulate the medium-term credit market. Some feelers were put out to individual central banks in order to find out whether there would be a practical scope for such an undertaking, but the response was at best lukewarm.[8]

The issue of medium- and long-term credits was put back onto the agenda of the BIS Board of Directors in February 1931. During 1930, the situation of the international capital markets had deteriorated rapidly. The feeling that something ought to be done to alleviate the credit crunch and revive long-term investments was widely shared. The only question was what? On this occasion the initiative came from the Bank of England. Governor Norman submitted a scheme, elaborated by Bank

---

[7] 'Rapport du Comité pour les crédits moyen-term', BISA, 1.3a(i) – *Minutes of the 6th meeting of the BIS Board of Directors*, December 1930, annex VI/E. The study committee consisted of Melchior (Reichsbank), Van Zeeland (National Bank of Belgium) and Addis (soon replaced by Siepmann – both Bank of England).

[8] Note by Karl Blessing, 12 December 1930, BISA 7.18(8) – *Papers Georges Royot*, folder 41.

of England director Robert Kindersley, for the creation of an international corporation authorized to issue bonds and use the proceeds for long-term credit operations. The underlying reasoning was that if the BIS itself was not in a position to act directly on the medium- or long-term credit market on any significant scale, then at least it could participate in raising the capital for a separate entity created for this purpose. The Kindersley Plan was discussed at the BIS Board meetings in February and March 1931. The reception was positive as far as the principle was concerned, but less enthusiastic when it came to the practicality of implementing the scheme. The 'Plan' (in reality it was not more than a four-page memorandum) was effectively sunk by the Governor of the Bank of France Clément Moret, who, after consultation with French commercial banks, concluded that it would not be wise for the BIS to 'give its patronage to the formation of an enterprise over which it could not exercise effective control'.[9] Its statutes prevented the BIS from 'acquiring a predominant interest in any business concern'.[10] There was a fear that the new corporation would mainly mobilize French capital – still comparatively buoyant – and redirect it to fund investment elsewhere.[11] As a sop to the proponents of the scheme – in particular the Bank of England and the Reichsbank – another ad hoc committee was created to elaborate practical recommendations as to how the BIS might best assist in the revival of long-term financing. At the same time, the BIS took some largely symbolic action by subscribing two loans for the amount of 500,000 Swiss francs each, issued by two recently created private, international institutes for mortgage financing, the Internationale Bodenkreditbank, Basel, and the Compagnie Centrale de Prêts Fonciers, Amsterdam.[12] This was no more than a drop in the ocean.

The ad hoc committee for long-term credit, created by the BIS Board, met in May and June 1931 in Brussels, under the chairmanship of Emile

---

[9] Letter from Moret to McGarrah, President of the BIS, 4 March 1931, BISA, 7.18(2) – *Papers McGarrah/Fraser*, box 2, folder 11.

[10] Article 25 of the 1930 statutes.

[11] As Barry Eichengreen has pointed out, the key problem to resolve for any international debt facility is that of finance and control. If private investors are expected to provide the bulk of the funds they will naturally want the control of the facility placed in private hands. If, on top of that, most funds are expected to come from one or only a few countries, their respective central banks and treasuries will likewise demand control on the allocation of the funds: Eichengreen (1991: 166–167). On the Kindersley Plan see also: Kunz (1987: 35–38).

[12] BISA, 3.8(a) – *Subscription of bonds of Internationale Bodenkreditbank, Basel*. And: 3.8(b) – *Subscription of bonds of Compagnie Centrale de Prêts Fonciers, Amsterdam*.

Francqui, the Belgian financier and elderly statesman who had already been closely involved with the Young Plan negotiations.[13] The participants were Melchior (Reichsbank), Beneduce (Bank of Italy), Farnier (Bank of France), Kindersley and Addis (Bank of England). No breakthrough was achieved. The committee discussed the option that the BIS should set aside important sums to rediscount the portfolios of various national institutions specializing in providing medium- and long-term trade finance. Alternatively, the Kindersley Plan was revived in the form of the adjusted Francqui Plan, calling for the creation of an International Credit Bank that would work in close relationship with the BIS, without, however, the BIS participating in its capital or in any way assuming responsibility. The committee was not able to reach unanimity on these proposals and put the ball back in the court of the BIS Board of Directors. In his report to a meeting of representatives of the BIS shareholding central banks, organized on 19–20 May 1931 on the occasion of the BIS's first Annual General Meeting, Ernst Hülse, Head of the BIS Banking Department, conceded that 'unfortunately the middle term credit operations of the BIS have so far not developed to the anticipated extent'.[14]

This disappointing outcome may have had something to do with the fact that the two most vocal and forthright proponents of the BIS had grown disenchanted with the institution. After the approval of the Young Plan in February 1930, Schacht had quit his desk at the Reichsbank, to be replaced by the rather uninspiring Hans Luther. For his part, Norman had come to distrust the BIS, which he felt had become dominated in its administration 'by American habits and by French ideas' (Kunz, 1987: 36).

In any case, notions for reviving the international capital markets were completely overtaken by events. In May 1931, the Austrian Creditanstalt collapsed, in June–July Germany succumbed to a twin currency and banking crisis, and in September the Bank of England was forced to take sterling off gold. Within a few months the monetary and financial system that had been painstakingly rebuilt during the 1920s on the basis of the gold exchange standard had completely unravelled. The reparation payments arrangements enshrined in the Young Plan were swept away.

---

[13] Baffi (2002: 169–172). In an introductory note, Francqui spoke of the 'heavy responsibility' resting on the central banks and on the BIS in the face of the grave difficulties with which the world economy struggled: 'Rapport présenté par M. Francqui', [undated], BISA 7.18(8) – *Papers Georges Royot*, folder 41.

[14] Bank for International Settlements (1931), *Meeting of Representatives of Central Banks Participating in the BIS, 2nd Committee – Credit, Reports*, Basel: BIS, p. 7.

The survival of the BIS itself was called into doubt. Under these circumstances, any thoughts of turning the BIS into a kind of development bank *avant la lettre* proved illusory.

4.3.2 Protecting the International Monetary System

During the latter part of the twentieth century, the IMF was best known – some might say notorious – for its country missions. Countries facing grave currency or balance-of-payments difficulties would turn to the IMF for help. An IMF mission would descend on the country's capital, advise the government, and arrange financial assistance in exchange for the adoption of rigorous budgetary and fiscal adjustment policies, in other words impose conditionality. That sovereign nations submitted, more or less willingly, to this kind of external discipline, accepting the multilateral surveillance that went with it, was a major achievement of the post-war order enshrined in the Bretton Woods agreements (Yago et al., 2015). Nevertheless, there had been pre-war precedents. In supporting financial reconstruction in Central Europe during the 1920s, the Finance Committee of the League of Nations had played a comparable role. After its creation in 1930, it looked briefly as though the Bank for International Settlements might take over and develop this role on an even broader scale.

Two examples of the BIS's activism in this field stand out: the attempted stabilization of the Spanish peseta in the winter of 1930–1, and the international support given to the Austrian National Bank in the wake of the Creditanstalt debacle in May–June 1931.

In 1930, Spain was the only major European country that had not yet stabilized its currency on the basis of the gold exchange standard. An economic slump, the continuous slide of the peseta on the foreign exchange markets and, finally, the collapse of the Prima de Rivero dictatorship in January 1930, prompted the Spanish government to tackle the country's precarious monetary situation. Given the chaotic political situation, the new Minister of Finance, Julio Wais, appointed his trusted collaborator Carlos Bas as Governor of the Bank of Spain with a mandate to seek international support for a stabilization of the Spanish peseta. Bas arranged a series of meetings from 16 to 20 October 1930 in Paris with Moret, Governor of the Bank of France, and with Gates McGarrah and Pierre Quesnay, respectively President and General Manager of the BIS.[15] During these meetings,

---

[15] Conversations de Paris entre la délégation de la Banque d'Espagne et les représentants de la BRI, 16–20 October 1930, BISA, 7.18(2) – *Papers McGarrah/Fraser*, MCG5, f39.

McGarrah and Quesnay advised Bas to stabilize the peseta at its current market value (between 40 and 50 pesetas to the pound), and to prepare a programme sustaining full convertibility at this fixed rate before the Cortes would reconvene in January 1931 to formalize Spain's adherence to the gold exchange standard. Bas agreed, and in exchange requested that the BIS should announce the granting of a loan supporting the peseta's formal stabilization. The BIS felt that this would be premature and that a credible stabilization programme ought to be worked out in detail first. For this it offered its help. Despite some initial reluctance from the part of Finance Minister Wais, BIS General Manager Quesnay travelled to Madrid twice in November and delivered a report recommending preparations for an early stabilization, by concentrating all foreign exchange operations at the central bank and earmarking part of the substantial Spanish gold reserves for supporting the external value of the peseta on the markets.

Quesnay's report was received well enough by the Spanish authorities. But the BIS's insistence that it would only grant an advance in pound sterling if the Bank of Spain first agreed to increase its gold stock held in London as collateral, proved to be a stumbling block. The shipment abroad of Spanish gold was a sensitive political issue in Spain, as it could easily be decried as a slight to Spanish sovereignty and pride. As the peseta continued its downward slide throughout December, relations between the Bank of Spain and the BIS became strained. A senior BIS employee, Michel Mitzakis (formerly at the Bank of France), was now dispatched to Madrid and took up office in the Bank of Spain. Initially, the prospects seemed dim. Governor Bas sternly reminded Mitzakis that 'Spain is a great country. I do not hesitate to fight the Minister and my own Board, but I cannot tolerate the BIS telling me what to do when the whole country is trembling and I am the general defending the Bank against the communists.'[16] Notwithstanding, consultations continued and before the end of the year agreement was reached. On 26 December 1930 the Board of the Bank of Spain gave the green light for an additional shipment of £1 million in gold to London, to be used as collateral. On 29 December, the BIS in return granted a three-month £1.5 million advance, made available through the Bank of Spain's Sterling sight account with the Bank of England.[17] In the meantime, Mitzakis had made a number

---

[16] Letter Mitzakis to Quesnay, 16 December 1930, BISA, 7.18(2) – *Papers McGarrah/ Fraser*, MCG5, f39.

[17] Exchange of letters between BIS Vice-President Leon Fraser and Bank of Spain Governor Carlos Bas, 30 December 1930, BISA, 2.81 – *Bank of Spain, Policy*, vol. 1.

of recommendations to help modernize the central bank, including the creation of a research department. With inputs from Mitzakis, a draft stabilization programme was finally committed to paper, and it was agreed that Governor Bas would travel to Basel to present the programme to the Governors gathered there for the February 1931 BIS Board meeting.

In the meantime, the Spanish Ministry of Finance had opened negotiations with J. P. Morgan and other private banks for an additional stabilization loan, only to be interrupted by a crisis in the cabinet. With a new government in power, and Governor Bas confirmed in his position, things seemed to be back on track by the end of February 1931. Quesnay travelled to Madrid to offer BIS support once again. On 26 March, the Bank of Spain concluded a loan agreement with J. P. Morgan and the Banque de Paris et des Pays Bas for £15 million. The BIS followed suit, extending its earlier credit for another three months and doubling the amount to £3 million. The expectation was that everything was now in place to announce the imminent formal stabilization of the peseta. But political events in Spain got in the way. Following the municipal elections of 12 April 1931, which revealed the strength of support for the republican parties, King Alfonso XIII fled the country, ushering in a provisional government that proclaimed the Second Republic. Governor Bas lost his position and stabilization was postponed indefinitely. This was no doubt for the best. Fixing the exchange rate of the peseta based on the gold exchange standard in the spring of 1931 would have been a monumental mistake in view of the financial and monetary turmoil that was about to be unleashed in Europe and across the world.

The failed Spanish stabilization laid bare some of the key challenges of multilateral central bank cooperation, and the role a new international organization such as the BIS might potentially play in defusing national sensitivities. Soon, the BIS was called upon to try to refine that role in the context of the Creditanstalt crisis. The Creditanstalt was more than Austria's largest commercial bank. It was a holding company with key stakes in Austria's main industrial and commercial companies. Therefore, when on Friday 8 May 1931 the Creditanstalt secretly informed the Austrian government that it faced a severe liquidity crisis, the alarm bells went off. An emergency package was quickly put together over the weekend, with the Austrian state, the Rothschilds, and the Austrian National Bank covering part of Creditanstalt's losses and making available additional liquidity. But this failed to convince the Austrian public. Withdrawals of funds from Creditanstalt gathered pace, forcing the central bank to open an unlimited discount window in favour of Creditanstalt. This, together with increased withdrawals from foreign creditors, began to eat into the Austrian National Bank's foreign exchange reserves. As a result, the published statements of the central bank showed a continuous drop in the cover ratio (gold and foreign exchange reserves) of the Austrian shilling. Fearing that if this went on for too long a panic and possibly a bank run might ensue, the Austrian National Bank appealed to its foreign partners for help.

To begin with the Austrians appealed to Bank of England Governor Norman, but he referred them to the BIS, which after all, he argued, had been created to coordinate the central banks' response to a situation of this nature (Schubert, 1991: 159). The initial plan was that the Austrian government would finance the rescue of the Creditanstalt by issuing Treasury bonds on the international market. Pending an agreement with the main international banks to place these bonds, the Austrian National Bank was tasked with obtaining a 150 million schilling standby credit from the central banks. The BIS responded swiftly. Francis Rodd, a BIS Manager formerly with the Bank of England, immediately left for Vienna to act as the BIS liaison man on the spot. He was soon followed by two more senior BIS staff members (among them Karl Blessing, who would become the President of the German Bundesbank in 1958) to gather information, and advise the Austrian National Bank as needed. Intense diplomacy ensued. Within days of the Austrian National Bank requesting assistance, the BIS rallied the main European central banks and the Federal Reserve Bank of New York to pledge contributions to a three-month 100 million schilling ($14 million) support loan. Austrian National Bank President Reisch travelled to Basel to meet with his counterparties, and the details of the loan were finalized just after the BIS Board of Directors' meeting on 18 May 1931, which, incidentally, coincided with the BIS's first Annual General Meeting.

Then, surprisingly, there was a delay of almost two weeks in executing the agreement. The main reason it would seem, was a growing suspicion among Austria's creditors, including the central banks, that Austria might call a unilateral moratorium on its foreign debt. While the Governors were meeting in Basel on 18–19 May, the BIS received a cable from the Austrian National Bank concerning the ongoing negotiations with the main international banks in the effort to persuade them not to withdraw their funds held with the Creditanstalt. The Austrian National Bank asked the BIS and the central banks to use their moral suasion to the same effect. It sounded as if the Austrians were preparing to impose a standstill on foreign credits. The central banks wanted to avoid this at all cost, as they feared it would have a knock-on effect on other central European countries, potentially threatening financial stability across the whole of Europe. Before committing emergency help, the central banks wanted additional assurances that a moratorium would not be called. By mid-May, the situation in Vienna had temporarily improved. The pace of bank withdrawals slowed considerably, somewhat reducing the sense of urgency. In the end, the planned issue of Austrian Treasury bonds to fund the Creditanstalt rescue was delayed as negotiations with the French banks, who were supposed to place the bulk of the issue, dragged on.

Towards the end of May, the Austrian National Bank began to sustain heavy foreign exchange losses once again. Vice-President Gustav Thaa called the BIS on 28 May with an urgent appeal to speed up the delivery of the assistance on offer. On 30 May 1931, the agreement regarding the 100 million schilling emergency credit package was finally signed in Vienna. The money was made available immediately to the Austrian central bank, which promptly drew on it to embellish its reserves position and currency cover ratio published a week later. As a quid pro quo, and to forestall the possibility of an Austrian moratorium, the BIS got the Austrian National Bank to agree to the appointment of a foreign advisor. The foreign creditors, for their part, insisted on the appointment of a foreign controller at the Creditanstalt. The Austrians consented to this too. The BIS had a hand in both of these appointments. They would prove crucial for getting the Creditanstalt crisis under control. The first was Gijsbert Bruins, who at the insistence of the BIS was appointed Foreign Technical Advisor to the Austrian National Bank for the duration of the crisis.[18] Bruins, a Dutch monetary expert, had been a League of Nations commissioner with the German Reichsbank from 1925 to 1930, and was therefore well-known in BIS circles. The second appointment was that of the flamboyant Dutch banker Adrianus Johannes van Hengel as special advisor to the Creditanstalt. Van Hengel had been invited to Vienna by the Austrian National Bank and soon became a representative on the international committee of the Creditanstalt's foreign creditors, set up in London. His name had originally been suggested by the BIS,[19] because of van Hengel's experience in reorganizing the failed Rotterdamsche Bankvereniging (Robaver) in the 1920s. In 1932, van Hengel went on to

[18] Letter Bruins to BIS President McGarrah, 3 June 1931, BISA, 7.18(2) – *Papers McGarrah/Fraser*, MCG1, f1.
[19] Telephone message (anonymous) from Vienna to the BIS, 1 June 1931, BISA, 7.18(2) – *Papers McGarrah/Fraser*, MCG1, f1.

assume the function of Director General of the Creditanstalt and steered the badly hit bank into calmer waters. As a further concession to its foreign creditors and the central banks, the Austrian parliament passed a decree on 28 May 1931 authorizing the government to guarantee all deposits and credits extended to the Creditanstalt. This further reduced the likelihood of a unilateral moratorium being declared.

Initially, these measures failed to produce the desired effect. The drain on the Austrian National Bank's reserves continued. At the suggestion of Bruins, the BIS Board meeting of 8 June 1931 discussed the granting of a second 100 million schilling credit. The Governors agreed in principle but made the release of this credit conditional on the successful issue of Austrian Treasury bonds on the international market. This became a sticking point. Just when agreement with the French banks seemed within grasp, the French government abruptly demanded that the Austrian government formally renounce a proposed customs union with Germany as a precondition for floating the loan in France. This placed the Austrian government in an impossible position. The ongoing run on the Creditanstalt threatened to spill over to the other main financial institutions and savings banks in Vienna. The Austrian central bank increased pressure on the government to declare a unilateral moratorium. Frantic diplomatic activity centered on Bruins and the BIS's Rodd in Vienna, McGarrah and Fraser at the BIS in Basel, and Siepmann, Kindersley, and Norman at the Bank of England. At the last moment, Norman stepped in, pledging a 150 million schilling ($21 million) renewable, seven-day advance to the Austrian National Bank. The condition was that the Austrian government would renounce its plans for calling a moratorium and finally declare a state guarantee for the Creditanstalt's foreign liabilities. The Austrian government complied, then announced its resignation on 16 June 1931. A moratorium had been avoided.

In his recent study on Austria, Marcus Nathan has argued that, in spite of its bad press, the Austrian rescue operation of May–June 1931, coordinated via the BIS, was comparatively successful (Nathan, 2018: 298–334). Despite many hiccups and delays, 'international central bank cooperation through the BIS had worked' (Nathan, 2018: 329). After the drama in mid-June, the financial situation quickly stabilized. The Creditanstalt's foreign creditors pledged to end withdrawals. The Austrian National Bank continued to see its foreign exchange reserves depleted, but at a much slower pace than before. Pressure on the Austrian schilling eased. Bruins concluded that the planned second BIS credit would not be needed after all. According to Nathan, the coordinated rescue operation had prevented the Austrian crisis from spilling over to other financial markets and international banks in any significant way. This, surely, is an over-generous assessment. Even if the Austrian rescue operation initially seemed to have warded off the crisis, the effect was short-lived. Within weeks, a far more severe banking and currency crisis took hold of Germany. This spelled renewed trouble for the already weakened Austrian banking sector. It also brought the entire Young Plan reparations settlement and the post-war gold exchange standard system crashing down.

The German crisis of summer 1931 effectively brought the BIS's fledgling role as an international crisis manager to an end. The key reason was that the German crisis became politicized almost from the outset. Germany's financial situation was inextricably linked to its capacity to meet its reparations obligations under the Young Plan. Any hint of financial difficulties inevitably risked rekindling the painful political dispute over reparations dating back to the 1920s. It was precisely for this reason that, when it was trying to stem a rapid surge in capital flight in June 1931, the Reichsbank initially turned to the Bank of England to request a bilateral credit, rather than calling on the BIS (Clement, 2002). The BIS had an institutional interest – yes, mission – to keep reparation payments flowing. The Bank of England, on the other hand, had previously demonstrated that it had sympathy for Germany's plight and was open to considering a substantial reduction in reparations. Nevertheless, the scale of Germany's problems was such that the Bank of England was keen to bring in other central banks, including the BIS, to fund a $100 million short-term loan, allowing the Reichsbank to meet its minimum reserve requirement in its next published statement. The emergency credit was provided in record time (barely a week after the Reichsbank had first approached the Bank of England), and came with no strings attached. The negotiations to put it together were coordinated from London, not from Basel, in spite of BIS President McGarrah's protestation that this was 'exactly the kind of credit which it is for the BIS to organise'.[20] Likewise, the BIS did not play a leading role in the denouement of the German crisis. When Hans Luther, the President of the Reichsbank, flew to Basel on 13 July 1931 to plead Germany's case before the central bank Governors gathered there, they sent him back empty-handed, pointing out that the crisis had become so politicized that it could only be solved

---

[20] Memorandum Siepmann, 24 June 1931, Bank of England Archive, Series OV34/80 – *Germany*.

at the political level. It was a telling recognition that the position of the central banks and of the BIS had become 'more and more that of helpless onlookers than of significant players' (Toniolo, 2005: 103).

The German banking and currency crisis of summer 1931, and the gradual demise of the gold exchange standard that followed, put an irrevocable end to any ambitions the BIS may have nurtured of establishing itself as a global – or even European – guardian of the international monetary system, or as the accepted, central location for providing emergency balance-of-payments and currency assistance as well as negotiating the conditionality attached to it. The BIS was not to be an IMF *avant la lettre*.

4.4 CONCLUSIONS

From more than one perspective, the birth of the BIS happened at the wrong time. Created at the end of an economic boom, with optimism regarding the world's economic, financial and political outlook still strong, the 'central banks' bank' made its first, tentative steps in an environment that was rapidly deteriorating. Much had been expected of the BIS, particularly by those who had played an important role in its creation, such as Montagu Norman and Hjalmar Schacht. These hopes foundered within the first two years of the BIS's existence. The BIS did not become the global development bank Hjalmar Schacht had envisaged, nor did it develop into the general headquarters coordinating the smooth functioning of the gold standard that Montagu Norman had envisioned.

There were many reasons for this. Timing played a decisive role. With the Great Depression wreaking havoc, the international cooperative spirit of the late 1920s soon gave way to overriding national self-interest, and even antagonism. Organizing effective support for those central banks and countries that got into trouble required the mobilization of considerable resources. The number of central banks that were still able to provide such resources shrank rapidly as the crisis dragged on and a self-preservation attitude took hold. For this reason, it became increasingly difficult to commit private creditors in any international bail-out or debt reduction scheme, as more and more of them faced mounting funding difficulties themselves. The fact that there was no agreed or rehearsed template for dealing with the rapid succession of financial and banking crises in 1930–1 did not help either. The BIS was a novice in the game and had to learn on the job.

However, the main reason why the BIS did not meet expectations in 1930–1 was due to the political environment. In the exceptional circumstances of the Great Depression any attempt at crisis resolution became unavoidably political as it had a bearing on the stability and even survival of banks and governments, as well as the livelihood of the people more generally. This was all the more true because domestic political constraints were often overlaid with international political tensions, many of which had their origins in the First World War (Bennett, 1962). The early disengagement of the United States from the Young Plan and from the BIS – for fear that it would confound the reparations and war debt issues – was a fatal blow to the ideal of far-reaching international central bank cooperation. The ongoing political tensions between France and Germany in particular, were also problematic. Norman and his colleagues had done their utmost to keep politics out, priding themselves in having created the BIS as a technical, non-political organization. Yet, as an institution dominated exclusively by central banks, it proved to be ill-suited to deal with the political backlash of the Great Depression. This became clear when the central bank community lost its unity of purpose and its common frame of reference with the partial collapse of the gold exchange standard in the late summer of 1931. As an organization committed to the gold standard ideology, and siding with the remaining members of the so-called Gold Bloc, the BIS could no longer speak for the central bank community as a whole. This diminished its role as an international centre for effective monetary and financial cooperation. This state of affairs was highlighted by the failure of the World Economic and Monetary Conference in London in July 1933, a last-ditch attempt to restore the international monetary system on a common footing, which the BIS had helped to prepare. As Eichengreen and Uzan have pointed out, it was the lack of a common conceptual framework among the main players – the United Kingdom, France, and the United States – together with their very different domestic policy constraints, that scuttled the London Conference (Eichengreen and Uzan, 1993). What the London Conference did demonstrate was that governments and heads of state had begun to assert their primacy in matters of monetary policy and international financial cooperation at the expense of the central banks. Under these circumstances, the scope for meaningful central bank cooperation was very narrow indeed.

In the end, the vision of Montagu Norman and Hjalmar Schacht to put high-level central bank cooperation on a firm institutional footing failed because of the lack of unified commitment when it was most needed. In the final analysis, it was the Great Depression that destroyed any common understanding, and thereby the chances of meaningful central bank cooperation. This provides a stark contrast to what happened in the wake of the 2007–9 Great Financial Crisis. After the failed London Conference, and for the remainder of the 1930s, the BIS would focus on what was directly useful to the central banks themselves, and what was realistically achievable given the political constraints: that is information exchange, cooperation on technical issues, provision of gold clearing and custody services, foreign exchange operations, and small-scale clearing operations on behalf of the Universal Postal Union.

In 1944, the Bretton Woods institutions were set up on a different premise. They were universal organizations through which governments and central banks cooperated but with the governments now taking the lead. Mindful of the damage caused by the Great Depression and by the Second World War, they benefitted from a regained unity of purpose and the renewed assertion of a common frame of reference.

REFERENCES

Unpublished (Archival) Sources

BISA – Bank for International Settlements Archives, Basel (Switzerland) (www.bis.org).

Published Sources

Ahamed, Liaquat (2009). *Lords of Finance: The Bankers That Broke the World*. New York: Penguin Press.

Baffi, Paolo (2002). *The Origins of Central Bank Cooperation: The Establishment of the Bank for International Settlements*. Rome: Editori Laterza.

Bennett, Edward W. (1962). *Germany and the Diplomacy of the Financial Crisis, 1931*. Cambridge, MA: Harvard University Press.

Borio, Claudio and Toniolo, Gianni (2008). 'One Hundred and Thirty Years of Central Bank Cooperation: A BIS Perspective,' in Claudio Borio, Gianni Toniolo, and Piet Clement (eds.), *Past and Future of Central Bank Cooperation*. Cambridge and New York: Cambridge University Press, 16–75.

Clarke, Stephen V. O. (1967). *Central Bank Cooperation 1924–31*. New York: Federal Reserve Bank of New York.

Clay, Henry (1957). *Lord Norman*. London: Macmillan and Co.

Clement, Piet (2002). 'Between Banks and Governments: the Bank for International Settlements and the 1931 Reichsbank credit', in Ton De Graaf, Joost Jonker, and Jaap-Jan Mobron (eds.), *European Banking Overseas, 19th–20th century*. Amsterdam: ABN-AMRO, 139–162.

Eichengreen, Barry (1991). 'Historical Research on International Lending and Debt'. *Journal of Economic Perspectives*, 5(2): 149–169.

Eichengreen, Barry (1992). *Golden Fetters: The Gold Standard and the Great Depression 1919–1939*. New York: Oxford University Press.

Eichengreen, Barry and Marc Uzan (1993). 'The 1933 World Economic Conference as an Instance of Failed International Cooperation,' in Peter B. Evans, Harold K. Jacobson, and Robert D. Putnam (eds.), *Double-Edged Diplomacy, International Bargaining and Domestic Policies*. Berkeley: University of California Press, 171–206.

Einzig, Paul (1932). *Montagu Norman: A Study in Financial Statesmanship*. London: Kegan Paul.

Flandreau, Marc (1997). 'Central Bank Cooperation in Historical Perspective: A Sceptical View'. *Economic History Review*, 50(4): 735–763.

Kunz, Diane B. (1987). *The Battle for Britain's Gold Standard in 1931*. London: Croom Helm.

Lüke, Rolf E. (1985). 'The Schacht and the Keynes Plans'. *Banca Nazionale del Lavoro Quarterly Review*, 152: 65–76.

Nathan, Marcus (2018). *Austrian Reconstruction and the Collapse of Global Finance, 1921–1931*. Cambridge, MA and London: Harvard University Press.

Schacht, Hjalmar (1953). *76 Jahre meines Lebens*. Bad Wörishofen: Kindler und Schiermeyer Verlag.

Schubert, Aurel (1991). *The Creditanstalt Crisis of 1931*. Cambridge, UK: Cambridge University Press.

Schuker, Stephen A. (2003). 'Money Doctors between the Wars', in Marc Flandreau (ed.), *Money Doctors: The Experience of International Financial Advising 1850–2000*. Routledge: London, 49–77.

Simmons, Beth A. (1993). 'Why Innovate? Founding the Bank for International Settlements, 1929–30'. *World Politics*, 45(3): 361–405.

Toniolo, Gianni, with the assistance of Piet Clement (2005). *Central Bank Cooperation at the Bank for International Settlements 1930–1973*. Cambridge, UK: Cambridge University Press.

Yago, Kazuhiko, Asai, Yoshio, and Itoh, Masanao (eds.) (2015). *History of the IMF, Organization, Policy and Market*, Tokyo-Heidelberg: Springer.

PART II

SPECIFIC

5

Central Bank Policy under Foreign Control

The Austrian National Bank in the 1920s

Hans Kernbauer

5.1 INTRODUCTION

The Austrian National Bank (ANB), the central bank of Austria, became operational on 1 January 1923. Its establishment was a pivotal part of the implementation of the League of Nations' scheme for the financial reconstruction of Austria. The once unified economic and currency zone of the monarchy had disintegrated after the end of the First World War, as 'successor states' strove for economic and financial sovereignty. The Austro-Hungarian Bank remained the central bank of the new republic until the end of 1922, continuing to finance the country's budgetary needs, as it had done during the war. The resulting hyperinflation was brought to an end in the last weeks of 1922 with the help of the League of Nations, which arranged state guarantees for an international loan to Austria. Representatives of the League's Financial Committee supervised the appropriation of the loan's net proceeds, while the League also appointed a special advisor to the president of the ANB, charged with overseeing monetary policy. Contemporary public opinion was highly critical of the League's activities and Austria was seen as 'a victim rather than a beneficiary of foreign interference' (Berger, 2003: 77). Both the commissioner general and the advisor were often used as scapegoats, blamed for the implementation of harsh financial measures which governments considered necessary, but were too weak to implement themselves.

This chapter is structured as follows: Section 5.2 covers the financial and economic situation of the Republic of Austria after the collapse of the monarchy. Section 5.3 describes the background of the League of

Nations' scheme for Austria, which formed part of a wider plan to shape the post-war monetary structure of Central Europe. The section includes a description of the specific features of the Geneva Protocols which, inter alia, defined the preconditions Austria had to fulfil in order to qualify for League members' state guarantees for an international loan. Section 5.4 is primarily concerned with the monetary development of Austria between 1923 and 1930, focusing on the cooperation (and lack thereof) between policy makers in Austria, Geneva, and London. It includes a short description of the Austrian banking system in the 1920s and the Creditanstalt crisis of 1931. Section 5.5 offers some concluding remarks.

5.2 THE ECONOMIC AND FINANCIAL SITUATION OF AUSTRIA AFTER THE FIRST WORLD WAR

The dissolution of the Habsburg monarchy was catastrophic for the Austrian economy. Market fragmentation caused widespread disruptions as successor states sought to develop industry behind high tariff walls, Austrian manufacturing lost access to markets and to raw materials and energy resources. In 1920, Austrian industrial production stood 50 per cent below its pre-war levels, while agricultural output covered less than half the domestic food demand; overall, real gross domestic product (GDP) had fallen by a third, compared with 1913.[1]

In the first years after the war, closed borders and the collapse of transport infrastructure (e.g., lack of rolling stock) throttled Austrians imports of food and coal. Exhausted and malnourished, the population succumbed to famine and disease. In 1919, as the Spanish Flu pandemic was ravaging the population, some additional 350,000 to 400,000 people also needed treatment for tuberculosis (Warnock, 2015: 33). Siegfried Beer describes the New Austria of 1918–19 more or less as a 'failed state'. 'It could not provide for its safety; it could not feed its population; it could not offer sufficient jobs for its people; and its citizens did not identify themselves with it; nor did they believe in its viability as a new state entity' (Beer, 2010: 111).

The state of public finances reflected the dismal state of the Austrian economy. Between November 1918 and June 1919, tax revenues still offset some 84 per cent of monthly expenditure, but by the second half of 1921, this ratio had dropped to 36 per cent (Gratz, 1949: 278). Key

---

[1] Kausel et al. (1965: 4–5), Matis (2005); comparisons based on the provinces of the Habsburg monarchy that would constitute the Republic of Austria after the war.

expenditures comprised food subsidies, interest payments on the national debt, and unemployment benefits – all obligations that were quite inelastic, as various Austrian governments of the time soon recognized. Given the significant scale of food imports, accelerated depreciation of the currency automatically widened the budget deficit. Debt service remained a heavy burden on government expenditure, at least until inflation eroded the national debt. The government upheld the principle that had been laid down by Joseph A. Schumpeter in his tenure as minister of finance, in 1919, when he stated that 'a crown is a crown', thus rejecting claims to adjust debt payments for inflation.[2] Similarly, to deprive soldiers returning from the frontline of their employment benefits seemed politically impossible.[3] Between 1919 and 1922, three-quarters of the Austrian federal budget deficit was financed by the printing press. The money supply increased 243-fold, causing hyperinflation.

Alexander Spitzmüller, the Austro-Hungarian Bank's final governor, felt there was no alternative to the monetary financing of the federal budget during the initial post-war years. In a letter to his Dutch counterpart, Simon Vissering, dated March 1920, Spitzmüller stressed that Austria would not be able to balance the budget on its own, nor was there any hope of raising domestic bonds. 'It is out of the question', he wrote, 'that we would be able to limit our spending to our tax receipts without provoking riots, anarchy and social chaos in Austria and, in consequence, in Central Europe' (Kernbauer, 1991: 38–39). It is worth remembering that, in the spring of 1919, Vienna had witnessed violent communist-inspired demonstrations that had been suppressed by force, at a point when communist worker's councils were seizing power in Hungary and Munich.[4]

The Austro-Hungarian Bank had become the central bank of the Habsburg monarchy in 1878, when it replaced the Chartered Austrian National Bank, which had been founded in 1816 (Jobst and Kernbauer, 2016: 112–141). After the war, the 'Austrian Management of the

---

[2] März (1984: 134). As a matter of fact, one gold crown of 1914 was equal to 14,400 paper crowns at the end of 1922. In 1925 the crown was replaced by the schilling at a rate of 1 schilling = 10,000 (paper) crowns.

[3] Comparably, Eichengreen and Temin (1997: 12–13) point to the reluctance of the British Government to reduce wages of returning soldiers and to implement deflationary policies immediately as was recommended by the Cunliffe Committee.

[4] In 1921, the Reparation Commission was still worried about the activities of Bolshevik agents in Vienna, even though the communist party had few followers in Austria; see Warnock (2015: 56).

TABLE 5.1 *Monetary circulation and the depreciation of the crown (monthly % changes)*

	Banknote circulation	Consumer prices (inflation)	US dollar ($) exchange rate
7/1914 – 11/1918	5	5	2
1/1920 – 8/1921	8	5	6
9/1921 – 9/1922	32	44	41

Source: Walré de Bordes (1924: 34–64, 65–106, and 107–145). Circulation data refers to the Austro-Hungarian Bank (AHB) until December 1919; as of January 1920, data refer to the Austrian Management of the AHB.

Austro-Hungarian Bank' continued to function as Austria's central bank, until it was liquidated in the end of 1922 (as per the provisions of the Treaty of St. Germain). The dissolution of the monarchy's monetary union, however, had started as early as January 1919, when the newly formed S. H. S. state (Yugoslavia), converted the crown banknotes in circulation into dinars (Garber and Spencer, 1994; Jobst and Kernbauer, 2016: 150–151). As mentioned earlier, the central bank mainly issued banknotes against Treasury bills. The steady increase in circulation was accompanied by rising prices and a depreciation of the external value of the currency (Table 5.1).

Table 5.1 shows that, during the war, the crown's external value had fallen much less than its domestic purchasing power. This was a consequence of the fall in international transactions and the gradual tightening of foreign exchange controls. From the end of the war until the summer of 1921, domestic inflation continued at the same pace, while the rate of depreciation (vis-à-vis the US dollar) accelerated. Hyperinflation struck in the summer of 1921, when it became apparent that the government's endeavours to achieve stabilization had come to nothing. As everyone fled the crown, the value of the US dollar rose at a monthly rate of 41 per cent, while domestic prices galloped to 44 per cent, surpassing the rise in circulation (32 per cent per month), due to the increasing velocity of circulation (Walré de Bordes, 1924: 34–145). The government's programme was doomed to fail because one of its essential components – the flotation of an international bond – was not possible: all of Austria's assets had been earmarked to secure reparations and 'relief loans' (credits for food imports, extended primarily by the United States, Britain, France, and Italy) and the government was unable to persuade those involved to waive their claims (Marcus, 2018: 35–112).

5.3 THE LEAGUE OF NATIONS AND THE
FINANCIAL RECONSTRUCTION OF AUSTRIA

The Austrian reconstruction scheme approved by the Council of the League of Nations in October 1922 served as the model for subsequent League aid packages to Hungary, Greece, Bulgaria, Estonia, and the city of Danzig (League of Nations, 1945: 10–16; Flores Zendejas and Decorzant, 2016). However, it was not the first scheme to be proposed by the League to stabilize Austrian finances.

At the International Financial Conference held in Brussels between 24 September and 8 October 1920, representatives from thirty-nine states had voted for an international credit scheme, dubbed the 'ter Meulen plan' after its author, the Dutch banker Carel Eliza ter Meulen. The plan aimed to remedy post-war financial disorder by supplying international commercial credits, since the reparation clauses in the Peace Treaties forbade the direct support of countries that lacked foreign credits (League of Nations, 1945: 7–9). However, several obstacles hindered the implementation of the ter Meulen plan:

On the one hand, the poorer States entitled to reparations were reluctant to relinquish their claims, however empty; on the other, foreign intervention in the affairs of a State, as required by the plan if any of that State's revenues had to be administered by an international body, raised thorny questions of sovereignty which might discourage even the most needy from entering into such commitments. (League of Nations, 1945: 15)

Being in dire need of foreign credits, Austria applied to participate in the ter Meulen plan in March 1921. One month later, a League delegation arrived in Vienna to discuss the details of a financial programme with politicians and local experts (Marcus, 2018: 87–97).[5] The reconstruction plan, published in May 1921, stipulated that, in order to qualify for League support, Austria had to increase excise taxes, tariffs, and the price of state monopoly products, introduce a general sales tax and a property tax, cancel food subsidies, downsize its administration, and curtail the number of public employees. A five-million-pound foreign loan would finance the current account deficit, while domestic bonds would cover the budget deficit. Income from the tobacco monopoly, public forests, and customs houses, as well as a mortgage on private real estate

---

[5] The delegation was headed by Drummond Fraser, a British banker accompanied by the Danish banker, Emil Gluckstad, and Joseph Avenol, an official of the French Treasury and member of the Financial Committee.

would be used to guarantee the foreign loan; internal debt would also be secured by a mortgage on private real estate. Finally, the plan envisioned the establishment of a new Austrian central bank, capitalized by domestic and foreign investors (Ausch, 1968: 21–22).

This League's 1921 reconstruction scheme failed, because the claims on Austrian assets could not be lifted, not least since the United States had withdrawn from the Reparation Commission. What is more, the Austrian government refused to accept foreign control over its domestic affairs (Marcus, 2018: 97). The failure of the stabilization plan led to extensive capital flight. Gaping budget deficits were financed by money creation, the exchange rate collapsed, and inflation shifted to overdrive. Hyperinflation only ended a year later, when the League of Nations and the Austrian government, headed by Chancellor Ignaz Seipel, agreed on a new financial reconstruction plan. On 15 August 1922, responding to Seipel's plea for help, an inter-Allied conference referred Austria to the League of Nations. The British cabinet had decided 'that no useful purpose would be served by advancing additional financial assistance to the Austrian government merely with a view to postponing what appeared to be an inevitable financial catastrophe' (Pauly, 1996: 14). Visiting neighbouring Czechoslovakia, Germany, and Italy, Seipel had recently warned that a 'collapse of Austria' was imminent, should financial assistance not be provided soon.

As the domestic situation deteriorated all roads pointed to the League of Nations in Geneva. Austrian negotiations with the League did not take long.[6] On 4 October 1922, three 'Geneva Protocols' were signed. The first stipulated that the signatories respected the political independence, territorial integrity, and sovereignty of Austria; conversely, Austria explicitly reaffirmed its acceptance of article 88 of the Treaty of St. Germain, which committed the country 'to abstain from any act which might directly or indirectly or by any means whatever compromise her independence, particularly, and until her admission to membership of the League of Nations, by participation in the affairs of another Power.'[7] The intended purpose was of course to prevent any affiliation with Germany which, according to article 80 of the Treaty of Versailles, had vowed to acknowledge and strictly respect Austria's independence.

---

[6] The head of the League's Economic and Financial Office, Arthur Salter, visited Vienna to discuss how the Financial Committee could help remedy Austria's problems.

[7] Staatsvertrag von Saint-Germain-en-Laye vom 10 September 1919. StGBl. Nr. 303/1920 [State Treaty of Saint-Germain-en-Laye of 10 September 1919. State Law Gazette, no. 303/1920].

The second Protocol contained the provisions for the issuance of an international loan of 650 million gold crowns. The loan's principal guarantors were France, Italy, Great Britain, and Czechoslovakia; other countries could participate in the bond, which outlined the loan's terms and conditions, along with the guarantors' obligations and the powers and duties of their representatives.

The third Protocol contained the list of measures that Austria agreed to implement. The parliament had to grant extraordinary powers to the government to implement the reforms necessary.[8] The federal budget should be balanced within two years and the gross revenues from the tobacco monopoly and the administration of customs houses should be given in pledge for interest and amortization payments on the new loan. Last but not least, the law of 24 July 1922 on the establishment of a new central bank should be amended to bring the bank's duties and legal provisions in line with the views of the League's Financial Committee (Kernbauer, 1991: 57).

Plans to replace the Austrian management of the Austro-Hungarian Bank had already been under way. The establishment of a new central bank had been expected to help put an end to the crown's continued depreciation, which made the import of essential food and raw materials more and more expensive. To overcome the lack of foreign exchange, Otto Bauer, a leading politician of the social democratic opposition party, had proposed to induce large Viennese banks to invest part of their gold and foreign exchange holdings in a new central bank. Vienna's major banks had agreed to contribute 24 of the 100 million Swiss francs needed to capitalise the new institution, and guarantee the subscription of another 36 million. But the Anglo-Austrian Bank and the Länderbank, which had recently come under British and French ownership, respectively, pulled out of the deal after Montagu Norman, the Governor of the Bank of England, declared that the creation of a new central bank would be ineffectual, unless it was accompanied by measures to balance the budget and issue a foreign loan to stabilize the crown (Clay, 1957: 185).

---

[8] This provision proved quite controversial. In the fall of 1922, a delegation from the League of Nations arrived in Vienna to help Seipel's efforts to rally the necessary parliamentary support for the Protocols and bolster support for the stabilization. The delegation was headed by the Belgian central banker, Albert Janssen, and comprised Joseph Avenol (French Treasury), Henry Strakosch (Union Corporation), Otto Niemeyer (British Treasury), Vilém Pospíšil (Czech banker), Maggiorino Ferraris (Italian senator), and Alfred Sarasin (Swiss banker).

The amendments to the central bank law demanded by the League of Nations were adopted by the Austrian parliament in December 1922. Article 1 of the National Bank Law charged the ANB with the primary task of creating the conditions necessary for a return to the pre-war gold standard. Until gold payments could be resumed, which would occur once the federal debt to the ANB had fallen to 30 million gold crowns (that is, the amount of the Bank's equity), 20 per cent of circulation (net of the loan to the federal state) had to be backed by the Bank's reserves, that is, gold and foreign exchange convertible into gold. This cover ratio would apply for the first five years and would gradually increase to 24, 28, and 33.33 per cent in five-year increments. Should the cover ratio ever fall below this statutory limit, the ANB would be charged with a 'banknote tax' on the excess circulation.

The ANB's note-issuing privilege in Austria was set to end on 31 December 1942. Independence from the state was provided by regulations prohibiting the monetary finance of federal, provincial, and municipal authorities. In addition, the government was restricted to a minority stake in the General Meeting, which elected the General Council, whose president and thirteen members managed the Bank. The Council set interest rates, appointed the managing committee (directorate), and chose the Bank's chief officers. No public employee or members of a legislative body could hold a seat on the General Council. Banks, savings banks, industry, trade and commerce, agriculture, and organized labour were each represented by one member on the Council. The president of the ANB was appointed by the president of Austria, upon recommendation by the federal government. A commissioner was appointed by the finance minister to monitor the bank's compliance with the laws and by-laws.

The money supply was mainly managed by transactions in gold and foreign exchange as well as the discounting of bills of exchange. Such bills were necessarily short-term (up to three months), had to be denominated in Austrian currency, and bear the signatures of at least two solvent debtors. Conversely, Lombard credits only played a minor role in managing the Austrian money supply (Federal Law Gazette no. 489/1922 and no. 823/1922; Kernbauer, 1991: 79–85).

The first president of the ANB was Richard Reisch, a professor of economics at the University of Vienna whose thesis had been supervised by the famous Austrian economist, Eugen von Böhm-Bawerk. Reisch, who had also served briefly as finance minister, sat on the board of Bodencreditanstalt, a renowned Viennese bank that had formerly managed the finances of the Habsburg family. His appointment was controversial as the League of

Nations and the Bank of England would have preferred a foreigner. Upon hearing of Reisch's appointment, Montagu Norman, the governor of the Bank of England, even considered withdrawing his support for Britain's participation in the League's loan. Sentiments in London are conveyed in a letter of Otto Niemeyer, controller of finance at the Treasury, to Arthur Salter, head of the League's Economic and Financial Section:

The Austrians' dilatoriness on the [reconstruction program] makes their recent bank of issue appointment not merely exasperating but rank folly. By this single piece of idiocy, they have put back any possible loans for many months. Nor is this only MY impression … Everyone here knows why the Austrian Banks (who are at the back of all this) want one of themselves. The Boden Credit actually sent people here to explain that they must have someone 'who would understand the needs of Austrian banking' … the Vienna Jews in their own interest have secured that the bad old traditions of inflated credits will go on … and that there will be no sound monetary policy. This of course is fatal for foreign interest in Austrian finance. (Quoted in Marcus, 2018: 149)

Unwilling to jeopardize Austria's financial reconstruction, Britain remained on board despite its frustration with the appointment of Reisch. To pour oil on troubled water, Chancellor Seipel informed the League's commissioner general of the government's intention to 'assign a first-rate foreign advisor with special authority to assist' the president of the ANB. The corresponding amendments to the statutes were implemented in the spring of 1923. The advisor was given the rank of co-president at the ANB whose consent was necessary to approve any measure related to bank policy, be it a motion to change interest rates, invest bank reserves, or strike an agreement with the federal state. The advisor was an agent of the Financial Committee of the League of Nations, represented in Vienna by the commissioner general. Charles Schnyder von Wartensee, vice-president of the Swiss National Bank, acted as advisor from June to December 1923; he was succeeded by Anton von Gijn, a former Dutch finance minister (May 1924 to January 1926), and Robert Ch. Kay, a confidant of Montagu Norman (January 1926 to June 1929).

The ANB's new rules and regulations mirrored the standards set by the Brussels conference of 1920 (Pauly, 1996: 7–9). All countries receiving League support had long been forced off gold; an immediate return to their old parities was considered too drastic a measure. As the League would later explain:

The Brussels Conference had recognized that in many cases it would be impossible to return to gold without radical deflation, and that deflation might have disastrous consequences unless carried out gradually. It was not recommended to attempt to stabilize the value of gold, or to set up an international currency or an international unit of account. (League of Nations, 1945: 20)

To economize gold reserves, in order to cover banknote circulation many countries opted not for a strictly gold-backed currency but for the gold-exchange standard: currency reserves were held in gold and convertible foreign exchange, that is, notes and bills in stable currencies that could be freely exchanged into gold. This system worked satisfactorily until the onset of the Great Depression when banks of issue lost gold and 'sound' currencies and were ultimately forced to suspend convertibility (Eichengreen, 1992: 191–221).

The League's financial reconstruction schemes provided for the appointment of commissioners mandated to withhold loan proceeds, should they believe the recipient country was not implementing the agreed reconstruction plan. In the case of Austria, article 4 of the second Geneva Protocol reads as follows: 'The yield of the loan may not be employed except under the authority of the commissioner-General appointed by the Council of the League of Nations and in accordance with the obligations contracted by the Austrian Government and set out in Protocol No. III' (League of Nations, 1922: 40). Alfred Zimmermann, a former mayor of the city of Rotterdam, was chosen as commissioner-General. In the eyes of the governor of the Bank of England, Montagu Norman, Zimmermann's credentials were impeccable as he shared many of his political and economic views: he was an uncompromising supporter of radical Manchester liberalism and he was against any form of 'social legislation, public welfare spending, capital taxation and trade unions' (Berger, 2007: 22–23). A paper of the advisor to the League of Nations, Adriaan Pelt, quoted by the Austrian economic historian, Peter Berger, expresses the widely held view that Austrian governments were too weak to implement the required policies for sound public finances on their own:

There is no avoiding the fact that the restoration of sound finances in Austria will necessarily entail considerable hardship on certain sections of the population. The responsibility for deciding which those sections shall be is the responsibility which the Controller is asked to assume. The kernel of the Austrian problem is this that no government has yet been found strong enough to assume this responsibility itself, and it is for this reason and this reason alone, when you come to the root of the matter, that a foreign Controller is required. (Pelt, cited in Berger, 2000: 23)

The Austrian governments shared most of the League's political objectives, but preferred to pin the blame for unpopular measures on the commissioner general. According to Chancellor Seipel, the government intended to get rid of the 'revolutionary rubble', that is, the socio-political reforms of the initial post-war years. These were laws that codified unemployment insurance and minimum annual leave, banned child labour, regulated collective bargaining, established a Chamber of Labour, and so on. 'Conservative Austrian politicians welcomed the League's role as executioner of these (ultra-orthodox financial) principles, mainly because responsibility for an anti-labour bias of economic reforms could be heaped on someone else's shoulders' (Berger, 2003: 77). Moreover, economists of the Austrian school whole-heartedly agreed with the dominant liberal tenor of an outright repeal of social legislation.[9]

Zimmerman's mission ended on 30 June 1926 after two experts appointed by the League, Walter T. Layton and Charles Rist, had delivered an encouraging report on Austria's economic and financial state (Layton and Rist, 1925). This report was approved by the Financial Committee and the League's Council decided to terminate the function of the commissioner general (League of Nations, 1926: 64–71). A member of Zimmermann's staff, Rost van Tonningen, stayed in Vienna to oversee the allocation of the remaining funds of the League loan. At the same time, the term of the advisor to the president of the ANB was prolonged for another three years.

In a pattern similar to that found in other recipient countries of League loans, the Austrian public perceived the commissioner general and other League staff as 'servants of foreign interests'. According to Marcus, however, foreign advisers:

generally sided with views held at the ANB and used their position to clarify misunderstandings and explain decisions and events to London. In fact, whereas the League's General Commissioner often held views diametrically opposed to those of the Austrian government, the foreign advisers seem mostly, though not always, to have agreed with their Austrian counterparts at the ANB. (Marcus, 2018: 248)

5.4 MONETARY POLICY IN AUSTRIA, 1923–1930

5.4.1 Rebalancing Macro-economic Aggregates

Seipel's successful negotiations in Geneva fostered expectations that the League of Nations would come to Austria's aid and halt the crown's depreciation. On 25 August 1922, the price of the US dollar peaked at 83,600

---

[9] For Austrian economist views on the subject, see Mises (1927, 1931), Klausinger (2002), and Wasserman (2019: 93–126).

crowns, 16,940 times its pre-war level. Subsequently, interventions by the Foreign Exchange Control Office (Devisenzentrale) brought a 15 per cent appreciation of the crown. As of mid-November 1922, the dollar exchange rate was stabilized at about 71,000 crowns, or 14,400 times its price in July 1914 (Walré de Bordes, 1924: 132–143; Marcus, 2018: 133–135). The financing of budget expenditures by the central bank continued until 18 November 1922. From late August to 30 November, Treasury bills held by the Austro-Hungarian Bank (Austrian Management) increased by 1,875 billion crowns, or 273 per cent (from 686 to 2,561 billion), while banknote circulation rose by 2,065 billion crowns, or 153 per cent (from 1,353 to 3,418 billion) (Pressburger, 1976: 2,296, 2,309).

Eight and a half years of inflation and hyperinflation, on top of profound changes in the economy's size, structure, and relationship with the rest of the world, confounded the interplay between different macroeconomic variables in Austria. The stabilization of the exchange rate initiated a search for a new equilibrium between the money supply and internal versus external prices. In the final quarter of 1922, the US dollar was quoted at a rate of 14,681 times above that of July 1914. During the same period, domestic prices had risen by a factor of 9,803, while the money supply had expanded 6,415 times (Walré de Bordes, 1924: 50, 83, 133–135). The process of achieving a new equilibrium between these variables was highly controversial: the country's fundamental territorial and economic changes since 1914 meant that pre-war comparisons were largely arbitrary. Inevitably, domestic and foreign observers disagreed in their assessment of monetary policy after the stabilization.

In 1923, the purchase of foreign exchange by the ANB along with, albeit to a lesser extent, the discounting of bills, led to a huge 74 per cent increase in the money supply (banknotes and demand deposits), which grew from 4,470.9 to 7,775.2 billion crowns. By the end of the year, the Bank's gold and foreign exchange reserves covered 50 per cent of the money supply, up from 27 per cent at the beginning of 1923. The share of bills of exchange and Lombard loans in the money supply remained roughly constant at 17 per cent, whereas the share of the outstanding central government debt fell from 57 to 33 per cent (Kernbauer, 1991: 126). Most of the foreign exchange sold to the ANB came from capital repatriation as well as from the hoards that had been built up during the hyperinflation.

Bank of England and League experts regarded the increase in the money supply to be inflationary, a continuation of the irresponsible monetary policy that had brought ruin to Austrian monetary affairs in the past, and demanded deflationary countermeasures (Marcus, 2018: 216–220). For his part, President Reisch argued that, compared to pre-war levels, the increase in the money supply was less than half the increase in the crown's dollar price, while Austria's per-capita money supply remained low by international standards. Moreover, Reisch pointed to the high interest rates and the shortage of loans as evidence that Austria did not suffer from any 'glut in the means of payment' (Reisch, 1924a: 93–106).

Walré de Bordes, a member of Zimmerman's staff, followed a similar line of argument in his dissertation, titled 'The Austrian Crown, its Depreciation and Stabilization'. According to his calculations, monetary circulation in Austria at the end of 1923 was commensurate to its pre-war level of approximately 500 million gold crowns. Of course, the country was poorer, so a reduction in circulation was required, but since many prices had risen faster than the price of the dollar, this 'would indicate that a circulation with a total value larger than before the War would not constitute inflation' (Walré de Bordes, 1924: 23). Keynes supported this argument in his *Tract on Monetary Reform*, reasoning that the increase in Austria's money supply did not threaten the stability of the crown, not least since renewed confidence in the currency had reduced the velocity of circulation: 'The fact of stabilisation, with foreign aid, has, by increasing confidence, permitted this increase of the note issue without imperilling stabilisation, and will probably permit in course of time a substantial further increase' (Keynes, 1924: 55).

In 1923, domestic prices edged upwards: the wholesale price index rose by 13 per cent, while the cost of living jumped by about 20 per cent (Statistische Nachrichten, 1924: 268). Financial experts in London and Geneva attributed the rise of prices to the increase of circulation. For his part, the president of the ANB blamed the price surge on the rise in global prices (and the high import content of consumption goods) as well as to increases in tariffs, excise taxes, and commercial rents (Reisch, 1924b: 1–12). Rost van Tonningen, serving on the commissioner general's staff at the time, argued that the crown had been stabilized 'so low that wages [and prices – HK] could subsequently be increased to a considerable extent without upsetting the equilibrium of the country' (Tonningen, cited in Berger, 2003: 79). Indeed, the 1923 spike in prices was an outlier; from 1924 to 1929, the private consumption deflator increased at an annual rate of 2 per cent.[10]

---

[10] This calculation is based on data from Kausel et al. (1965: 41–44).

The repatriation of capital that boosted the ANB's foreign exchange holdings and the money supply also fuelled a boom on the Viennese stock exchange that had been underway since 1922. At the time, many investors had believed that the stock market was pricing listed companies far below their net asset value, offering lucrative opportunities. Between January and December 1923 Vienna's domestic stock price index rose almost 13-fold, from 56 to 719 (first half 1914 = 100). The boom peaked in January 1924, when the index reached a level of 2,680, before stock prices collapsed again; by the end of 1924 the index stood at 1,194 or 55 per cent below its peak.[11]

When stock prices started to fall in early 1924, investors switched to speculating against the French franc by, inter alia, buying US dollars against francs on the forward market or term purchasing French goods. Thus, when the franc was stabilized with the help of a Morgan bank loan, speculators incurred significant losses (Aldcroft, 1978: 170; Eichengreen, 1992: 172–183). In order to safeguard monetary stability, the ANB and the government supported a consortium of Viennese banks who sought to minimize the losses incurred by speculators (Jobst and Kernbauer, 2016: 163–164). Despite being approved by the commissioner general, this intervention drew heavy fire from the Bank of England (see Section 5.4.3).

5.4.2 The League of Nations Loan

The League of Nations Loan was a bond issued by the Republic of Austria, guaranteed by various states of the League of Nations. It was issued in June 1923 in eleven tranches, denominated in ten different currencies and offering nominal yields between 7.7 and 8.5 per cent. Its par value of 650 million gold crowns was calculated to cover the budget deficits of 1923 und 1924 and the repayment of bridging loans. Net proceeds amounted to 631 million gold crowns, which were credited to an ANB account of which the commissioner general could dispose exclusively. Funds that were not cleared by the commissioner general for fiscal use had to be invested with foreign banks or placed in short-term financial instruments of the countries where bond tranches had been issued. Such transactions were unfavourable to Austria, since the return on such foreign investment was 6 to 7 percentage points below the interest rate on the bonds (Jobst and Kernbauer, 2016: 158).

---

[11] All data are taken from various issues of Statistische Nachrichten (1923: 7; 1924: 3, and 1925: 4).

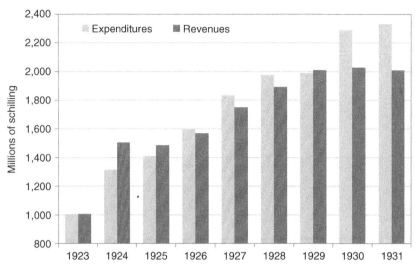

FIGURE 5.1 Austrian federal budget revenues and expenditures, 1923–1931
Source: Fibich (1977: 170–178).

An unforeseen marked increase in tax revenues balanced the budget by 1923. This generated a surplus of loan proceeds, whose utilization prompted lengthy discussions between the Austrian Government and the Financial Committee of the League of Nations. The League's representatives continued to press for further fiscal retrenchment (Marcus, 2018: 230–234), even though between 1923 and 1929, Austria's federal budgets generated an aggregate surplus of 87 million schilling (see Figure 5.1). Pressures to cut public spending were not confined to the federal level, but were extended to provincial governments, too. However, since the Geneva Protocols did not bind Austria's provinces and municipalities, the commissioner general had no direct control over their finances. Nevertheless, Zimmerman extended his effective sphere of control by deterring foreign (mainly US) banks from placing provincial or municipal loans (Marcus, 2018: 235).

5.4.3 Interest-Rate Policy

As mentioned in Section 5.4.1, in 1924 some Austrian banks got into difficulties as a result of the fall in stock prices and the failed speculation against the French franc. The largest bank to file for bankruptcy was the Depositenbank. This bank had been established in 1871 and,

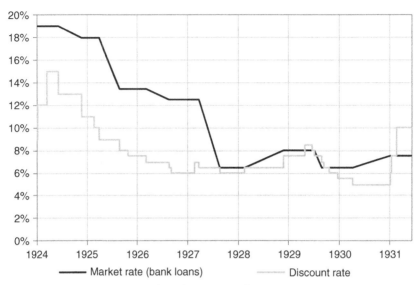

FIGURE 5.2 Discount rate and market rates in Austria, 1924–1931

Source: *Mitteilungen des Direktoriums der Oesterreichischen Nationalbank* [Minutes of the Board of Directors of the Austrian National Bank]; Institute for Business Cycle Research 6/1938: 140.

since 1918, it had been under the control of Camillo Castiliogni, 'the richest, most powerful and most influential of all speculators during the war and inflation period, the uncontested King of the nouveau riches' (Ausch, 1968: 157; Stiefel, 2012). To avoid jeopardizing the currency's new-found stability, a bank syndicate was hastily set up to support other financial institutions that had also incurred substantial losses. The commissioner general placed 300 billion crowns at the syndicate's disposal and the ANB added another 5 million US dollars of credits. Furthermore, the ANB increased its discounts by 89 per cent, raising its portfolio of bills from 1,759 to 3,328 billion crowns between April and August 1924 (Kernbauer, 1991: 131–132).

Despite the heavy drain on its credit facilities and foreign exchange reserves, the ANB was reluctant to raise the discount rate. This policy was strongly criticized by its foreign advisor, as well as the commissioner general and the Bank of England. Finally, in July 1924, the bank rate was raised from 9 to 12 per cent, only to be pushed up to 15 per cent in August (Marcus, 2018: 183–185) (Figure 5.2). The delay in the Bank's reaction was caused mainly by opposition from representatives of financial institutions on the General Council. To prevent this from happening again, the League of Nations asked the Austrian Government to amend the ANB statutes to transfer the responsibility for determining interest rate setting from the General Council to the board of directors. This, the government refused to do. Instead, rate setting was delegated to an Executive Committee that comprised the president, the two vice-presidents, the general director, and his deputy (Jobst and Kernbauer, 2016: 165). During the same meeting, in September 1924, the League of Nations asked the Austrian Government to instruct the ANB to pursue an interest rate policy to guarantee the value of the crown not only in relation to gold, but also in terms of domestic goods prices. President Reisch interpreted this as a sign of mistrust against his leadership and tendered his resignation. Chancellor Seipel refused to accept it and assured the president that the ANB's policy enjoyed the League's approval (Kernbauer, 1991: 147).

In the 1920s, nominal interest rates in Austria were high. In 1923, stock market speculators were prepared to borrow at rates of 60 to 70 per cent per annum, effectively crowding out commercial and industrial borrowers. In 1924, as the consumer price index rose by 17 per cent, real interest rates were about 2 per cent. Real rates increased in the second half of the 1920s, as annual inflation dropped below 2 per cent between 1926 and 1929 – lower still, if one includes 1930 (Butschek 1999: Table 8.1). The ANB's official discount rate remained high and out of line with developments in the price level. Still, in the eyes of foreign observers, the bank's policy was insufficiently restrictive. The General Council minutes reveal numerous occasions when business cycle considerations or changes in the volume of discounts favoured lowering the discount rate, but the ANB chose to leave rates unchanged, in deference to international financial circumstances. In January 1925, for example, the General Director reiterated 'the known fact that, for the time being, a reduction [in the bank rate] is not welcome in English circles, whom we have to respect given our credit relations with foreign countries, particularly England'.[12] Two months later, Vice-President Gustav Thaa objected to a motion to lower the bank rate for similar reasons. Given the importance of foreign finance to Austria, Thaa said, 'it would be unwise to annoy them by emphasizing our own position', before reminding his colleagues that negotiations were currently under way to secure a new loan in London.[13]

---

[12] ANB-Archive, Minutes of the 26th meeting of the General Council, 23 January 1925.
[13] ANB-Archive, Minutes of the 27th meeting of the General Council, 20 February 1925.

Indeed, Austrian Railways were attempting to float a 22 million US-dollar loan to continue the electrification of the country's railway system. During a meeting at the Bank of England between Montagu Norman, President Reisch, and the general director of the ANB, Viktor Brauneis, the Bank of England refused to support the loan, referring Austria to the Reparations Commission, the general secretary, and the Financial Committee of the League (Kernbauer, 1991: 179–181).

ANB officials were well aware of the need to toe the line set by the Bank of England. Given Austria's need for long-term foreign loans, the Austrian central bank's policy had to enjoy the approval of the City's financial circles in general, and Montagu Norman's in particular. Austria's ambassador in London, Georg Franckenstein, put it quite bluntly in a letter to the minister of finance, Heinrich Mataja:

> It might well be that in theoretical knowledge we are more or less superior to the English ... The overpowering question is however: do we require British sympathy, Anglo-Saxon capital, foreign confidence and the help of the most powerful financier, our proven and great friend Mr. Norman? If so, we must shed vanity, sensitivity and suspicion for the good of our Fatherland and accept the current power-relations with courage and determination. (Franckenstein, cited in Marcus, 2018: 219)

5.4.4 Short-term Debt and the Money Supply

The broad disparity (by as much as four percentage points at the turn of 1924–1925) between short-term rates for sterling in Vienna and London induced many foreign banks to deposit funds with Viennese banks. Initially, this was seen as proof of the success of the League's stabilization programme and of restored confidence in Austria's finances. In its annual report for 1926, the ANB welcomed the significant increase of its foreign exchange holdings, which 'fully guarantees that the economy can provide the necessary foreign currency to repay short-term loans if needed'. 'However', the report continued, 'a further considerable increase in Austrian short-term external liabilities is not desirable, as it would lead to too strong a dependence of our domestic economy on the development of money markets abroad and would seriously hinder the ANB's monetary and lending policies.'[14]

---

[14] Quoted in Jobst and Kernbauer (2016: 170). Austria's total short-term debt in 1930 amounted to 1,700 million schilling (Wärmer, 1936: 282).

TABLE 5.2 *The Austrian National Bank's money supply and its components (in millions of schilling*), 1924–1930*

	1923 (end of year)	1930 (end of year)	Change (absolute, total)	Change (%, annual)
Money supply	777.5	1,182.8	405.3	5.4
Gold and forex reserves	391.5	929.8	538.3	11.4
Bills of exchange	132.3	148.0	15.7	1.4
Government debt	253.5	101.2	-152.3	-10.8

* The shilling replaced the crown in 1925 at a rate of 10,000 crowns = 1 schilling.
Source: Mitteilungen des Direktoriums der Österreichischen Nationalbank [Minutes of the Board of Directors of the Austrian National Bank], published monthly.

Between 1924 and 1930, purchases of foreign exchange and gold were the main factor driving the expansion of the Austrian money supply. As a matter of fact, given the offsetting impact of the reduction in government debt, the ANB's foreign exchange holdings ended up increasing by a third more than the money supply (Table 5.2). On the other hand, the Bank's portfolio of bills of exchange barely changed. The Bank of England and London bankers disapproved of the growth in the Austria's money supply, arguing that a deflationary economic policy was more appropriate for the country. Deflation, they argued, would help balance the federal budget, while the fall in prices would improve export competitiveness and thus reduce or even eliminate the country's trade deficit (Marcus, 2018: 179–199).

It is not obvious how the ANB could have accomplished a lesser increase in the money supply, given the need to maintain convertibility. Deflation as recommended by the Bank of England would have entailed comparatively higher interest rates; these, in turn, would have induced further capital imports by foreign banks. The ANB could not sterilize such inflows because open market operation, that is, the buying and selling of bonds or other financial instruments to manipulate the money supply, were not included in the exhaustive list of operations the ANB was legally allowed to perform. As for the suggestion that deflation would automatically reduce the budget deficit, this is less straightforward than its advocates presumed. Lower prices would certainly reduce budgetary expenses on goods and services, but tax revenues would also fall. At the same time, rising unemployment would entail additional public sector spending. The relative price elasticity of public spending and revenues is an open, empirical question.

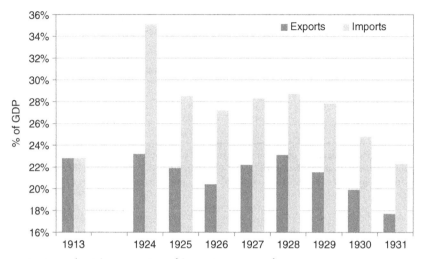

FIGURE 5.3 Austrian exports and imports, 1913 and 1924–1931
Source: Data from Kausel et al. (1965: 41).

5.4.5 Foreign Trade, Investment, and Economic Growth

During the Brussels Conference the architects of the post-war monetary system had underlined the critical role of trade liberalization for the success of the reconstruction efforts: the delegates were convinced that financial remedies alone could not secure prosperity. If the European economy was to recover fully, wartime trade restrictions would have to be lifted. In reality, Europe moved in the opposite direction. As the League of Nations would bemoan in retrospect:

It was assumed that trade would start again on the old scale between the States all or part of whose territories formerly belonged to the same Customs unit, as soon as exchange difficulties had been disposed of. But instead of this, the stronger the successor States' financial position grew, the less they traded with one another. Efforts were made to reverse this tendency, both in and outside the League, but to no avail. Failure to apply the Brussels Conference principles in this field was one, and perhaps the most powerful, of the reasons that caused the breakdown of the 1919–1920 Settlement in Central and South-Eastern Europe. (League of Nations, 1945: 21)

Figure 5.3 plots the evolution of Austrian exports and imports of goods and services as a share of GDP in the 1920s. This was a period when overall trade declined significantly. Deflation would have suppressed imports, without necessarily boosting exports. But customs barriers remained high, since several initiatives to reduce tariffs in the Danube region had failed

(Marcus, 2018: 226–230). Between 1924 and 1929, Austria's exports to its neighbours (Hungary, Poland, Czechoslovakia, Yugoslavia, Romania, and Bulgaria) fell from 47 to 40 per cent of its total exports, and the corresponding import share shrank from 51 to 46 per cent. Given widespread trade restrictions in Central and Eastern Europe, it is hard to imagine how lowering prices by pursuing a deflationary policy would have improved the Austrian balance of payments significantly.

High interest rates at home and the loss of markets abroad discouraged domestic investment at a time when the need to restructure the Austrian economy and adapt the productive capacity to post-war realities was highest. In the 1920s, gross investment as percentage of GDP peaked at 10 per cent in 1929, 22.6 per cent below its level in 1913. During the interwar 'growth period' (1924–9) the average share of investment in GDP was 8.3 per cent, marginally above the rate of capital depreciation.[15] Real economic growth averaged 3.5 per cent in these six years. By 1929, GDP in Austria stood at a meagre 5 per cent above its corresponding level in 1913 (Kausel et al., 1965: 40). Nevertheless, unemployment remained elevated: in 1929, 283,000 people or 12.3 per cent of the dependent labour force were without a job. By 1933, unemployment had jumped to 27.2 per cent (Butschek, 1999: Table 3.3).

5.4.6 Weaknesses of the Austrian Banking Sector, Lending of Last Resort

Vienna had been the political, administrative, and financial centre of the Habsburg monarchy. In 1913, Viennese banks accounted for more than two-thirds of the equity capital of all banks in Cisleithania, the western part of the monarchy.[16] Given that the Republic of Austria barely exceeded a quarter of Cisleithania's economic size, Austrian banks were comparatively large relative to the post-war domestic market. Unwilling to limit the range of their activities to the new Austrian territory, large Viennese banks made every effort to retain their position in their pre-war business areas (März, 1984: 333–345; Weber, 2016: 69–112), often with the support of western financial institutions, 'for whom the Viennese banks

---

[15] Kausel et al. (1965: 42–43). To put these figures into perspective, one might point out that in the two decades following the State Treaty of 1955 real gross investment exceeded 20 per cent of GDP.

[16] Named after Leitha, the border river between the Austrian and the Hungarian part of the monarchy.

continued to be the major players when it came to lending to the Central European market' (Wärmer, 1936: 8). Foreign banks granted short-term loans to their Viennese counterparts, which they used to maintain and expand their business in other parts of the former empire. They frequently did so through long-term loans, thereby creating a maturity mismatch between their assets and liabilities, which came on top of the foreign exchange and default risk they were already facing on those investments.

The financial strength of Vienna's financial institutions had been drained by protracted inflation and the break-up of the monarchy. When the crown was replaced by the Austrian schilling in 1925, all enterprises were asked to reassess the actual values of their assets and liabilities. Banks' financial statements (Goldbilanzen) revealed the enormous losses they had suffered: the equity capital and reserves of the seven largest banks were down 76 per cent from 1913; total assets had shrunk by 71 per cent.[17] Many of the banks established during the post-war inflation period had become insolvent soon after speculation had subsided. Yet older institutions had also failed due to mismanagement, speculation, and the intertwining of politics and business which had fostered corrupt practices (Ausch, 1968: 247–306).

The Anglo-Austrian Bank, whose main shareholder was the Bank of England, was liquidated in 1926. Its management was not prepared to follow the continental banking practice of extending long-term credits to industry and – in the event of debtor illiquidity – swapping debt for equity, as was common practice in Austrian banking since the last quarter of the nineteenth century. A substantial part of the Anglo-Austrian Bank was taken over by Creditanstalt, an institution dominated by the house of Rothschild. Stockholders were compensated with Creditanstalt shares; thus, the Bank of England acquired a 23 per cent share in the capital of the largest bank in Austria and Central Europe (Natmeßnig, 1998; Weber, 2016: 295–306).

On several occasions, the ANB came to the aid of struggling banks by discounting their bills, backing mergers or – as seen in the case of losses incurred after the stock market slump – supporting bank syndicates by providing liquidity (Kernbauer, 1991: 255–282). Yet this attitude, echoing Bagehot's principles concerning a central bank's lender-of-last-resort functions, was strongly criticized by the country's foreign advisers. When, in 1924, the distinguished Depositenbank ran into trouble, the

---

[17] Mitteilungen des Direktoriums der Oesterreichischen Nationalbank [Minutes of the Board of Directors of the Austrian National Bank], 1926: 234–237.

commissioner general refused to provide any assistance and allowed the bank to go bankrupt; Zimmerman 'was no longer convinced interventions would end the rout and expressed fears about the risk of inflation from further increases in credit and circulation' (Ausch, 1968: 157; Marcus, 2018: 180). Bankers at the City of London, including Norman, were also opposed to supporting struggling Austrian banks. Conversely, President Reisch believed such actions were part of 'the higher duties of a bank of issue, particularly in times of crises ... Crises have a tendency to swell up like avalanches and drag down healthy institutions as well, if their development is not obviated in good time.' Reisch appreciated that the right measure of intervention was a touchy and an invidious task. In his opinion, the decision to support an ailing bank depended on the circumstances prevailing in each country: 'It will be different in the City of London, characterized by a stable banking structure with a long tradition, from the situation in Budapest or Vienna, who have a less developed, unconsolidated credit organization' (Reisch, 1925: 202).

After his resignation in February 1932, the weekly journal *Der Österreichische Volkswirt* [The Austrian Economist] blamed Reisch for the 'serious sin' of having supported the practice of taking over insolvent banks by other financial institutions, over the course of many years. According to the journal, these rescue operations covered up fraudulent behaviour in banks whose activities often involved government politicians. Thus, Reisch's behaviour may have been motivated, at least in part, by 'his political relations with the Christian-Social Party, particularly the circle intimately connected with Seipel'.[18]

The Bank of England and the Financial Committee of the League of Nations believed that the president of the ANB was too soft vis-à-vis the Austrian banks. The commissioner general's decision to block the ANB's plans to restructure the Austrian banking system in 1924 is indicative of such concerns. Thus, a joint proposal by the ANB and the Austrian Government to encourage mergers so as to deliberately reduce the number of banks and restructure the financial system was dismissed by the commissioner general. After the collapse of the Depositenbank, the government and the ANB wanted to set up a new institution (Geldinstitutszentrale) endowed with 200 billion crowns of capital, to recapitalize mid-sized banks, take over three or four other institutions thus reducing the number of banks and bank employees. The ANB endorsed the plan because

---

[18] *Der Österreichische Volkswirt*, 6 February 1932; see also Ausch (1968: 155–334).

for the bank it meant sharing the burden of lender-of-last-resort opera-tions with the government. Parliament approved the bill in July 1924, but Zimmermann vetoed the release of the necessary federal funds, argu-ing that 'the budget is not yet in a solid state and without any doubt we will feel the feedback of the economic crisis during the next month' (Kernbauer, 1991: 144–145). In retrospect, blocking the downsizing of a bloated banking sector for budgetary reasons seems to have been a missed opportunity for aligning the Austrian banking sector with the business opportunities of post-war Central Europe.

In the second half of the 1920s, several illiquid or insolvent banks were taken over by the two largest Viennese banks, the Creditanstalt and Bodencreditanstalt (BCA) (Weber, 2016: 223–256). In 1926, the Postsparkasse (Postal Savings Bank) was recapitalized, after specula-tion, mismanagement, and political interference in its business affairs had caused losses to the tune of 319 million schilling, a sum equal to 3.1 per cent of the country's GDP (Wagner and Tomanek, 1983: 229–234). In the autumn of 1929, the BCA itself had to be merged with the Creditanstalt to avoid insolvency. The ANB, whose president used to be on the BCA's Board of Directors, supported the merger by plac-ing 15 million US dollars in foreign banks that held deposits with the Creditanstalt (cross-deposits). The ANB also offered the bank a three-year grace period to settle BCA's debt from discounts to the ANB. In a bout of optimism, the ANB's General Manager claimed that 'the merger provides the Creditanstalt with great profit opportunities and the bank will not regret taking this step' (Jobst and Kernbauer, 2016: 173). Less than two years later, the losses incurred by taking over BCA would play a key role in bringing down the Creditanstalt.

In its 1929 annual report, the ANB listed some of the most serious banking mistakes that had sealed the fate of the Bodencreditanstalt. Thus, the bank had neglected:

to adapt its business model to the dramatic downsizing of Austria in a timely man-ner. Instead, it sought to hold onto higher dividends and share prices, pursuing a policy of prestige that was ill-suited to the new, difficult circumstances. Above all, however, it maintained, on the advice of its industrial experts, the aspiration to keep its affiliated industries, which were among the largest in Austria, in their previous dimensions. Time and again, it advanced considerable funds, as needed, increasingly immobilizing itself, hoping to be able to recoup these funds through industrial debt and equity issues once the stock market situation improved.[19]

[19] ANB-Archive, 363/1931.

These critical remarks are appropriate for the management of Creditanstalt, too which, in May 1931, announced a loss of 140 million schilling in its balance sheet for 1930 (about 20 million US dollars). Neither the bank's management, nor its supervisory board seem to have been aware of Creditanstalt's precarious financial situation before the spring of 1931. Louis Rothschild was chairman of the supervisory board of Creditanstalt that included two members of the League's Financial Committee – Otto Niemeyer (Bank of England and Chairman of the merchant bank Lazard Brothers & Co) and Henry Strakosch (Union Corporation, London) – as well as other prominent bankers, like Peter Bark (Anglo-International Bank, London), Max Warburg (Bankhaus Warburg, Hamburg) and Eugène Schneider-Creuzot (Paris) (Schubert, 1992: 11). Upon hearing of the Creditanstalt's losses, Harry Siepman, one of Norman's senior advisors at the Bank of England, observed: 'This, I think, is it, and it may well bring down the whole house of cards in which we have been living' (cited in Ahamed, 2009: 404).

The crisis of the largest bank in Austria and Central Europe was 'the straw that broke the camel's back' (Eichengreen, 1992: 19). Seen in an international context Creditanstalt's short-term liabilities were not excessive: the bank owed foreign banks about 76 million US dollars, or 0.8 per cent of the aggregate short-term international indebtedness.[20] Creditanstalt's failure had primarily psychological effects: when the reputable Rothschild bank in Vienna ran into difficulties, many asked themselves, how sound are other financial institutions? Indeed, confidence in the stability of the international financial system quickly evaporated.

The Creditanstalt crisis has been discussed extensively in the literature, so a few words should suffice here.[21] The government, the ANB, and the Vienna Rothschilds quickly recapitalized the bank, but it was soon rumoured that the asset write-down had not gone far enough. Deposits were withdrawn – financed by discounting bills of exchange at the ANB – and converted into foreign exchange. To discourage foreign banks from withdrawing all their capital, the government was forced to guarantee the bank's deposits. A loan by the Bank for International Settlements was quickly used up and additional credits were blocked when France sought to attach conditions that were unacceptable to the Austrian Government. A bridge loan by the Bank

---

[20] At the start of 1931, the Bank for International Settlements estimated total short term international indebtedness at about 50 billion Swiss francs, or 9.6 billion US dollars; Bank for International Settlements (1932: 11).

[21] For an introduction into this voluminous literature, see Marcus (2018: 298–334), Weber (2016: 404–536), Schubert (1992), and Eichengreen (1992: 264–270).

of England temporarily restored the ANB's foreign exchange reserves, but the banking crisis in Germany soon led to further capital flight.[22] When, in September 1931, the Bank of England 'temporarily' left the gold standard (Morrison, 2016: 19), Austria introduced foreign exchange controls.[23] On the black market, the schilling was quoted up to 30 per cent below par. The devaluation was only officially recognized in 1934. In 1932, a second international reconstruction loan was necessary to prop up Austria's finances (Klingenstein, 1965). A loan of 300 million schilling was guaranteed by England, France, Italy, and Belgium. The Austrian Government was obliged, inter alia, to restore balance to its budget immediately, eliminate the existing disparity between the value of its currency at home and abroad, remove foreign exchange restrictions and obstacles to international trade, and reduce the federal debt to the ANB by issuing domestic bonds. The use of the proceeds from the loan and the proper implementation of the budgetary and financial reform programme were monitored by a representative of the League of Nations, while the ANB received again an 'advisor', much like the one who had followed the 1923 League loan (Kernbauer, 1991: 331–333).[24]

5.5 CONCLUDING REMARKS

Britain's departure from the gold standard was a shocking policy shift that signalled the end of the monetary regime established after the First World War. Many contemporaries were taken aback and expected, like Chancellor Philip Snowden, a drastic reduction in the living standards of the working population (Morrison, 2016: 2). This is how Ahamed describes the dominant economic paradigm at that time:

> After the war, there was a universal consensus among bankers that the world must return to the gold standard as quickly as possible. The almost theological

---

[22] The outbreak of the crisis prompted Peter Bark (the BoE representative on the Creditanstalt board) and Francis Rodd (BIS) to visit Vienna to get a clear picture of the financial situation. They were soon followed by Robert Kindersley (BoE and Lazard Frères) and James Gannon (Chase National Bank), both representatives of Creditanstalt's foreign creditors, who arrived to hasten the emission of Treasury bills.

[23] Causing fears of a general moratorium, the announcement led Carel Eliza ter Meulen and Otto Niemeyer to visit Vienna, on behalf of the League of Nations, to assess the situation.

[24] The new commissioner general was the Dutchman Meinoud Marinus Rost van Tonningen, who had previously served on Zimmerman's staff; the ANB's advisor was the Dutch professor Gijsbert Weyer Jan Bruins, who was succeeded by the Belgian Maurice Paul Frère, in 1932; their appointments lasted till 1936.

belief in gold as the foundation for money was so embedded in their thinking, so much a part of their mental equipment for framing the world, that few could see any other way to organize the international monetary system. Leading that quest were Montagu Norman and Benjamin Strong.[25]

Norman was convinced that the reconstruction of pre-war monetary relations was of utmost importance for the restoration of London's financial pre-eminence, so much so that the burden of realigning domestic costs and prices to the pre-war exchange rate between sterling and the dollar could be ignored (Péteri, 1992). Thus, he told the Macmillan Committee that the 'ill effects [of deflationary policy – HK] are greatly exaggerated and they are much more psychological than real.'[26] This is consistent with Keynes's claim that, under Norman, the Bank of England held 'the extreme form of the quantity theory, in which the only effect of monetary change is on prices, without disturbing production or employment' (Wood, 2005: 283). For his part, Moggridge describes the Bank of England's attitude in the 1920s as follows: 'Policy-making depended almost exclusively on the use of rules of thumb, often disguised as general principles, derived from an earlier, less complicated and more benign age. It rested on instinct rather than analysis' (Moggridge, 1972: 242).

We have already discussed how the Bank of England attributed Austria's inflation in 1923 to an excessive increase in the money supply. President Reisch considered this interpretation of the quantity theory to be 'too one-sided' and expressed 'the fear that the theory can overestimate the influence of central banks; in my opinion, under no circumstances can rising prices be tackled decisively by the technical instruments of the central bank alone.'[27] Returning from a visit to the Bank of England, in December 1924, Reisch lamented that London misunderstood Austria's economic and political problems:

Naturally enough, the comparatively peaceful development of English economic life and the well-known conservatism of the English people makes it difficult to understand the fundamental upheavals which the revolution and the period of inflation brought to Austria, the results of which are still felt. (Reisch, 1925: 202)

Bank of England experts certainly had difficulties understanding. To them, questioning the validity of the quantity theory, even in its strictest

---

[25] Ahamed (2010: 155); Strong was Governor of the Federal Reserve Bank of New York from 1914 to 1928.
[26] Quoted in Wood (2005: 284); the Macmillan Committee was set up after the stock market crash in 1929, to explore the root causes of the economic depression in the United Kingdom.
[27] ANB-Archive, Minutes of the 25th meeting of the General Council, 18 December 1924.

interpretation, bordered on sacrilege. Commenting on Reisch's discussions, the London *Times* remarked that 'A Gilbertian situation would indeed be created if the country whose reconstruction was based upon certain economic principles, of which the quantity theory is the most important, were seriously to challenge their validity,' only to add the stern warning that 'the Austrian people would be unwise to ignore the consequences that must follow, if the policy pursued is not approved in countries where Austria desires to borrow.'[28]

Indeed, controlling the access to the London capital market gave the Bank of England considerable leverage to ensure the compliance of those countries whose financial reconstruction was supported by the League of Nations. We have already mentioned how, in the spring of 1925, Norman flatly rejected Austrian entreaties to back a loan for the further electrification of the Austrian railways. Much later, in October 1927, after the League's loan had been exhausted, Austria secured the approval of the Control Committee which watched over the interests of the countries which had guaranteed the 1923 League loan to float a 725 million schilling loan to finance public investments. The so-called *Internationale Bundesanleihe* (International Federal Bond) was issued not before 1930 and the amount of the issue reduced to 60 per cent of its originally intended value. The strains in the relationship between the Bank of England and the Austrian central bank probably contributed to the delay. As early as 1928, the ANB's annual report complained about the 'impossible situation a country can get into, when compelled to seek, in long drawn-out deliberations, the consent of a great number of authorities, before carrying out any credit operation – especially if the country is dependent on the arbitrary discretion of these authorities and the momentary political attitude prevailing in each one' (Kernbauer, 1991: 218–220). This statement shows as well how difficult it was for Austrian policy makers to come to terms with the fact that Vienna was no longer the core of the Habsburg monarchy, but part of inter-war Europe's periphery.

On the other hand, the senior management of the ANB shared many of the Bank of England's views on monetary policy and the economy. After all, pro-market liberalism was typical of the Austrian school of economics and of President Reisch, who was once a student of Böhm-Bawerk. Reisch, however, disagreed with Norman's views on the short-term

---

[28] *The Times*, 22 December 1924.

relationship between money aggregates and other macroeconomic variables. To him, it seemed obvious that this relationship was different in an economy with a well-established structure as in the United Kingdom from the Austrian one which was cut out of an integrated economic area and which had undergone eight years of inflation and hyperinflation. At the same time, financial circles in both countries shared the distinct desire to a return to the pre-war status quo. Unfortunately, it was this fatal belief that the conditions of the late nineteenth century could be replicated which led to the collapse of the inter-war economic and monetary system. Keynes's description of the difficulties of solving economic problems during the Great Depression is true of the general attitude of the ruling strata during the interwar years:

The obstacles to recovery are not material. They reside in the state of knowledge, judgment, and opinion of those who sit in the seats of authority. Unluckily the traditional and ingrained beliefs of those who hold responsible positions throughout the world grew out of experiences which contained no parallel to the present, and are often the opposite of what one would wish them to believe today. (Keynes, 1932: 86–87)

The sterling devaluation of September 1931 fundamentally changed British monetary policy. The 'policy of deflation, debt repayment, high taxation, large sinking funds and Gold Standard' had been, as Churchill lamented in 1927, 'almost entirely unsatisfactory in its reaction upon the wider social, industrial, and political spheres' (cited in Wood, 2005: 291). After leaving the gold standard Britain introduced a policy of cheap money, setting the bank rate at 2 per cent and intervening in the foreign exchange markets via the Exchange Equalization Fund. The economy recovered rapidly; by 1937 British GDP was more than 16 per cent higher than in 1929 (Mitchell et al., 2011: 14). Writing privately in 1932, Churchill pleaded for the removal of Norman, whom he saw as the pivot, the *spiritus rector* of the unsuccessful monetary policy of England after the war: 'Surely it will become a public necessity to get rid of Montagu Norman. No man has ever been stultified as he has been in his fourteen years' policy.'[29] Still, the Governor remained at the helm of the Bank of England till 1944. But the Bank had lost its influence on monetary and exchange rate policy. The same was true of central banks in many countries, which had lost their independence 'because of their disastrous performance in the depression' (Singleton, 2011: 79–86).

---

[29] Quoted in Wood (2005: 293); at the time, Churchill was a Member of Parliament and did not hold any ministerial position.

In Austria, President Reisch was replaced by Viktor Kienböck in February 1932. Kienböck had served as finance minister in the governments led by Seipel in 1922–4 and 1926–9. He became Austria's chief economic policy maker in the 1930s, only to continue his predecessor's deflationary policy. One may wonder why, unlike other countries, Austria did not witness a change in its economic policy paradigm after the collapse of the post-war monetary order in 1931. Part of the answer is financial: Austria needed further international loans, guaranteed by League members, therefore it had to accept the strings attached to such loans. Borrowing abroad was necessary for the long-term refinancing of the bridge loans which had been granted by the Bank for International Settlements and the Bank of England at the height of the Creditanstalt crisis in 1931. What is more, the Austrian state had guaranteed deposits with the Creditanstalt and needed foreign exchange to repay foreign investors. As far as the League of Nations was concerned, balancing the budget was a pre-condition for further support to Austria. In a report on interwar reconstruction measures, the League stated:

> The fall in prices necessarily brought about a heavy decrease in receipts, involving budgetary disequilibrium. However painful it might be to make ruthless cuts in expenditure, there was no other way to recover stability. (League of Nations, 1945: 24)

After the outbreak of the Creditanstalt crisis, the ANB had freely discounted bills of exchange, pumping liquidity to Creditanstalt and other banks faced with extensive deposit withdrawals. Some of the funds withdrawn were immediately converted into foreign exchange, draining ANB's reserves. In October 1931, exchange controls were introduced, only to be gradually relaxed in the course of 1932. By the end of 1933, the exchange rate was stabilized at 78 per cent of its gold parity. Debt service of the 1923 loan was interrupted briefly in 1932, with amortization and interest being paid out of reserves; by September 1933, all transfer arrears had been liquidated and, two years later, normal service for private foreign debt, too was resumed (League of Nations, 1945: 59–61).

Another part of the answer goes back to economic and political ideas, as conditioned by inflationary experiences. As already mentioned, most Austrian school economists and policy-makers espoused liberal economic principles and believed in the strict necessity of balancing the budget. The memory of wartime and post-war inflation, fuelled with the money created by the central bank, reinforced their conviction that any deviation from orthodox principles would lead back to an uncontrollable rise in prices. Large parts of the population shared this inflation phobia. Political reasons also turned price stability into a key domestic policy objective. In 1933, Austrian democracy was abolished as the conservative government, dominated by the Christian-Social Party, dissolved parliament and gradually banned all other political parties. Modelled after Italian fascism, the new regime lacked wide-spread support and was attacked vehemently by the Nazi-party, whose support had been growing since its coming into power in Germany, in January 1933. Inasmuch as inflation eroded real incomes, the government was anxious a further reduction of the living standard could mobilize the clandestine opposition, particularly trade unions and supporters of the outlawed social democratic party[30]. Therefore, in the eyes of the government, price stability was crucial for the political stability of the regime (Talos and Neugebauer, 1985).

The consequences of this policy for economic development were dismal: by 1937, GDP was 14 per cent below its 1929 level and 9 per cent below its level in 1913 (Kausel et al., 1965: 38). In this year more than 20 per cent of the Austrian labour force was unemployed (Butschek, 1999: Table 3.3). The government, for its part, celebrated the schilling as the 'alpine dollar'.[31] Poor economic performance weakened Austria's resistance against propaganda from Nazi Germany, which regarded the unutilized resources in Austria as a welcome support for its armament programme. In 1938, Austria was occupied by Nazi Germany.

REFERENCES

Unpublished (Archival) Sources

Austrian National Bank Archive (ANB-Archive), Vienna (Austria).

Published Sources

Ahamed, Liaquat (2009). *Lords of Finance: The Bankers Who Broke the World*. London and New York: Penguin Press.
Aldcroft, Derek H. (1978). *The European Economy: 1914–1970*. London: Croom Helm.
Ausch, Karl (1968). *Als die Banken fielen. Zur Soziologie der politischen Korruption*. Vienna: Europa Verlag.

---

[30] In the interwar period the Social-Democratic Party was the largest political party in Austria with a share of about 40% of the electorate.
[31] One US-dollar equaled 7.2 schilling 1927, 4.5 schilling in 1937!

Bank for International Settlements (1932). *Second Annual Report April 1, 1931 – March 31, 1932*. Basel: Bank for International Settlements.

Beer, Siegfried (2010). 'Selectively Perceived Legacies of World War I: The Little-Known Halstead Mission in Austria, 1919', in Günter Bischof, Fritz Plasser, and Peter Berger (eds.), *From Empire to Republic: Post-World War I Austria*. New Orleans: University of New Orleans Press, 110–122.

Berger, Peter (2000). *Im Schatten der Diktatur. Die Finanzdiplomatie des Vertreters des Völkerbundes in Österreich, Meinoud Marinus Rost van Tonningen 1931–1936*. Vienna: Böhlau.

Berger, Peter (2003). 'The League of Nations and Interwar Austria: A Critical Assessment of a Partnership in Economic Reconstruction', in Günter Bischof, Anton Pelinka, and Alexander Lassner (eds.), *The Dollfuss/Schuschnigg Era in Austria: A Reassessment*. New Brunswick, NJ: Transaction Publishers, 73–92.

Berger, Peter (2007). *Kurze Geschichte Österreichs im 20. Jahrhundert*. Vienna: Universitätsverlag der Hochschülerschaft an der Universität Wien.

Butschek, Felix (1999). *Statistische Reihen zur österreichischen Wirtschaftsgeschichte. Die österreichische Wirtschaft seit der industriellen Revolution*. Vienna: Österreichisches Institut für Wirtschaftsforschung.

Clay, Henry (1957). *Lord Norman*. London: Macmillan.

Eichengreen, Barry (1992). *Golden Fetters: The Gold Standard and the Great Depression, 1919–1939*. New York: Oxford University Press.

Eichengreen, Barry and Peter Temin (1997). 'The Gold Standard and the Great Depression'. NBER Working Paper Series. Working Paper 6060.

Fibich, Alexander (1977). 'Die Entwicklung der österreichischen Bundesausgaben in der Ersten Republik (1918–1938)'. PhD diss., University of Vienna.

Flores Zendejas, Juan and Decorzant, Yann (2016). 'Going Multilateral? Financial Markets' Access and the League of Nations Loans, 1923–8'. *The Economic History Review*, 69(2): 653–678.

Garber, Peter M. and Spencer, Michael G. (1994). *The Dissolution of the Austro-Hungarian Empire: Lessons for Currency Reform*. Essays in International Finance, No. 191. Princeton, NJ: Princeton University Press.

Gratz, Alois (1949). 'Die österreichische Finanzpolitik von 1848 bis 1948', in Hans Mayer (ed.), *Hundert Jahre österreichischer Wirtschaftsentwicklung 1848 bis 1948*. Vienna: Springer, 222–309.

Jobst, Clemens and Kernbauer, Hans (2016). *The Quest for Stable Money: Central Banking in Austria, 1816–2016*. Frankfurt: Campus.

Kausel, Anton, Nemeth, Nandor, and Seidel, Hans (1965). *Österreichs Volkseinkommen 1913 bis 1963*. Vienna: Monatsberichte des Österreichischen Institutes für Wirtschaftsforschung.

Kernbauer, Hans (1991). *Währungspolitik in der Zwischenkriegszeit. Geschichte der Oesterreichischen Nationalbank von 1923 bis 1938*. Vienna: Oesterreichische Nationalbank.

Keynes, John Maynard (1924). *A Tract on Monetary Reform*. London: Macmillan and Co.

Keynes, John Maynard (1932). *The World's Economic Crisis and the Way of Escape*. Halley Stewart Lecture, 1931. London: George Allen & Unwin, 69–88.

Klausinger, Hansjörg (2002). 'The Austrian School of Economics and the Gold Standard Mentality in Austrian Economic Policy in the 1930s'. Working Paper 02–2, Vienna University of Economics and Business. Department of Economics.

Klingenstein, Grete (1965). *Die Anleihe von Lausanne*. Vienna-Graz: Stiasny.

Layton, Walter T. and Rist, Charles (1925). *La Situation Économique de L'Autriche. Rapport présenté au Conseil de la Société des Nations.* Geneva: Publications de la Société des Nations.

League of Nations (1922). *The Restoration of Austria. Agreements arranged by the League of Nations and Signed at Geneva on October 4th, 1922 with the Relevant Documents and Public Statements.* Geneva: League of Nations Publications.

League of Nations (1926). *The Financial Reconstruction of Austria: General Survey and Principal Documents.* Geneva: League of Nations Publications.

League of Nations (1945). *The League of Nations Reconstruction Schemes in the Inter-War Period.* Geneva: League of Nations Publications.

Marcus, Nathan (2018). *Austrian Reconstruction and the Collapse of Global Finance, 1921–1931.* Cambridge, MA: Harvard University Press.

März, Eduard (1984). *Austrian Banking and Financial Policy: Creditanstalt at a Turning Point, 1913–1923.* London: Weidenfeld and Nicholson.

Matis, Herbert (2005). 'Österreichs Wirtschaft in der Zwischenkriegszeit: Desintegration, Neustrukturierung und Stagnation', in Oliver Rathkolb and Ulrike Zimmerl (eds.), *Bank Austria Credit-Anstalt: 150 Jahre österreichische Bankgeschichte im Zentrum Europas.* Vienna: Zsolnay, 125–147.

Mises, Ludwig (1927). *Liberalismus.* Jena: Gustav Fischer.

Mises, Ludwig (1931). *Die Ursachen der Wirtschaftskrise.* Tübingen: J. C. B. Mohr.

Mitchell, James, Solomou, Solomos, and Weale, Martin (2011). 'Monthly GDP Estimates for Inter-War Britain'. www.econ.cam.ac.uk/research-files/repec/cam/pdf/cwpe1155.pdf

Moggridge, Donald E. (1972). *British Monetary Policy 1924–1931: The Norman Conquest of $4.86.* Cambridge, UK and New York: Cambridge University Press.

Morrison, James Ashley (2016). 'Shocking Intellectual Austerity: The Role of Ideas in the Demise of the Gold Standard in Britain'. *International Organization*, 70(1): 175–207.

Natmeßnig, Charlotte (1998). *Britische Finanzinteressen in Österreich: Die Anglo-Österreichische Bank.* Vienna: Böhlau.

Pauly, W. Louis (1996). *The League of Nations and the Foreshadowing of the International Monetary Fund.* Essays in International Finance, No. 201. Princeton: Princeton University Press.

Péteri, György (1992). 'Central Bank Diplomacy: Montagu Norman and Central Europe's Monetary Reconstruction after World War I'. *Contemporary European History*, 1(3): 233–258.

Pressburger, Siegfried (1976). *Das österreichische Noteninstitut 1816–1966.* Part II. Vol. 4. Vienna: Oesterreichische Nationalbank.

Reisch, Richard (1924a). 'Meine Duplik in Causa "Geldwertpolitik"'. *Mitteilungen des Verbandes österreichischer Banken und Bankiers*, 6(3/4): 93–106.

Reisch, Richard (1924b). 'Stabilisierung oder Steigerung des Kronenwertes'. *Mitteilungen des Verbandes österreichischer Banken und Bankiers*, 6(1/2): 1–12.

Reisch, Richard (1925). 'Die höheren Aufgaben einer modernen Notenbank, insbesondere in Krisenzeiten'. *Mitteilungen des Verbandes österreichischer Banken und Bankiers*, 7(7/8): 193–207.

Schubert, Aurel (1992). *The Credit-Anstalt Crisis of 1931*. Cambridge, MA: Cambridge University Press.

Singleton, John (2011). *Central Banking in the Twentieth Century*. Cambridge, MA: Cambridge University Press.

Statistische Nachrichten (1923, 1924, 1925). *Statistische Nachrichten*. Vienna: Bundesamt für Statistik.

Stiefel, Dieter (2012). *Camillo Castiglioni oder Die Metaphysik der Haifische*. Vienna: Böhlau.

Talos, Emerich and Neugebauer, Wolfgang (eds.) (1985). '"*Austrofaschismus.*" *Beiträge über Politik, Ökonomie und Kultur 1934–1938*. Vienna: Verlag für Gesellschaftskritik.

Wagner, Michael and Tomanek, Peter (1983). *Bankiers und Beamte. Hundert Jahre Österreichische Postsparkasse*. Vienna: Österreichische Postsparkasse.

Walré de Bordes, Jan (1924). *The Austrian Crown: Its Depreciation and Stabilization*. London: P. S. King & Son, Ltd.

Wärmer, Gustav (1936). *Das österreichische Kreditwesen*. Vienna: Verlag des Bankenverbandes.

Warnock, Barbara Susan (2015). 'The First Bailout – The Financial Reconstruction of Austria 1922–1926'. PhD diss., University of London.

Wasserman, Janek (2019). *The Marginal Revolutionaries: How Austrian Economists Fought the War of Ideas*. New Haven and London: Yale University Press.

Weber, Fritz (2016). *Vor dem großen Krach. Österreichs Bankwesen der Zwischenkriegszeit: Am Beispiel der Credit-Anstalt für Handel und Gewerbe*. Vienna: Böhlau.

Wood, John H. (2005). *A History of Central Banking in Great Britain and the United States*. Cambridge, MA: Cambridge University Press.

6

Sneaking Nationalization

Hungary and the Liberal Monetary Order, 1924–1931

György Péteri

6.1 INTRODUCTION

In the comparative analysis of economic systems, the interwar years are usually portrayed as a period clearly divided between two phases: the "conservative 1920s" and the "revolutionary 1930s" (Polányi, 2001: chapter 2). Of course, the 1930s is seen as the postliberal era of "managed money," national isolationism, beggar-thy-neighbor practices, and trade block building, which was accompanied by the growing popularity for state interventionism, macroeconomic planning, and so on. By contrast, the 1920s have been seen as the decade which saw a "return to normalcy," and the restoration of the liberal economic order that had been prevalent before the First World War, characterized by the relatively (or increasingly) free movement of goods, capital and, to a lesser extent, people. On the monetary side of things, the gold standard or, at least, the gold exchange standard held sway – a monetary regime that worked "automatically" by tying the value of the national currency to gold and/or to currencies more or less convertible into gold. Central banks were asked not to stand in the way of the adjustment process triggered by balance of payments imbalances, but rather, to promote and facilitate such adjustment, discouraging any national measures and actions that threatened to impede the "automatic" process expected to restore equilibrium in international payments.

In this chapter, I use the case of Hungarian monetary policy to argue that this contrast between the 1920s and 1930s has been greatly exaggerated. I will discuss what I term the sneaking nationalization of monetary management, providing empirical evidence as to how the central bank of a small peripheral economy like Hungary responded to the international pressure exerted through the gold exchange standard. Specifically, I shall demonstrate that the Hungarian National Bank tried to abide by the rules of the game, while at the same time seeking to get around them whenever they seemed to hurt national economic interests.

The rest of the chapter proceeds as follows.[1] Section 6.2 provides some context in terms of the political and economic situation prevailing in Hungary after the First World War. Section 6.3 offers a brief review of the 1924 stabilization, which was carried out under the auspices of the League of Nations, as well as the concomitant crisis that affected the Hungarian economy in 1924–5, when the korona followed sterling's appreciation. Section 6.4 focuses on the structure of the balance of payments after the crisis and Hungary's dependence on the international capital market. Inevitably, this dependence affected the Hungarian National Bank, which was forced, at least in principle, to prioritize its external commitment to the gold standard, rather than pay attention to domestic economic and monetary conditions. Whether it did so in practice is examined in Section 6.5, which applies – and extends – the methodology of Ragnar Nurkse and Arthur Bloomfield (Brown and Nurkse, 1944; Bloomfield, 1959) to identify the extent to which the Hungarian National Bank deviated from the rules of the game. Finally, Section 6.6 offers some conclusions.

6.2 HUNGARY'S POSTWAR REALITY AND THE "RETURN TO NORMALCY"

Left with less than a third of its territory and hardly more than a third of its population compared with the prewar years, and bearing the deep scars of war, two revolutions, and a bloody counter-revolution, Hungary emerged from the First World War with no clear sense of what "a return to normalcy" might involve. Did it mean being part of the Austro-Hungarian Empire, both politically and economically? Should the pre-war Kingdom of Hungary be thought of as representing an ideal one should strive to recover? Or should Hungarians accept and become resigned to a "mutilated Hungary": the outcome of the territorial rearrangements imposed by the Trianon Peace Treaty?

---

[1] In writing this chapter, I have drawn extensively on my own previous writings, particularly Péteri (1980, 1995, and 2002). Thus, many additional references are suppressed in what follows.

For those on the radical right, who demanded an immediate revision of the Treaty of Trianon, the return to normalcy meant prioritizing the restoration of the country's pre-1914 borders. The rest of the populace were said to inhabit what the counter-revolutionary sociopolitical order defined as the field of "legitimate politics," and thus tempered their revisionism with gradualism. They argued Hungary should abstain from revisionist adventures and focus on consolidation; this was considered vital for the emerging rightist-conservative and authoritarian sociopolitical order which sought to promote the interests of the Christian-national middle classes.[2]

In practice, gradualism meant two things. First, Hungary needed to win international approval and secure the patronage of a great power. This would help defend Hungary against the hostile successor states of the defunct Habsburg empire that had been enlisted in the Little Entente[3]. Second, the gradualists believed that Hungary should pursue a policy of economic recovery to enable it to re-assert its pivotal economic role in East Central Europe. In the long run, it was believed, these measures would lead to the restoration of pre-Trianon Hungary, at least in terms of hegemony, if not territorial sovereignty. This kind of gradual revisionism was endorsed by Count István Bethlen's government (1921–1931) which put an end to the Hungarian White Terror, disciplined and tamed rightist extremism, dethroned the Habsburgs, and came to terms with the Social-Democratic Party, thereby securing domestic political stability, which was a key precondition for securing the monetary stabilization loan in 1924.

The war, together with the postwar political upheaval, and the loss of both lands and people had caused severe economic dislocation. The integrated and relatively well-functioning imperial market of the dual monarchy, comprising a population of 53 million had given way to a series of structural mismatches between supply and demand, along with major supply chain disruptions since the new political boundaries had distributed productive capacities, resources, and markets unevenly. To give but one example, most of Hungary's production capacity in milling – a

---

[2] This is a contemporary term (*keresztény-nemzeti középosztály*) used to describe the social base of the interwar authoritarian, nationalist, and anti-semitic Horthy-regime. Typically non-Jewish and "gentry," the Christian-national middle class comprised middle-sized landowners, descendants of such landowning nobility who had lost their properties, and those serving in various positions of the officers corps in the military, the police, the gendarmerie, and public administration, etc.

[3] The Little Entente was an alliance formed in 1920 and 1921 by Czechoslovakia, Romania, and the Kingdom of Serbs, Croats, and Slovenes, with the support of France, against potential Hungarian attempts to regain their lost territories and Habsburg attempts to restore the empire.

major export industry before the war – remained within the country's new borders, but the amount of grain produced domestically was now limited to about one-third of the industry's processing capacity. During the 1920s, this situation was responsible for the emergence of sizeable current account deficits. Under the gold exchange standard, implemented between 1924 and 1931, these deficits caused frequent headaches to Hungary's monetary managers (Péteri, 2002: 138).

6.3 STABILIZATION AND ADJUSTMENT

Ever since the country had experienced soaring inflation in the early 1920s, Hungarian policymakers had been convinced that Hungary would come to depend on the regular influx of foreign capital to secure monetary stability and economic growth. What is more, the accumulation of foreign liabilities also meant that a significant foreign power was committing its resources – and thus developing a stake – in the country's political and economic future. This dovetailed with Hungary's major foreign policy objective, which consisted of doing away with her postwar international status as a pariah state. In 1924, following an abortive attempt to approach Paris, Hungary turned to Great Britain for help with achieving monetary stabilization and reintegration within the international financial system. Britain's stance was profoundly influenced by the main architect of Central Europe's post-Habsburg and post-Wilhelmine monetary and financial reconstruction, the governor of the Bank of England, Montagu Norman. The stabilization took place in the spirit of the liberal program "to return to normalcy" under the aegis of the League of Nations.

In the long run, the shift in Hungary's politics towards right-wing nationalism, together with the pressures of economic adjustment, shifted Hungary's interwar economic and monetary policies away from engagement with the international economy, and towards greater insularity. Paradoxically, the 1924 stabilization loan achieved under Montagu Norman's patronage would serve to reinforce this tendency, inasmuch as it tied up Hungary's monetary management to a system of fixed exchange rates under the gold-exchange standard. The paradox stems from the circumstances in which the Hungarian National Bank was established, and currency stabilization took place. By the end of May 1924, stabilization efforts under the aegis of the League of Nations had reached a critical turning point.[4]

---

[4] Arthur Salter and Joseph Avenol had visited Hungary on behalf of the League's Secretariat as early as 1923, to prepare the ground; details of the stabilization plan and new bank

The stabilization plan called for a £12 million foreign loan, to be issued in three equal tranches in Paris, London, and New York. Despite facing some difficulties, the London and Paris tranches were placed successfully, chiefly thanks to the support of the British government and the Bank of England. But when New York showed no interest in investing in the sovereign bonds of a Central European country, the whole project was threatened with collapse. At this juncture Norman swept in to save the Hungarian stabilization scheme. He encouraged the British government to send him a letter, asking the Bank of England to advance the missing £4 million; in doing so, the Bank would be defending the reputation of Britain and the League of Nations as promoters of Europe's postwar reconstruction. With the government's request in hand, Norman convinced the Bank of England's Board to approve a £4 million advance to the Hungarian National Bank, which was about to be established, on the security of Hungarian Treasury bills. Since the credits were meant to bridge the gap caused by the failure to float the League of Nations loan in New York, and the loan was meant to finance the Hungarian government's budget deficit to stem inflationary monetary finance, the decision to advance the £4 million was far from straightforward for the Bank. Indeed, the Board reacted to Norman's proposal with a mixture of apprehension and concern, one Board member going so far as to dissent during the final vote. At the time, the Bank of England was Europe's leading central bank and still controlled the continent's largest capital market. Under Norman's leadership, the Bank had sought to disseminate and internationally impose a code of conduct that, among other things, emphatically discouraged central banks from doing business with their own governments, or those of other countries, or politicians in general.

In making his case for the advance to Hungary, Norman probably highlighted a number of considerations that lay close to his heart at the time. Under the League's stabilization scheme, a former British civil servant, Harry Siepmann, was expected to become senior advisor to the new Hungarian National Bank, thus exercising considerable control over monetary policy. While nominally appointed at the League's behest, Siepmann was expected to work closely with the Bank of England. In fact, no sooner had he received tidings of his anticipated new appointment, he wrote to Norman asking to be taken on as his pupil so that

statutes were negotiated in March 1924, when a League delegation headed by Henry Strakosch, arrived in Budapest. Additional members included Joseph Avenol, Arthur Salter, Giuseppe Bianchini, C. E. ter Meulen, Vilem Pospíšil, and Marcus Wallenberg. Albert Janssen, originally meant to chair the delegation, could not attend on account of other duties.

Norman could serve as mentor in matters of central banking. No doubt, Norman also hoped that the Hungarian advance would give him an opportunity to widen the transnational network of cooperating banks of issue prepared to hold true to what he believed to be the right ethos of central banking. So long as part of the advance remained outstanding, Threadneedle Street would have additional leverage over the new Bank which it could use to tailor its discount rate to whatever London deemed necessary. Furthermore, the advance would help guarantee that sterling would be used as the standard for the Hungarian currency's stabilization.

This last condition, which became clause no. 11 of the agreement between Norman and the newly appointed president of the Hungarian National Bank, Alexander Popovics, must have been as gratifying to Threadneedle Street as it was unsettling to the managers of Hungary's new central bank. During the war, Britain had suspended convertibility; the dominant view in the early 1920s was that sterling would soon return to the gold standard at its prewar parity, that is, at $4.86 to the pound (the dollar being the only currency still freely convertible into gold). For the better part of 1923–4, however, the sterling exchange rate hovered well below its gold parity, fluctuating between $4.40 and $4.50 per pound. Thus, with the korona pegged to sterling and sterling set to appreciate back to parity, Hungary was destined to experience two full years of severe deflationary pressure (Table 6.1).

Clause 11 helped London in its efforts to return to parity; without this arrangement, the Hungarian National Bank would have wanted to transfer the proceeds of the loan to New York or, in any case, convert them into dollars. More importantly, it boosted Norman's efforts to cement the global position of sterling and London vis-à-vis the dollar and New York, at a critical period when sterling was off gold and a growing number of international transactions were being conducted through New York. As Norman himself would put it, in early 1924, in connection with another one of his attempts to support Central Europe's monetary reconstruction on the condition of pegging the region's currencies to the pound, this was "All for the good of Sterling!"[5].

In Budapest, however, "the good of sterling" brought sustained deflationary pressure for almost two full years. In what became known at the time as the *Sanierungskrise*, the pegging of the Hungarian korona to sterling depressed the Hungarian price level by about 15 percentage points

---

[5] Norman to W. H. Clegg, the governor of the South African Reserve Bank, 10 January 1924, copy, Bank of England Archives (henceforth BOEA), OV34/117.

TABLE 6.1 *Hungarian price level, pound sterling, and korona exchange rates (June 1924=100), 1923–1925*

	1923			1924			1925		
	Prices	Pound	Korona	Prices	Pound	Korona	Prices	Pound	Korona
Jan	–	107.7	3,554.5	46.5	98.6	354.5	104.5	110.7	127.3
Feb	–	108.6	3,463.6	83.3	99.7	300.0	100.5	110.5	127.3
Mar	–	108.7	2,627.3	94.1	99.3	136.4	95.9	110.6	127.3
Apr	–	107.8	1,972.7	96.7	100.7	127.3	94.1	110.0	127.3
May	–	107.1	1,736.4	102.8	100.9	109.1	91.8	112.4	127.3
Jun	–	106.8	1,272.7	100.0	100.0	100.0	92.1	112.5	127.3
Jul	–	106.1	881.8	103.9	101.2	109.1	88.7	112.5	127.3
Aug	–	105.6	509.1	101.5	104.2	118.2	87.6	112.4	127.3
Sep	–	105.1	500.0	101.3	103.3	118.2	88.4	112.2	127.3
Oct	–	104.7	490.9	103.5	103.9	118.2	85.6	112.1	127.3
Nov	–	101.4	490.9	104.6	106.7	118.2	84.3	112.2	127.3
Dec	3.6	100.9	472.7	106.3	108.7	118.2	85.3	112.3	127.3

Note: Exchange rates as quoted in New York, in terms of dollars per pound sterling or Hungarian koronas; a rise in the index value suggests an appreciation of the pound or korona vis-à-vis the dollar.
Source: League of Nations (1926).

between June 1924 and December 1925 (Péteri, 2002: 119). This wreaked havoc on the economy: business contracted, unemployment surged, and crisis struck various industries, as described in detail by Iván T. Berend and György Ránki in their early book on the 1920s (Berend and Ránki, 1966: 240–244). Upon reading a draft of the Norman–Popovics agreement, Siepmann was taken aback and wrote to Norman:

> from this end, your conditions seem stiff. Imagine a government in power here at a time of trade depression, after a bad harvest with plenty of unemployed. The winter is bitter cold and the destructive elements which still exist in this country threaten to give trouble. Just at this time, shall we say, you are linking yourself gradually up with gold again. In order to maintain parity with sterling, the Hungarian government is to see a contraction of the currency, a further disturbance of the price level, a further setback to business. All this on account of an agreement between two central banks with which the sovereign government is in honour bound not to interfere. It takes some believing that the ruling classes would stand idle (sic) by. The same would be true, I admit, of stabilisation in terms of gold, but your calling it sterling adds a risk of an additional 10% of price depression. Still, beggars cannot be choosers ...[6]

[6] Siepmann to Norman, Budapest, 3 June 1924, BOEA OV33/71.

The shift to right-wing nationalism fueled by post-1920 revisionist sentiment and the sustained adjustment pressure weighing on the country's
economy constitute two principal features of interwar Hungary. Along
with the deflationary crisis experienced in the first two years after switch-
ing to a fixed exchange rate regime, these forces combined to forge the
context within which practices of "limping neutralization" emerged. It is
to these practices that this chapter now turns.

6.4 THE STRATEGIC DEPENDENCY OF THE CENTRAL BANK

On the eve of stabilization, Hungarian policymakers expressed concerns
about the weakness of domestic capital accumulation and the threat
posed by the country's persistent balance of payments deficit. The League
of Nations responded in reassuring tones. Addressing Hungary's finance
minister, Tibor Kállay, on November 16, 1923, Arthur Salter, the head
of the League's Economic and Financial Section, explained how these
problems would "resolve themselves by the state becoming viable and
by stabilizing the korona. If the budget is balanced, foreign capital will
come. This, however, is not the task of the present lenders, but that of
private enterprise in the future."[7] On 20 March 1924, during yet another
League mission visit to Budapest, Hungarians were warned that:

The Bank should not aim to raise the rate of the Korona. If the rate falls because
of the lack of foreign exchange, it should be allowed to fall. Up till now it has
been falling because of the inflation and, to a smaller extent because of the balance of payments, since equilibrium in the latter gets restored by itself on the
longer run. Now that the inflation will no longer be a problem, with regard to the
balance of payments the only thing that needs to be done is to see to it that there
are no more restrictions and the [Bank's] discount rate should help.[8]

While undergoing the adjustment pressure of the 1920s, however,
Hungarian policymakers were soon confronted with a dilemma, the solution to which set them on a course that was hard to reconcile with the
norms of a market-regulated economy. This dilemma was clearly articu-
lated in the correspondence exchanged between Siepmann, the Hungarian
National Bank's senior advisor, and the head of the Department of
Statistics and Economic Studies, Béla Imrédy.

---

[7] Point 10/b in "My notes from the negotiations with the representatives [of the Financial
Committee of the League of Nations]," November 13–14, 1923, by Minister of Finance
Tibor Kállay, Hungarian National Archives (henceforth MOL), K275, 8. Cs. VII/3.
[8] Finance Minister Tibor Kállay's handwritten note dated March 20, 1924, Papers of
Finance Minister Tibor Kállay, MOL K 275, 9. cs.

In the course of their correspondence between 1926 and 1927, Imrédy wrote to Siepmann expressing his concern that agriculture was losing much of its income-generating capacity worldwide. At the same time, Imrédy argued, under the current prevailing conditions of a liberal economic order, a predominantly agricultural economy such as Hungary faced steep if not insurmountable obstacles on its path to industrialization, which was the only means to secure the employment and livelihood of an increasing (and increasingly "superfluous," that is, underemployed) rural population. Since emigration to North America – a familiar population release valve during the nineteenth century – was no longer an option, the situation seemed to be hopeless, "perhaps, then, it would be easier to just gas Hungary with cyanide" Imrédy wrote in exasperation.[9] Siepmann, who considered Imrédy's outburst to have been overly dramatic, responded: "Why do you go on worrying about the population of Hungary? It strikes me as the poorest possible excuse for keeping alive a whole lot of economically wasteful industries."[10]

Yet politicians and policymakers, whether democratically elected or authoritarian, can seldom afford to stop worrying about the population living under their watch. Hungary's newly established central bank therefore seems to have sought and found ways and means to ease the pressure of adjustment on the economy and society, without explicitly questioning the "rules of the game." The appropriation and taming of the gold standard's rules are what I describe as the sneaking nationalization of monetary management under a fixed rate of exchange regime.

Between 1924 and 1931, Hungary was on a de facto gold-exchange standard. In line with legal provisions to that effect, this was considered a stepping stone to a pure gold standard, by which the Hungarian National Bank would resume gold payments, that is, stand by to convert, on demand, Hungarian currency (the pengő, as of January 1, 1927) into gold, at a legally prescribed rate of exchange with the precious metal. Under the Bank's statutes its task was "above all ... to prepare

---

[9] Béla Imrédy's letter to Harry A. Siepmann, Budapest, September 9, 1926 (in German), Papers of Béla Imrédy, Ministry of Finance, MOL K 278, 6. cs. 33. d.; Béla Imrédy's letter to Harry A. Siepmann, Budapest, April 3, 1927 (in German), Papers of Béla Imrédy, Ministry of Finance, MOL K 278, 6. cs. 33. d. An extract from the letter, translated into English is also found in BOEA, OV 33/2. Imrédy would go on to become a leading personality of Hungarian rightist politics in the 1930s and orchestrated the first attempt to introduce macroeconomic planning to Hungary.

[10] Harry A. Siepmann to Béla Imrédy [London], September 15, 1926 (in English), Papers of Béla Imrédy, Ministry of Finance, MOL K 278, 6. cs. 33. d.

to make gold payments (to convert banknotes into metal) by storing gold and claims on foreign currencies of fixed value, and to ensure the maintenance of gold payments once they have been legally instituted" (Magyar Törvénytár, 1924: 50). During most of the period under consideration, that is, until the reintroduction of exchange controls in July 1931, the Hungarian National Bank guaranteed the convertibility of the pengő in relation to other nations' currencies and claims upon those currencies. Or, as the president of the Bank, Sándor Popovics, put it in 1929, "the Hungarian National Bank is a gold payer in foreign exchange."[11] The Bank's overall policy objective during this time was the defense of the country's exchange rate, that is, the maintenance of the korona (subsequently pengő) exchange rate in international transactions: "the question of currency stability can be taken as the primary and most important consideration. To guarantee the fixed value of the korona is the Bank's first and foremost task."[12] Indeed, this was the Bank's legal duty as laid down in its statutes: "The Bank is obliged to ensure by every available means that until the legal establishment of the convertibility of paper currency (banknotes) into metal, the value of notes issued, expressed in the rate of exchange of bills of countries with gold-based currencies or fixed-value currencies, should remain stable" (Magyar Törvénytár, 1924: 50). Radical changes only took place in 1931, the year of the financial crisis, when exchange controls were introduced, and the international gold-exchange standard collapsed. At that point, the Bank's managing director declared that "the Bank's present task is to maintain not the foreign parities of the pengő but its domestic purchasing power."[13]

Stability of the pengő's value expressed in foreign, gold-convertible currencies directly assumed that the pengő could be freely converted into those currencies, that is, that the supply of pengő (emanating from claims of foreign-currency creditors on the Hungarian economy) and the demand for pengő (springing from claims of Hungarian economic

---

[11] Hungarian National Bank, Board of Directors meeting May 28, 1929. Minutes, MOL Z8, 1. cs.

[12] Hungarian National Bank, Board of Directors meeting June 20, 1924. Minutes, MOL Z6, 1. cs. Document 8 – Hungarian National Bank, Board of Directors meeting, October 30, 1931, Minutes, MOL Microfilm Collection, Box nr. 13388, pp. 2–3. Document 9 – Hungarian National Bank, Board of Directors meeting, May 22, 1929, and August 30, 1929, Minutes, MOL Microfilm Collection, Box nr. 13388, pp. 14–17 and 15–17.

[13] Hungarian National Bank, Board of Directors meeting, November 25, 1931, Minutes, MOL Microfilm Collection, Box nr. 13388, p. 20

TABLE 6.2 *Hungary's balance of payments (in millions of US dollars),*
1926–1931
($1=5.7176 pengős)

	1926	1927	1928	1929	1930	1931
Trade balance	−16.28	−60.88	−64.73	−7.15	10.76	2.47
Interest and dividends	−15.29	−19.80	−24.96	−27.42	−31.78	−35.57
Other current items	2.76	−3.22	1.94	−2.76	−3.15	−6.19
= Current account	−28.81	−83.90	−87.75	−37.33	−24.17	−39.29
Repayments and amortization	−4.84	−3.85	−6.94	−7.75	−19.52	−36.71
Buying/selling of securities	2.62	−4.48	3.04	−0.42	−4.44	−3.85
New foreign loans	29.51	51.53	52.43	41.00	56.02	87.57
Issue of new shares	1.38	5.40	6.40	5.33	2.61	1.99
Buying/selling of real estate	0.65	0.00	0.21	0.03	−0.03	−0.05
Change in reserves*	−2.75	−4.84	17.33	10.06	0.98	18.73
Net short-term credits	−0.91	40.14	15.39	−11.89	1.05	−17.49
Balancing item	3.19	0.00	0.11	−0.97	12.50	10.90
= Capital movements	28.81	83.90	87.75	37.33	24.17	39.29

* Note that, the sale (decrease) of foreign exchange reserves is recorded as a receipt (+), whereas the purchase (increase) of foreign exchange reserves is recorded as a payment (−).
Source: Hungary's balance of payments in 1923–1937 [probably from 1946], OL Ministry of Foreign Affairs, Peace Preparation Section, III-33. There are no data for 1925.

actors on foreign countries) would not differ substantially. Obviously, the pengő's position on the international money market and the stability of its exchange rate depended on Hungary's balance of payments. The credit side of this balance (the current liabilities of foreign countries vis-à-vis the Hungarian economy) strengthened the pengő, while the debit side (current liabilities of the Hungarian economy to foreign countries) weakened it. Clearly, a chronic current account deficit would tend to cause serious difficulties for guardians of currency stability like the central bank. Indeed, during the years under consideration, Hungary's balance of payments exhibited chronic imbalances (see Table 6.2).

Hungary's persistent current account deficit stemmed mainly from its negative trade balance and more specifically, from the country's low export capability, which was exacerbated by deteriorating terms of trade. The other important factor, particularly after 1929, was the increasing sums absorbed by interest and dividend payments abroad, along with amortizations and repayments on capital account. These demonstrate that from 1924–5 onwards, the rapid increase in capital imports had not contributed sufficiently to the strengthening of Hungary's international position, at least in terms of its current account. The data in Table 6.2 also show that throughout the period under consideration, Hungary's deficit on its current account was only financed through the steady inflow of foreign capital. Till 1929, the surplus on capital account financed an average of 90 percent of the main debit items, that is, merchandise trade, plus interest and dividends, plus amortizations and repayments. Over the whole 1926–31 period, the ratio of net capital inflows to debit items was 108.1 percent – only a small fraction of net capital inflows was left freely available after trade and (increasingly) debt service had been paid for.

In the light of this, the stability of Hungary's currency in the seven years of belonging de facto to the gold-exchange standard rested on the volume of foreign exchange made available by the international capital and money markets: year after year, the country's international liquidity was dependent on the supplies of short- and long-term capital from abroad. In other words, the chronic balance-of-payments deficit, which had structural causes, made the external stability of the Hungarian currency dependent upon the state of capital and money markets in New York and London. Market "demand" and "firmness" became determinants of the Hungarian National Bank's gold and foreign exchange reserves and thus of the country's capacity to act as a "payer in gold or foreign exchange." This explains why, in 1931, the Bank informed the Economic and Financial Commission of the League of Nations that:

A radical change in the country's present position is not a problem of financial methods but of economics ... The country's present indebtedness is of such a nature that the requirement deriving from it can only be covered by incurring further debt, and to alter the present position our aim must consequently be to change the country's economic structure in a manner that after a while allows the balance-of-payments deficit to be ameliorated by an increase in our production and exports, so that the deficit may one day be eliminated altogether.[14]

Since currency stability was based on the inflow of foreign capital, the Hungarian National Bank focused its attention primarily on external indicators: it kept its eyes fixed on fluctuations in international money and capital markets, as well as foreign borrowing by domestic economic

---

[14] Hungarian National Bank, Board of Directors meeting, October 30, 1931, Minutes, MOL Microfilm Collection, Box nr. 13388, pp. 2–3.

actors, all of which affected its gold and gold-exchange reserves; by contrast, the Bank appeared to be paying less attention to interest rates and credit policy requirements deriving from domestic economic processes and changes. This precarious currency stability would soon be rendered untenable; the crucial turning point was the moment when additional foreign capital would become equal to interest and amortization on accumulated past indebtedness. Early indications of such a position were already present in the second half of 1928. They had grown by summer 1929, when the position of the Bank as a "gold-payer" was temporarily maintained only thanks to a £500,000 credit from the Bank of England, followed by a $10 million gold credit raised in equal shares by the Bank of England, the Federal Reserve Bank of New York, the Banque de France, the Banque Nationale de Belgique, and the Nederlandsche Bank.[15]

While this stabilization mechanism demonstrates both the instability of the gold-exchange standard and the strategic dependency of Hungarian monetary policy, it does not tell us whether the adoption of the gold-exchange standard, which succeeded in stabilizing the exchange rate for a few years, really meant that considerations of domestic economic stability and prosperity were downgraded in the short run. This question can be examined by analyzing the link between the central bank's international liquidity, its credit base, and the money supply.

6.5 GOLD RESERVES, MONEY SUPPLY, AND THE CREDIT BASE

Orthodox, classical economic theory sees the gold standard as a mechanism whereby disequilibria in the balance of payments are automatically adjusted, through a mechanism where central banks play a somewhat passive role.

According to this interpretation, which constituted the accepted policy norm of the time in Britain and at the League of Nations, disequilibria induced processes that lead to an automatic adjustment of the balance of payments. Current account deficits, which arise when goods and services sold abroad and the international receipts from capital imports fail to cover the liabilities deriving from the import of goods, services, and securities, cause a decrease in the supply of means of international payment (whether reserves of gold or convertible foreign exchange) available to the country's central bank. As domestic debtors convert their assets into gold

---

[15] Hungarian National Bank, Board of Directors meeting, May 22, 1929 and August 30, 1929, Minutes, MOL Microfilm Collection, Box nr. 13388, pp. 14–17 and 15–17.

or foreign exchange, the domestic money supply (banknotes in circulation plus central bank sight liabilities) shrinks. Since the fall in gold and foreign exchange reserves threatens currency stability, the central bank is forced to respond by taking defensive measures.[16] The bank raises the discount rate, and (if necessary) introduces credit restrictions, lowering credit ceilings, applying stricter controls on bills of exchange, decreasing the number of those authorized to present bills of exchange, and so on. These, in turn, cause effective demand to shrink, producing a drop in the domestic price level, which triggers an automatic correction in the trade balance, raising the international competitiveness of domestic goods and services compared to imports. The increase in the discount rate, and the concomitant increase in market interest rates that is also encouraged by the flight of gold, induce an equilibrating process on capital account: higher interest rates attract (mainly short-term) capital into the country from the international money markets, where the supply of capital flows in the direction of positive interest-rate differentials. Over time, the current account returns to equilibrium, or a surplus may even be formed, setting in motion the same automatic processes, albeit in the opposite direction.

Clearly the central bank's role in this mechanism is not entirely autonomous. It is expected to follow the "rules of the game," which require the bank to accelerate and strengthen automatic equilibration (Brown and Nurkse, 1944: 68) in such a way as to decrease the bank rate and institute a policy of credit expansion when its international reserves increase, and to raise the cost and limit the volume of central bank credit in the opposite case. For the purposes of the present study, we are interested in determining whether the Hungarian National Bank adhered to the "rules of the game," and if so, in what way? Did the Bank simply allow the changes in the international position of the Hungarian economy to affect domestic economic activity through the credit system, and did it strengthen or try to dilute these effects? If the "rules" were not adhered to, can one talk of a deliberate neutralization of the changes in the national economy's performance as reflected in the foreign exchange reserves, to defend domestic economic activity, prosperity and employment? Or does the explanation lie in some extraneous automatic factor not considered in the preceding discussion?

---

[16] The same course of action was also motivated by concerns over profitability, as negative deviations from the legally prescribed cover ratio, that is, the ratio of gold and gold-exchange reserves to banknote circulation and central bank sight liabilities, were penalized through progressive penalty taxes.

Ragnar Nurkse examined the correlations between the international and domestic assets of central banks in twenty-six countries between 1922 and 1938, using their end-of-year figures. His remarkable conclusion has been quoted many times since:

From year to year, central banks' international and domestic assets, during most of the period under review (1922–1938) moved far more often in the opposite than in the same direction … the negative correlation was much more frequent than the positive. (Brown and Nurkse, 1944: 68)

But Nurkse himself added a word of caution: it would be rash to conclude that the central banks were following a deliberate policy of neutralization, since it is possible that using annual intervals between observations may have masked a delayed alignment (over a period of more than a year) of domestic assets (short-term credits against bills of exchange and securities) with changes in international assets (gold and foreign exchange reserves). Second, it is not improbable that the negative correlation may have been due to inactivity rather than to a deliberate policy to neutralize foreign asset flows. For example, an increase in reserves may well have resulted from an inflow of foreign capital, gold or foreign exchange, which would raise the liquidity of both the central bank and the domestic money market (the private banks), thus enabling the latter to repay or liquidate credits due to the central bank (causing a contraction in central bank credit). Conversely, a decrease in international assets caused by the withdrawal of foreign credits would decrease the central bank's reserves as well as the liquidity of the entire money market, increasing the latter's dependency on central bank's lending (Brown and Nurkse, 1944: 69–70).

In making a reassessment of Nurkse's argument one should add that annual observation can mask short-term changes in domestic assets: within a year, several short-term changes in international assets may take place – fairly probable, given the nature of such assets and the preponderance of short-term foreign loans at the time. Indeed, the central bank may well have reacted to such changes within the same year by changing its credit policy. It also seems worth pointing out that Nurkse, in explaining automatic, non-discretionary neutralization, failed to take one aspect into account: in the case of a decrease (outflow) of gold and foreign exchange available to the money market and the central bank, an increase in central bank credits can hardly be considered automatic neutralization, since a central bank does not automatically increase its investments in accordance with the demands of the money market, but makes a conscious decision to pursue a policy of credit expansion (or contraction). Whenever the central bank increases (or maintains) its lending to the money market, in the face of dwindling foreign reserves, it is following a deliberate neutralization policy. On the other hand, the central bank would obviously enjoy no discretion in the opposite case, that is, when gold and foreign assets are flowing into the country. But while the country remained on a gold, or gold-exchange, standard, the central bank would not be able to refuse the conversion of foreign assets flowing into the country into domestic currency.

Another point worth mentioning is that Nurkse ran his survey until 1938, although the system he was examining had effectively ceased to operate as an international monetary regime much earlier, in 1931. In the context of the post-1931 circumstances, a decrease in the central bank's credit base can be attributed to an automatic process of neutralization. In these circumstances, it may well be that the fall in central bank credits in response to an increase in foreign reserves is not the product of a deliberate policy decision, but the consequence of increased liquidity in the domestic money market and commercial banks. In short, to analyze the conduct of monetary policy along these lines, one must assess the extent of central bank autonomy under different scenarios.

The data on the Hungarian National Bank presented in Table 6.3 have been compiled following Nurkse's method, albeit with the difference that they are on quarterly averages derived from the Bank's weekly public reports (Weekly Reports, 1924–1931) rather than on the Bank's balance on December 31 of each year. Figure 6.1 uses this data to plot the percentage changes in short-term credits (granted against bills of exchange and securities granted by the Bank), against the corresponding percentage changes in the Bank's gold and foreign exchange reserves. According to the Bank's statutes, gold and gold-exchange reserves could only comprise assets in foreign currencies that were on the gold standard and/or stable, that is, free of exchange-rate fluctuations (Magyar Törvénytár, 1924: 67). The last column of Table 6.3 ($\Delta C/\Delta R$) records the ratio of percentage fluctuations in domestic and international assets. A ratio is negative if the domestic credit base and the Bank's international assets have moved in opposite directions, signaling a potential breach in the "rules of the game." Conversely, a positive ratio suggests changes were in the same direction. Similarly, negative ratios correspond to points on the first and third quadrant of Figure 6.1, while positive ratios correspond to points in the second and fourth quadrants.

TABLE 6.3 *Changes in central bank international assets (reserves) and domestic credit in Hungary, 1924–1931*

		Domestic credit base (C)		International assets (R)		
		Change in Koronas	% change (ΔC)	Change in Koronas	% change (ΔR)	Ratio ΔC/ΔR
1924	Q4	522,214,500	17.3	641,166,570	21.3	0.81
1925	Q1	-194,513,700	-4.7	276,978,500	6.6	-0.71
	Q2	-278,040,500	-6.5	184,947,700	4.3	-1.51
	Q3	119,648,500	2.9	15,813,230	0.4	7.25
	Q4	58,434,800	1.4	510,736,270	11.9	0.12
1926	Q1	174,747,900	3.6	-128,652,140	-2.6	-1.38
	Q2	133,684,600	2.7	-204,258,340	-4.2	-0.64
	Q3	46,583,400	1.0	97,727,200	2.0	0.50
	Q4	368,460,000	7.4	439,126,300	8.8	0.84
1927	Q1	46,460,800	0.8	-62,865,000	-1.1	-0.73
	Q2	526,350,700	9.1	-147,467,300	-2.6	-3.50
	Q3	586,970,900	9.5	135,926,500	2.2	4.32
	Q4	339,630,000	4.9	357,400,400	5.2	0.94
1928	Q1	-160,300,700	-2.1	-19,784,700	-0.3	7.00
	Q2	12,502,000	0.2	-197,935,300	-2.7	-0.07
	Q3	501,077,700	6.9	-318,418,370	-4.4	-1.57
	Q4	954,542,300	12.9	-11,038,070	-0.1	-129.00
1929	Q1	-1,155,385,600	-13.9	-96,660,860	-1.2	11.58
	Q2	441,064,600	6.2	-563,486,730	-7.9	-0.78
	Q3	-653,202,600	-9.4	-56,255,370	-0.8	11.75
	Q4	76,347,300	1.2	25,508,100	0.4	3.00
1930	Q1	-808,553,300	-12.7	-260,855,490	-4.1	3.10
	Q2	-414,869,300	-7.8	-11,802,350	-0.2	39.00
	Q3	-328,780,400	-6.8	224,319,900	4.6	-1.48
	Q4	687,313,790	14.4	-204,252,010	-4.3	-3.35
1931	Q1	-218,000,400	-4.2	-89,180,680	-1.7	2.47
	Q2	201,248,100	4.1	-448,180,630	-9.1	-0.45
	Q3	1,608,143,300	34.3	-225,296,710	-4.8	-7.15
	Q4	408,899,600	6.7	25,729,430	-0.4	-16.75

Source: Weekly Reports of the Hungarian National Bank carrying the Bank's balances every 7th, 15th, 23rd, and 31st (30th or 28th) day of each month, as published in: *Budapesti Közlöny*, Hungary's official gazette, 1924–1931.

Of the twenty-nine ratios calculated, fifteen are negative and fourteen are positive. The results are therefore mixed, implying that, between 1924 and 1931, the Hungarian National Bank could neither be accused of steadfast neutralization, nor of using its international liquidity position as the decisive criterion guiding its credit policy.

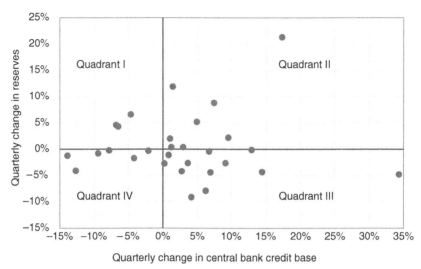

FIGURE 6.1 Playing by the rules in Hungary? Quarterly changes in central bank reserves and credits, 1924–1931
Source: Data in Table 6.3.

Nevertheless, it is worth considering these data a little longer. It is striking that in twelve out of the fifteen cases where the correlation is negative (quadrant III in Figure 6.1), the Bank's international assets have decreased, compared to only three instances where gold and gold-exchange reserves increased (quadrant I in Figure 6.1). Thus, one can safely conclude that when the Bank appears to neutralize the effects of changes in its international reserves, it does so precisely when the liquidity position has deteriorated, that is, when the "rules of the game" would have required credit restrictions and an increase in interest rates, tantamount to a "deflationary" policy that might have caused economic activity to contract! By contrast, the fourteen instances of positive correlation are more evenly distributed between quadrants II and IV, although once again, there appears to have been a slight bias toward increasing (rather than decreasing) the domestic credit base: In eight out of fourteen cases (57%), the domestic credit base was increased along with the Bank's reserves (quadrant II).

In other words, the Hungarian National Bank was far more willing to follow the rules of the game when this exerted additional stimulus and a favorable influence on domestic economic activity than when this mandated the imposition of contractionary measures. This becomes even clearer if the data are grouped differently. In eighteen out of twenty-nine cases (62%), the Bank's gold and gold-exchange reserves fell; in twelve of these cases (67%) the Bank's reaction was to neutralize the effect, while only on six of the remaining occasions did the Bank follow the "rules of the game." Conversely, the Bank's reserves rose on eleven instances; here, the Bank's most common reaction (73% of the time) was to adhere to the "rules" and favor domestic economic expansion.

Neither Nurkse, nor Bloomfield (1959), who applied Nurkse's methodology to his analysis of the pre-1914 gold standard, approached the data in this way. This alternative approach, however, offers additional insights into the policy of the Hungarian National Bank and lends itself to generalization. The more general point is that, within the framework of the gold (exchange) standard, the way in which a central bank reacts to changes in its international reserves cannot be fully explained by juxtaposing neutralization with the rules of the game. The Hungarian experience demonstrates that the assertion of domestic economic considerations is not necessarily bound up with the wish to neutralize reserve changes. When international liquidity improves, adherence to the rules of the game coincides with the interests of stimulating domestic economic activity (or, at the least, with the desire to avoid plunging the economy into a downward spiral). The Hungarian central bank seems to have had no objection to the rules of the game when its reserves were increasing and only pursued a neutralizing policy when its reserves were dwindling.

6.6 CONCLUSION

Tying the external value of a national currency to something beyond the central bank's control, whether this might be gold, gold-exchange, or any other foreign currency, such as the pound sterling or the dollar, imposes tangible limitations upon the central bank's "sovereignty," that is, its discretionary powers. The delicate balancing act performed by the Hungarian National Bank, as described in this chapter, whereby adherence to the rules of the game was combined with neutralization, was one of the few options available to a central bank seeking to attempt a renationalization of monetary management. This was particularly true under circumstances where open defiance against the gold exchange standard was both politically and economically out of the question. Of course, to ascertain exactly how much of this sneaking nationalization might have been due to deliberate policy decisions and how much was driven by automatic processes, one would have to examine the archival sources pertinent to the Bank's decision making at different levels; such a detailed investigation lies beyond the scope of this chapter. Nevertheless, there can be little doubt that, in the Hungarian case (and, quite probably, numerous others), Robert Triffin's apt observation on developments in the 1930s was already applicable in the 1920s:

The most significant development of the period ... was the growing importance of domestic factors as final determinants of monetary policies. ... Central bank power [was] no longer used to transmit automatically to the domestic economy the upward or downward pressures of surpluses or deficits in the balance of payments, regardless of national policy objectives. On the contrary, central banking policies came to be defined less and less with reference to the state of the gold reserves or the prerequisites of international balance, and more and more in terms of domestic price stability, the promotion of fuller employment, etc. (Triffin 1946: 57)

Inasmuch as this chapter goes beyond the mere demonstration, verification, and, perhaps, extension of the claims of Nurkse and Triffin, as applied to the Hungarian case, it highlights that Hungarian monetary practice, which on a tactical level was independent and oriented towards the domestic economy, did not embody a policy of pure neutralization, but an "optimum" combination of neutralization and the application of gold-standard rules, with a view to protecting domestic economic activity.

Choices made between various systemic options for conducting transactions with the rest of the world inevitably come with economic, as well as social and political costs and stress. Even at best, a choice may entail both pain and gain. In this respect, time horizons are important. In 1931 it may have felt like a relief to make the divorce from the gold-exchange standard open and official – at least in the short term. If, however, we consider that this was one of the first steps along the trajectory that eventually pushed the country, along with the whole East-Central and South-Eastern Europe, into the orbit of Nazi Germany and subsequently the Soviet Union, both in systemic terms as well as in terms of foreign political and military alliances, the longer-term costs might rightly be considered to have been unbearably high.

REFERENCES

Unpublished (Archival) Sources

Hungarian National Archives (Magyar Országos Levéltár, MOL), Budapest (Hungary).
    Section K – Records of Government Organs between 1867 and 1945, Ministry of Finance
    Section Z – Business Archives,Archives of the Hungarian National Bank

Microfilm Collection, Box nr. 13388
Bank of England Archives (BOEA), London (United Kingdom).
OV33 Overseas Department – Hungary
OV34 Overseas Department – Germany

Published Sources

Berend, Iván T. and Ránki, György (1966). *Magyarország gazdasága az első világháború után 1919–1929* [The economy of Hungary after the First World War 1919–1929]. Budapest: Akadémiai Kiadó.

Bloomfield, Arthur I. (1959). *Monetary Policy under the International Gold Standard, 1880–1914*. New York: Federal Reserve Bank of New York.

Brown, William Adams and Nurkse, Ragnar (1944). *International Currency Experience: Lessons of the Inter-War Period*. Geneva: League of Nations (Economic, Financial and Transit Department).

League of Nations (1926). *Mémorandum sur les monnaies et les banques centrales, 1913–1925*, Vol. 2. Geneva: League of Nations.

Magyar Törvénytár (1924). [Hungarian Statutory Record], Act V, 1924: 'A Magyar Nemzeti Bank létesítése és szabadalma' [The Establishment and Charter of the Hungarian National Bank].

Péteri, György (1980). 'Nemzetközi likviditás és nemzetgazdasági szempont a magyar monetáris politikában 1924–1931 között' [International liquidity and national economic aspects in Hungarian monetary policy between 1924–1931]. *Közgazdasági Szemle*, 27(10): 1203–1215.

Péteri, György (1995). *Revolutionary Twenties: Essays on International Monetary and Financial Relations after World War I*. Trondheim, Norway: University of Trondheim.

Péteri, György (2002). *Global Monetary Regime and National Central Banking: The Case of Hungary, 1921–1929*. Wayne, NJ: Center for Hungarian Studies and Publications.

Polányi, Karl (2001). *The Great Transformation: The Political and Economic Origins of Our Time*. Boston, MA: Beacon Press.

Triffin, Robert (1946). 'National Central Banking and the International Economy'. *Review of Economic Studies*, 14(2): 53–75.

Weekly Reports of the Hungarian National Bank carrying the Bank's balances every 7th, 15th, 23rd, and 31st (30th or 28th) day of each month in: *Budapesti Közlöny*, Hungary's official gazette, 1924–1931.

7

The Bank of Poland and Monetary Policy during the Interwar Period

Cecylia Leszczyńska

7.1 INTRODUCTION

The purpose of this chapter is to conduct an analysis of Polish monetary policy during the interwar period. Poland – like other developing countries – based its monetary policy on the gold exchange standard system, created by the conference in Genoa in 1922. The basic principles of this system were as follows: a fixed exchange rate under the gold standard and monetary circulation in proportion to the volume of gold and foreign currency reserves. If the market rate of the currency deviated from the parity rate, the central bank was obliged to intervene. The state governments were to move as quickly as possible away from issuance to finance budget deficits, reduce state spending, liberalize commodity and capital flows, and ensure central banks' independence from governments. Poland participated in the Genoa Conference and implemented the principles of the gold standard system in response to the great hyperinflation of 1923. In 1924 the Bank of Poland was established, and it began issuing Polish złoty within the gold exchange standard system.

The chapter answers questions about the determinants of the Bank of Poland's monetary policy in the years 1924–38. Two main facts are analysed: 1. the ability to comply with the gold exchange standard – here the internal economic situation was important, as well as capital flows and financial relations with Poland's most important partners; 2. the stance of the monetary authorities on the directions of monetary policy – here the Bank of Poland, Treasury Ministers, and the highest authorities of the State indicated the basic guidelines. The following sections analyse the economic and financial conditions and the motives that informed the monetary policy adopted by the Bank of Poland.

The structure of the sections is as follows: in Section 7.2 I present the general political and economic situation in which the Polish central bank (the Bank of Poland) functioned. In Section 7.3 I analyse the period of hyperinflation between 1919 and 1923. In Section 7.4 I present the principles of the 1924 reform, how the Bank of Poland was set up, and the creation of a new Polish currency – the złoty (zł). In Section 7.5 the 1925 economic and financial crisis and the economic, social, and political costs of financial destabilization are discussed. Section 7.6 describes the new stabilization programme launched in 1927. Section 7.7 covers the Great Depression and in Section 7.8 I examine the exchange restrictions, while Section 7.9 presents conclusions.

The case of Poland is interesting for several reasons. First, it reveals the difficulty faced by this newly formed country, lacking both a financial track record as well as significant gold and foreign exchange reserves, and little known to the international financial markets. Poland's situation was further complicated by the difficult political and economic relations with its largest trading partner, Germany. The other sizeable neighbour was the newly founded USSR, with whom economic relations were de facto frozen. In these difficult circumstances, Poland sought to gain international credibility through good financial relations with France, the United Kingdom, and the United States. It was believed that the implementation of the gold exchange standard and a stable exchange rate would increase the confidence of foreign investors and financial markets.

Polish monetary experiences are very interesting for one more reason. They show the importance of bad monetary experiences on decision-making processes. I mean the hyperinflation of 1919–23 and the second inflation of 1925 created the belief that any easing of monetary policy would trigger an inflationary spiral. A stable exchange rate became the imperative of all macroeconomic and financial policy.

7.2 POLITICAL AND ECONOMIC CONTEXT LEADING UP TO 1924

The defeat of Russia, Germany, and Austria in the First World War resulted in a disintegration of the Central European ancien régime and the establishment of several new states, including Poland. New boundaries caused frictions between neighbours. In the aftermath of the Polish–Soviet war (1919–20), over contested terrain in Belarus and Ukraine, relations between Poland and the USSR were frozen. Relations with Germany – Poland's main economic partner – were also complicated by

border issues: a part of Upper Silesia was incorporated into Poland while
the historically Polish city of Gdańsk became an autonomous district
(Free City of Danzig), under strong German influence. The 1925 Treaty
of Locarno and the German–Soviet pact of 1926 both strengthened
Germany's geopolitical position. Poland sought alliances and economic
cooperation with the United Kingdom, the United States, and France, a
country it had particularly friendly relations with. International tensions
were matched by domestic political instability. Between 1919 and 1924,
the government changed on average every six months, since no political
faction could establish a firm parliamentary majority.

Comprising regions that had previously belonged to Austria,
Germany, and Russia, the Republic of Poland was the sixth largest country in Europe in terms of area (388.6 thousand km²) and population (in
1921: 27.4 million, in 1939: 35.1 million). The most important task after
1918 was to integrate the regions into a unified state, centralize the legal
system and build new institutions.

Polish GDP per capita stood between a third and half that of rich
West European countries. What is more, post-war reconstruction started
from a very low level: as late as 1929, total GDP was more than 20
per cent below the 1913 level. Regional disparities were acute, with the
eastern and south-eastern provinces being particularly underdeveloped;
overall 60 per cent of the population earned their living from agriculture.
Industrialization was seen as the only way to raise living standards and
relieve rural overpopulation. The country was in urgent need of major
investment in industry and infrastructure, but this required substantial
capital and favourable economic conditions. Given the paucity of domestic resources, Polish reconstruction would largely have to rely on foreign
capital, so the Poles sought to woo foreign lenders and investors.

At the same time, Poles were acutely sensitive to the potential political dangers of foreign capital and dreaded falling under the economic
domination of a revived Germany. They thus sought to develop financial
ties with countries that posed fewer political risks, such as France, the
United Kingdom, and the United States, which became a special target
of Polish financial courtship, especially in the second half of the 1920s
(Pease, 1986).

The history of Polish central banking reveals discontinuities that ema-
nate from the history of the Polish state itself. The first bank of issue,
the Bank Polski (Bank of Poland), was established in 1828 and operated for almost sixty years; it was closed by the Russian authorities in
1886. Henceforth, note-issuing functions in the provinces belonging to

Austria, Germany, and Russia were performed by the central banks of those countries.

Polish central banking was rebuilt during the First World War and its immediate aftermath. In 1916, German authorities established the Polish National Loan Bank (Polska Krajowa Kasa Pożyczkowa, or PKKP). Once Poland became independent, it faced the dual challenge of achieving monetary unification and stabilization. The country inherited four distinct monetary systems: formerly German, Austrian, and Russian territories used the mark, krone, and rouble respectively; those areas that had been occupied by Germany used Polish marks (PM), issued by the PKKP, a government bank established in 1916. Late in 1918, the Polish government decided that the PKKP would remain the bank of issue for an interim period, until the establishment of the new Bank of Poland and the introduction of the złoty. The war against Bolshevik Russia (1919–20) caused further delay and monetary instability; the establishment of the Bank of Poland was postponed until 1924.

7.3 HYPERINFLATION (1919–1923)

In the first years of independence, Polish public finance came under enormous pressure: economic reconstruction, the need to establish a new public administration and set up an educational system, not to mention fund the new state's armed forces required substantial public outlays. Ordinary taxes could not cover these expenses and the budget deficit rose from PM 58.5 billion in 1920 to PM 113.7 thousand billion in 1923. Expenditures were financed with loans from PKKP, which put its printing press to work (Table 7.1).[1]

A budget deficit recorded just after a war can be justified on several grounds: wartime destruction and expenses incurred in war, together with the disruption in tax collection, and so on. Once the situation stabilizes, however, the impact of these causes wanes and the deficit is expected to diminish. In Poland, things followed a different course: year after year, the nominal deficit kept increasing. Responsibility rested primarily with the *Sejm* (parliament), which refused to agree to radical measures such as raising taxes or cutting budget spending. Successive governments

---

[1] Legally, the PKKP extended interest free-loans to the Treasury, pursuant to a decision of the Council of Ministers, approved by the Chief of State (Naczelnik Państwa), Józef Piłsudski, and – as of January 1919 – by the Sejm. After 1921, PKKP was allowed to collect interest on a portion of the loans extended. The Sejm set the upper lending limit.

TABLE 7.1 *Circulation and State Treasury debt with the Polish National Loan Bank (PKKP) (in millions of PM, end of year balances), 1918–1924*

Years	Notes in circulation	State Treasury debt
1918	1,024.3	119.9
1919	5,316.3	6,825.0
1920	49,361.5	59,625.0
1921	229,537.6	221,000.0
1922	793,437.5	675,600.0
1923	125,371,955.4	111,332,000.0
1924 III	596,244,205.6	291,700,000.0

Source: Zdziechowski (1925).

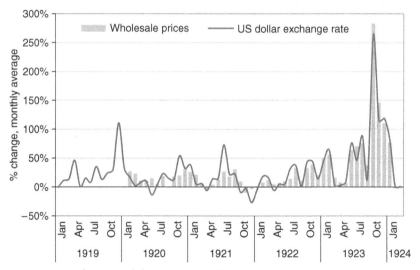

FIGURE 7.1 Inflation and depreciation in Poland, 1919–1924
Source: Taylor (1926).

collapsed, Treasury ministers came and went, and proposals for fiscal stabilization failed to gain broad political support.

Printing quantities of paper currency triggered high inflation (Figure 7.1). In the autumn of 1923, panic caused by German monetary developments pushed Poland into hyperinflation. The Polish mark depreciated and the price of one US dollar rose from PM 9 in 1918 to PM 110 in 1919, PM 590 in 1920, PM 17.8 thousand in 1922 and PM 6.4 million in 1923.

Economists and historians have discussed Polish hyperinflation at length (von Thadden, 1994). Its causes were numerous. Initially, it was the wartime monetary overhang which (after 1918) was converted into Polish marks.[2] Afterwards, circulation kept growing due to the PKKP's loans to the government. What is more, since its statutes permitted business loans, the PKKP had the remit to function as a commercial bank, accepting deposits, issuing loans, and carrying out transfer and clearing operations. After 1921, business loans increased to become the second largest cause of an increase in circulation (Leszczyńska, 2011). By 1923, the inflationary spiral had become entrenched, causing widespread panic on the money market.

Foreigners were critical of Polish financial policy. As one historian writes:

American observers placed the blame for Poland's hyperinflation on an unwillingness to submit to fiscal self-discipline; her public finance, in the verdict of the Wall Street Journal, could 'only be called the finest bid for bankruptcy ever made by any modern State in Europe with the sole exception of Russia'. Warsaw objected, with some justice, that the inflation was as much the result of six years of unbroken warfare as of faulty management, but the steady degeneration of politics and finances discouraged foreign capital. (Pease, 1986: 14)

American investors shunned Poland, believing it to be too risky. When a British mission led by Hilton Young visited Warsaw on 7 October 1923, 'Young repeatedly advised Kucharski (Minister of Treasury) to postpone the establishment of a central bank and the issue of a new currency until after the balancing of the budget' (Allen, 2020: 13).

In the autumn of 1923, a sudden wage drop followed by worker strikes led the government to declare a state of emergency. In November, street fights broke out, costing the lives of more than thirty people. The government could no longer procrastinate. Poland was in urgent need of internal financial reorganization to balance the budget and end inflation.

7.4 THE 1924 STABILIZATION AND THE ESTABLISHMENT OF THE BANK OF POLAND

In December 1923, the president of the state, Stanisław Wojciechowski, summoned all recent Treasury ministers to discuss the next course of action. The president's initiative was important, as earlier reforms had been undermined by inter-party rivalry while current circumstances

---

[2] This has been estimated to approximately PM 7 billion; the unification of circulation took place between 1918 and 1921.

mandated urgent action. The president appointed his friend, Władysław Grabski, to the post of prime minister and minister of the Treasury. Grabski was entrusted with putting the state's finances in order, introducing a new currency and setting up the new central bank. Parliament granted his government special powers to implement reforms over a short period of time.[3] An erstwhile proponent of gradualism, Grabski now had to implement reforms at speed. By June 1924, a package of new legislation had been approved.

The first measures concerned the budget and foreign exchange. In January 1924, the Polish mark was stabilized at a rate of PM 9.1 million to the US dollar. Use of the printing press to finance the budget ceased, and fiscal policy was tightened: taxes were indexed to inflation and a property tax was introduced, while military and civilian spending was curtailed. At the same time, however, the government resisted recommendations by the Hilton Young mission to reassure foreign lenders by ceding a measure of control over its public finances to foreign financial advisers.[4]

The second pillar of the Grabski stabilization was monetary reform and the establishment of the Bank of Poland. In April 1924, the złoty replaced the Polish mark at a rate of 1.8 million PM/zł. The gold content of the new currency was set on a par with the Latin Union franc (0.29 gr), so that 1 franc = 1 złoty and 1 US dollar = 5.18 złoty. The rationale for reaching this decision remains unclear. Historians attribute it to psychological factors: since the franc was a stable currency the intention may have been to convince Poles that the złoty would also be reliable. Political ties with France may also have played a role; some may even have expected the Latin Monetary Union to survive in some form.

The new monetary system comprised three types of money subject: paper notes issued by the Bank of Poland; gold, silver, nickel and bronze

---

[3] Grabski belonged to no political party; he demanded (and received) from parliament the freedom to enact special decrees on fiscal and budgetary matters for a period of six months. Armed with more authority than any prime minister, Grabski formed a non-partisan government of centre-right complexion.

[4] When, Young returned to Warsaw on 25 January 1924 and met Grabski, the latter informed him 'that he did not intend to appoint a financial mission or a financial adviser at the present time; he might however ask for a manager for the central bank, and an adviser on government accounts or funding'. The final mission report, dated 10 February 1924, recommended balancing the budget and appointing foreign controllers; this was deemed necessary to secure a new foreign loan. As for the central bank, the Young mission recommended establishing a 100 per cent privately owned institution with 'as large a fund as possible of currencies with stable exchange rates ..., to be used as reserve for the protection of Polish currency from undue fluctuation' (quoted in Allen, 2020: 16).

TABLE 7.2 *Monetary units in Poland's monetary system*

Accepted with no restrictions	Accepted up to specific amounts
• *Notes of the Bank of Poland* (10, 20, 50, 100, and 500 zł) • *Gold coins* (20 and 50 zł, though none were minted eventually)	• *Silver coins* (1, 2, and 5 zł) [issued up to 8 zł per capita; accepted up to 100 zł per transaction] • *Nickel and bronze coins* (1, 10, 20, and 50 grosz; 1 zł = 100 grosz) [issued up to 4 zł per capita; accepted up to 10 zł per transaction] • *Treasury notes* (for the interim period) (1, 2, and 5 złotys) [issued up to 150 million zł; accepted up to 10 zł per transaction, raised to 1,000 zł after 1926]

Source: Leszczyńska (2013).

coins produced by the mint for the Ministry of the Treasury; and paper notes issued by the Ministry of the Treasury (Table 7.2). Banknote circulation was limited by the Bank's gold and foreign currency reserves; gold coin minting was determined by the Treasury's gold reserves (eventually, no gold coins were minted), and statutory limits applied to Treasury notes and all other coins.

The Bank of Poland opened its doors on 28 April 1924. Its operations were set forth in its articles of association, which set out the main principles of monetary and credit policy. The Bank was granted the exclusive note issuing privilege until 31 December 1944 (in 1939, this was extended until 1954) and tasked with keeping the złoty stable. Stability was ensured through the gold exchange standard. The Bank had to maintain convertibility of its own notes at a fixed exchange rate. At least 30 per cent of circulating banknotes had to be covered by gold or (convertible) foreign exchange; this cover ratio could only be changed by an act of parliament (Leszczyńska, 2011). The Bank could provide interest-free credits to the government, but only up to a maximum of 50 million zł.

The Bank of Poland also carried out credit operations. Besides granting discount and Lombard loans to other banks, it also lent directly to industrial and trading companies at low interest rates. As one might expect, private banks considered such competition harmful to their interests (Morawski, 1996). The Bank of Poland, however, wanted to exert downward pressure on commercial lending rates, which were capped at 24 per cent by a law against usury (Leszczyńska and Lisiecka, 2006). Throughout the entire 1924–38 period, the Bank thus offered interest

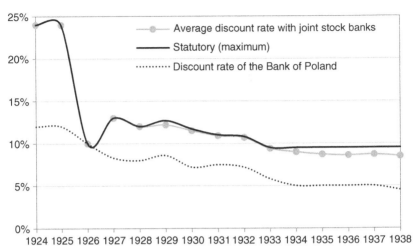

FIGURE 7.2 Money market interest rates in Poland, 1924–1938
Source: GUS (1939).

rates below the market equilibrium, rationing loans to those banks and businesses that had the best credit standing (see Figure 7.2).

The Bank of Poland availed itself of traditional credit tools: lending quotas, reviews of bills of exchange and promissory notes, as well as the discount rate.[5] The discount rate, however, was not key to the Bank's policy. The interbank money market was underdeveloped and, like many central banks on the Continent, the Bank of Poland was not allowed to conduct open market operations to avoid monetizing public debt (Karpiński, 1958: 231). Thus, interest rates were influenced by the legal caps established to combat usury, which were usually set at twice the level of the Bank's discount rate (Leszczyńska, 2013).

The Bank of Poland was established as a joint stock company and its shares were listed on the Warsaw stock exchange. Share capital was 100 million złoty, divided in one million shares of 100 złoty each. At first, the Treasury only held about 1 per cent of capital, with banks, enterprises, organizations, and natural persons being the main shareholders. Shareholders comprised the Bank's Council, which elected the director general, senior management, and Discount Committee members. The

---

[5] Quotas specified the maximum loan for each industrial/commercial enterprise or banking institution; review involved quality assessment of bills and notes; the discount rate was determined in line with the Bank's lending capability, the rates abroad, and the requirements of government's economic policy.

Council also set the Bank's discount and Lombard rates, established lending rules, and provided a forum to discuss monetary and credit policy. The Bank's president was proposed by the prime minister and appointed by the president of Poland for a term of five years. He supervised the Bank's operations and had the right to suspend the Council's resolutions, if he believed they were contrary to state interests or Bank statues. The Treasury also approved senior management and appointed a commissioner to 'liaise' with the Bank.[6]

In its first two years of operation, the Bank of Poland enjoyed considerable freedom from political interference. Loans to the state were capped, the Bank had its own budget and paid a special tax based on note circulation. However, its independence, was eroded after Józef Piłsudski's coup d'état in 1926. The status and independence of Bank Polski was strengthened by the Stabilization Plan that was signed by Poland in October 1927. As a result, the Bank remained independent until 1930 (Landau, 1992; see Sections 7.6 and 7.7).

Monetary policy in the first two years was mainly aimed at stabilizing the złoty by keeping the exchange rate fixed. In April 1924, reserves amounted to 285.9 million złoty (or $55.2 million), of which 71.7 million złoty were held in gold, and the rest in foreign exchange. With circulation at 245 million złoty, the cover ratio was more than 70 per cent, which was close to the European average at the time (Figure 7.3). However, domestic money supply was quite limited and every increase in circulation led to a lower cover ratio.

The first phase of the reform was positive: after the exchange rate was fixed, prices remained stable. However, in the second half of 1924, prices began to rise once again. By December, inflation was about 6 per cent, spreading doubts about the success of the reform.

One of Grabski's main objectives had been to stabilize the economy without help from outside; 'by our own efforts' had been his slogan. His reforms were implemented without foreign loans or League of Nations assistance.[7] He believed that if the young Polish state wanted to be

---

[6] Commissioners included Leon Barański and Adam Koc. Barański became deputy director-general in 1931 and director-general in 1934 (formally 1935); Barański played an important role in creating the monetary policy of the Bank of Poland. Adam Koc was the president of the Bank for several months in 1936 (Leszczyńska, 2011).

[7] Grabski approached the League in February 1925, but was informed that any loan would require the consent of the Bank of England and the establishment of an independent controller at the Polish Ministry of Finance (Allen, 2020: 21).

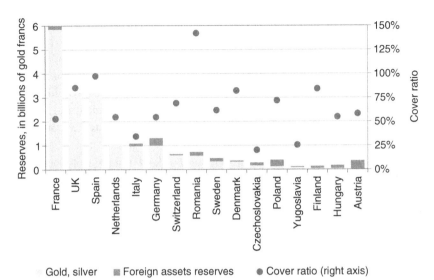

FIGURE 7.3 Reserves and cover ratio of select European central banks, end of 1924
Source: League of Nations (1927).

independent, it could not condone foreign interference.[8] Grabski pointed to the experiences of Austria and Hungary, who had been forced to accept foreign supervision in exchange for stabilization loans. Financial autonomy was also important to the National Party and the Left, which harboured misgivings about foreign capital. And yet, perhaps ironically, Grabski soon faced a crisis that forced him to seek foreign funds to defend his stabilization.

7.5 ECONOMIC AND CURRENCY CRISIS (1925)

The cracks in the façade of the 1924 stabilization became deeper in the first half of 1925. With the economy in recession, the government came under increased fire. Critics argued that fiscal policy was too restrictive and trade policy too liberal (Leszczyńska, 2013). With price competitiveness in

---

[8] As a matter of fact, Poland did receive external loans, but these were quite small. In September 1924, the Bank Gospodarstwa Krajowego (National Economic Bank) agreed to issue bonds of $9.7 million; the loan was arranged by Ulen & Co. of New York to finance public works projects and was quite expensive: 8 per cent interest and 15 per cent commission for Ulen & Co. In January 1924, Poland also agreed to obtain a military loan from France. This could reach a maximum of 400 million French francs, but Poland renounced a quarter of those in April 1925, after the Dillon loan had been agreed (Allen, 2020).

decline, trade deficits started to accumulate, threatening the stability of the exchange rate.[9] Grabski believed difficulties were inevitable, but temporary; many countries, including Britain, had experienced similar recessions during their post-war stabilization (Grabski, 1924, 1925b). The Bank of Poland agreed. Polish policy makers redoubled efforts to secure new foreign loans to finance the country's current account deficits: in February 1925, after a long and tortuous negotiation, Poland raised 35 million dollars in New York through investment bank Dillon, Read and Co.[10]

The situation deteriorated in June 1925, when Germany announced its intention to impose customs duties on Polish products. A trade war broke out, which acted as a 'signal for the general recall of large German short-term credits, and to some extent of other credits also. The second issue of Dillon's loan fell through, owing mainly to the tariff war' (Zweig, 1944). Western newspapers reported that Poland was headed for 'financial catastrophe' (Kowal, 1995: 17–21) and foreign banks were put off by uncertainty (Landau 1961: 158–159). Germany was trying to undermine the stabilization and use Poland's financial difficulties to revise bilateral territorial arrangements.

In late July, the złoty started declining – first in foreign, and then in domestic markets as well (Figure 7.4). The Bank of Poland intervened, but relief was only temporary. The Bank used its own reserves as well as credits from the Federal Reserve Bank of New York (up to $10 million), Bank Suisse (CHF 20 million), the British Overseas Bank (£250,000) and the Bank Franco-Polonaise ($600,000) (Landau, 1970: 522). Pressed for additional credits, Grabski turned once more to the League of Nations. The League's terms, however, were still deemed unacceptable: they included the placement of a British comptroller at the Polish Ministry of Finance, if not the Bank of Poland as well; what is more, German participation in the loan scheme seemed contingent on territorial concessions that Polish independence would not accept.[11]

---

[9] In a pattern typical of Central and Eastern Europe at the time (Łazor, 2018), Poland's economy remained relatively closed compared to Western Europe (its foreign trade per capita was low and protectionism was high).

[10] Arranged by Dillon, Read and Co., the loan was for a total of $50 million; $35 million would be available immediately, with Dillon's retaining the option to offer the remaining bonds on 1 August. Moreover, Dillon's extracted (and subsequently enforced) a promise from Poland to purchase up to $7.5 million of any unsold bonds. Interestingly enough, the governor of the Bank of England, Montagu Norman, discouraged lending to the Polish government (Allen, 2020).

[11] Montagu Norman's diary describes that Polish officials continued trying to raise money, including from the Bank of England and the Federal Reserve; Poland wanted to avoid

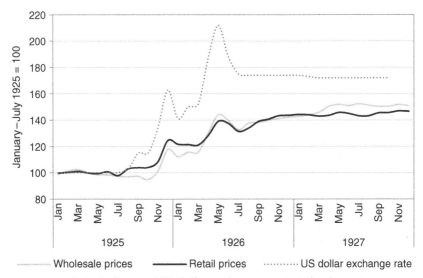

FIGURE 7.4 Price indices and US dollar exchange rate in Poland, 1925–1927
Source: Ministerstwo Skarbu (1928).

Without additional credits, the Bank informed the government that its reserves were running low and foreign exchange interventions would soon have to stop. Grabski opposed abandoning the stabilization. However, on August 25 the government and the Bank agreed to suspend interventions temporarily. Panic gripped the market as people fled the złoty to purchase dollars; as people withdrew their deposits, several small banks went bust (Landau, 2001: 89).[12]

By 10 November, the Bank had tightened restrictions on foreign transactions and stabilized the dollar at 5.98 złoty, thus hoping to prevent the exchange rate from crossing the psychological barrier at 6 złoty (Grabski, 1925a: 2–3). Foreign exchange interventions continued to drain the Bank's reserves, which dropped from zł91.5 million (zł72.8 million net)

the League of Nations for fear that it carried the stigma of destitution and receivership, and that a loan from the League might be used as a means of advancing Germany's territorial claims. Germany would be willing to lend Poland $250 million but only on condition that Poland ceded the Corridor to Germany. Norman wrote to Benjamin Strong: 'I see no prospect of loan or credit operations in this Market except possibly under effective foreign control' (Allen, 2020: 27–30, 33).

[12] By the end of 1925, the total assets of all private banks had decreased by 32 per cent compared with 30 June; the total assets of state banks increased by 100 per cent. The government provided credit of zł25 million to the 'most important' banks affected by the crisis, mainly for the repayment of international short-term deposits.

TABLE 7.3 *Bank of Poland notes and reserves (millions of złoty, at the end of each month), 1924–1925*

		Note circulation	Reserves in gold	Reserves in foreign exchange	Cover ratio (%)
1924	V	245.0	71.7	214.2	105.4
	XII	550.9	103.4	269.0	65.1
1925	I	553.2	104.2	242.1	60.6
	VII	461.6	121.7	91.5	43.2
	X	382.4	132.3	61.0	40.7
	XII	381.4	133.6	69.7	38.0

Source: Ministerstwo Skarbu (1928).

in July to zł61 million (zł10–15 million net) in November.[13] The Bank of Poland decided that depreciation was inevitable. Grabski was informed on 12 November 1925. Convinced that the success of his reforms rested on the stability of the złoty – 'my whole authority rested on the złoty', he would write later (Grabski, 2003: 203) – the prime minister sought to avert a depreciation; having failed, on 13 November 1925 he submitted his resignation. Within a few weeks the dollar price rose to 9 zł/$. After a temporary respite in early 1926, the złoty continued to decline, falling to 11 zł/$ during the May coup d'état, before stabilizing around 9 zł/$ again.

Grabski's reforms sparked much controversy at the time. Today, Polish historians appreciate his efforts to lead the Polish economy out of hyperinflation. Nevertheless, the 1925 crisis also revealed that Poland had not been ready to join the gold exchange standard in 1924. Full convertibility and foreign trade liberalization had been premature. This was especially true given the level and composition of the country's reserves (Table 7.3): the Bank of Poland was unwilling to sell gold, which made up a considerable portion of its reserves; once gold was excluded, however, reserves only covered a fraction of circulation and could finance less than a month's worth of imports.[14] Thus, the official

---

[13] Foreign currency reserves amounted to zł53 million while liquid reserves were only zł8 million (zł45 million were to be repaid to foreign banks); by comparison, in December 1924, reserves had stood at zł269.0 million (zł254.1 million net).

[14] In the first half of 1925, average monthly reserves amounted to zł302 million (including foreign currency reserves of zł187 million), in August–December 1925, on the average zł198 million (foreign currency reserves zł65 million). Imports in 1925 amounted to zł1,603 million.

FIGURE 7.5   Banknote and Treasury money circulation in Poland, 1924–1926
Source: Lipiński (1928).

cover ratio, which remained above the statutory limit of 30 per cent throughout the crisis, did not offer genuine protection against a currency crisis. Moreover, Treasury notes circulating on top of Bank of Poland banknotes, which were not covered by gold or foreign exchange and thus constituted a de facto violation of the 'rules of the game', probably contributed to the inflationary expectations that helped unravel the stabilization (Figure 7.5).

The 1925 crisis was the first time Poland experienced a conflict between the external objective of maintaining a fixed exchange rate and the needs of the domestic economy. The experience would be repeated during the Great Depression of 1929–33. In the meantime, the country would attempt its second stabilization.

7.6 A NEW STABILIZATION PLAN (1927–1930) AND THE SECOND MONETARY REFORM

In 1926, the Polish economy started to recover. A weaker złoty and a year-long strike by British miners had bolstered the price of coal, as well as other exports. No sooner had the economic situation begun to improve than the Polish government resumed its efforts to secure a sizeable foreign loan. The crisis of 1925 had shown that credible stabilization required adequate foreign exchange reserves and these would only be replenished with foreign capital.

Loan negotiations were tortuous. They involved financiers and central bankers from the United States, Britain, France, and Germany, as well as League of Nations' representatives – not all with the same interests or objectives. The extent of foreign control over Poland's finances, the advantages and disadvantages of issuing the loan under the auspices of the League, and the question of whether an adjustment to the Polish–German border should be a precondition for any assistance were all hotly debated, not least between Montagu Norman, governor of the Bank of England and Benjamin Strong, governor of the Federal Reserve. The president of the Reichsbank, Hjalmar Schacht, also became involved, hoping to exploit the loan negotiations to exact territorial concessions from Poland. The complicated politics of a League Loan discouraged Poland from accepting the League oversight advised by Norman; early in 1926, around the time Norman began talking to German diplomats about Poland, Strong decided to break with the Bank of England and support a loan to Poland outside the auspices of the League (Allen, 2020: 193–194).

In the meantime, the political situation in Poland was unravelling. Grabski's resignation in November 1925 had led to another cycle of short-lived governments; the cycle was broken in May 1926, when Marshal Józef Piłsudski seized power in a successful coup d'état, which put the country on a path of greater political stability, albeit at the cost of increasing authoritarianism. Piłsudski became the effective head of state and his movement was called Sanation (taken from the word Sanacja, or 'healing').

Loan negotiations were not derailed by the coup. Americans were well-disposed toward Piłsudski, who reassured the US government of his intention to stabilize the złoty. The Sanacja regime was chiefly concerned with retaining Poland's territorial integrity and fending off German aggression; to this end, monetary stabilization was meant to strengthen the economy and keep foreign investment flowing into the country (Wolf, 2007). On 28 May 1926, the new cabinet reaffirmed a plan to invite the American 'money doctor', Edwin Kemmerer, along with representatives of the Bankers Trust Company, to advise on stabilization (Pease, 1986: 76–79). This would be Kemmerer's second mission to Poland, the first having been in 1925, when Dillon, Read and Co. had employed him as an advisor. Kemmerer's mission began in early July and lasted eleven weeks. Tasked with assessing the country's financial situation and making recommendations for monetary reform, Kemmerer's report provided the basis for the new stabilization plan, including the decision to devalue the currency to approximately 9 zł/$.[15]

By early 1927, Poland had made considerable progress towards securing a loan in New York and had already brought the New York Fed and the Bank of France to its side. The Fed was trying to secure the support of other European central banks, notably the Bank of England and the Reichsbank. Negotiations dragged on till May 1927; their successful conclusion was largely due to Strong and his representative, George Harrison.

The new stabilization plan was published on 13 October 1927. It was a three-year plan (1927–30), during which Poland would strive to establish the economic and institutional conditions necessary for a permanent stabilization. The government promised to open up foreign trade, liberalize capital flows, and balance its budget. The Bank of Poland, which had already been intervening to maintain the exchange rate around 9 zł/$, officially devalued the currency to 0.16879 gr of gold, thus pegging bilateral exchange rates at to 8.91 zł/$ (up from 5.18 in 1924), 1.72 złoty to the Swiss franc, and 43.38 złoty to the pound. The new parities would be maintained until the Second World War.

The stabilization plan also entailed changes in the Bank's statutes, with a view to restoring the operation of the gold exchange standard. Treasury notes were withdrawn from circulation, which would henceforth be made up of banknotes and coins, but only gold coins and banknotes could be used in transactions without any limits. The statutory cover ratio, that is, the minimum percentage of Bank of Poland notes and other demand liabilities that had to be covered by gold and foreign exchange reserves (currencies convertible into gold such as the British pound, the US dollar, the Swiss franc)[16] was set to 40 per cent; should the cover fall below that limit, the Bank would have to raise the discount rate and pay a special tax to the Treasury. At least three-quarters of the Bank's reserves had to consist of gold coins and bars, two-thirds of which were to be kept

---

[15] Kemmerer's report proposed de facto and, subsequently, de jure stabilization at 9 zł/$; it also recommended a gradual withdrawal of currency issued by the Treasury, which was held responsible for the failure of the 1924 stabilization (Kemmerer, 1926).

[16] It should be added that the convertibility of the Polish złoty to foreign currencies was full (the Polish people had the right to exchange the złoty for any foreign currency at the official rate; this rule did not apply to gold, despite the Polish authorities' declaration that they did not introduce gold coins into circulation).

domestically. Interest free advances by the Bank to the Treasury were capped at 100 million złoty.

The stabilization plan was followed by 71.73 million dollar loan (62 million dollars and 2 million pounds) loan carrying a 7 per cent coupon rate, collateralized by Polish customs revenues. The subscription was carried out from 18 October 1927 in New York, London, Paris, Amsterdam, Basel, Stockholm, and Warsaw; the loan was syndicated by a consortium of more than forty banks, with US banks (Bankers Trust Company, Chase Securities Corporation, and Blair & Co.) playing first fiddle. About three-quarters of the loan was earmarked for the stabilization of the złoty, the balance to be used for investment. The Bank of Poland increased its share capital to 150 million złoty and replenished its reserves: in December 1927, reserves totalled 1,415 million złoty (895 million in foreign exchange); the cover ratio thus rose to 73%, far above the new 40% statutory limit.[17]

Polish authorities felt the conditions imposed by the lenders were tough, but the loan was badly needed to stabilize the currency and thus attract further foreign investment (Landau, 1963). Compliance with the terms of the loan and the new stabilization plan was to be monitored by a financial adviser chosen by the country's creditors. Former Assistant Secretary to the US Treasury and banker Charles Dewey was selected for the job and became a member of the Council at the Bank of Poland between 1927 and 1930.

Dewey's reception in Warsaw was frosty. Piłsudski ignored him and most people resented his supervision, which they felt was an affront to the country's sovereignty. Nevertheless, Dewey soon developed an affection for Poland and persuaded himself of the merit and reliability of Piłsudski's government. His periodic reports and public appearances became 'paeans to the virtues of Poland's government' (Pease, 1987: 88) and the attractions of doing business with Poland.[18] Still, his efforts to secure additional foreign credit were unsuccessful and his departure from

---

[17] The Bank of Poland received a special stabilization loan, which was organized by the European central banks and the Fed. The negotiations were held over several months. The agreement was signed on 17 June 1927, fourteen central banks participated in the loan $20 million, the Federal Reserve Bank NY played a major role. Allen (2020) describes the difficult negotiations in detail. It should be added that in 1928 the loan was extended, although Bank of Poland did not use it (Leszczyńska, 2013).

[18] At the same time, Dewey developed a pronounced antipathy towards Germany, which refused to relinquish its territorial claims and continued to wage a trade war against Poland.

Warsaw, in November 1930, was followed by a sigh of relief. As Pease comments:

The state department was glad to be rid of a figure considered a meddlesome dilettante, and although the Poles paid him fulsome public compliments, their private opinions were more reserved. (…) Many Poles blamed him personally for the failure of the stabilization plan to lead to more and greater loans and even his Polish defenders could rouse themselves to no more than faint praise. As one of them put it, though Dewey had not managed to do Poland much good, at least he had done no real harm. (Pease, 1987: 91–92)

Even his supporters acknowledged he had not managed 'to do Poland much good' (Pease, 1987: 92).

The second stabilization plan reaffirmed the Bank of Poland's formal independence from government interference; the presence of a creditor representative (Dewey) on the Bank's council discouraged outright meddling in the Bank's business. Over time, the Bank's independence became a point of friction with the government. In June 1929, during a meeting with the Polish President Ignacy Mościcki and Treasury minister Ignacy Matuszewski, Marshall Piłsudski, who held the post of minister of military affairs but was the de facto leader of the regime, stated: 'We have to do our best to see to the appointments of the Bank of Poland, so that we would be sure that the people holding the head positions conduct a policy in the interest of the government, and not in the interest of the Bank itself' (Landau, 2001: 91). Piłsudski was clearly thinking about the president of the Bank, Stanisław Karpiński, whose five-year term was soon coming to an end. The American financial advisor Dewey was the only remaining obstacle; as Piłsudski explained in October 1929, once Dewey's three-year term is over 'we should stage a war to subjugate the Bank of Poland to the government' (Landau, 2001: 92). The highest authorities were highly critical of Bank of Poland's decision to raise interest rates in April 1929 without consulting the government.

Piłsudski's plan was carried out. Władysław Wróblewski was appointed president and the Bank of Poland became totally dependent on the Treasury. While formally still a private joint stock company with a minority government stake, the Bank became a part of the state sector. As Zygmunt Karpiński, former director to the Bank, would write in his memoirs: 'The new President of the Bank never showing any independent thinking in connection with the bank matters, implemented the wishes of the government and Ministry of Treasury' (cited in Landau, 2001: 91–92). Government interference would become even more pronounced after the introduction of exchange controls, in 1936 (see Section 7.8); but this was still a few years in the future.

In the meantime, after the 1927 stabilization, economic growth picked up. The złoty exchange rate was stabilised, the budget was balanced and convertibility was restored. Having improved Poland's international credit standing, the government was looking forward to the large inflows of foreign capital the Polish economy needed for its development. Still, despite being offered additional tax and administrative incentives, foreign investors were not particularly keen on directing their capital into Poland. Landau (2001: 50) attributes this to two factors: first, geopolitical concerns about the future of Poland, as a new state flanked by Germany and the Soviet Union; second, a preference, on behalf of foreign investors, to acquire existing Polish companies, rather than establish new ones or open up new markets and opportunities. US entrepreneurs also seem to have been discouraged by concerns over Poland's longevity, with one sympathetic US diplomat admitting that he would not advise anyone to invest in Polish securities unless he 'was so terrifically rich that [he] did not mind what happened to the money'(quoted in Pease, 1987: 93). Intended to be the first of a series of American capital investments into Poland, the 1927 stabilization loan also turned out to be the last. Foreign capital inflows may have helped stabilize Poland's currency and balance of payments, but they were not sufficient to bring about substantial economic development; after all, the Great Depression was just around the corner.

7.7 THE BANK OF POLAND'S MONETARY POLICY DURING THE GREAT DEPRESSION

The Great Depression hit Poland in 1930. The scale of economic collapse, comparable only to Germany and the United States, was surprisingly large for a semi-industrial country. GDP per capita fell by 25 per cent and industrial output by 40 per cent, as Poland's industry was strongly affected by the slump (see Figures 7.6 and 7.7).

Investment collapsed and unemployment rose steeply, especially in urban areas, where around 40 per cent of industrial workers were out of a job. Rural regions provided a buffer, as many of the unemployed relocated to the countryside. Prices dropped by 50 per cent, agricultural prices even more. Many farmers were pushed off the market and returned to self-sufficiency. Faced with mounting debt burdens and shrinking revenue, several large enterprises filed for bankruptcy. Foreign

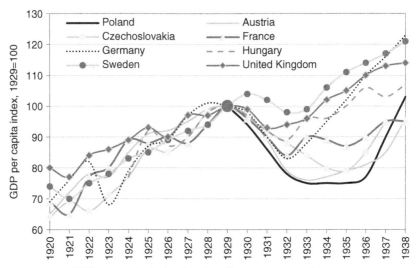

FIGURE 7.6 GDP per capita index in select European countries, 1920–1938
Note: Poland data for 1929–1938, Czechoslovakia for 1920–1937, and Hungary for 1924–1938.
Source: Maddison (2006).

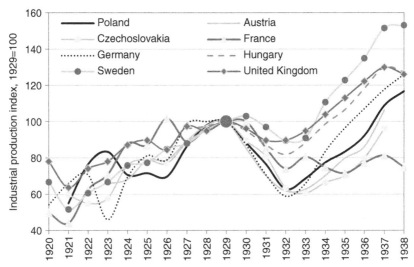

FIGURE 7.7 Industrial production index in select European countries, 1920–1938
Source: Mitchell (2007); Polish data based on Polish statistics, Jezierski and Leszczyńska (2003).

trade shrank by 70 per cent (relative to 1929), with imports falling faster than exports. Imports were curtailed through quotas and tariffs, while exports were encouraged with dumping and customs duty refunds (Landau, 1984).

Poland's financial distress was exacerbated by faulty economic policy, which combined fiscal and monetary retrenchment. The government prioritised the stability of the złoty and pursued deflationary policies in an effort to remain on the gold standard. Piłsudski felt that a strong złoty projected the image of a strong Poland, while monetary stability and external convertibility were considered necessary to maintain the trust of foreign investors, even in the face of a mass exodus of foreign capital from the country.[19] The Bank of Poland considered that devaluation of the złoty was needed, or control of capital flows. The government was against it. The government's views remained prevalent and monetary authorities followed suit. As the crisis deepened, this liberal orthodoxy became increasingly untenable, but it was not until after Piłsudski's death, in 1935, that policy shifted.

During the early years of the Great Depression, Polish fiscal policy was contractionary. Spending cuts were combined with modest tax hikes in an effort to balance the budget. Deficits were traditionally covered by foreign loans, but these became increasingly difficult to secure after 1929, and entirely impossible between 1932 and 1935 (Landau, 1984).[20] With external finance running dry, the Treasury turned to the domestic market, raising a series of internal loans, which funded the deficit but squeezed liquidity from the market. By 1 April 1936, the state's domestic liabilities stood at 1,705 million złoty, up from 477 million on 1 January 1930 (GUS, 1939).

Just as foreign lending was becoming scarce, capital flight was exerting pressures on the balance of payments and the banking system. The financial crises that swept through Central Europe in the summer of 1931 and the subsequent sterling devaluation only accelerated financial outflows. Still, the government opposed both devaluation and the imposition of capital controls, fearing that these would trigger inflation (similar to

---

[19] Wolf (2007) argues that this policy may have been economically costly, but it also altered the structure of foreign investments, favouring French investment just as the role of German capital went into decline.

[20] Amongst the last foreign loans obtained were a $32.4 million match-monopoly loan negotiated with Swedish financier Ivar Kreuger in 1930, and a 400 million French franc (about 129 million złoty) loan raised by the Franco-Polish Railway Society in 1931, both at 6.5 per cent interest.

that of 1925) and undermine financial relations with the West.[21] Thus, at a time when Germany and other neighbouring countries were introducing capital controls, Poland maintained full convertibility and suffered heavy withdrawals that strained its banking system.

Capital flight drained the Bank of Poland's foreign exchange reserves and lowered its cover ratio close to its statutory limit (Table 7.4).[22] This was the basis for the Bank's contractionary monetary policy, which began in 1930 and became even stricter in response to the Austrian and German crises of the following year. From 1932 onwards, the Bank of Poland stabilized the narrow money supply. But as the commercial banking system continued to struggle, bank money continued to fall; this explains why the M1 ended up falling more than M0 (Figure 7.8). Wishing to avert a complete financial meltdown, the government came to the aid of private commercial banks, which had lost more than half their deposits until 1935. The government used a special Credit Institutions Relief Fund, which had been established after the 1925 crisis. A special bank relief law of 1932 had permitted the government to acquire parts of the stock of banks to which it had given loans to financial support. Between 1931 and 1935, 158 million złoty were allotted to bolster Polish banks while in two of the largest private banks (Bank Handlowy in Warsaw and Bank Związku Spółek Zarobkowych), the majority shares was held by the Ministry of Treasury (Landau, 2001). The Bank of Poland increased loans to banks, but they were not large. The authorities of the Bank were afraid of loosening the issuing policy. They focused on keeping the złoty issue coverage in line with the statute.

In February 1933, Polish authorities sought to mitigate the deflationary pressures created by their adherence to the gold standard by changing the Bank's statutes. Henceforth, złoty banknotes and the Bank's sight liabilities would not be backed by a minimum of 40 per cent gold or foreign exchange, but only 30 per cent of pure gold; what is more, 100 million złoty of sight liabilities would require no gold cover. The combined effect

---

[21] The Bank of England envoy, L. E. Hubbard, visited Poland late in 1932 and recorded that Poland was determined to 'keep the złoty on gold to the last gasp', because 'confidence in the currency is rather a sensitive plant and it takes very little to cause a flight from the złoty' (Allen, 2020: 99).

[22] Reserves also took a substantial hit in 1931, when sterling devalued, since the Bank had held considerable reserves with the Bank of England; this reinforced the Bank's tendency to protect – if not increase – its holdings in pure gold. Following sterling's devaluation, the Bank of Poland withdrew most of its deposits and gold from the Bank of England (Allen, 2020: 93–94).

TABLE 7.4 *Bank of Poland banknote circulation and cover ratio, 1930–1938 (end of year)*

	1929	1930	1931	1932	1933	1934	1935	1936	1937	1938
Bank of Poland banknotes and reserves (millions of zł)										
Banknote circulation and short-term liabilities	1,808	1,538	1,431	1,223	1,266	1,222	1,217	1,326	1,419	1,657
... of which banknotes	1,340	1,328	1,218	1,003	1,004	981	1,007	1,034	1,059	1,406
Gold and foreign exchange reserves	1,229	975	813	639	564	531	471	423	471	464
... of which in gold	701	562	600	502	476	503	444	393	435	445
... of which in foreign exchange	526	413	213	137	88	28	27	30	36	19
Cover ratio (reserves as % of circulation and other short-term liabilities)										
Gross reserves (gold and foreign exchange)	67.8	63.4	56.9	52.2	44.5	43.5	38.7	31.9	33.2	28.0
Gold reserves (gold alone)	38.7	36.6	42.0	41.1	37.6	41.2	36.5	29.6	30.7	26.9

Source: Leszczyńska (2013) and Karpiński (1958).

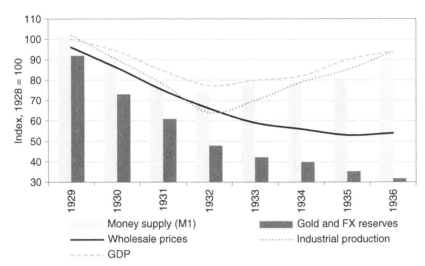

FIGURE 7.8 GDP, industrial production, prices, and money in Poland, 1929–1936
Note: GDP was calculated as an average from several GDP estimates published
in the relevant literature. The wholesale price index was published as annual
average values.
Source: Wyczański (2006) and GUS (1939).

of these measures was to release 146 million złoty in gold and foreign
exchange and thus 'create powerful reserves for the people and enable the
Bank of Poland to revive the economy once it has, at long last, started to
recover' (Jezierski and Leszczyńska, 1994: 72). At the same time, Polish
authorities reiterated that the złoty was one of the world's soundest
currencies and no one would 'go for inflation'.[23] In reality, of course,
złoty banknotes were not convertible into gold and the Bank of Poland's
foreign exchange reserves continued to fall, especially after President
Roosevelt announced that the United States would also be leaving the
gold standard. After devaluations of the dollar, the złoty appreciated and
the exchange rate returned to the level of 5.3 złoty per US dollar.

Following the dollar devaluation and the failure of the 1933
International Financial Conference, Poland joined the Gold Bloc, a
small group of countries headed by France, who continued to defend
the principles of the gold exchange standard.[24] The deal was sweetened

---

[23] Foreign reactions to the change were generally positive – see Allen (2020: 101–102).
[24] For a discussion about monetary policy and interwar gold standard, see Bernanke and
James (1991), Feinstein et al. (2008).

by a trickle of foreign credits, most of them from the Bank of France, aimed at replenishing the reserves of the Bank of Poland.[25] Under the circumstances, these credits could only provide a temporary stop-gap. The Bank's bodies and the government opposed a further 'loosening' of the issuing policy. The Polish monetary policy was as conservative as the economic one, although many countries were heading towards flexible monetary policies. This policy resulted in deflation, which deepened the slowdown of economy (see Figure 7.8).

In conducting its monetary policy, the Bank of Poland had to reconcile two conflicting interests. On the one hand, the loss of reserves forced it to cut circulation through lending restrictions. On the other, distressed enterprises were hoping for easier credits. Pressure from various government bodies as well as different economic groups represented on the Bank's Council also had an impact. The Bank endeavoured to show very little flexibility: in 1929, the Bank's promissory note portfolio (bill of exchange) amounted to 704 million złoty, in the following years the bill case would fluctuate reflecting the lending policy, it usually exceeded 650 million złoty (1930 – 672 million, 1931 – 670 million, 1932 – 586 million, 1933 – 688 million, 1934 – 654 million, 1935 – 689 million, 1936 – 681 million) (Leszczyńska, 2013: 320).

Despite mounting financial difficulties and a deepening recession, Polish authorities refused either to impose capital controls or to allow the złoty to devalue. Unlike the majority of the countries, Poland did not stop making foreign payments, as it sought to maintain foreigners' trust. In spite of that, significant capital was withdrawn by foreign investors, and Poland's reserves were almost completely exhausted.

7.8 POLISH MONETARY POLICY CHANGES, 1936–1938

Józef Piłsudski's death on 12 May 1935 marked a turning point in Polish interwar history. After his death, the Sanacja movement was split in two principal factions: a moderate, civilian faction supporting President Ignacy Mościcki, and a nationalist, military faction headed by General Edward Rydz-Śmigły. An uneasy power-sharing agreement between the two groups forged the basis of what became known as the 'Colonel's Government' that ruled until the German invasion of Poland in 1939 (Koryś, 2018).

---

[25] The Bank of France opened credits worth 185 million złoty at the end of 1936 (on top of another 100 million złoty opened in mid-1931); up to 12 million złoty were raised from a group of French banks headed by the French-Polish Bank (Leszczyńska, 2013).

The change in government also brought about a shift in economic policy. Early in 1936, Eugeniusz Kwiatkowski, the newly designated deputy prime minister and minister of the Treasury, presented a 'Four-year Plan' for economic recovery; the plan entailed extensive public-investment projects that would make the state the owner of key industrial sectors. Indeed, between 1936 and 1939, public investment rose to 10–20 per cent of annual GDP. Markets were still respected, but the new policy marked a shift toward centralized decision making and state intervention (Jezierski and Leszczyńska, 2003). The new emphasis on industrialization, particularly investments in the arms industry, was also consistent with Poland's geopolitical concerns in the face of the rising military power of Germany and the USSR. Such concerns underpinned the 1936 'renewal' of the Franco–Polish alliance, which was bolstered by renewed French credits through the Rambouillet Accord.[26]

At the same time Kwiatkowski was announcing his Four-year Plan, conditions on foreign exchange market were deteriorating.[27] In March 1936 the Bank of France, which had been supplying the Bank of Poland with foreign exchange credits, signalled its reluctance to offer additional advances. Furthermore, the government's ambitious investment plans were expected to put additional pressure on the balance of payments, at least in the short run (Szempliński, 1938: 1787). Polish monetary authorities started contemplating a change in the Bank's policy. Adam Koc, president of the Bank of Poland, and Leon Barański, the Bank's director, favoured a 25–30 per cent devaluation, after which the złoty would be tied to sterling. Kwiatkowski, the Treasury minister, and President Mościcki, however, feared that devaluation would cause inflation and spark a new round of demands for wage increases and social unrest. Instead, they favoured imposing exchange controls and negotiations to reduce Poland's external debt service. At a key meeting held in the president's office on 21 April 1936, Mościcki stated that devaluation would

---

[26] The Rambouillet credit entailed 2,600 million French francs over the years 1936–40, of which 1,350 million represented cash and 1,250 million were export credits. Cash payments were partly in złoty and partly in francs; by the end of 1938, 950 million francs had been granted in cash.

[27] In December 1935 an advance was granted by the Bank of France to the Bank of Poland for 50 million złoty against gold held in Warsaw (in addition to the existing facilities of 500 million francs against gold held in Paris). In February 1936 the Bank of France had extended for a three months 25 million złoty of the 50 million złoty that they had advanced to the Bank of Poland. In March the Bank of France had refused to renew more than that amount.

be a 'disaster' for Poland (Landau, 1986); most of those present agreed and favoured controls on foreign payments rather than any 'monetary experiments' (Landau, 1986). Finding himself at odds with the government, Koc resigned from the presidency of the Bank of Poland.

Having imposed its will on the central bank, on 26 April 1936 the government imposed strict controls on foreign exchange and gold transactions. Financial transfers were either prohibited or controlled, and both imports and exports were regulated, with exporters obliged to sell their foreign exchange earnings to state banks. The new regulations were meant to limit speculation and protect the country's foreign currency reserves. Kwiatkowski said that he obtained a possibility for mechanical restoration of equilibrium in the balance of payments. It became possible to administratively determine the amount of outflow of foreign currencies by controlling imports and inflow by promoting exports. (Kwiatkowski, 1938). In a declaration to the public, the government explained how:

For ten years, Polish financial policy has rested on the two major principles: stability of the currency and freedom of capital flows. ... By introducing temporary exchange controls, the government declares that they have been conceived of solely as a means of protecting the society from attempts at profiteering and economic defeatism (...). Poland's liabilities due to foreign trade as well as loan liabilities will continue to be respected.[28]

Controls may have been announced as 'temporary', but they were soon tightened and maintained indefinitely, signalling Poland's de facto departure from the gold exchange standard. Nevertheless, there was little support for a formal devaluation of the złoty, whose stability was seen as a test of strength for the Polish state itself. France's decision to devalue, in September 1936, did not change this attitude. Addressing the Parliament three months later, Kwiatkowski dismissed rumours of an impending złoty devaluation and reiterated Poland's commitment to 'prudent' monetary policy.

At the Bank of Poland, Adam Koc was replaced by Władysław Byrka, whose appointment was orchestrated by Kwiatkowski. Kwiatkowski wanted the Bank run by someone who shared his monetary policy views. According to the Polish economist Ferdynand Zweig, minister of finance Kwiatkowski's appointment of Byrka limited the Bank of Poland's independence. Monetary policy was determined by Kwiatkowski and the Bank of Poland became 'a subjugated tool in the hands of the Ministry' (Zweig, 1944: 113).

---

[28] Cited in Leszczyńska (2011: 33).

Byrka's appointment was part of a broader conflict between the civilian and military factions that dominated Polish politics after Piłsudski's death. The conflict also concerned monetary policy: whether to use traditional rules or use moderate inflation. The former group was led by Kwiatkowski and Byrka, while the latter consisted of the military and their allies; Kwiatkowski defended monetary orthodoxy, whereas the army representatives demanded the introduction of 'fiat money'. Kwiatkowski's views prevailed and his Ministry assumed control over monetary policy and foreign financial relations. Between 1938 and 1939 the proponent of 'inflationism' gained predominance (Zweig, 1944: 113).

Despite formal adherence to monetary orthodoxy, the Bank of Poland gradually increased its role in the economy and the scale of its credit operations. After 1936 the money issue grew in connection with the development of an extensive investment programme by the government. In 1935, the statutes of Bank Polski were amended to allow the Bank to buy Polish bonds up to 150 million złoty (previously there had been a limit of 10 per cent of the Bank's capital, that is, 10 million złoty). After the statutes were amended in 1938, the amount was raised to 200 million złoty. It should be remembered that since 1924 Bank Polski had been granting the government a loan of 100 million złoty without interest (and in 1938 this was increased to a loan of 150 million złoty). What is more, the Bank could now purchase up to 400 million złoty-worth of Treasury notes. Previously, the Bank accepted them for discounting, their value not exceeding 100 million złoty.

From 1936, the Bank extended special loans to the Treasury and state banks (mainly to the Bank Gospodarstwa Krajowego). They were also directed at financing investments. In 1936 the liabilities of the State Treasury and state banks amounted to 797 million złoty (63 per cent of total loans). These amounts increased in 1938 and 1939. Leon Barański, general director of the Bank of Poland, commented on the situation as follows: 'The Bank of Poland has changed its principles of activity just like foreign banks. These banks have increased their loans to the State Treasury in recent years.' He gave the example of the Bank of France, the Bank of England, and the Fed (Jezierski and Leszczyńska, 1994: 103).

Having maintained the size of its short-terms loan portfolio while private banks were deleveraging, by 1936 the Bank already controlled a larger share of the market; between 1936 and 1938, loans granted by the Bank of Poland grew by 18 per cent, compared with 4 per cent for private banks, 2 per cent for state banks and 12 per cent for municipal

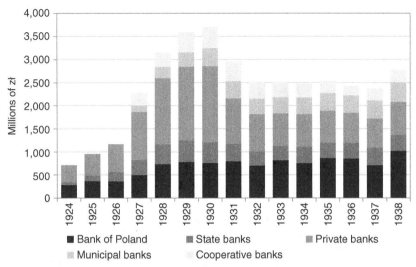

FIGURE 7.9 Short-term loans of the Bank of Poland and other banks, 1924–1938
Note: These are short-term Lombard loans and bills of exchange loans for the
Bank of Poland; figures on other banks exclude bills of exchange rediscounted at
the Bank of Poland.
Source: Morawski (1996) and GUS (1939).

banks; cooperative bank loans actually fell by 2 per cent (Figure 7.9). As
a result, for the first time in its history, the Bank of Poland became the
largest player in the short-term-loan market (Karpiński, 1958).[29]

In the autumn of 1938, the Sudeten crisis in Czechoslovakia and the
Munich Conference caused a bank run, and some 500 million złoty were
withdrawn from the Polish banks. Assuming the role of the lender of
last resort, the Bank of Poland provided liquidity support and circulation reached 1.4 billion złoty (Figure 7.10).[30] This was the first intervention on such a large scale. During the banking crisis of 1925 and
the crisis of 1931–3 there was little aid: priority was given to the rules
of the gold standard, the protection of foreign exchange reserves, and
the złoty exchange rate. After 1936, the foreign exchange market came
under state control.

[29] Deposits also increased across the banking system, but these were channelled primarily
to state-owned banks, that were perceived as more trustworthy, at times of financial
distress (Landau, 2001: 96–97).
[30] A further run on Polish bank deposits occurred in March 1939, and circulation reached
2.0 billion złoty (Jezierski and Leszczyńska, 1994).

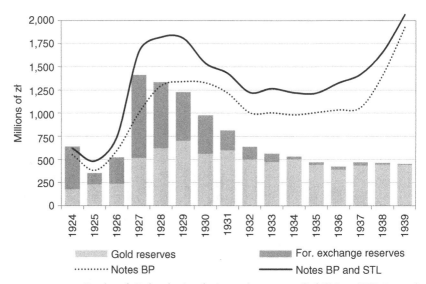

FIGURE 7.10 Bank of Poland circulation, short-term liabilities (STLs), and reserves, 1924–1939
Note: The złoty value of gold reserves is calculated on the basis of the 1927 parity.
Source: Karpiński (1958) and GUS (1939).

The Bank's monetary activism meant that, by the end 1938, the cover ratio had fallen below its statutory threshold of 30 per cent. But this was no longer treated as a critical standard and the money supply remained unchanged. Instead, government responded by amending the statutes of the Bank of Poland to facilitate the pursuit of looser monetary policy: rules of issue were relaxed and the possibilities for the government to use credits from the Polish Bank were expanded.

The Bank of Poland's statutes were amended in February 1939. The legal minimum gold cover was raised to 40 per cent of sight liabilities, but this only applied to liabilities in excess of 800 million złoty, a fiduciary issue that the Bank's Council could raise to 1.2 billion złoty, if the Treasury Minister approved. At the time, these 800 million złoty were roughly tantamount to the total of state obligations toward the Bank of Poland, which also converted 515 million złoty of state obligations assumed on behalf of state banks (some dating back as far as 1931) into a new, consolidated loan. Statutory limits on the purchase of state and municipal bonds, as well as interest-free advances to the Treasury were also increased (Jezierski and Leszczyńska, 1994: 75–76). Sweeping statutory amendments were also introduced immediately after the German invasion, in September 1939, but the economy did not have time to benefit from these.[31]

The shift in economic policy after 1936 helped the economy recover; between 1936 and the outbreak of the Second World War, Polish GDP per capita grew by more than 11 per cent annually.

Summing up, Poland's monetary policy was characterized by caution, and a fear of experimentation. Inherently conservative, Kwiatkowski believed the results of other countries' policy experiments had not been uniformly positive and was reluctant to jeopardize the stability of the złoty. He believed that orthodox rules – a balanced budget and fixed exchange rate – were preferable and that the country's investment policy should be realistic and respect the lending capacity of the money market. Thus, the implementation of the four-year investment plan in 1936–7 was not accompanied by any substantial loosening of monetary policy. The situation was changed from 1938 under the influence of internal and international factors. During this period we can talk about an expansionary monetary policy.

7.9 CONCLUSIONS

This chapter has presented the monetary policy conducted by the Bank of Poland and successive Polish governments during the interwar years. Poland based its monetary policy on the gold exchange standard, which gained momentum after the Genoa conference of 1922. In this period Poland experienced rampant inflation caused by financing the state's expenditure with money emission, and in 1923 this turned into hyperinflation. The result was a flight from domestic money, great social protests, and a political crisis. Currency reform, which had been postponed several times, became necessary, and it was already being carried out by neighbouring countries such as Austria and Germany.

The 1924 stabilization aimed at balancing the state budget and achieving monetary stability. Seen as an important symbol of Polish statehood, the new currency (złoty) had to be strong and backed by

---

[31] The Bank of Poland's statutes were last amended on 2 September 1939. According to the balance sheet, on 30 August 1939, the total amount of loans was 1.4 billion złoty. The money circulation at that time was 2.6 billion złoty, of which the circulation of banknotes of the Bank of Poland was 2.1 billion złoty (Jezierski and Leszczyńska, 1994: 106, 115; Kwiatkowski, 2003: 139).

gold. To that end, monetary policy was tight. Success was only partial, however, as a crisis in 1925 and adverse balance of payment developments weakened the currency. In the autumn of 1925 there was a sudden outflow of capital, a flight from the złoty, withdrawal of deposits from banks, and purchases of foreign currency. The pressure on the foreign exchange reserves of the Bank of Poland forced it to resort to foreign intervention loans, which only raised devaluation expectations. The official exchange rate of the dollar was 5.18 złoty, the market rate was 7–8 zł/$. The slump of the złoty exchange rate and recession in the economy in 1925 would foster Poland's long-term aversion to a weak currency. The Bank of Poland found itself in a difficult situation and should have defended the złoty exchange rate, but it had insufficient reserves. The Bank's authorities therefore decided that intervention on the currency market was impossible. Prime Minister and Treasury Minister Grabski had a different position: he demanded that the exchange rate be defended. The conflict was resolved by Stanisław Wojciechowski, president of Poland, and the offended Grabski resigned. The price of the dollar rose temporarily to 11–12 złoty, in what was typical panic and currency speculation. Afterwards, the price of the dollar stabilized at around 9 złoty. Polish society at large saw each change to the exchange rate as evidence of major economic problems. For these reasons, both economists and politicians developed the conviction that a strong and stable currency was a value in itself. From November 1925 to October 1927 the market price of the dollar oscillated around 9 złoty, the parity rate was 5.18 złoty.

A second reform was needed and a new official rate for the złoty was established. In 1927, Poland obtained a large international stabilization loan and announced a three-year stabilization plan (1927–30). Poland returned to a 'strong' gold exchange standard with complete freedom in foreign exchange markets and international capital movement. The złoty was stabilized approximately 40 per cent below its previous parity. These were three stable years for the Polish economy. The monetary policy of the Bank of Poland was aligned with the rules of the gold standard system.

When the stabilization plan expired in 1930, the economy was in a state of economic crisis. The basic problem was the outflow of capital and the decline in the reserves of the Bank of Poland. It was expected that the crisis situation was temporary, monetary policy was passive and when the decrease of currency reserves occurred, the issue of złoty was lowered and credits to the economy were reduced. While many countries abandoned gold after 1931, Polish monetary authorities believed it was necessary to avoid devaluation and stick to gold. In 1933, the country joined the Gold Bloc and it was only in April 1936, after the Gold Bloc had collapsed, that Poland decided to restrict external transactions and impose controls on the foreign exchange market. The decision to remain on gold for so long contributed to the persistence and severity of the Great Depression (and deflation) in Poland, relative to other countries.

What were the sources of this policy? There were several. The first was the memory of inflation and the failure of the first stabilization of 1925 and the crisis of the złoty. This had made a serious impact on the way the monetary authorities thought, but also on social attitudes. The stable exchange rate became an unshakeable dogma constituting the foundation of economic policy. The prevailing belief was that devaluation must be followed by inflation. This was the main barrier to a change in monetary policy between 1930 and 1933.

The second reason was related to the previous one and can be called conscientious adherence to the rules of the game. This is, of course, about the gold exchange standard. Poland wished to comply with the principles of the gold exchange standard in order to convince foreign investors and financiers that it was a reliable partner. Poland's case may be treated as an example of a peripheral country that attempted to comply with the gold exchange standard principles, even with very difficult external and internal circumstances. The principles prevailed in Poland's monetary and exchange rate policies until 1936.

Polish monetary policy during the interwar period did not provide a stimulus to the economy. The logic of the gold exchange standard system imposed the described policies, implying deflationary effects. During the years of the Great Depression, Polish authorities tried to reduce this deflationary bias by amending the Bank's statutes on numerous occasions, but such actions were of negligible importance. Only the April 1936 regulation that introduced exchange controls provided a significant modification to the monetary framework, making other changes in the Bank's policies possible. This was, nonetheless, done much later than in other countries.

The next reason was related to fears that the devaluation of the złoty and monetary easing would cause capital flight and a decline in Poland's credibility. Lacking a long financial history, the new Polish state had to establish a reputation for financial stability. After all, a strong currency would also symbolize a strong state. Participation in the gold exchange standard was considered the most effective way to assure such strength; other economic needs and objectives came second. Economic and political shocks, however, produced capital outflows that threatened to destabilize the currency. This strategy was revised after 1936.

In the 1930s, the Bank gradually lost its independence to the extent that after the 1936 imposition of exchange controls, it simply followed the government's instructions. Monetary policy was de facto conducted by the government. It should be added that the authorities of the Bank of Poland accepted it. The expansion of the money supply went hand in hand with increases in the amount loans granted by the Bank of Poland to the state. This situation was reinforced in 1938–9. The act of the Bank of Poland was amended in February 1939, allowing for the fiduciary issue of the złoty. The processes that took place between 1936 and 1939 strongly changed the status of the Bank of Poland and Polish monetary policy.

REFERENCES

Allen, William A. (2020). 'Poland, the International Monetary System and the Bank of England, 1921–39'. NBP Working Paper, No. 328.

Bernanke, Ben and James, Harold (1991). 'The Gold Standard, Deflation, and Financial Crisis in the Great Depression: An International Comparison', in Hubbard, R. G. (ed.), *Financial Markets and Financial Crises*. Chicago: University of Chicago Press, 33–68.

Feinstein, Charles H., Temin, Peter, and Toniolo, Gianni (2008). *The World Economy between the World Wars*. New York: Oxford University Press.

Grabski, Władysław (1924). *Równowaga budżetowa w świetle sytuacji gospodarczej. Expose wygłoszone na plenarnym posiedzeniu Sejmu w dniu 10 czerwca 1924 r.* [Budget balance in the light of the economic situation: Expose delivered at the plenary session of the Parliament on June 10, 1924]. Warsaw: Drukarnia Państwowa.

Grabski, Władysław (1925a). 'Mowa Prezesa Rady Ministrów Władysława Grabskiego w dniu 10 września na posiedzeniu komisji skarbowo-budżetowej Senatu' [Speech by the Prime Minister, Władysław Grabski, on September 10, at the meeting of the Senate's treasury and budgetary committee]. *Monitor Polski*, 210: 2–5.

Grabski, Władysław (1925b). *Program walki z kryzysem gospodarczym w Polsce. Mowy Prezesa Rady Ministrów i Ministra Skarbu Władysława Grabskiego* [Program for combating the economic crisis in Poland: Speeches by the Prime Minister and Treasury Minister, Władysław Grabski]. Warsaw: Drukarnia Państwowa.

Grabski, Władysław (2003). *Dwa lata pracy u podstaw państwowości naszej, 1924–1925* [Two years of work on the foundations of our statehood, 1924–1925]. Warsaw-Rzeszów: SGGW, WSIiZ.

GUS (1939). *Mały Rocznik Statystyczny 1939* [Concise Statistical Yearbook 1939]. Warsaw: Główny Urząd Statystyczny.

Jezierski, Andrzej and Leszczyńska, Cecilia (1994). *Bank Polski 1924–1952* [Bank of Poland 1924–1952]. Warsaw: Narodowy Bank Polski.

Jezierski, Andrzej and Leszczyńska, Cecilia (2003). *Historia gospodarcza Polski* [Economic History of Poland]. Warsaw: KeyText.

Karpiński, Zygmunt (1958). *Bank Polski 1924–1939* [Bank of Poland 1924–1939]. Warsaw: Polskie Wydawnictwa Gospodarcze.

Kemmerer, Edwin Walter (1926). *Poland, Reports Submitted by the Commission of the American Financial Experts*. Warsaw: Ministerstwo Skarbu.

Koryś, Piotr (2018). *Poland from Partitions to EU Accession: A Modern Economic History*. London: Palgrave Macmillan.

Kowal, Stefan (1995). *Partnerstwo czy uzależnienie? Niemieckie postawy wobec stosunków gospodarczych z Polską w czasach Republiki Weimarskiej* [Partnership or dependence? German attitudes to economic relations with Poland during the Weimar Republic]. Poznań: Wydawnictwo Naukowe Uniwersytetu Adama Mickiewicza.

Kwiatkowski, Eugeniusz (1938). 'Przemówienie Pana wicepremiera i ministra skarbu Eugeniusza Kwiatkowskiego w sejmie' [Speech by Deputy Prime Minister and Treasury Minister, Eugeniusz Kwiatkowski in the Parliament]. *Polska Gospodarcza*. 49: 1741–1757.

Kwiatkowski, Eugeniusz (2003). *Dziennik lipiec 1939-sierpień 1940* [Diary, July 1939-August 1940]. Rzeszów: Wydawnictwo Wyższej Szkoły Informatyki i Zarządzania.

Landau, Zbigniew (1961). *Polskie zagraniczne pożyczki państwowe 1918–1926* [The foreign loans of the Polish State 1918–1926]. Warsaw: Książka i Wiedza.

Landau, Zbigniew (1963). *Plan stabilizacyjny 1927–1930. Geneza, założenia, wyniki* [The stabilization plan 1927–1930. Genesis, assumptions, results]. Warsaw: Książka i Wiedza.

Landau, Zbigniew (1970). 'Dwie stabilizacje złotego (1924–1927)' [Two stabilizations of the złoty (1924–1927)]. *Studia Historyczne*, 13(4): 511–536.

Landau, Zbigniew (1984). 'Poland's Finance Policy in the Years of the Great Depression (1930–1935)'. *Acta Poloniae Historica*, 49: 133–155.

Landau, Zbigniew (1986). 'The Polish Government's Monetary Policy in 1936–1939'. *Acta Poloniae Historica*, 58: 103–130.

Landau, Zbigniew (1992). 'Rząd a Bank Polski w latach 1924–1939' [The government and the Bank of Poland in the years 1924–1939]. *Materiały i Studia, NBP*, 28: 3–21.

Landau, Zbigniew (2001). 'State Sector in the Banking of the Interwar Poland'. *Studia Historiae Oeconomicae*, 24: 87–98.

League of Nations (1927). *International Statistical Yearbook 1926*. Geneva: League of Nations.

Leszczyńska, Cecilia (2011). *An Outline History of Polish Central Banking*. Warsaw: Narodowy Bank Polski.

Leszczyńska, Cecilia (2013). *Polska polityka pieniężna i walutowa w latach 1924–1936: W systemie Gold Exchange Standard* [Polish monetary and currency policy in 1924–1936: In the Gold Exchange Standard system]. Warsaw: Wydawnictwa Uniwersytetu Warszawskiego.

Leszczyńska, Cecylia and Lisiecka, Łucja (2006). 'Useful or harmful? Money usury law in the 2nd Republic of Poland'. *Studia Historiae Oeconomicae*, 26: 67–88.

Lipiński, Edward (ed.) (1928). *Koniunktura gospodarcza w Polsce 1924–1927* [Economic situation in Poland 1924–1927]. Warsaw: Główny Urząd Statystyczny.

Łazor, Jerzy (2018). 'From Economic Nationalism to the Open Market. Polish Trade Policy in the 20th and 21st Century'. *Kwartalnik Kolegium Ekonomiczno-Społecznego Studia i Prace*, 3(35): 81–100.

Maddison, Angus (2006). *The World Economy*, Vol. 1. Millennial Perspective, Vol. 2. Historical Statistics. Paris: OECD.

Ministerstwo Skarbu (1928). *Rocznik Ministerstwa Skarbu* [Yearbook of the Treasury Ministry]. Warsaw: Ministerstwo Skarbu.

Mitchell, Barry Richard (2007). *International Historical Statistics: Europe 1750–2005*. London: Palgrave Macmillan.

Morawski, Wojciech (1996). *Bankowość prywatna w II Rzeczypospolitej* [Private banking in the Second Republic of Poland]. Warsaw: Oficyna Wydawnicza SGH.

Pease, Neal (1986). *Poland, the United States, and the Stabilization of Europe, 1919–1933*. New York: Oxford University Press.

Pease, Neal (1987). 'Charles Dewey as the United States financial adviser to Poland, 1927–1930'. *International History Review*, 9(1): 85–94.

Szempliński, Zygmunt (1938). 'Rozwój polskiej polityki inwestycyjnej' [Development of Polish investment policy]. *Polska Gospodarcza*, 50: 1783–1787.

Taylor, Edward (1926). *Inflacja polska* [Polish inflation]. Poznań: Poznańskie Towarzystwo Przyjaciół Nauk.

Von Thadden, Goetz Henning (1994). 'Inflation in the Reconstruction of Poland 1918–1927'. PhD thesis, London School of Economics and Political Science.

Wolf, Nikolaus (2007). 'Should I stay or should I go? Understanding Poland's adherence to gold, 1928–1936', *Historical Social Research*, 32(4): 351–368.

Wyczański, Andrzej (ed.) (2006). *Historia Polski w liczbach, vol. 2. Gospodarka* [History of Poland in numbers, Vol. 2. Economy]. Warsaw: Główny Urząd Statystyczny.

Zdziechowski, Jerzy (1925). *Finanse Polski 1924 i 1925* [Poland's finances 1924 and 1925]. Warsaw: Biblioteka Polska.

Zweig, Ferdynand, (1944). *Poland Between Two Wars: A Critical Study of Social and Economic Changes*. London: Secker and Warburg.

8

From Banking Office to National Bank

The Establishment of the National Bank of Czechoslovakia, 1919–1926

Jakub Kunert

8.1 INTRODUCTION

At the first General Meeting of shareholders at the National Bank of Czechoslovakia, held on 21 March 1926, the decision was taken to establish a new central bank of the Czechoslovak Republic. This signalled the end of an interim period of more than seven years when the country's currency had been administered by a Banking Office. The Office had been part of the Ministry of Finance, and its most important body, the Banking Committee, was headed by the finance minister. The Banking Office's main task was to stabilize the Czechoslovak currency both domestically and internationally by aiding the transition from a state-backed paper currency (treasury notes) to a currency covered by the assets of a private bank of issue (banknotes). Initially, the Banking Office had been seen as a stop gap. Indeed, the Act of the National Bank of Czechoslovakia (passed some years before, in 1920), had envisaged the rapid establishment of a central bank, immediately after the introduction of the gold standard. However, due to the post-war economic situation, the Banking Office would remain in operation for seven years.

This chapter describes the events surrounding the establishment of the National Bank of Czechoslovakia, focusing on how thinking changed between 1924 and 1926, two key years during the formation of this new institution. It emphasizes the external factors that led the Czechoslovak political and economic authorities to decide to establish a bank of issue prior to the introduction of the gold standard, a significant deviation from the timeline set by the National Bank of Czechoslovakia Act 1920. It reveals the main differences between the Banking Office and the new National

Bank of Czechoslovakia and considers whether the model chosen for the new-born central bank helped uphold its independence in the 1930s.[1]

Section 8.2 focuses on the circumstances of the creation of the Czechoslovak currency and the establishment of the first Czechoslovak bank of issue. Section 8.3 describes the reasons that led the Czechoslovak government to publish the National Bank of Czechoslovakia Act and outlines the basic parameters of the bank of issue to be established under this Act. Section 8.4 explains why the Act did not take effect in the following almost six years and summarizes the attempts to establish the bank of issue during the first three years. The key foreign stimulus for establishing the bank of issue is discussed in Section 8.5. Section 8.6 focuses on an amendment to the National Bank of Czechoslovakia Act and on the resulting changes. Section 8.7 describes the preparatory work on the establishment of the bank. Section 8.8 deals with the functioning of the National Bank of Czechoslovakia after the adoption of the gold standard and during the parallel outbreak of the Great Depression.

8.2 THE CREATION OF THE CZECHOSLOVAK CURRENCY AND THE BANKING OFFICE OF THE MINISTRY OF FINANCE

For all the extensive preparations for the establishment of an independent Czechoslovakia, the constitution of the new state on 28 October 1918 and the changes associated with the transition from war to peace were unpredictable, especially on the economic front. Initial planning for the post-coup period included the establishment of a 'Bank of the Czech Lands' which would take over the note-issuing privileges of the Austro-Hungarian Bank.[2] This turned out to be impractical, however, since notes and coins in circulation could not be replaced at such short notice. Thus, the Austro-Hungarian koruna, which was administered by the Austro-Hungarian Bank, remained valid in the Czech lands for another four months (until 8 March 1919), and even longer in Slovakia and Carpathian Ruthenia.[3]

---

[1] For more details on the establishment of the National Bank of Czechoslovakia, see Kunert (2013).

[2] Archive of the Czech National Bank (hereinafter only 'ACNB'), archive collection Národní banka Československá (hereinafter only 'NBČ'), NBČ/753/1, Korespondence Viléma Pospíšila, file Předválečné období, Návrh zákona hospodářského – původní redakce, cat. no. 753.

[3] The Czechoslovak currency was separated pursuant to Act No. 84/1919 Coll., which empowered the Minister of Finance to order the stamping of banknotes and make a property inventory for the purposes of imposing a property levy. Pursuant to Ministry of

Still, the Austro-Hungarian Bank's activities in the new state were limited. The minister of finance, Dr Alois Rašín, whose name is synonymous with the introduction of the new currency in the Czech Republic, refused to allow the Bank to conduct certain business (for example the provision of Lombard loans) and hence restricted its privileges.[4]

During an interview granted to American journalists in April 1926, soon after the establishment of the National Bank of Czechoslovakia, Vilém Pospíšil, the Bank's first governor and one of its leading architects, explained that the plan he and Rašín had devised for monetary reform had been based on the concept of gradualism. In other words, they had envisaged a gradual process that would start with currency independence, to be followed by the establishment of the bank of issue and, finally, by the fixing of the currency to gold.[5] As a matter of fact, the original idea

Finance Regulation No. 86/1919 Coll. of 25 February 1919, stamping of existing Austro-Hungarian banknotes circulating in the territory of the Czechoslovak state was chosen. This was performed between 3 and 8 March 1919 in the Czech lands and by 12 March 1919 in Slovakia. Due to the later assignment of Carpathian Ruthenia, stamping there did not happen until 1920. Extraordinary legislative measures setting further stamping deadlines were adopted for territories transferred additionally under the Treaty of Versailles. The process of currency separation also involved the withdrawal of a part of the currency held by individuals, which was converted into a compulsory state loan. According to Alois Rašín, the aim was to create a credit market, something which had not been necessary in a period of excess cash. The stamping process was formally ended by Act No. 67/1921 Coll. of 10 February 1921 on the circulation of Czechoslovak treasury notes in the Hlučín, Vitoraz, and Valčice and Czechoslovak Těšín regions and in Carpathian Ruthenia and Slovakia if no stamping had been performed in those two territories under Act No. 84 Coll. of 25 February 1919.

[4] The Czechoslovak currency unit – the Czechoslovak koruna (Kč) – was established de jure with Act No. 187/1919 Coll. of 10 April 1919 which governed the circulation and administration of banknotes and coins in the Czechoslovak state and amended the empowerment of the Ministry of Finance under Act No. 84 Coll. of 25 February 1919. However, the koruna was still considered an interim currency, as policymakers envisioned the creation of a gold-backed currency (a franc or Czechoslovak franc) to circulate alongside the koruna, which was covered by government debt. For this reason, Act No. 347/1920 Coll. (14 April 1920) on the joint-stock bank of issue, for example, set the amount of capital of the proposed central bank in francs. The idea of having two parallel currencies was abandoned on 23 April 1925, when No. 102/1925 Coll., amended Act No. 347/1920 Coll.

[5] 'Dr. Rashin's wisdom explains why there has not been hitherto a national bank, and why the Czechs did not adopt a fresh currency unit and also why, even today, they have no gold coin and no gold balance sheets. Time had to ripen the experience of the Republic, and time was needed to show when it was best to introduce these changes. Nothing has been abrupt and, consequently, it may be said that probably nothing will have to be undone.' ACNB, NBČ/3918/1, Výstřižkový archiv – Národní banka Československá a Vilém Pospíšil, article: 'Czechs found National bank,' *The Christian Science Monitor* (9 April 1926), cat. no. 3918.

entertained by Rašín and Pospíšil had been the exact opposite, at least when it came to the last two stages of the reform: gold stabilization had been meant to precede the establishment of a new bank of issue.

Gradual or not, the new monetary regime needed an institutional framework to administer the interim currency. Austro-Hungarian banknotes were stamped to distinguish them from those circulating outside Czechoslovak territory. Most of these notes were backed by debt issued during the First World War, which was subsequently taken over by the Czechoslovak state. Given the size of the debt overhang, it was decided that the Ministry of Finance should administer the currency and function as a bank of issue.[6] This was effected through Government Decree No. 119/1919 Coll., which regulated relations with the Austro-Hungarian Bank. To perform its new role, the Ministry of Finance would set up a Banking Office under the direction of 'a Banking Committee at the Ministry of Finance', chaired by the finance minister himself.

The Banking Office operated both as a quasi-independent branch of the Ministry and as a public credit institution. Its key decision-making body, the Banking Committee, consisted of eleven members: the minister of finance (or his deputy) and a further ten members appointed by the minister, who was complemented by a representative of the committee of the National Assembly.[7] The Banking Committee supervised all the Office's business and managed currency reform and public debt. It administered the circulation of banknotes and coins, set the level of discount and lending rates, and determined the purchase prices of precious metals. As an advisory body to the minister of finance, it also drafted various reports, either in response to ministerial questions or at its own initiative.

Day-to-day operations would be handled by 'expert business management', that is, clerical staff with relevant banking expertise. Charged with implementing the Banking Committee's resolutions and decrees, management stood at the top of the Office's internal hierarchy and issued guidelines and instructions to the head and branch offices. Its members were appointed by the minister of finance, following a hearing with the Banking Committee. The organization of the Banking Office was complemented

---

[6] The note debt consisted of banknotes, giro accounts, and Treasury bills in circulation and was expected to be reduced gradually over time, not least through the liquidation of assets of the Austro-Hungarian Bank.

[7] The representative of the National Assembly was a member of a seven-strong committee under Article 17 of Act No. 84/1919 Coll. empowering the Finance Minister to order the stamping of banknotes and make a property inventory for the purposes of imposing a property levy.

by a network of branches, offices, and subsidiary offices, whose establishment and powers were decided by the Banking Committee. The same applied to the appointment of 'censors', who worked as advisers to individual offices.[8] To carry out its functions, the Banking Office would use the buildings and facilities of the Austro-Hungarian Bank in Czechoslovakia.

The decree envisaged that the Banking Office would be established immediately upon the date of promulgation – 6 March 1919. In practice, it was not until 11 March 1919, when the minister of finance, Rašín, recruited several of the Austro-Hungarian Bank's former clerks, that the Banking Office commenced its operations. Over the next two months, the Office operated under the direct supervision and guidance of Rašín. On 12 May 1919, the Office's final statutes were published and Rašín appointed the ten members of the Banking Committee.

The Banking Committee was instrumental in maintaining the Office's independence. Committee membership was honorary and lasted indefinitely (unless revoked). Between 1919 and 1926, it was chaired by no fewer than seven Ministers from several political parties, representing different policy views. Still, no attempt was ever made alter the Committee's composition, which explains why the press frequently referred to the Banking Committee as a 'group of unelected cardinals for life'.[9] Even Rašín, who first appointed the Committee members in 1919 and enjoyed considerable popularity, often found himself in the minority. As one member would later write in his memoirs: 'when we voted and the majority was of a different opinion than the deceased Dr Rašín, he went so far as ... to say that he would never cancel a decision of the Banking Committee, even if it were very harmful in his opinion.'[10]

[8] Government Decree No. 246/1919 Coll., on the organization of the Banking Office of the Ministry of Finance, the charter of the Banking Committee at the Ministry of Finance, the business of the Banking Office of the Ministry of Finance, the assumption and settlement of Lombard loans and T-bills, the settlement of giro accounts of the Austro-Hungarian Bank, and the takeover of employees of that bank.

[9] ACNB, ŽB/449, Kniha výstřižků k otázce Národní banky Československé, 'Cedulová banka a naše finanční politika,' *Právo Lidu* (22 March 1925): 51–55. Karel Engliš (Minister of Finance between 1920–1921 and 1925–1928) deserves special mention. He represented a stream of economic policy favouring the export industry and rejecting the deflationary process promoted by Alois Rašín, who conversely held economic policy views presented by the most important Czechoslovak financial institution, Živnostenská banka. Their dispute about the koruna exchange rate basically continued even after Rašín's death in 1923 and extended until the 1930s, when it was concluded in favour of Karel Engliš with the first devaluation of the Czechoslovak koruna (1934). The circumstances leading up to the devaluation are discussed later in this chapter.

[10] ACNB, NBČ/47/9, Protokol o schůzi Bankovního výboru při ministerstvu financí, 26 September 1924, 22, cat. no. 47.

Thus, the Banking Office's personal independence was respected throughout its existence. As for the other three areas of independence, whether institutional, functional, or financial, archival evidence, particularly the minutes of the Banking Committee's own meetings, suggest that all three were respected by government representatives. Whenever an attempt was made to violate the Office's independence, as in the case of the draft Government Decree No. 206/1924 Coll., which sought to count the Office as a state enterprise, thus making it possible to transfer its profits to the state budget, Banking Committee members reacted and the 'inappropriate' initiative was soon withdrawn.[11]

8.3 THE ACT ON THE JOINT-STOCK BANK OF ISSUE 1920

Initially, the plan had been to wait until the koruna exchange rate had stabilized and sufficient gold reserves had been accumulated before converting the treasury notes administered by the Banking Office into banknotes convertible into gold. In other words, the original assumption had been that the new bank of issue would be established after the introduction of the gold standard. However, sharp exchange-rate fluctuations on international markets during 1919 – when the value of the koruna in the Zurich Stock Exchange rose from an initial 21 Swiss franc (CHF) centimes to a high of 34.25 centimes, on 16 May 1919, only to then plummet to 7 centimes (Figure 8.1) – rendered any thoughts of establishing an independent bank of issue impossible (Národní banka Československá 1937: 423). In December 1919, Alois Rašín, by then no longer minister of finance but still a member of the Banking Committee,[12] dismissed the possibility of establishing a bank of issue. In his opinion, with seven billion korunas' worth of treasury notes still in circulation, it was quite premature to discuss the establishment of a new central bank, especially since the Banking Office had hardly performed any of the functions of a central credit institution. Instead, the Office had essentially been administering the national debt.[13]

---

[11] ACNB, NBČ/28/4, Zápis o schůzi bankovního výboru při ministerstvu financí, 24 October 1923, 15–16, cat. no. 28.

[12] Rašín was Minister of Finance and Chairman of the Banking Committee between 6 March 1919 and 7 July 1919; he then served as an ordinary member of the Banking Committee until 7 October 1922, when he became Minister of Finance again (until 17 February 1923).

[13] ACNB, NBČ/1/9, Protokol o schůzi Bankovního výboru při ministerstvu financí, 22 December 1919, 5–6, cat. no. 1.

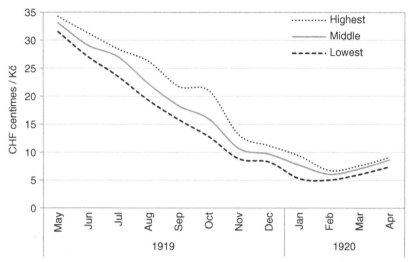

FIGURE 8.1 Koruna–Swiss franc exchange rate, May 1919–April 1920
Source: Žekulin (1927: 46).

The slump of the Czechoslovak koruna in late 1919 forced the government to take action. The minister of finance, Kuneš Sonntag, initially tried to 'talk up' the currency by declaring that 'the proposal for a joint-stock bank of issue was an urgent matter.'[14] However, his statements failed to alter expectations and the koruna continued to depreciate during the early 1920s (Figure 8.1). The government therefore decided to signal its determination to defend the currency and, on 27 January 1920, submitted a bill to 'establish a bank of issue' to the Chamber of Deputies. Nevertheless, the move was still intended mainly as a declaration directed at the Czechoslovak and international public. No sooner had the koruna rebounded from its trough of 5 centimes (recorded on 5 February 1920; see Žekulin, 1927: 46), than the government decided to withdraw the bill in the middle of March 1920.[15]

The proposed bill only consisted of four articles, declaring the establishment of the bank of issue and announcing that its statutes would be published shortly. To take account of the views of socialist deputies, however, the intended statutes would also enable the bank to be nationalized. Much more important was the bill's explanatory memorandum, which went at length to explain why the legal form of a joint-stock company, rather than a state bank, had been preferred. This was part of

[14] Ibid.
[15] Protokol 130. schůze Národního shromáždění československého ve čtvrtek dne 18. března 1920. Tisk 2582 (www.psp.cz/eknih/1918ns/ps/tisky/t2582_01.htm).

an effort to separate currency administration from political interference and thus protect 'the future legal tender [the expected franc currencies – JK] from forced intervention by the state'. To this, the memorandum's authors added: 'Our new legal tender must have private guarantees to prevent changes undertaken by the state from spilling over into the private economy together with changes in the soundness of the currency.'[16]

Following the government's proclamatory bill, an editorial group of economists, headed by Josef Fořt, was established under the auspices of the minister of finance. Despite resistance from a circle of economists who regarded such initiatives as premature, the Fořt group was tasked with preparing an actual bill for the establishment of a new central bank.[17] The preparatory process involved a debate whether the bank should be private or state-owned. Arguments for the public ownership of the bank invoked the non-profit character of the bank of issue. On the other hand, it was argued that a state-owned bank would be subordinate to the state and could end up being misused to finance the budget. Despite the recent example of the Austro-Hungarian Bank, which had ended up financing war debt despite being a private institution, it was still believed that private ownership would ensure the inviolability of the currency by the state. The debate ended in a compromise: the new institution would be established as a mixed private joint-stock bank, that is, a private bank with significant state participation. The state would acquire one-third of the new bank's capital, along with the right to appoint the governor and some board members. The statutes of the new bank, included in the draft law, were modelled on those of its Austro-Hungarian predecessor, albeit with influences from the statutes of the German Reichsbank and the National Bank of Belgium (Palkovský, 1925: 84). On 18 March 1920, the government submitted its proposal to the National Assembly, where it was approved on 14 April 1920.[18]

The Act on the Joint-Stock Bank of Issue 1920 consisted of two sections and three annexes and contained a total of 142 articles.[19]

---

[16] Tisk 2265. Vládní návrh ze dne 27. ledna 1920. Zákon ze dne ... 1920, kterým zřizuje se akciová banka cedulová.

[17] Early in 1920, the speedy transition to the new regime was opposed by Cyril Horáček, a professor of statistics at Charles University and the second Czechoslovak finance minister; this was paradoxical, since Horáček had demanded the establishment of a national bank of Czechoslovakia in the National Assembly as early as 13 December 1918 (print no. 167/1918); cf. Horáček (1920).

[18] 144. schůze Národního shromáždění československého ve středu dne 14. dubna 1920 (www.psp.cz/eknih/1918ns/ps/stenprot/144schuz/s144001.htm).

[19] Act No. 347/1920 Coll., on the Joint-Stock Bank of Issue.

The first section mentioned the right of the state to regulate currency circulation and authorized the government to establish a National Bank of Czechoslovakia. The second section contained the new bank's statutes. They set its equity capital at 75,000,000 'currency units in gold', to be divided into 150,000 shares of 500 units per share. The law set out the composition of the Bank Board (to be comprised of the Governor and nine members), a select committee of the Bank Board, sections of the Bank Board, a five-member Audit Committee, and the General Meeting of shareholders as the supreme administrative bodies. Given the state's share in the Bank's capital, the governor and three of the Board members were to be appointed by the president of the Republic, following the government's proposal. The remaining six board members were to be elected by the General Meeting of the shareholders. One of these members was, at the government's proposal, subsequently appointed deputy governor by the president of the Republic. Members of the Audit Committee, the Bank's main auditing body, were also elected by the shareholders' General Meeting.

These main bodies aside, the new bank would also have a Board of Censors, whose members were appointed to individual branches. The Board of Censors functioned as an advisory council for the discounting of bills and as a board of secretaries, submitting proposals regarding the economic needs of specific regions. The Bank would be staffed and administered by its business management, headed by a directorate. State supervisors were appointed by the minister of finance to ensure that the Bank complied with legislation. As in the case of the Banking Office, the Bank's affairs would be handled by its business management, which was a professional board of officials.

Parliamentary approval for the Act on the Joint-Stock Bank of Issue in 1920 did not mean that the time when the new central bank would be established was getting any closer. Article 43 of the Act left the final decision up to the minister of finance, and no minister appeared to be in any particular rush.

8.4 THE DISCUSSION ABOUT ESTABLISHING THE NATIONAL BANK OF CZECHOSLOVAKIA TO THE END OF 1923

The publication of the Act on the Joint-Stock Bank of Issue 1920 certainly contributed to the appreciation of the koruna on international financial markets in the summer of 1920. Whether the renewed slump of the currency in the second half of the year was a response to the failure

TABLE 8.1 *(Some) assets and liabilities of Czechoslovakia's Banking Office, 1920–1921 (Kč millions, on 31 January of each year)*

	31.1.1920	31.1.1921
Assets		
Precious metals reserve	–	164.9
Claims abroad and foreign currency reserves	25.9	165.4
Bills	150.9	1,794.0
Lombard loans	569.2	2,206.9
Uncovered treasury note debt	8,829.0	8,236.8
Other assets	145.3	554.8
Liabilities		
Circulation (treasury notes)	5,574.7	10,888.3
Giro	1,099.5	857.1
Treasury bills in circulation	266.3	286.3
Other liabilities	81.8	514.0

Source: Stavy Bankovního úřadu Rekapitulace výkazů Národní banky Československé, *Zprávy Národní banky Československé*, 1(1) (October 1926): 4–5.

to put the law into practice, or vice versa, is harder to determine. In any case, the prospect of adopting the gold standard and establishing a new central bank posed an obvious challenge for Czechoslovakia: out of a total circulation of more than 10 billion koruna, 8.2 billion were covered by government debt while fewer than 330 million koruna were covered by precious metals and gold-backed foreign currencies (Table 8.1); as a matter of fact, uncovered note issue was probably higher, given that total liabilities exceeded the assets reported by the Banking Office.[20]

There was another aspect to the passing of the new central bank law, related to the country's efforts to tap international capital markets. Czechoslovakia was trying to demonstrate that, when negotiating with international lenders for new loans, the country could offer a private monetary institution, able (if necessary) to assume private obligations.[21] When it came to international financial matters, the deputy chairman of the Banking Committee, Vilém Pospíšil, was one of the country's main negotiators. His experience had convinced him that Czechoslovakia

[20] The list of assets and liabilities in Table 8.1 is not complete, causing the two sides of the balance sheet to diverge; unfortunately, this is the only data source available for the Banking Office at the time.

[21] ACNB, record group Živnostenská banka (hereinafter only 'ŽB'), ŽB/449/1, Kniha výstřižků k otázce Národní banky Československé, Karel Karásek, 'Zřízení čsl. cedulové banky', *Venkov* (2 September 1924): 23–25.

would not succeed in obtaining any foreign credits unless it had an independent bank of issue.

Nevertheless, external pressures to establish a central bank that would be independent of the state did not appear in the minutes of the Banking Committee's meetings until October 1920, one month after the conclusion of the Brussels Financial Conference. The conference, attended by thirty-nine delegates, ended with a resolution that clearly set out the need for a gradual transition to gold coverage of national currencies and the establishment of central banks free of political influence.[22] The talks in Brussels had been organized by the League of Nations but its decisions were non-binding, as those attending did not have the necessary political mandates. By contrast, the summit convened in Genoa by the British prime minister, David Lloyd George, in April 1922 was a highly political event.[23] Its conclusions reiterated the need for each country to establish independent central banks. Previously in 1920, the Banking Committee had opted for a milder formulation outlining the need to establish an independent central bank at some future date. After Genoa, it actively began working on ways to enhance its independence, in line with the conference conclusions.

Questions regarding the independence of the Czechoslovak bank of issue were not only raised at international conferences, where the issue was discussed at a very general level, but also in bilateral talks with representatives of the – mostly British – banks, from whom Czechoslovakia hoped to obtain international loans. The main obstacle during these talks appeared to be the reluctance, on behalf of potential foreign creditors, to accept that the Banking Office was genuinely independent and not just 'a Ministry of Finance department doing banking business'.[24] Foreign bank

---

[22] ACNB, NBČ/1/22, Protokol o schůzi Bankovního výboru při ministerstvu financí, 25 October 1920, p. 11, cat. no. 1. On the creation and motives of the resolution, see Capie et al. (1994: 53).

[23] Pospíšil (1930: 178–180) and Stibral (1930: 190–196).

[24] ACNB, NBČ/36/3, Protokol o schůzi Bankovního výboru při ministerstvu financí 26 February 1923, 8, cat. no. 36. The same stance on the Banking Office was presented in 1922 by Jiří Kosek, who made a study trip to several major banks of issue together with Ministry officials. Reporting to the management of the Banking Office, Kosek wrote: 'the study trip provided us with the knowledge that the prestige of our state would benefit extraordinarily from the establishment of a bank of issue fully independent of the state administration. It is hard to convince foreigners that the Banking Office is just such an independent institution, and the author's arguments, regardless of their soundness, could not entirely eliminate the doubts of the foreigners involved in the matter, as the very name of our institution gives the impression that the Banking Office is merely a department of the state financial administration.' ACNB, NBČ 845/2, Korespondence s

representatives felt that a currency dependent on the political composition of government bodies did not provide sufficient guarantee against potential devaluation, whereas a bank of issue would 'always vigorously defend its stance and its independent position towards the state'.[25]

Between 1920 and 1924, therefore, the Banking Office went to great lengths to convince its foreign partners that it was, to all intents and purposes, the equivalent of an independent central bank. Among other things, it even considered changing the English translation of its name from 'the Banking Office of the Ministry of Finance', which belied its functional attachment to the Ministry, to the 'Banking Establishment of Issue', so as to highlight its independence. Concerns that foreign institutions might misinterpret this as an attempt to postpone the establishment of the new central bank, however, led the Office to keep its original name.[26] Another tactic was to transfer the Czechoslovak gold reserves from Brussels to London. The rationale was that if the Bank of England were to take the reserves under its administration, the prestige of the Banking Office would increase to the extent that other central banks would accept it as a peer institution. Initial attempts to sound out the Bank of England were unsuccessful, and the Office's request was rejected. It was not until February 1923, during a confidential tête-à-tête with Montagu Norman, that Pospíšil convinced the governor that the Banking Office was, in fact, a central bank whose gold reserves could be administered by the Bank of England.[27] Norman reportedly changed his mind solely because Pospíšil promised him to make every effort to establish a bank of issue as quickly as possible.[28]

cedulovými ústavy-Ministerstvo financí v Praze-vyslání expertů do ciziny-zpráva tajemníka Jiřího Koska r. 1922, Zpráva tajemníka Jiřího Koska o studijní cestě do zahraničí vykonané z rozkazu vlády Československé republiky v době od 25. září do 26. října 1922, zpracováno 3. 11. 1922, 44–45.

[25] ACNB, NBČ/32/2, Protokol mimořádné schůze Bankovního výboru, 9 February 1925, 13, cat. no. 32.

[26] ACNB, NBČ/103/1, Protokol o schůzi zvláštní komise konané dne 29. května 1923 za účelem projednání prováděcího nařízení k zákonu ze dne 18. prosince 1922 č. 404, 4–6, cat. no. 103.

[27] ACNB, NBČ/36/3, Protokol o schůzi bankovního výboru při ministerstvu financí 26 February 1923, 8, cat. no. 36.

[28] ACNB, NBČ/99/37 Protokol o schůzi komitétu bankovního výboru konané dne 14 February 1923, 8, cat. no. 99. From Norman's diaries we can deduce that the meeting took place on 6 February 1923. Its content was subsequently confirmed by a visit of the Czechoslovak Ambassador to London, Vojtěch Mastný, on 20 February 1923. Unfortunately, the fragmented entries do not reveal the content of the conversation. Bank of England Archives (BOEA), ADM34/12, Montagu Norman Diaries, 6 February 1923 and 20 February 1923.

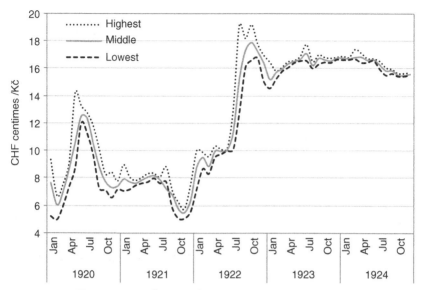

FIGURE 8.2 Koruna–Swiss franc exchange rate, January 1920–December 1924
Source: Zprávy Národní banky Československé (1926).

While Pospíšil was in London Alois Rašín was in hospital. On 10 October 1922, he had resumed his post as minister of finance pursuing a contractionary policy that had led to significant price and wage deflation. The koruna exchange rate had increased (Figure 8.2), but so had unemployment and hostility toward Rašín and his policy. In the morning of 5 January 1923, the minister of finance was shot by a radical Anarcho-Communist, Josef Šoupal, who later claimed to have been targeting supporters of the banking plutocracy; on 18 February 1923, Rašín succumbed to his injuries. At a meeting of the Banking Committee held a few days later, Pospíšil argued that Rašín's memory would best be honoured by organizing a campaign to collect the deposits to make up the capital for the new central bank. After all, the new institutions had always been intended as the crowning glory of Rašin's monetary work.

Due to excessive currency volatility (Figure 8.2) Pospíšil's proposal was never carried out, which gave rise to justified concerns that the depositors (and future shareholders) might be harmed in the process of stabilizing the koruna.[29] The protection of shareholders' assets, however,

---

[29] ACNB, NBČ/36/3, Protokol o schůzi bankovního výboru při ministerstvu financí, 26 February 1923, 17–21 and the text in the proposal in annex H, cat. no. 36.

was not the only thing Czechoslovak economists, especially the members of the Banking Committee, were concerned about. Prior to the end of 1921, monetary policy had been dominated by efforts to stabilize the koruna on the basis of the 'natural exchange rate', which corresponded to the ratio of Czechoslovak to foreign prices. Early in 1922, a policy of artificially revaluing the exchange rate, with the intention of bringing down Czechoslovak prices, gradually started to prevail in policy circles.[30] All foreign exchange reserves, including costly funds from international loans (the first tranche of the Czecholoan and the loan to the City of Prague) were gradually used for interventions in foreign exchange markets until the middle of 1923 (Kubů and Šouša, 2010).

The Czechoslovak economy had become export-oriented immediately after the creation of the new state, as almost three-quarters of all the industry in Cisleithania was located in its territory, whereas most its customers lived outside the borders of the new state. Indeed, almost one-third of production was exported during the boom. For this reason, the 1922 interventions to revalue the koruna in the foreign exchange market had a significant impact on the economy. The school of thought promoted by Alois Rašín saw such interventions as a way of lowering the price level, as a high koruna exchange rate would generate downward pressure on production costs. It even counted on the occurrence of a small economic crisis which would clear the economy of inefficient firms. However, the scale of the economic crisis, which soon spilled over to financial institutions, surprised and shocked many of his supporters. The experiment resulted in large losses mainly for the export industry, on which the Czechoslovak economy was dependent, and a deep banking crisis. In late 1922, they therefore convinced him to end the policy of conducting foreign exchange interventions and maintaining a high and unspecified exchange rate of the Czechoslovak koruna. Over the following years, the Czechoslovak economy struggled to recover from the crisis, as did its public finances, which were plagued by a shortfall in revenues and a series of extraordinary rescue measures after the deflationary crisis

---

[30] In the second half of 1921, the average monthly exchange rate fluctuated between 5.53 and 7.90 CHF centimes to the koruna; by contrast, in the first half of 1922, it moved between 8.84 and 10.08 CHF centimes. In the second half of 1922, the koruna was fully influenced by the Banking Office's deflationary policy and the average exchange rate fluctuated between 11.35 and 17.87. The highest level recorded was 19.20 CHF centimes to the koruna on 10 October 1922 (Žekulin, 1927: 49–51). At that time, 10 centimes to the koruna was considered the natural exchange rate level for the Czechoslovak economy. See Národní banka Československá (1937: 41).

(for example, the bailout of some financial institutions) (Národní banka Československá, 1937: 41–43, 158–159).

Interventions to revalue the koruna caused the Banking Office to incur an internal loss of half a billion koruna in foreign exchange reserves. This raised the fundamental question of whether the state or the new central bank would bear losses if the new institution was established amidst continued currency interventions. The Banking Committee debated this matter at length, as early as December 1922. The decision to establish a bank of issue prior to stabilizing the currency was probably influenced by the views of Erik von Frenkell of the Bank of Finland (Suomen Panki), who, during a meeting with the Bank Office, drew on the Finnish experience and warned against rushing to establish the bank of issue too soon.[31]

8.5 FOREIGN PRESSURE TO ESTABLISH THE NATIONAL BANK OF CZECHOSLOVAKIA

As time elapsed without any news concerning the establishment of Czechoslovakia's new central bank, foreign financial institutions started getting impatient. During talks with the Ministry of Finance, delegations of foreign banks, such as the National City Bank, the Guaranty Trust Company, and Lee, Higginson & Co., inquired about the timeline of monetary reform.[32] After all, Czechoslovakia was one of the last European nations without its own bank of issue.[33]

Foreign capital was expected to play a key role in Czechoslovakia's post-war reconstruction. As in the case of other countries in the European periphery, monetary reform became entwined with negotiations to secure foreign loans. Unlike other countries, however,

---

[31] NBČ/103/1, Protokol o schůzi zvláštní komise konané dne 29. května 1923 za účelem projednání prováděcího nařízení k zákonu ze dne 18. prosince 1922, no. 404, 10 cat. no. 103. According to a statement made by its Deputy Chief Executive Director, Karel Kučera, the Banking Office and the Bank of Finland had forged a special relationship. Kučera had received from Erik von Frenkell 'a confidential message that the Finns will share with us their experience of the path towards a gold currency, which they want to have in four to five years, and are asking us to share ours with them' (ibid.). Unfortunately, there is no detailed information in the documents of the National Bank of Czechoslovakia about negotiations and information exchange between the two institutions.

[32] ACNB, NBČ/32/2, Protokol mimořádné schůze Bankovního výboru z 9 February 1925, 13, cat. no. 32

[33] For the nature and the establishment of banks of issue in Europe and around the world cf. Dědek (1925: 102–106, 214–219, 256–260).

Czechoslovakia was reluctant to approach the League of Nations for assistance, and negotiated directly with private financial groups instead. An appeal to the League would have been considered a domestic policy failure: League programmes were reserved for countries like Austria and Hungary, who were in dire straits – or so it was believed, at least. What is more, some Czech economists and members of the Banking Committee had participated in negotiations for the League's stabilization loan to Austria, and this experience had made them quite sceptical of League interference.[34]

Foreign pressure ultimately played a key role in hastening the establishment the new central bank. In 1924, the second tranche of the Czechoslovak foreign loan was under negotiation. On 14 May 1924, Vilém Pospíšil and Augustin Novák met with Bank of England governor, Montagu Norman. According to Pospíšil, Norman was quite critical: 'Mr. Pospíšil here travels all around the world telling everyone that no one will speak to you unless you have a bank of issue – and is there one in his home country?'[35] Trying to defend the Banking Office's position, Pospíšil and Novák argued that the necessary legal framework was already in place and Czechoslovakia was just waiting for the right moment to join the gold standard. They also pointed to the general risks surrounding the European economy, at a time when it was uncertain, for instance, whether Germany would be able to stabilize with the Deutsche Golddiskontbank.

Norman expressed his understanding but 'resolutely insisted on his stance'[36] that the existence of a private central bank was pivotal to the conduct of monetary policy. For his part, Pospíšil, argued that the establishment of the new central bank was hindered by the paucity of the foreign exchange and gold reserves necessary to cover the new currency. According to Banking Office reports, foreign reserves accounted for less than 25 per cent of circulation in 1922–1925; by contrast, more than 70 per cent of circulation was backed by public debt, that is, treasury notes (see Table 8.2).

---

[34] This was particularly true of Dr Emil Roos, who was a member of the League of Nations control committee for the Austrian stabilization loan and had access to details. See, for example, ACNB, NBČ/770/1, JUDr. Vilém Pospíšil, guvernér Národní banky – Zprávy kontrolního komitétu pro Rakousko, cat. no. 770. For more on Czechoslovak foreign loans (the Czecholoan) in general, see Kubů and Šouša (2010: 11–26).

[35] ACNB, NBČ/47/5, Protokol o schůzi bankovního výboru při ministerstvu financí, 27 May 1924, 15, cat. no. 47.

[36] ACNB, NBČ/47/5, Protokol o schůzi bankovního výboru při ministerstvu financí, 27 May 1924, 16, cat. no. 47.

TABLE 8.2 *Composition of circulation cover in Czechoslovakia (%),*
1922–1925

Circulation covered by:	31.01.1922	31.01.1923	31.01.1924	31.01.1925
Gold and foreign exchange	12.9	13.3	24.4	21.1
Government debt	70.7	77.8	68.9	70.5
Other assets	16.4	8.9	6.7	8.4

Source: Stavy Bankovního úřadu Rekapitulace výkazů Národní banky Československé,
Zprávy Národní banky Československé, 1(1): 4–5 (October 1926).

Norman agreed that 'the situation … [was] not yet ripe' for the stabilization of the Czechoslovak currency on a gold base, at which point
Pospíšil and Novák proposed establishing a central bank and introducing inconvertible banknotes prior to the accumulation of sufficient gold
and foreign exchange reserves. What happened then surprised both of
them because Norman was open to the idea, and he 'expressed complete agreement with our view that a bank of issue could be established
without introducing the gold standard'. At the end of their conversation, Norman 'expressed the hope that by the time we met again, he
would be pleased to hear about the progress of this idea', and warned
that if Czechoslovakia hesitated any further, this would jeopardize its
access to foreign capital. Henceforth, whenever it turned to 'the international market, the absence of a bank of issue would be an unfavourable factor for Czechoslovakia'.[37] Norman's entry into his personal
diary reveals how the Governor of the Bank of England perceived the
outcome of their meeting: 'They will urge setting up Central Bk [*sic*]
quickly.'[38]

Their conversation with Norman led Pospíšil and Novák to conclude
that Czechoslovakia's chances of obtaining further international loans
were starting to dwindle. The two men decided to take prompt action
and immediately informečd Prime Minister Antonín Švehla and Finance

[37] ACNB, NBČ/47/5, Protokol o schůzi bankovního výboru při ministerstvu financí, 27
May 1924, 15–18, cat. no. 47.
[38] BOEA, ADM34/13, Montagu Norman Diaries, 14 May 1924. Norman's uncompromising stance probably stemmed from his general views on central banking as well as a
recent press campaign run by *The Times*, concerning the huge size of the Czechoslovak
reparations, especially the 'contribution to the liberation'. Norman had probably started
to worry that Czechoslovakia would not be able to meet its obligations and that a loan
of any amount would turn out to be a risk. See ACNB, NBČ/47/5, Protokol o schůzi
bankovního výboru při ministerstvu financí, 27 May 1924, 15–18, cat. no. 47.

Minister Bohdan Bečka of the urgent need to proceed with the establishment of a central bank.[39] In the summer of 1924, the issue was added to
the agenda of the meeting of the 'Five', an important unofficial body made
up of leading representatives from Czechoslovak government parties;[40]
it was discussed further at a meeting of leading politicians held in the
town of Mariánské Lázně. These meetings were also attended by Jaroslav
Preiss, the managing director of the most important Czechoslovak commercial bank, Živnostenská banka, who also functioned as a technical
adviser.[41] During those meetings, it was ultimately decided to postpone the fixing of the koruna to gold and proceed with preparations
for the establishment of a new central bank right away.[42] The success of
Pospíšil's campaign was confirmed by the September issue of the Finance
Ministry's bulletin, which announced that an amendment to the bank act
had been prepared and would be submitted to the Chamber of Deputies
in the upcoming spring session.[43]

8.6 ACT NO. 102/1925

Penned by Pospíšil himself, the new version of the Act on the Bank of
Issue, was approved in April 1925.[44] Eager to project Czechoslovakia's
compliance with international central banking standards, authorities
immediately sent copies to the Bank of England. A few weeks later, on 21
May 1925, when the bill was signed into effect by the president, Pospíšil
telegraphed Norman to let him know.[45]

---

[39] ACNB, NBČ/32/2, Protokol mimořádné schůze Bankovního výboru z 9 February 1925,
2, cat. no. 32.

[40] ACNB, ŽB/449, Kniha výstřižků k otázce Národní banky Československé, Vondrák
(1924: 20–21).

[41] Ibid.; Málek (1924: 21).

[42] The last step was to convince the general public, which had been stirred up by the leftist press; many one the left considered any step toward establishing a gold peg would
lead to inflation, at least in the short run. The campaign against the postponement of
the introduction of the gold standard was ultimately suppressed with help from Foreign Affairs Minister, Edvard Beneš. ACNB, NBČ/225/1, Act on the Bank of Issue, file
1, Dotazy na zákon a stanovy cedulové banky, Dopis Augustina Nováka na ministra
zahraničí Eduarda Beneše z 7. 8. 1924, cat. no. 225.

[43] 'Přípravy k cedulové bance,' Věstník ministerstva financí státu Československého, Part
II., review section, vol. 1924, no. 9 (September1924): 292.

[44] Act No. 102/1925 Coll., amending Act No. 347 Coll. of 14 April 1920.

[45] 'Governor Norman Bank of England LONDON. With reference to our conversation a
year ago we beg to inform that president of republic has signed today additional bill to
bank of issue law stop this is achievement of the legal basis on which preparatory steps
for actual establishing have already begun stop compliments pospisil novak' ACNB,

The new law contained twenty-eight articles revising the previous version. Article 2, stipulated that the hitherto undefined currency unit of future banknotes was to be the 'Czechoslovak koruna' (Kč). Article 3 defined a target range for the koruna's exchange rate against foreign gold-backed currencies (that is, the US dollar), to be based on the range of fluctuations over last two years (USD 2.90–3.03 per Kč 100). Setting a target zone for the koruna exchange rate relative to the US dollar was seen as a first step toward the adoption of the gold standard. Act No. 102/1925 thus emphasized that the koruna would almost be brought to an indirect parity with gold via a (convertible) foreign currency. The future central bank was also charged with maintaining a cover ratio of 20 per cent, raising it by one percentage point each year over the next fifteen years, with the target 35 per cent cover ratio to be achieved by 1941.

Perhaps the most significant changes concerned the new bank's capital and organization. At the time the act was approved, the US dollar was the only convertible currency; thus, the bank's equity capital was denominated in dollars. The original 75 million currency units (theoretically, gold francs) were converted into USD 15 million. To take account of the country's population, however, this was reduced to USD 12 million with an option to increase capital to the original amount (although this never happened). Capital was divided into 120,000 shares of USD 100 each.

An important change was also made to the composition of the Bank's Board, which took into consideration the interwar trend for foreign creditors to install representatives at their debtors' central banks. The nine original Board members could now be joined by a tenth, who – unlike everyone else – did not have to be a Czechoslovak citizen. What is more, the new act eliminated the government's rights to approve the Board and Audit Committee members chosen by the shareholder's General Meeting, thus curtailing state authority over the Bank's administration. Clearly, the intention was to reassure the foreign financial community that Czechoslovakia's new central bank enjoyed considerable independence from the executive.

NBČ/225/1 Act on the Bank of Issue, file 1 Dotazy na zákon a stanovy cedulové banky, Zápis pro pamět' Viléma Pospíšila, 21 May 1925, cat. no 225. The Bank of England replied: 'Whilst writing, I am to tender the Governor's congratulations and to express the hope that this foreshadows full co-operation in the sense of the Genoa Resolutions between the Banks of Issue of our two Countries.' Ibid., Letter of the Bank of England (Chief Cashier) to the NBC, 21 May 1925, cat. no. 225.

8.7 THE PROCESS OF ESTABLISHING THE NATIONAL BANK OF CZECHOSLOVAKIA

Pursuant to Act No. 102/1925, on 24 April 1925, Finance Minister Bohdan Bečka tasked the Banking Committee with establishing the new central bank. The Committee, in turn, delegated the task to a special board, 'charged with the preparatory work for the establishment of the bank of issue'. Preparations included organizing the issuing and distribution of the new bank shares among investors. Despite the initial sense of urgency that surrounded the matter, subscriptions for the new shares did not open until 2–7 November 1925; prospectuses and advertisements were published six months after the approval of the Act, symbolically on 28 October 1925, the date of the establishment of Czechoslovak state seven years earlier.[46]

Two reasons contributed to this delay. First, authorities waited until the autumn sugar beet harvest had been brought in. Traditionally, this placed considerable strain on domestic financial institutions, and authorities did not wish the stock offering to coincide with a period of limited liquidity.[47] Second, negotiations with the United States on the consolidation of war debt had to be concluded before the second Czechoslovak foreign loan could be issued. These dragged on till October, because American officials refused to approve any new long-term loans until all outstanding issues concerning the war debts had been resolved.[48] Negotiations were finally concluded in October, largely thanks to the intercession of Pospíšil.[49] In the intervening six months, however, Banking Office representatives ran a number of promotional campaigns throughout Czechoslovakia to ensure the success

[46] Cf.: ACNB, NBČ/25/4, Protokol o schůzi Bankovního výboru, 26 November 1925, annex Q – Pozvání k upisování and annex P – Prospekt, cat. no. 25.

[47] 'K emisi akcií Národní banky čsl. dojde až v listopadu,' Národní listy (3 October 1925): 6.

[48] The main problem concerned the amount of debt to be recognized by Czechoslovakia, since part of the war material commissioned by representatives of the future Czechoslovak Republic had been taken over by Italy and France. At the time, it was claimed that $11 of the $91 million of debt were in dispute; ACNB, NBČ/32/8, Protokol o schůzi Bankovního výboru z 25 September 1925, 7, cat. no. 32.

[49] The second foreign loan aimed at converting internal short-term treasury debt into long-term foreign liabilities. The loan agreement was signed on 26 October 1925. The $50 million loan was payable in 20 years was issued by the National City Bank group, in cooperation with Kidder & Peabody, Kuhn, Loeb & Co., Lee, Higginson & Co., and Marshall Field & Co. in New York and Hope & Co. in Amsterdam. Hope & Co. then sold bonds from the first tranche worth $25 million in New York and Amsterdam. See, for example, Compass. Finanzielles Jahrbuch 1927, Čechoslovakei, Bd. II., Prague 1927, vol. 60, 125.

of the subscription. These included preliminary, unofficial subscriptions, since the official subscription period itself was expected to be quite short.[50]

The campaigns proved successful, as investors finally subscribed for a total of 217,912 shares, compared to the 80,000 that were on offer. A special repartition formula allocated shares on the basis of three criteria: the number of shares subscribed, the subscriber's nationality, and the economic sector or activity represented, thus private individuals ended up with 43.3 per cent of the capital, savings banks and credit unions secured another 17.9 per cent, while industrial, trade, and transport companies obtained 17.4 per cent. The small share of independent agricultural concerns was offset by rural credit unions, through which rural investors ended up controlling almost 10 per cent of the central bank. Shares allocated abroad accounted for less than 1 per cent of the initial public offer. Thus, the newly established National Bank of Czechoslovakia was a wholly Czechoslovak institution.[51]

Once shares had been allocated, two steps remained before the new central bank could be formally established. The first was to appoint the institution's first Governor. To no one's surprise, on 16 January 1926, the post was assumed by Pospíšil. Second came the convening of the first General Meeting of the shareholders, which took place on 21 March 1926. Besides adopting the resolution to establish the National Bank of Czechoslovakia, the meeting elected the members of the Bank's statutory bodies, the Bank Board and the Audit Committee. Three members representing industry (one for German shareholders), two members representing agriculture and one representative of the credit union movement were elected to the Board. The Audit Committee comprised two representatives from agricultural credit societies and cooperative banks, as well as another three members, each one representing industry, agriculture, or self-employed craftsmen and traders. Board members were subsequently joined by the three state representatives (one representative from the savings banks, one from workers' credit unions, and one from public banks), as well as a Slovak representative. The first meeting of the Bank Board was held on 1 April 1926, when the National Bank of Czechoslovakia first

---

[50] See, for example, ACNB, ŽB/449, Kniha výstřižků k otázce Národní banky Československé, *Die Subskription der Zettelbankaktien*, Prager Presse (6 October. 1925): 82.

[51] ACNB, NBČ/198/1, Výkaz úpisu akcií a jejich přídělu podle skupin českých a německých, Slovensko, cizina, státní úpisy, Důvěrný výkaz úpisu a přídělu akcií Národní banky Československé podle skupin upisovatelů, cat. no. 198.

opened for business.[52] A subsequent agreement with the Czechoslovak government, dated 2 February 1927, transferred all assets and liabilities of the Banking Office of the Ministry of Finance on 31 December 1925 to the newly established National Bank of Czechoslovakia.[53]

8.8 THE NATIONAL BANK OF CZECHOSLOVAKIA UNDER THE GOLD EXCHANGE STANDARD (1929–1934)

True to the goals set by Alois Rašín in 1919, the new central bank prioritized the formal adoption of the gold standard. The peg to gold was encouraged by the extraordinary boom experienced by the Czechoslovak economy in the second half of the 1920s, which manifested itself, among other things, in a sizeable trade surplus. What is more, participation in the gold standard was expected to help the National Bank of Czechoslovakia become accepted as a shareholder of the new Bank for International Settlements (BIS). Ironically, the final decision to peg the exchange rate at the koruna's legally defined gold content – 44.58 mg of pure gold per koruna – was taken on 7 December 1929, that is, shortly after the onset of the Great Depression.

Initially, the Czechoslovak economy appeared quite resilient to the Great Depression; over time went however, its effects became deeper (Figure 8.3). By 1931, the crisis had hit Czechoslovakia at full strength, prompting the central bank to respond. Exchange controls were introduced, all foreign exchange transactions were carried out through the National Bank, and payments abroad were placed under strict control. Nevertheless, Bank authorities were proponents of deflationary policy and thus refused to implement any unorthodox monetary solutions. Since maintaining its export capacity was crucial to the Czechoslovak's economy, Bank authorities leaned toward Rašín's policy of a gradual price decreases. In their opinion, such deflation would foster intensification of labour efforts and, in turn, increase the competitiveness of Czechoslovak products abroad.[54]

---

[52] The official opening date was later moved back to 1 January 1926, when the Bank (retroactively) took over almost all business from the former Banking Office of the Ministry of Finance.

[53] ACNB, NBČ/235/1, Dohody a smlouvy, Úmluva mezi vládou Československé republiky a Národní bankou československou o vyúčtování a z něho plynoucí úpravě práv a závazků, 2 and 4, cat. no. 235.

[54] Cf.: ACNB, NBČ/21/15, Zápis o řádné schůzi bankovní rady Národní banky Československé, 24 January 1933, pp. 26 and 49, cat. no. 21, and NBČ/7/13, Zápis o řádné schůzi bankovního výboru při ministerstvu financí, 21 December 1922, 9, cat. no. 7.

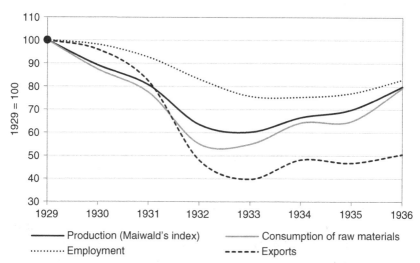

FIGURE 8.3 Economic activity indicators (1929 = 100) in Czechoslovakia, 1929–1935
Source: Zprávy Národní banky Československé (1937).

However, it gradually became clear that the standard tools promoted by the Bank Board, such as interest rates and an internal softening of the conditions for censoring discounted commercial bills, were not sufficient. Moreover, there were concerns that further interest rate cuts would squeeze Czechoslovak banks' profitability beyond repair, causing them to curtail credit rather than help finance economic activity. At the same time, the Bank Board also rejected the new ideas circulating abroad, especially in the Anglo-Saxon world, where reflationary deviations from orthodoxy were gaining traction. Instead, the Board reiterated its belief that 'monetary interventions extend a crisis rather than resolve it.'[55] Before long, this brought the central bank in conflict with the former minister of finance, Professor Karel Engliš, who had become one of the chief proponents of policy activism to reflated the economy and resolve the crisis.[56]

After sterling's departure from gold, in September 1931, Engliš started emphasizing the positive effects of suspending convertibility and allowing the koruna to depreciate. Over time, such ideas gained support beyond academia, especially in agricultural circles. In a country where

[55] ACNB, NBČ/14/1, Zápis o řádné schůzi bankovní rady Národní banky Československé, 24 April 1933, 13, cat. no. 14.
[56] ACNB, NBČ/387/2, Zápis o řádné schůzi bankovní rady Národní banky Československé, 24 November 1930, 10, 13–14, cat. no. 387.

the Agrarian Party, representing the interests of Czechoslovak farmers, regularly obtained the highest number of parliamentary seats and was the strongest member of the government coalition, this shift in policy opinion was important.[57] Early in 1932, the leading representatives of the Agrarian Party launched a campaign to devalue the currency, arguing that such a measure would 'ease the burden on farmers'.[58] Similar proposals to save the economy through devaluation appeared elsewhere in the public arena; in May 1932, rumours circulated in the press that the government coalition was considering replacing Pospíšil with a Governor more inclined to broaden the credit base of the National Bank of Czechoslovakia.[59]

Talk of devaluation had petered out by 1933, as if in expectation of the results of the monetary experiments announced by Franklin D. Roosevelt in the United States, only to re-emerge in the second half of the year. Once more, Engliš was at the helm of the campaign, writing several articles on the subject. Echoing Gustav Cassel, Engliš offered a monetary interpretation of the crisis, blaming the valuation of gold in particular. His recipe for combating the crisis was therefore price adjustment to the global situation, but no longer via deflation, but through a change in the currency's conversion rate or bonuses paid to exporters on imported goods. While the Bank Board had rarely commented on Engliš's views before, by 1933 his ideas were being discussed widely at its meetings.[60] Clearly, the Board now saw them as a direct threat to its independence and as a route to monetary anarchy.[61] It was argued that if devaluation were allowed, the central bank would become subservient to various interest groups who would hardly be satisfied with a single devaluation, but would gradually push the economy toward a string of competitive devaluations that would ultimately damage domestic industry.[62]

---

[57] After 1920, the Agrarian Party regularly secured the largest number of parliamentary seats and got to appoint the prime minister. A key member of government coalitions, it was also in charge of important ministries such as the Ministry of the Interior, the Ministry of Defence, and the Ministry of Agriculture.

[58] ACNB, NBČ/41/7, Zápis o řádné schůzi bankovní rady Národní banky Československé, 24 May 1932, 35, cat. no. 41.

[59] ACNB, NBČ/41/8, Zápis o řádné schůzi bankovní rady Národní banky Československé, 24 June 1932, 24–25, cat. no. 41. Kolářík (1937: 531–532). No such considerations were ever recorded in the minutes of Bank's Board.

[60] For a rare exception to the rule, see ACNB, NBČ/387/2, Zápis o řádné schůzi bankovní rady Národní banky Československé, 24 November 1930, 10, cat. no. 387.

[61] ACNB, NBČ/20/2, Zápis o řádné schůzi bankovní rady Národní banky Československé, 24 November 1933, 21–22, cat. no. 20.

[62] See, for example, ACNB, NBČ/27/1, Zápis o řádné schůzi bankovní rady Národní banky Československé, 24 January 1934, 77, cat. no. 27.

Sticking to monetary orthodoxy, Pospíšil emphasized that any change in the exchange rate would bring about concomitant adjustment to a host of nominal prices, thus raising inflation.[63]

Things snowballed in January 1934, when Prime Minister Jan Malypetr summoned the governor for a consultation and demanded that the central bank come up with solutions to the key problems facing the Czechoslovak economy, if gold convertibility was to remain in place.[64] In response, the National Bank of Czechoslovakia prepared an extensive memorandum.[65] Still, the Bank of could no longer overturn the government's intention to devalue the currency and adopt the policy championed by Engliš.

On 17 February 1934, the gold content of the koruna was reduced from 44.58 to 37.15 mg and the statutory cover ratio (consisting solely of gold), was reduced to 25 per cent.[66] The koruna was thus devalued by one-sixth, although all remaining provisions of the Act on the Joint-Stock Bank of Issue of 1920/1925 were left intact. Devaluation helped economic recovery; by 1935, production was up 16.1 per cent relative to its 1933 trough and even exports were showing signs of recovery. In retrospect, even opponents of Engliš's policy had to admit that the koruna devaluation, combined with maintaining a conservative credit policy, was the right step that gave the necessary impetus to the troubled economy.

The shift in monetary policy inevitably brought changes to the central bank. On the eve of the devaluation, Pospíšil informed the Bank Board of the government's intentions and announced his resignation from the post of governor. Senior management also announced they were leaving the Bank, while other Board members put their mandates at the disposal of the groups they represented.[67] The architect of the devaluation, Karel Engliš, became the new governor.[68] As minister of finance back in 1926,

[63] NBČ/27/1, Zápis o řádné schůzi bankovní rady Národní banky Československé, 24 January 1934, 24, cat. no. 27.

[64] Malypetr's demands covered the following areas: 1) support for exports, 2) the need for municipal budgets, 3) accessible and affordable credit for the private sector, and 4) stabilization of German savings banks. ACNB, NBČ/27/1, Zápis o řádné schůzi bankovní rady Národní banky Československé, 24 January 1934, 40–41, cat. no. 27.

[65] ACNB, ŽB/81/4, Devalvace, Devalvace československé koruny, memorandum of 24 January 1934, cat. no. 81.

[66] Act No. 25/1934 Coll., amending Some Measures of the Standing Committee of 7 November 1929, Act No. 166 Coll., on the Final Framework for the Czechoslovak Currency, and Act No. 347 Coll. of 14 April 1920, on the Joint-Stock Bank of Issue.

[67] ACNB, NBČ/27/2, Zápis o mimořádné schůzi bankovní rady Národní banky Československé, 16 February 1934, 67, cat. no. 27.

[68] ACNB, NBČ/27/3, Zápis o řádné schůzi bankovní rady Národní banky Československé, 24 February 1934, 7 and 50, cat. no. 27.

he had been present when the National Bank of Czechoslovakia was first established; several years later, he was placed in charge of the institution to put an end to a long phase in the history of Czech central banking – one that had started during Rašín's tenure at the Ministry of Finance.

8.9 CONCLUSION

The birth of the National Bank of Czechoslovakia was long and laborious. Plans for the establishment of an independent monetary institution may have emerged prior to the country's independence, but their implementation took almost eight years. This was partly because of Alois Rašín's conviction that a stable currency could only be achieved in gradual steps.

Whereas the separation of the Czechoslovak currency from the Austro-Hungarian one in 1919 had been fully in the hands of the Czechoslovak government, the stabilization of the koruna and the introduction of a currency anchor in the form of gold were simply impossible to achieve in the post-war situation. Up until the summer of 1921 completion of the process of stabilizing the Czechoslovak currency was thwarted by the volatility of the koruna on international markets, as international investors associated it with the fate of other Central European currencies, especially the German mark. Subsequently it was impeded by the deflationary policy in the form of foreign exchange interventions in 1922. Likewise, the ratio of coverage by precious metals and gold-backed foreign currency to circulating treasury notes gave no grounds for optimism that sufficient metal coverage of the Czechoslovak currency could be achieved quickly.

The key impetus for the establishment of the central bank ultimately came from the international financial groups Czechoslovakia repeatedly approached to secure foreign loans. Foreign bankers reiterated their distrust of the country's finances and their concerns of their impact on monetary stability. Anglo-Saxon financial circles believed that an independent, private central bank would guarantee a return on their investments, especially in the unfamiliar and potentially unstable nations of Central and Eastern Europe. Despite Czechoslovak assurances, foreigners were not convinced that the Banking Office, a body attached to the Ministry of Finance, could perform this role independently. If Czechoslovakia wanted to secure additional foreign loans, it had to establish a central bank soon, even if that meant joining the gold standard at a later date.

The National Bank of Czechoslovakia was finally established in 1926. It was tasked with keeping the value of the Czechoslovak koruna stable within a target range determined by the exchange rate of the previous two years. Still, the koruna was expected to become a gold currency before this date. Ironically perhaps, the switch to a gold peg coincided with the onset of the Great Depression in 1929. Once the Bank of International Settlements (BIS) was established in Basel, Czechoslovakia came under pressure to join the gold standard. It is worth wondering when (or whether) the country would have joined the gold standard in the absence of such pressure, given how the Great Depression was already dismantling the international currency system that had been reconstructed after the First World War.

It is debatable whether the central bank that replaced the state-run Banking Office of the Ministry of Finance brought any significant enhancement to monetary policy independence, as the interwar money doctors were wont to suggest. From what we know about the inner workings of the two institutions, it would seem that change was minimal and private ownership did not really prevent the state from trying to influence monetary policy. In fact, the government did not hesitate to devalue the koruna twice, once in 1934 and again in 1936, disregarding the strength of objection from the National Bank of Czechoslovakia (Kunert, 2018).

REFERENCES

Unpublished (Archival) Sources

Archive of the Czech National Bank (ACNB), Prague (Czech Republic).
    Archive Collection Národní banka Československá (NBČ)
Bank of England Archives (BOEA), London (United Kingdom).

Published Sources

Capie, Forrest, Goodhart, Charles, Fischer, Stanley, and Schnadt, Norbert (1994). *The Future of Central Banking*. Cambridge: Cambridge University Press.
Dědek, Vladimír (1925). 'Několik poznámek k organisaci cedulových bank' [Some comments about the organisation of central banks]. *Obzor národohospodářský*, 30(3): 102–106 (15 March); 30(5): 214–219 (28 May); 30(6): 256–260 (25 June).
Horáček, Cyril (1920). 'Ještě o naší budoucí bance cedulové' [Once again about our future central bank]. *Obzor národohospodářský*, 25(3):110–115 (15 March).
Kolářík, Jaroslav (1937). *Peníze a politika* [Money and Politics]. Prague: Fr. Borovy.
Kubů, Eduard and Šouša, Jiří (2010). 'The Czechoslovak Loan of 1922: Meeting Place of Financial Elites of London and Prague'. *Prager wirtschafts- und sozialhistorische Mitteilungen – Prague Economic and Social History Papers*, 11: 11–26.

Kunert, Jakub (2013). 'Zřizování Národní banky Československé 1920–1926' [Establishment of the National Bank of Czechoslovakia]. *Sborník archivních prací*, 63(1): 131–200.

Kunert, Jakub (2018). 'Měnová politika Národní banky Československé v období deflace (1929–1934)' [Monetary policy of the National Bank of Czechoslovakia in the deflationary period (1929–1934)]. *Prager wirtschafts- und sozialhistorische Mitteilungen – Prague Economic and Social History Papers*, 27: 24–74.

Málek, Josef (1924). 'Národní banka československá [National Bank of Czechoslovakia]'. *Právo Lidu* [The People's Right], 15 August, 21.

Národní banka Československá (1937). *Deset let Národní banky Československé* [Ten Years of the National Bank of Czechoslovakia]. Prague: National Bank of Czechoslovakia.

Palkovský, Břetislav (1925). *Národní banka Československá a náprava měny* [National Bank of Czechoslovakia and the reformation of currency]. Prague: Vesmír.

Pospíšil, Vilém (1930). 'Hlavní zásady měnové v díle Společnosti národů' [Main monetary principles in the work of the League of Nations], in František Weyr (ed.), *Sborník prací k padesátým narozeninám Karla Engliše* [Collection of articles in honour of the 50th anniversary of birth of Karel Engliš]. Prague: Orbis, 178–180.

Stibral, Karel (1930). 'Měnová politika a měnově technická opatření Dra. K. Engliše' [Monetary policy and technical monetary measures of Dr. K. Engliš], in František Weyr (ed.), *Sborník prací k padesátým narozeninám Karla Engliše* [Collection of articles in honour of the 50th anniversary of birth of Karel Engliš]. Prague: Orbis, 190–196.

Vondrák, Karel (1924). 'Národní banka československá' [National Bank of Czechoslovakia]. *Tribuna*, 3 August: 20–21.

Žekulin, Nikolaj Sergejevič (1927). *Československá měna od reformy dra Rašína až do zřízení československé národní banky* [Czechoslovak currency from the reform of Dr. Rašín to the establishment of the National Bank of Czechoslovakia]. Prague: Vesmír.

Zprávy Národní banky Československé [Bulletin of the National Bank of Czechoslovakia], various issues.

9

'Nobody's Child'

The Bank of Greece in the Interwar Years

Andreas Kakridis

9.1 INTRODUCTION

History was not kind to Greece's central bank in the interwar years. Born at the behest of the country's foreign creditors during a time of financial distress and political rancour, the Bank of Greece was treated with a mixture of suspicion and hostility from the very beginning. Soon after its creation on 15 September 1927, the new institution was tested by the US stock market crash in 1929 that thrust it into the limelight, as the Great Depression rattled the international financial system. Charged with defending Greece's exchange rate in the face of capital flight, the central bank faced a dilemma that became all too familiar to monetary authorities after 1929; one that required the Bank to reconcile the external objective underpinning the country's access to foreign capital against the internal incentive to support domestic liquidity and reflate the economy.

Historians reviewing the Bank's first years of operation have not been particularly kind either. The Bank's early policy has often been described as either ineffectual or detrimental.[1] The Bank is accused of failing to respond to the international financial crisis or responding in a restrictive fashion that pushed the economy further into recession. The 'battle for the drachma', as the futile attempt to retain the gold exchange standard after the British sterling crisis became known, is regarded as the

---

[1] See Kostis (1986, 2003, 2018), Pepelasis-Minoglou (1993), Lazaretou (1996), Christodoulakis (2013); Mazower (1991) adopts a less critical stance, which is shared by Psalidopoulos (2019). Those interested in contemporary accounts of monetary policy could start with Pyrsos (1936, 1946), Vouros (1938), Pyrris (1934), and Zolotas (1936).

culmination of this folly. The subsequent decision to re-peg the drachma to gold in 1933, less than a year after devaluation, is taken as further evidence of an unhealthy 'obsession with orthodoxy' (Kostis, 2003: 477; 2018: 256). More recently, Greece's financial woes have rekindled interest in the interwar years, which are now viewed through the lens of the country's sovereign debt crisis (Chouliarakis and Lazaretou, 2014). In this context, some have used the battle for the drachma to question the wisdom of Greece's attachment to the euro, while others have taken the opposite stance, arguing that devaluation failed to produce genuine recovery (Christodoulakis, 2013). As is often the case, this use of history to settle modern debates has proved to be a mixed blessing.

This chapter provides a comprehensive account of the Bank of Greece's establishment and the policy decisions that were made during the Great Depression.[2] The aim is to contribute to the comparative literature on the Great Depression as well as to ongoing debates regarding the role of the League of Nations and the effectiveness of money doctoring. In what follows, several aspects of the conventional narrative surrounding the Bank's role are revised. First, it is argued that Greek monetary policy was neither as ineffective nor as restrictive as critics suggest; this was partly due to the continued trickle of foreign loans, and partly due to the bank's decision to sterilize foreign exchange outflows, thus breaking with the 'rules of the game' in a way consistent with Nurkse's (1944) findings. Second, it revisits the battle of the drachma, to add some context to what is all too often denounced as a critical policy failure. Last but not least, it argues that Greece is no exception to the rule that holds that countries who shed their 'golden fetters' recover faster (Eichengreen and Sachs, 1985; Eichengreen, 1992).

The chapter combines qualitative and quantitative sources. National archives aside, extensive use is made of the hitherto underutilized material in the Bank of England, which received weekly confidential updates on developments in Athens and orchestrated the international response through the League of Nations.[3] On the quantitative front, the chapter draws on numerous sources, challenging the reliability of some frequently

---

[2] Making this narrative accessible to those who don't have access to the Greek literature and sources is a second objective; to this end, priority is given to references – including archival documents – in English (or French); cf. Dertilis and Costis (1995).

[3] The main archives used are the Tsouderos Archive held at the Bank of Greece Historical Archives (henceforth IATE), the Venizelos Archive held at the Benaki Museum (VA) and the Bank of England Archive (BOEA). Bank of England archives have previously been used by Dritsa (2012), Christodoulaki (2015), Kakridis (2017), and Pantelakis (2018).

used figures and constructing new series where necessary. Despite recent efforts to compile long-term data, notably by Kostelenos et al. (2007) and Lazaretou (2014), data problems persist. Government budgets counted loans as revenue and failed to distinguish between primary and total expenditure; commercial banks channelled assets to foreign branches and refused to share data with authorities; volume indices were unweighted, and composite indicators were often arbitrary. To this day, annual estimates of GDP growth remain sketchy. A better understanding of the data sources and their limitations would help reduce some of the contradictions present in some of the empirical work. While this chapter does not aspire to address all these shortcomings, it does caution against overreliance on questionable figures.

The rest of the chapter is structured as follows. Section 9.2 provides the necessary context by explaining how the new central bank emerged as the unintended by-product of Greece's request for a foreign loan. The peculiar circumstances of its establishment contributed to a series of built-in weaknesses, including limited liquidity, which would hamper the central bank's ability to control the domestic money market; with priority given to separating the bank from public finance, its relationship with commercial banks was disregarded. This ended up hobbling the new institution, as the government conducted its financial operations through other banks that the Bank of Greece was unable to supervise (Section 9.3). At the same time, however, these built-in weaknesses offered a handy excuse to break the rules of the game. Section 9.4 covers the period from 1929 to the eve of Britain's departure from the gold standard. Without questioning the inherent limitation of its clout, it argues that the weakness of the Bank of Greece was often exaggerated in order to deflect criticism and strengthen its position in the financial system. In practice, the bank systematically sterilized foreign exchange losses, probably contributing to Greece's relative resilience in the face of the global recession. Section 9.5 focuses on the few months between sterling's devaluation and the country's default, in April 1932, during which Greece struggled in vain to remain on gold. What appears in retrospect to have been a costly mistake, was a calculated delay to try to salvage the country's loan-financed development strategy; there was never any true intention to deflate the economy and the Bank of Greece duly injected liquidity to bolster the banking system, precipitating the country's departure from gold. Section 9.6 concludes with a brief review of the post-default years, challenging the notion that monetary policy was unduly restrictive or that Greece failed to recover after the 1932 devaluation.

9.2 AN UNEXPECTED BIRTH

Greece entered the Roaring Twenties with a roar of pain. After a decade of almost uninterrupted war, the collapse of the Asia Minor front in the summer of 1922 had left the country exhausted and flooded with refugees. The forced population exchange mandated by the Treaty of Lausanne served as the final act in a drama that had seen Balkan people and borders in constant flux since 1912. In Greece, reconstruction came with the dual challenge of integrating the country's new territories to the north and settling more than a million refugees from the east. For a poor, agricultural country with a per capita GDP less than half the West European average at the time, the challenge was formidable.

Two thirds of the population still lived on the land, where 60 per cent of output and 90 per cent of exports – mostly tobacco and currants – were produced. Roads were fewer than rivers, though often hard to tell apart; floods were commonplace, and malaria was endemic. Cities lacked proper water and sewage, let alone electricity; housing was sparse, even before the arrival of the refugees. The sweeping land reforms of the 1920s had helped ease social tensions in the countryside but hardly improved agricultural yields, which remained low. Despite devoting 70 per cent of cultivable land to cereals, interwar Greece was unable to feed itself. Its gaping trade deficit was financed by a steady inflow of invisibles, notably emigrant remittances from the United States. But as emigration options narrowed and population growth accelerated, economists and politicians agonized over the country's viability.[4]

The quest for viability promised to be expensive. Like other European countries, Greece was financially drained in the aftermath of the First World War. Its budget and currency lay in tatters. Despite significant tax increases, deficits remained high and were financed through the printing press. Between 1920 and 1927, prices rose five-fold and the drachma lost more than 90 per cent of its pre-war value (Figure 9.1). Domestic funding alternatives were limited. Having twice resorted to cutting banknotes in half to convert a portion of the circulation into a forced loan, the government had run out of ways to force the population to hold more of its bonds.

Foreign capital was the obvious solution, but not an easy one. Thanks to the operation of the International Financial Commission (IFC), a body set up by the country's creditors in 1898 and administered by Britain,

---

[4] Mazower (1991) and Kostis (2018) offer the necessary details; viability concerns are discussed in Kakridis (2009), with Ploumidis (2013) drawing interesting parallels with other Balkan countries.

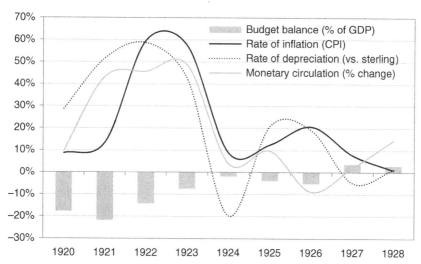

FIGURE 9.1 Greece's post-war stabilization: money supply, inflation, depreciation, and fiscal balance, 1920–1928
Source: See Appendix.

France, and Italy, national debt had continued to be serviced during the war. The IFC maintained direct control over a portion of state revenue, which it channelled for interest and debt repayment (Tunçer, 2015; Kakridis, 2018). Still, political and financial instability – not to mention the uncertainty of wartime reparations and inter-allied debt settlement – hardly inspired confidence in capital markets, where Greek bonds traded at heavy discounts. In the aftermath of the Asia Minor debacle, the League of Nations helped Greece secure a £10 million loan (net) in London and New York at an effective rate of 8.5 per cent. Issued soon after similar League initiatives for Austria and Hungary, the 1924 Refugee Loan was to be serviced by the IFC and managed by another autonomous agency under foreign administration, the Refugee Settlement Commission (RSC). The strict terms helped raise the loan, together with the hope of Greece's financial rehabilitation. In 1925 the military coup dashed those hopes and soured relations with the League, causing London to impose an effective loan embargo on Greece.[5]

---

[5] The Refugee Loan is discussed at length in Tounta-Fergadi (1986) and Pepelasis-Minoglou (1993: 64–93), who offers details on the British loan embargo and the poor relations with the regime of General Pangalos (pp. 101–115); cf. Norman to Niemeyer (Treasury), 1 February 1926, BOEA OV80-1/6; on the RSC, see Kontogiorgi (2006).

Democracy was restored in 1926 and the new coalition government re-opened negotiations for a supplementary refugee loan. Over the course of the following year, war debts were settled with Britain, the United States, and France – the latter proving most intransigent, not least since the French disliked the prospect of another British loan initiative.[6] But the message from London, echoed by Geneva, was clear: further assistance to Greece would come part and parcel with fiscal and monetary stabilization. The former meant budget reform and a cap on public expenditure; the latter entailed a de jure return to gold and the establishment of an independent central bank.[7]

These terms were reaffirmed by the League's financial experts who visited Greece in the spring of 1927 and reported to the Financial Committee at its June session in Geneva. The mission, which comprised staff members Arthur Elliott Felkin, Jan van Walré de Bordes, and the young Jacques Rueff, was headed by the League's Deputy Secretary General, Joseph Avenol and fit neatly into the pattern of interwar money doctoring (Schuker, 2003). In a lengthy appendix to their report, the experts described how the country's largest commercial bank, the National Bank of Greece, was also the sole note-issuing authority and worked in tandem with the government.[8] Established as a commercial bank with limited note-issuing rights in 1841, the National Bank had gradually expanded to providing a wide range of financial services: everything from discounts and business advances to agricultural credits, state loans, and mortgages. Encouraged by the small size of the Greek market, the concentration of financial services in a single institution reflected the National Bank's skilful exploitation of political leverage. Its role in state finance – however perilous at times of overborrowing – guaranteed frequent cabinet appointments for its senior management and provided a steady stream of

---

[6] War debts were settled with Britain on 9 April 1927 and the United States on 8 November 1927 (Pantelakis 1988). Poincaré threatened to use the French member of the IFC to block any new loans unless Greece accepted the French estimates of its obligations; Norman and Siepmann's attempts to mediate through the Banque de France merely reinforced the French conviction that the Financial Committee was controlled by the Bank of England; see Siepmann to Quesnay, 22 September 1927, BOEA OV80-2/36 and the subsequent exchange between Moreau and Norman in the same file. The matter was eventually settled through arbitration, as agreed in December 1927.

[7] The negotiations leading to the establishment of the Bank of Greece have been the subject of several monographs – see, amongst others, Pyrsos (1936), Pepelasis-Minoglou (1993: 121–171), Kostis (2003: ch. 11) and Christodoulaki (2015); in what follows, references are kept to a minimum.

[8] See *The National Bank of Greece*, 6 June 1927 in IATE A3-S1-Y1-F4/1; this is the third note accompanying the report submitted to the Financial Commission.

special privileges that helped reinforce its monopoly; by 1920, the Bank had also become the country's sole note-issuing authority.[9]

By interwar monetary standards the National Bank's multiple roles were highly unorthodox. The bank's governor, Alexandros Diomidis, may have insisted that its dominance made it 'the most independent central bank in Continental Europe', but few took him seriously.[10] In Geneva, the Greek government was asked 'to bring the National Bank into closer conformity with Modern Central Banking'; that meant stripping it of commercial activities and severing its ties with the treasury. The government agreed in principle and submitted its official loan application on 14 June 1927.[11]

When news of the deal reached Athens, Diomidis was incensed. The bank was not prepared to shed the most lucrative part of its business, nor could the Greek financial system be 'tailored to the designs conceived by simple yet misty Nordic minds', that were hardly applicable to a country where 'credit was still in its infancy'.[12] The government, for its part, was also reluctant to jeopardize the integrity of the country's largest commercial bank; it hoped to keep the reform on hold for a few years. As the prospect of such a delay dimmed, negotiations came to an impasse.

Emmanouil Tsouderos, the deputy governor of the National Bank, came up with a solution: instead of giving up its commercial portfolio, the bank could transfer the note issue – along with the foreign exchange reserves and a sizeable chunk of the public debt – to establish a new, separate central bank. The proposal was initially made to Financial Committee members in London, Otto Niemeyer and Henry Strakosch, but soon gained traction in Athens and Geneva.[13] Only the Swiss member of the Financial Committee, Léopold Dubois, predicted that the government would continue to rely heavily on the National Bank and questioned whether the new institution would be strong enough to stand its ground; his concerns were to prove prescient, but they were brushed aside.[14]

[9] On the early history of the National Bank, Valaoritis (1902) remains a classic, while Thomadakis (1985) offers a rare contribution in English; cf. Kostis and Tsokopoulos (1988).

[10] H. Siepmann, Note of Conversation with Mr Al. N. Diomede, 14 February 1927, BOEA OV80-1/27.

[11] See the list of questions posed 'privately' by the Financial Commission to the Greek minister of finance on 12 June 1927 (along with his answers) in BOEA OV80-2/23; the official application, dated 14 June, is appended to the *Report to the Council of the Proceedings of the 27th Session of the Financial Commission* (C.335.M.110.1927.II).

[12] Diomidis to Tsouderos, 22 and 23 June 1927 in IATE A3-S1-Y1-F40/13 and Y2-F25/68.

[13] Tsouderos to Diomidis, 29 June 1927, IATE A3-S1-Y2-F25/71; cf. Pyrsos (1936: 69ff) and Venezis (1955: 37–43).

[14] Mentioned in a letter by de Bordes to Strakosch, 14 July 1927, BOEA OV9-190/93.

July 1927 was spent drafting the new statutes.[15] The League had recently helped to establish the Bank of Estonia, and this provided a blueprint, while further inspiration was drawn from the newly created Bulgarian and Austrian National Banks, as well as the Indian Reserve Bank. Limits on treasury bill discounts and state advances were copied from the Reichsbank. Tsouderos intervened to weaken the government's hold on management, while Strakosch added a 7 per cent minimum reserve requirement for commercial banks, which the Greek side eliminated from subsequent drafts.[16] In retrospect, it is striking how little thought was given to the institution's relationship with other banks, as opposed to its independence from government. Interwar bankers were still haunted by the spectre of fiscal dominance and inflation.

Negotiations continued through the summer, before the final drafts were submitted to the Financial Committee to become the Geneva Protocol, which was signed on 15 September 1927. Banking reform aside, Greece promised to stabilize the drachma at the prevailing rate, cap public spending, and overhaul its public accounting practices; it also agreed to submit quarterly progress reports, endure continued IFC and RSC control and even appoint a suitable 'technical advisor' to the new bank.[17] Opposition parties in Athens rushed to accuse the government of capitulating to foreign interests without exploring other loan options. In fact, records show the government welcomed alternatives, not least because they helped improve its negotiating position. Much to London's frustration, a competitive Swedish loan was put forward during the negotiations.[18] Given how these alternatives came with fewer strings attached, why did Greece end up choosing the League's proposal?

---

[15] IATE A3-S1-Y1-F7 contains successive annotated drafts, identifying the source of each article; similar files appended to letter from Osborne to Niemeyer, 12 July 1927, BOEA OV9-190/1.

[16] The requirement was limited to the National Bank, and only in cities where the Bank of Greece had a branch (that is, Athens); all other commercial banks were exempt, effectively being allowed to continue the existing practice of depositing excess reserves with the National Bank; see *Remarques du gouvernement Grec et de la Banque Nationale de Grèce sur les projets de loi monétaire, statuts de la Banque etc.*, September 1927 in IATE A3-S1-Y1-F8/2.

[17] The idea was hardly new and paralleled the appointment of special commissioners that accompanied other stabilization loans; Greece objected strongly to the prospect of embedding yet another foreigner with veto power into its administration and managed to keep the role advisory.

[18] The offer, which did not involve any League supervision, was for a £9,000,000 loan at an effective rate of 8%. Much like the League loan, it would be serviced through the IFC. This meant British, French, and Italian governments would have to approve of the scheme and charge the IFC with the new task (Pepelasis-Minoglou, 1993: 162f).

Both Santaella (1993) and Flores Zendejas and Decorzant (2016) have argued that League supervision helped countries access cheaper credit by improving credibility and promoting much-needed reforms; the latter maintain that the League's multilateral approach was superior to the bilateral deals used elsewhere. Much of this rings true for Greece. Tied to monetary stabilization, the League's loan was conceived as part of a broader reform package that would act as a 'good housekeeping seal of approval', smoothing the country's return to capital markets.[19] External enforcement would make reforms more credible abroad, while deflecting some of their political cost at home. Politicians saw Geneva as a potential scapegoat for unpopular austerity; the National Bank regarded it as an ally against government pressure.

Other aspects of the Greek case, however, are less consistent with this argument. The IFC had already provided Greece with an external enforcement mechanism that could be used to tap foreign markets at competitive rates and even orchestrate monetary stabilization.[20] The Swedish loan offer, predicated on IFC guarantees, was a case in point. What ultimately undermined these alternatives was London's unwillingness to allow Greece to fall into the financial orbit of any other country. Wielding considerable leverage, Britain was opposed to any plan that did not go through the Financial Committee, where the Bank of England held most sway. Greek policymakers were well aware of this; in response to a French suggestion to explore alternatives in Paris, Tsouderos asked:

Is it worth pursuing financial restoration without the League's cooperation? Could we succeed? What would our position be vis-à-vis the big central banks, whose help we need, especially the Bank of England and the New York Fed? These banks are working together and – for better or worse – control global markets. I'm sure we can obtain loans elsewhere [...] But pursuing an almost unilateral stabilisation without the blessing of [these] central banks would make the attempt short-lived.[21]

Coercion was thus an essential part of the process whereby Greece chose the League. Niemeyer's threat was thinly veiled, when he described the

---

[19] The 'seal of approval' reference points to Bordo and Rockoff (1996), who investigate the effects of gold-standard participation in the pre-war era; Lazaretou (2005) extends this framework to the Greek case.

[20] In fact, the IFC had already drafted two stabilization plans, both of which envisioned handing control of the money supply to a department of the National Bank under IFC supervision; see L. G. Roussin, *Stabilisation of the Drachma*, dated 12 July 1925, and updated 15 March 1926, in BOEA OV80-1/8–9. Both notes were circulated and discussed at the Treasury and the Bank of England at the time.

[21] Tsouderos to Diomidis, 29 September 1927, IATE A3-S1-Y2-F25/71.

Swedish loan to Tsouderos as a 'foolish and short-sighted' idea, which threatened to upset Greece's relationship with the League and 'those who are anxious to be her friends'.[22] London could not only veto IFC involvement in the servicing of the Swedish loan; less conspicuously and more ominously, it could also direct the City bankers to turn a deaf ear to Greece's subsequent loan requests. By extension, it is worth considering whether the different interwar loan experiences do not reflect the superiority of the League's multilateralism, but rather the superior firepower the Bank of England and the City of London could bring to bear to help its friends or intimidate its foes.[23]

Ratification of the Geneva Protocol, along with an improved budget and the de facto pegging of the drachma (Figure 9.1), opened the door to negotiate a 'tripartite' loan of £9 million, to be split in three equal tranches: one for refugees, another to settle budget arrears and a third to boost the foreign exchange reserve of the new central bank. The loan was successfully floated in January 1928, setting the stage for the de jure stabilization of the drachma.[24] On 12 May 1928, the currency was fixed at 375 drachmas to the sterling as the country joined the gold exchange standard. Close to the average since 1926, the exchange rate was widely believed to undervalue the drachma, thus offering policymakers additional leeway.[25] Henceforth, the note issue would be controlled by the new central bank, which was mandated to hold gold or convertible foreign exchange reserves at no less than 40 per cent of circulation. Diomidis became the first governor, with Tsouderos as his deputy. At Niemeyer's

---

[22] Niemeyer to Tsouderos, 3 October 1927, IATE A3-S1-Y2-F51/16.
[23] This is especially true of comparisons with such cases, like Romania and Poland, where bilateral loans were made that deliberately by-passed the Bank of England. On the imperial rivalries and concomitant central banks disagreements underpinning such loans, see Meyer (1970); cf. Tooze and Ivanov (2011) on the Bulgarian case.
[24] By that time, the US government had also agreed to advance Greece $12,167,000 (£2,500,000) at 4 per cent for refugee settlement. Thus, only the remaining £6,500,000 (net) were raised through public subscription in London and New York, some bonds being taken up in Italy, Sweden, Switzerland, and Greece. The loan was issued at 91 (85.5 net of commission) with 6 per cent coupon, raising the effective interest rate to 7 per cent.
[25] Christodoulakis (2013: 278) claims, rather unconvincingly, that the drachma was overvalued, compared to its trough value in August 1926. Why the month a military regime was toppled by another coup and the exchange rate dipped two standard deviations below its 1926 average should be taken as the drachma's equilibrium value is not explained. Nor is the possible overvaluation of sterling relevant, given that the drachma did not seek to restore its pre-war parity, but rather re-pegged at one-fifteenth of its pre-war sterling rate.

behest, Horace G. F. Finlayson, a Treasury official stationed at the British embassy in Berlin, was chosen to be the technical advisor.[26] On 14 May 1928, the Bank of Greece opened its doors to the public for the first time. The quest for a supplementary refugee loan, had led to the creation of a new central bank.

9.3 'NOBODY'S CHILD'

The unexpected birth was followed by a difficult childhood. Created at foreign behest, the Bank of Greece was treated with a mixture of suspicion and hostility within Greece, as it struggled to establish a foothold in a market dominated by its predecessor.

The Bank of Greece was afflicted by some serious disadvantages: 47.5 per cent of its assets were tied up in unmarketable, low-interest loans to the state; with gold and foreign exchange reserves taking up another half its balance sheet, only about 1 per cent was left for liquid drachma assets such as commercial bills or marketable securities. This meant the new central bank was effectively cut off from the market it was expected to control and was unable to rely on rediscounting (a practice unfamiliar to most Greek banks) or open market operations to reign in money and credit.[27]

Some of these disadvantages were inherent: a decade of fiscal profligacy had left much of the drachma issue covered by forced state loans. For those to be liquidated, Greece would have to issue more foreign bonds, effectively replacing cheap domestic credit with expensive foreign loans. A compromise was struck: the Bank of Greece would assume

---

[26] Finlayson's career details are provided by Leith Ross to Niemeyer, 13 August 1927 in BOEA OV9-190/109. The same folder contains correspondence concerning negotiations with the Greek side to secure Finlayson's post; for the flip side to these negotiations, see IATE A3-S1-Y2-F44 and F45. When the choice was announced to the Financial Committee, the French representative was the only one to grumble, no doubt since Finlayson's presence in Athens would solidify British influence; see Comité Financier, 29ème Session, Procès-verbal de la 14ème séance tenue à Genève le 7 Décembre 1927, IATE A3-S1-Y1-F9/1. Finlayson's initial appointment was meant to lapse in three years, but was renewed several times, until April 1937.

[27] Percentages are based on the Bank's opening balance sheet but still held on 31 December 1928; see Pyrsos (1936: 100) and Bank of Greece (1929: 52); cf. the discussion in Lazaretou (2015: 74–78). The limited effectiveness of discounts in markets inundated with government securities was common to many of the interwar central banks; what made the Greek case different was the fact that the central bank was burdened with non-securitized debt, which meant it could not perform contractionary open-market operations either.

about 3,800 million drachmas of debt and the government would repay it in instalments of no fewer than 200 million drachmas annually. Thus, as Dubois put it in September 1927, 'the new bank would not be a bank of issue in the strict sense of the word, but it had been necessary to adapt to circumstances.'[28]

Other disadvantages, however, were due to the circumstances of the Bank's establishment: weary of foreign intervention, the government had allowed the National Bank to tailor monetary reform to suit its own interests. Thus, when the two institutions were separated, the National Bank transferred the most unprofitable and indigestible public loans (including some 1.1 billion drachmas unrelated to the note issue) to the new central bank, keeping the most lucrative and marketable securities to itself. As the anonymous author of a party pamphlet would later put it, 'the National Bank secured all the meat for its stockholders, leaving the bones to the Bank of Greece.'[29] What is more, the National Bank clung on to several old privileges, most notably the sole right to hold the deposits of the country's public agencies. By leaving a sizeable portion of public savings under National Bank control, the government thus 'sold the birth right of the Bank of Greece', breaching the spirit, if not the letter of the Geneva Protocol.[30]

The upshot of all this was the new central bank with a 108-million drachma portfolio in an eight billion drachma market, which had just received a considerable liquidity boost, not least due to the tripartite loan. The elephant in the room was the National Bank, which controlled almost half the deposits and a third of short-term credits. A few months after the Bank of Greece had opened its doors, the National Bank spearheaded an initiative to establish the Hellenic Bank Association (HBA),

---

[28] Comité Financier, 28ème Session, Procès-verbal de la 10ème séance tenue à Genève le 7 Septembre 1927, IATE A3-S1-Y1-F8/1. For a succinct formulation of the trade-off involved, as seen from the Greek side, see the anonymous memo (probably drafted by Tsouderos) titled *Signification de la Stabilisation*, n.d., in IATE A3-S1-Y2-F173/1.

[29] Petridis (2000 [1932]); see also Tsouderos to Varvaressos, 19 May 1928, IATE A3-S1-Y1-F32/1 and Kyrkilitsis (1935: 30).

[30] The formulation belongs to Finlayson, as recorded in Comité Financier, 38ème Session, Procès-verbal de la 2ème séance tenue à Genève le 8 Mai 1930, IATE A3-S1-Y1-F25/2, p. 27. The decision to keep these deposits – which amounted to some 450 million drs. – with the National Bank led to acrimonious debates with the Financial Committee. The compromise reached in July 1929 was mainly a face-saving exercise, inasmuch as the Bank of Greece merely got to 'rubber stamp' the deposits, which remained with the National Bank until 1950; cf. the heated debate at the Comité Financier, 35ème Session, Procès-verbal de la 3ème séance tenue à Paris le 5 Juin 1929, IATE A3-S1-Y1-F21/2.

which served to regulate the market and represent commercial bank interests. Liberated from the state's stifling embrace, the National Bank would only see its dominance grow over the next years.[31]

Of course, none of this had seemed problematic in 1927, when Diomidis and Tsouderos were negotiating in London and Geneva. Their objective had been to conform to the League's prescriptions and protect Greece's note issue from government interference. Inasmuch as the Financial Committee also insisted on bank reform, their priority had been to keep the National Bank from harm's way. Neither of them foresaw any trouble between the new and old banks of issue. In fact, their private correspondence reveals that their primary concern was the potential reaction of rival banks, notably the Bank of Athens, who might attempt to convert substantial amounts of drachmas into foreign exchange; Diomidis even went so far as to approach the Bank of England for a stand-by credit facility to stave off potential speculative attacks.[32] But the National Bank was beyond suspicion, expected to work in harmony with the Bank of Greece. After 1928, Diomidis and Tsouderos would come to realise just how optimistic their expectations had been.

Most of the Bank of Greece's early policy initiatives can be seen as attempts to overcome the inherent flaws in its makeup: the operation of clearing houses to reduce cash transactions and encourage banks to keep reserves with the Bank of Greece; the establishment of local branches to absorb foreign exchange in agricultural export towns; the elaborate plans to set up a nation-wide Savings Bank to drain liquidity from commercial banks or repackage state loans into marketable short-term securities; the legislative campaigns to force data disclosure and revive Strakosch's 7 per cent minimum reserve requirement – each reflect the Bank's efforts to

---

[31] The numbers cited refer to discounts and other short-term credits outstanding on 31 December 1928, for the Bank of Greece and commercial banks, as published in Table 11 of the Bank of Greece Monthly Bulletin, 1(1), January 1930, p. 15. On the meteoric rise of the National Bank *after* 1928, see Kyrkilitsis (1935) and Kostis (2003: chapter 17, aptly titled 'The empire strikes back'); for a history of the HBA see Kostis (1997).

[32] Diomidis had always pressed for such credits to support the stabilization 'psychologically'. As he explained to Siepmann 'what he must have is a soldier dressed in gold from head to foot, standing at the door of a room which contains nothing whatever' (Note by H. A. Siepmann, 24 February 1927 in BOEA OV80-1/36). Demands became more persistent on the eve of stabilization, as speculative attacks were feared (Note of conversation between Siepmann and Tsouderos, 30 January 1928, in BOEA OV80-3/34), only to be rebuffed each time as 'wholly absurd' (Niemeyer to Diomede, and Niemeyer to Finlayson, both on 23 March 1928, in BOEA OV9-190/183–184).

reinforce its position.[33] Despite support from the Financial Committee, most initiatives failed to yield the desired results. What is more, they provoked hostility from commercial banks, who viewed the institution's actions as antagonistic (Mazower, 1991: 147). According to Tsouderos, one senior National Bank official even threatened him with an attack on the central bank's reserves, should it continue to set up new branches and compete for foreign exchange and discounts on the open market (Venezis, 1966: 63).

Relations with the government were also fraught with difficulties. Mandated to report to the Financial Committee on a quarterly basis, the Bank was often the unwitting harbinger of uncomfortable news from Geneva. This strained its relationship with the government, which expected the Bank of Greece to do its bidding. Thus, senior government officials occasionally made 'improper excursions into bank rate policy', which led to further rounds of protest from abroad.[34] Inevitably, as Dubois had predicted, the government continued to rely heavily on the advice and resources of the National Bank, often leaving the central bank on the side-lines.

Politics also played a part. From the very start, bank reform had been controversial. In August 1927, the conservative People's Party had withdrawn from the coalition government, ostensibly because it disagreed with the proposed reform; henceforth, the party would remain hostile to the Bank of Greece, periodically proposing its abolition.[35] Soon thereafter, the leader of the progressive Agricultural Labour Party and minister of agriculture, Alexandros Papanastassiou, threatened to withhold support for the Geneva Protocol, unless steps were also taken to establish an Agricultural Bank (Kostis, 2003: 305f). Another campaign to avert bank reform was waged a few months later by another party leader, Georgios Kondylis, albeit to no effect.

---

[33] Pyrsos (1946) offers the most detailed discussion of the early years of the Bank's policy; Finlayson's confidential annual reports are also useful windows into the operation of the Bank, as are the minutes of Financial Committee meetings with Bank representatives. The *Annual Report to the Governor of the Bank of Greece*, 6 April 1929, in BOEA OV9-192/2, the *Memorandum* dated 2 October 1930, in IATE A3-S1-Y2-F60/1 and the *Notes on statement to the Financial Committee*, 11 May 1931 in BOEA OV80-4/107b offer key summaries.

[34] Niemeyer to Finlayson, 27 November 1928, in BOEA OV9-191/142, in reply to Finlayson's complaints that Venizelos had pressured the Bank to lower its discount rate too soon.

[35] The deeper reasons for its withdrawal were probably internal to the party; an unwillingness to share responsibility for the austerity measures concomitant of stabilization may also have played a role; Dafnis (1997 [1974]: 381f); Pepelasis-Minoglou (1993: 149); cf. Tsouderos to Agnides, 10 August 1927, in IETA A3-S1-Y1-F35/16.

The most significant blow came in June 1928, when the former prime minister and founder of the Liberal Party, Eleftherios Venizelos, voiced his opposition to the handling of negotiations in Geneva. The coalition government was forced to resign, paving the way for Venizelos's return to the premiership. British officials in Athens informed the Treasury and the Bank of England that 'the old man [was] on the war path', proposing the de facto merger of the Bank of Greece with the National Bank.[36] By July, Athens was rife with rumours of Diomidis's impending dismissal and the reversal of the bank reform. In what was to become an oft-repeated manoeuvre in coming years, London and Geneva put their foot down, pointing out that central bank independence had been an integral part of the 1927 Protocol and a precondition for continued League support.

As it turned out, Venizelos was merely using the Bank of Greece as a stalking horse to attack the National Bank and renegotiate the division of the spoils created by the revaluation of its foreign exchange reserves at the new parity. Over the coming months, he attacked the National Bank for defrauding the state of its rightful 'surplus value' gains and threatened it with new taxes. The dispute was settled in June 1929, when the National Bank was forced to cede half the gains to the state.[37] The unexpected upshot of this compromise was the Agricultural Bank, financed largely by the state's share of the spoils, which started its operations in early 1930 and became the second most important new bank of the interwar years. Much like the Bank of Greece, its early years were spent in the shadow of the National Bank.

All this controversy did not help bolster the position of the Bank of Greece, at a time when 'important political and business sections assumed a definitely hostile attitude to the new institution', as wrote Finlayson in

[36] Lorraine (Minister Plenipotentiary to Greece in Athens) quoted by Waley to Niemeyer, 28 June 1928, in BOEA OV9-191/90a. See also Finlayson, Memorandum, 2 July 1928, in BOEA OV9-205 and his letter to Niemeyer of 4 July 1928, in BOEA OV9-191/98. Having spent three years abroad, Venizelos returned to Greece in April 1927; about a year later – and less than a fortnight after the de jure stabilization – on 23 May 1928, he announced his intention to return the leadership of the Liberal party.

[37] The National Bank argued these gains were its rightful compensation for having lost the note issue. Venizelos thus proposed the return of the note issue to the National Bank, to eliminate the need for any compensation. The 'gold covers dispute' raged for over a year and was ultimately a power-struggle between the country's top bank and its top politician. Pyrsos (1936: chapter 7) and Kostis (2003: chapter 16) offer excellent summaries; for a peek into the negotiations themselves, see Finlayson to Niemeyer, dated 3 August 1928, in VA Φ357-36-37, as well as the exchanges between Niemeyer, Finlayson, and Strakosch between October 1928 and January 1929 in BOEA OV9-206.

autumn 1928. Things might have been different if the government had made a public declaration in support of the newcomer:

> Unfortunately, no such declaration was ever made public and the private banks still assume an attitude of sullen hostility to the Central Institution. This is bound to continue so long as the Bank of Greece continues to work in a position of semi-complete isolation. For the time being, it is nobody's child and its real activities are little more than those of a rather pretentious exchange-shop.[38]

9.4 AN UNEXPECTED CRISIS

Following his triumphant return to the political centre-stage in 1928, Venizelos won the August elections in a landslide. During his campaign, he promised to modernize the country, introduce sweeping reforms, and promote public investment. Over the next few years, extensive drainage and irrigation works either reclaimed or protected some 300,000 hectares of land, and total cultivable area rose by 30 per cent; road networks expanded by 15 per cent; port infrastructure was improved, and more than 3,000 new school buildings were erected, just as the major projects to provide Athens with adequate water and power were concluded. Many of these projects were kept off budget, being financed by contractors, who undertook to raise the necessary foreign capital. With the drachma back on gold, Greece rushed to tap international markets: between 1928 and 1932, public and private borrowing from abroad amounted to some £23.8 million, or about a quarter of GDP.[39]

The rapid accumulation of foreign liabilities did not go unnoticed in London. As early as September 1928, Niemeyer warned Venizelos that 'as experience has shown elsewhere, a newly stabilized economy at once becomes the happy hunting ground for foreign contractors and bond sellers, each anxious to sell his own particular interest.'[40] Eyebrows may

---

[38] Finlayson, Relations between the state and the central bank of issue, 10 October 1928, in BOEA OV9-206/2.

[39] This figure comprises foreign lending ('assistance from abroad') plus *net* bank credits (receipts minus payments), as recorded on the Balance of Payments for 1929–32, Table XIX of Bank of Greece (1934); GDP figures are from Kostelenos et al. (2007). Besides the tripartite loan (partially credited in 1929), the largest public loans credits in 1932 were two loans for productive works (1928, 1931) and one for school buildings, worth a total of £7.9 million net (Dertilis 1936: 134). Pepelasis-Minoglou (1993) surveys public works financed with foreign capital, including some major private loans. For summaries of Venizelos's economic policy, see Mazower (1991: 108ff) and Dafnis (1997 [1974]: 497–514).

[40] Niemeyer to Venizelos, 6 September 1928, in VA Φ332-07. Niemeyer's letter came at a time when Venizelos was flirting with Seligman, a New York investment bank, for a new

have been raised, but no alarms went off, not least since many of those happy hunters were British contractors and financiers. Besides, ever since Greece had re-opened negotiations with the League in 1926, the country had been fairly candid about the role of foreign capital in its development strategy: few of the League's terms would have been tolerated without the prospect of securing foreign loans.

In the long run, public works would boost agricultural production and close the country's trade deficit, thus securing the foreign exchange necessary to service the debt incurred. In the short term, continued access to capital markets would ensure the steady refinancing of foreign liabilities. In other words, Greece's outward-oriented development strategy was predicated on its short-term ability to secure enough foreign exchange to service its debt. The strategy was both risky and ambitious, but it was hardly original. Many European countries, including most recipients of League loans, were following a similar path of action. There was just one problem: the year was 1928. The sands of international capital mobility were about to run out – not just in Greece, but everywhere.

No country escaped the grip of the Great Depression that swept the world after 1929.[41] Greece was no exception, although the insular nature of its more traditional sectors, coupled with the stimulus provided by foreign lending, shielded the economy from a deep recession (Table 9.1).

Greece felt the onset of the crisis through the collapse of primary product prices and trade. By 1932, its exports had shrunk by 30 per cent in volume and 60 per cent in value, taking a heavy toll on rural income from such crucial cash crops as tobacco and currants. Bad weather and a succession of crop failures, the worst in 1931, further depressed rural incomes, prompting the government to suspend taxes, raise tariffs, and guarantee higher minimum prices for farm products. Deflation was mild compared to other countries, but it was enough to increase real debt, which became unbearable for most farmers and many businesses. Stock-market prices tumbled, and defaults multiplied, as manufacturing production shrank by about 10 per cent. Heavily concentrated, the financial

loan, which the British actively sought to quash; cf. Niemeyer to Leith Ross (Treasury), 29 November 1928, in BOEA OV9-196 and Finlayson to Niemeyer, 17 January 1932, in BOEA OV9-206/32. Needless to say, competition between different foreign interests was closely monitored by diplomatic missions in Athens.

[41] This paragraph can't do justice to the literature on the Great Depression in Greece; Kostis (1986) and Mazower (1991) remain classics but see also some chapters in Kakridis and Rizas (2021).

TABLE 9.1 *Greece and the Great Depression: economic activity, prices/wages, monetary, bank, and fiscal data, 1928–1932*

	1928	1929	1930	1931	1932
Economic activity (1928=100)					
Gross Domestic Product (real)	100	104.7	102.2	97.9	106.3
% change		4.7	−2.4	−4.1	8.5
Agricultural production	100	90.1	97.0	87.2	117.4
% change		−9.9	7.6	−10.1	34.6
Manufacturing production	100	105.6	97.8	94.6	93.2
% change		5.6	−7.4	−3.2	−1.5
Industrial production	100	107.8	103.9	103.3	102.8
% change		7.8	−3.6	−0.6	−0.5
Prices and wages (1928=100)					
Wholesale price index (WPI)	100	105.3	95.7	85.5	102.7
% change		5.3	−9.1	−10.7	20.1
Consumer price index (CPI, Athens)	100	100.7	95.0	91.3	97.5
% change		0.7	−5.7	−3.8	6.8
Average wages in manufacturing	100	98.2	96.3	90.0	89.4
% change		−1.8	−1.9	−6.6	−0.6
Monetary and bank data (end of year, 1928=100/bn. drs.)					
Forex reserves (1928=100)	100	73.5	71.0	41.6	37.7
% change		−26.5	−3.4	−41.4	−9.5
Banknote circulation (1928=100)	100	91.3	84.4	70.4	82.9
% change		−8.7	−7.5	−16.6	17.8
Monetary base [M0] (1928=100)	100	90.5	88.2	74.7	80.7
% change		−9.5	−2.5	−15.2	8.0
Money supply [M3] (bn. drs.)	:	:	22.3	21.8	20.7
% change		:	:	−2.5	−4.9
Commercial bank deposits (bn. drs.)	:	:	18.1	17.1	16.4
% change		:	:	−5.4	−4.1
Commercial bank credits (bn. drs.)	:	:	15.3	15.2	14.7
% change		:	:	−1.0	−3.0
Fiscal data (% of GDP)					
Primary balance	12.2	10.5	8.9	5.4	2.2
Budget balance	3.0	−1.1	−3.1	−6.6	−3.1

: not available (in the course of 1930, the Bank of Greece changed its data collection methodology, forcing commercial banks to report activity in all currencies and branches; this creates a data discontinuity that makes comparison with previous years problematic).
Sources: See Appendix.

sector proved quite resilient, although several smaller banks did not survive.[42] The fall in imports offset the loss of exports, but not the collapse of invisibles, which traditionally financed the country's trade deficit; as foreign exchange reserves began to shrink, the first seeds of doubt about the drachma's ability to stay on gold were planted.

Inevitably, the Bank of Greece found itself at the centre of the maelstrom. Worried about its cover ratio, the bank responded to the loss of reserves by allowing note circulation to fall (Table 9.1), fuelling complaints of 'monetary stringency'. In the press, the Bank was accused of strangling business at the very moment it needed liquidity most; in parliament, the government was interpellated over monetary policy, just as financial circles were abuzz with 'hysterical rumours that the National Bank is out to bust [the central bank] and take over again'.[43] Conscious of Geneva's watchful gaze, Venizelos gave a half-hearted defence of the Bank in public. Privately, he kept pressing it to let the cover ratio drop to its legal minimum and inject additional liquidity. When Finlayson and Tsouderos demurred, he accused them of 'gold fetishism'.[44]

These accusations were exaggerated. The fall in circulation was modest compared to the loss of reserves; aggregate bank deposits and loans continued to increase and bank liquidity remained high – hardly a sign of 'monetary stringency'. Inasmuch as complaints were incited by the National Bank, they might have been an attempt to deflect attention at a time when the government was pressing for moratoria on farmers' debt.[45] Either way, the dispute was revealing of the continued tension between the new bank of issue, the government, and commercial banks; as for the prime minister, Finlayson was quite certain there would be 'trouble with the old man'.[46]

Trouble, however, was also brewing in Geneva. Unlike the Bank's critics at home, the Financial Committee felt Greek policy had been far

---

[42] Bank bankruptcies are discussed in Kyrkilitsis (1934: 12–14) and Alogoskoufis and Lazaretou (1997: 130). The stock market crash strained those with loans backed by securities, including stockbrokers, who pleaded for additional credits; see Finlayson to Niemeyer, 3 December 1929, in BOEA OV9-207/1.

[43] Finlayson to Niemeyer, 13 February 1930, in BOEA OV9-192/71A; the same letter contains details on the parliamentary interpellation. Details of the press campaign on 'monetary stringency' in Finlayson's Memorandum dated 25 November 1929, in BOEA OV9-206/78.

[44] Finlayson to Niemeyer, 14 February 1930, in BOEA OV9-192/72. Government pressure had started as early as October 1929; see Finlayson to Niemeyer, 29 October 1930, in BOEA OV9-206/68.

[45] Finlayson to Niemeyer, 29 October 1929, in BOEA OV9-206/68.

[46] Finlayson to Niemeyer, 14 February 1930, in BOEA OV9-192/76.

too complacent: the discount rate had remained unchanged, the drachma had not depreciated to its gold export point and the central bank's own discounts had increased. As Niemeyer put it, 'during the latter part of 1929, the Bank of Greece went to sleep'.[47] As of 1930, the need to tighten domestic credit became a recurrent theme in the letters from London and Geneva.

The Bank of Greece pleaded innocence and pointed to its inherent weaknesses: given the size of its portfolio, neither a higher discount rate nor open market operations could have influenced domestic credit. Commercial banks, and especially the National Bank, were too strong, and could safely ignore – or even threaten the central bank.[48] Working closely with the government, the National Bank was injecting additional cash to support farm prices; it spearheaded efforts to stabilize the stock market, bail out major industrial concerns, and take over troubled banks. In many respects, the National Bank was acting as Greece's lender of last resort (Kostis, 2003: 423ff).

This line of defence has since become a staple of the literature and is overdue for reassessment. During the crisis, the Bank of Greece deliberately exaggerated its weakness, in order to deflect criticism and strengthen its position in the financial system. Commercial banks may have determined the money multiplier, but the Bank of Greece still controlled the monetary base and could – at the very least – reduce circulation *pari passu* with the drain in foreign exchange. Inasmuch as it sterilized part of this drain, it was making a deliberate policy decision.

Given its statutory obligation to keep foreign exchange reserves at 40 per cent of circulation, the bank would have to withdraw 2.5 drachmas for every (equivalent) drachma of reserves lost in order to stabilize the cover ratio. Without an adequate portfolio to carry out open market operations, the bank was indeed unable to contract as much. Its own data, however, reveal it was also unwilling to contract even at a one-to-one rate: between May 1928 and the sterling crisis of September 1931,

---

[47] Notes of interview with O. Niemeyer in London, 25 January 1930, in BOEA OV9-192/70. The Bank kept the discount rate at 9 per cent from late 1928 till September 1931. On the Bank's reluctance to use the gold points, see Comité Financier, 37ème session, Procès-verbal de la troisième séance tenue à Genève, le 21 January 1931 in IATE A3-S1-Y1-F24/2.

[48] For a succinct formulation of the argument by Greek representatives, see Comité Financier, 42ème session, Procès-verbal de la huitième séance tenue à Genève, le 7 Septembre 1931, p. 10 in IATE. A3-S1-Y1-F29/1; see also Pyrris (1934: 85ff) and Pyrsos (1946: 326ff).

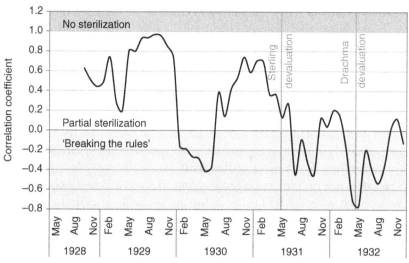

FIGURE 9.2 Playing by the rules in Greece? Correlation between monthly changes in foreign reserves and circulation (previous six months)
Source: See Appendix.

the bank lost reserves worth 1,622.6 million drachmas, but only withdrew 1,096.8 million from circulation, or 67.6 per cent of the loss; by the time Greece left gold, that ratio had fallen to 27.4 per cent. The Bank of Greece was actively leaning against the wind by injecting additional drachmas into the market whenever foreign exchange transactions drained the money supply.[49]

The motive behind this policy is obvious: a more aggressive contraction would have hurt the economy. As a senior bank official would explain, in January 1930, 'the situation in Greece is different from that in other countries; there is the refugee question to be dealt with, and efforts must be made not to create unemployment.'[50] Figure 9.2 tracks the coefficient of correlation between monthly changes in reserves and circulation over a six month 'moving window'; a more conventional plot of the cover ratio can be found in Figure 9.4 (discussed later) Apart from a few months in mid-1929, the coefficient never approached unity. The

---

[49] A more detailed version of the argument, which dates back to Nurkse (1944) and Bloomfield (1959) is found in Kakridis (2021); the Greek case fits neatly into Eichengreen's (1990) cross-sectional estimates.
[50] Comité Financier, 37ème session, Procès-verbal de la quatrième séance tenue à Genève, le 21 Janvier 1930, p. 20 in IATE A3-S1-Y1-F24/2.

Bank was systematically attempting to cushion the domestic money supply from changes in reserves. The timing of these interventions is telling: whenever the country was buffeted by international shocks – late in 1929, during the Creditanstalt crisis, or after the sterling devaluation – the Bank of Greece responded by increasing domestic circulation.[51] This was not a sign of weakness – it was a deliberate policy choice.

Priority to internal objectives, however, jeopardized the country's external commitment to the gold standard. The Bank of Greece tried to have its cake and eat it: it attempted to stay on gold but shied away from strict adherence to the rules of the game. As its foreign reserves became depleted, it resorted to various accounting tricks to inflate the cover ratio and pleaded with the IFC to defer foreign exchange purchases for debt service.[52] Criticism abroad was deflected by exaggerating the institution's inherent defects. In retrospect, this strategy helped Greek monetary policy steer clear from a deeper recession. At the time, it was used to absolve the central bank of responsibility and garner support for its efforts to tighten control over the financial system. Bank of Greece officials blamed the loss of reserves on the 'continued fight of [commercial] banks against us, which is carried on either out of spite or out of a bad estimation of things', the National Bank invariably being the prime suspect.[53]

Diomidis was more cautious. He agreed that 'clipping the National Bank's wings was advisable' but attributed the loss of reserves to more fundamental macro-economic imbalances. Writing to Tsouderos, in May 1931, he explained how 'the cover keeps shrinking because of successive [current account] deficits; certainly, if other banks followed a healthier policy, our position would be better, but I doubt it would make a large difference, for our entire economy is constantly in deficit.'[54]

The governor was right. Convenient as it may have been to blame the banks, they were not the main culprits for what was ultimately the effect of an international credit squeeze. As late as 1931, Greece borrowed a total of

---

[51] The impact on broader money (M3) is, as one might expect, less pronounced, not least since the shocks also affected the money multiplier, an effect the Bank of Greece was trying to dampen.

[52] The attempts to convince the IFC to defer foreign exchange purchases, reminiscent of the BIS mandate to minimize reparations-related shocks to Germanys' foreign exchange market, led to a bitter conflict between the Bank and the IFC, documented in Pepelasis-Minoglou (1993: 181–184).

[53] Tsouderos to Niemeyer, 10 February 1931, in BOEA OV80-4/83· cf. Tsouderos to Diomidis, Diomidis Archive owned by N. Pantelakis, F1-SF1-SE4-FI24-IT5.

[54] Diomidis to Tsouderos, 23 May 1931, in Diomidis Archive owned by N. Pantelakis, F1-SF1-SE4-FI24-IT10; see also Pantelakis (2018: 303) and Venezis (1966: 76).

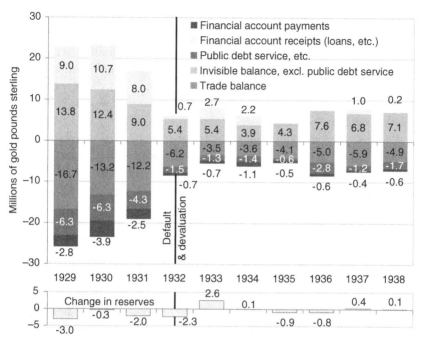

FIGURE 9.3 Greece's balance of payments, 1929–1938
Source: See Appendix.

£8 million to cover 42 per cent of the foreign exchange needs (Figure 9.3). With both exports and net invisibles shrinking, without continued access to foreign capital, the loss of reserves was guaranteed – no matter how commercial banks responded. But Diomidis was only half-right. The only bank that could have responded was the central bank, which he governed, but he was reluctant to sacrifice domestic economic activity to defend the cover. By mid-1931 Greece's outward-oriented development strategy was rapidly unravelling, along with expectations of the country's ability to remain on gold. Under these circumstances, neither commercial banks nor investors could be blamed for walking away from the drachma. In September 1931, the walk turned into a stampede.

9.5 THE BATTLE FOR THE DRACHMA

Sterling's devaluation on 21 September 1931 sent shockwaves through the global financial system. At an emergency meeting held at the Bank of Greece, government and bank representatives agreed that the drachma would remain on gold.[55] Having long touted the benefits of stabilization, authorities were loath to abandon the linchpin of their externally financed development strategy, not least since devaluation was tantamount to default: debt service was largely payable in gold and absorbed 40 per cent of budget revenue.[56] The drachma was immediately re-pegged to the dollar, though no additional restrictions were imposed. The 'battle for the drachma' was on.

Panic gripped markets almost immediately. Asset prices collapsed and on Wednesday, trading on the Athens stock market was suspended. By Friday, the Bank of Greece had lost $3.6 million and was forced to swallow its pride and ask the National Bank for emergency credits to prop up its cover ratio (Figure 9.4). Exchange controls and import restrictions were hurriedly introduced over the weekend. The discount rate, which had been kept at 9 per cent since November 1928 was raised to 12 per cent, only to be throttled back to 11 per cent the next month; given the size of the Bank's portfolio, the changes were largely meant to provide a signal, rather than exert any direct influence. The signal was picked up and commercial discount rates, which had hitherto followed an independent path, followed suit. Taken aback by the violence of capital flight and eager to pin the blame on someone, Venizelos forced, the bank's governor, Diomidis to resign. After a few weeks of political intrigue, he was replaced by Tsouderos, who found himself at the helm of the bank he had helped establish, just when calls for its abolition were making headlines again.[57]

---

[55] At the time of sterling's devaluation, the Bank of Greece held roughly a quarter of its reserves in sterling (£1.6 million); losses were later estimated at 174.7 million drachmas, or 7.5 per cent of the country's reserves (Pyrsos, 1946: 101). The statutory implication that sterling could no longer be considered part of the official reserves was a much greater challenge; in practice, this provision was ignored, and the Bank of Greece kept its sterling, albeit at its market parity.

[56] Most Greek foreign loans were either payable in currencies that were still pegged to gold or carried gold clauses; interestingly enough, this is rarely mentioned by those who favoured a Greek devaluation in September 1931, including Niemeyer, who seems to have had the sterling tranche of the League loans in mind when he proposed that the drachma follow sterling but continue servicing its debt. The composition of Greek foreign debt is discussed in L. Palamas, *Note on the mode of service of the external Greek loans*, 2 November 1931, in BOEA OV80-5/74. Greek authorities were acutely aware of the legal complications that would arise should the country seek to pay in depreciated currency; see the various memos drafted in the fall of 1931 in IATE A5-S1-Y5-F15.

[57] For a more detailed chronicle, see Venezis (1955: 97ff), Mazower (1991: 143ff), Kostis (2003: 376ff) and Kakridis (2017: 68ff). For the English translation a headline-making newspaper article calling for the Bank of Greece to be re-absorbed by the National Bank, written by the senior economic advisor to the Liberal party, Dimitrios Maximos, see BOEA OV80-5/94c; for reactions to the Maximos plans by Diomidis, see OV80-6/29.

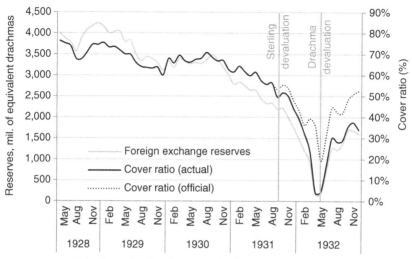

FIGURE 9.4 Flight from the drachma: Bank of Greece foreign exchange reserves and cover ratio, 1928–1932
Source: See Appendix.

With the introduction of exchange controls, Greece joined the scores of countries that – while nominally still on gold – were already drifting away from their official parity (Eichengreen, 1992: 231). Controls throttled capital outflows but also discouraged remittances and other invisible inflows; the current account was deep in the red and expectations of an impending devaluation became widespread. Within weeks, the drachma was trading at a heavy discount on the black market.

Economic historians have criticized Greek policymakers for 'adhering to a legalistic view of the economy' (Kostis, 2003: 376), and acting as 'late proselytes', willing to 'choke off liquidity' to defend the gold standard (Christodoulakis, 2013: 282), 'naively believing they would be able to further tap international capital markets' (Pepelasis-Minoglou, 1993: 186). Justified as they may be in hindsight, these critiques ignore both the conditions and mindset of the times, while overestimating the stringency of the Bank's policy.

Greece's ability to defend its parity hinged on its ability to plug its current account deficit (Figure 9.3). In theory, this could be attempted through a massive contraction in domestic liquidity and imports; alternatively, as the French member of the Financial Committee unabashedly suggested, Greece could dismiss civil servants, cut salaries by 20 per

cent and close down some of its schools.[58] Fortunately, Greek authorities
never contemplated such a contraction, especially on the eve of an election
year. Fiscal measures were modest, import volumes dipped only mildly,
and the Bank of Greece continued its policy of sterilization (Figure 9.2).
The only alternative acceptable to the Greek side was to find some combination of debt relief and renewed capital injections. By autumn 1931,
this was precisely what Athens was expecting.

As late as April 1931, Greece had floated a £4.6 million loan to
fund its public works through an international bank syndicate headed
by Hambros. Placement had been difficult, with the British tranche
being under-subscribed. However, the operation was considered a success and even the governor of the Bank of England, Montagu Norman
expressed his surprise.[59] Having thus confirmed the country's financial standing, authorities were confident that (once the sterling crisis had blown over) access to international capital would be restored.
Meanwhile, the country would continue to play by the rules of the
game – or at least appear to be doing so. As the crisis drew on, authorities in Athens pinned their hopes on a coordinated initiative, presumably under the auspices of the League. By January 1932, Venizelos was
touring European capitals advocating a five-year debt moratorium and
a $50 million loan to complete his public works initiative.[60] The battle
for the drachma now resembled a siege, whose outcome hinged on the
defenders' ability to hold the fort until a foreign relief party came to
the rescue.

Venizelos's demands were unrealistic although plans for an international relief operation were not without adherents in Geneva. Meeting in
March 1932, the Financial Committee offered a sanguine assessment of
the situation in Austria, Hungary, Bulgaria, and Greece and proposed a

---

[58] As reported in Tsouderos to Venizelos, 12 March 1932, in IATE A3-S1-Y2-F2/3.

[59] H. Finlayson, *Report on recent loan negotiations in London, 1st March-19th April*, 30
April1931, in BOEA OV80-4/101b and Pepelasis-Minoglou (1993: 388–392). The loan
carried an effective interest rate of 7.3 per cent; £2 million were floated in London, £1
million was taken up by the National Bank in Athens, the balance being sold in Sweden,
Switzerland, Holland, and Italy. New York banks were also approached but refused
to participate; Speyer and the National City Bank, however, agreed to advance cash
against £1.5 million-worth of Greek Treasury bills, thus renewing past advances for
another year.

[60] Venizelos's proposals are contained in *Memorandum on Greek financial situation*,
20 January 1932, in BOEA OV80-6/4. London's reactions are hardly encouraging, as
shown in the reply by Neville Chamberlain to Venizelos, 28 January 1932, in BOEA
OV80-6/18.

'concerted effort' to guarantee loans to these countries, giving them some 'breathing space' until the international situation improved.[61] In Greece's case, the proposed loan was $10 million and was accompanied by strict fiscal terms and a temporary transfer moratorium on amortization. Fears of contagion certainly informed the Committee's attitude. Niemeyer, who had recently visited Athens to assess the situation in person, had told Venizelos not to 'monkey around' with League loans. Devaluation and default were all the more unpalatable to Geneva, since Greece appeared to be in better shape than other League debtors who were still clinging on to gold. A decision to suspend Greek debt service was bound to trigger further defaults.[62]

Between 1929 and 1931, Greece's economy had shown some resilience. The slump in agricultural prices had increased the country's debt burden, but since Greece mainly imported food and raw materials, its terms of trade had not deteriorated. Thanks to a reserve army of urban refugees, wages were flexible and absorbed most price changes, just as tariffs offered manufacturing increased protection. The same tariffs propped up the budget, which had not come under serious strain before the imposition of exchange controls. Most significantly, foreign loans had provided external stimulus and funded extensive public works. Thanks to those loans, and the willingness of the Bank of Greece to sterilize foreign exchange outflows, the financial system remained liquid and both credits and deposits continued to grow, albeit in nominal terms, until August 1931. Legal protections afforded to foreign exchange deposits meant commercial banks did not witness extensive withdrawals over the summer.[63] In this context, it is less surprising that Greek policymakers felt the country could hold the fort for some time.

---

[61] League of Nations Financial Committee, *Report to the Council on the Work of the Forty-Fifth Session of the Committee* (Paris, 3–24 March 1932), 29 March 1932, C.328.M.199.1932.II.A.

[62] Niemeyer to Loveday, 29 January 1932, in BOEA OV80-6/17; a few days earlier, Niemeyer had noted that 'the Greek position is by no means as bad as that of certain other countries which we know' (BOEA OV80-6/5); see also Tsouderos to Venizelos, 12 March 1932, in IATE A3-S1-Y2-F2/3.

[63] Deposits in foreign exchange, a legacy of the pre-stabilization years and testimony to many people's continued mistrust of the drachma, were payable in foreign exchange or their *market* equivalent in drachmas; parliament had imposed a five-year moratorium on any law concerning such deposits, which was due to expire on 8 June 1932. Incidentally, this explains why no commercial bank was eager to abandon gold in September 1931: their extensive foreign exchange liabilities, many of them backed by gold-backed Greek sovereign bonds, meant that a devaluation would hurt commercial banks, especially if it were accompanied by a default. See also footnote 70.

To critics of the Bank's policy, none of this mattered, since no relief party was coming to lift the siege. Sooner or later, Greece would have to abandon the gold standard. The battle was merely postponing the inevitable, wasting valuable time and foreign exchange. In hindsight, there is no doubt the critics were right. Greek authorities misread the prospects of international cooperation and underestimated the shift in investor sentiment (Accominotti and Eichengreen, 2016). In September 1931, however, few in Greece could have been so clairvoyant as to opt for immediate devaluation and default – not least since the prospect of foreign retaliation had not been ruled out. It is no accident that, for all their complaints about specific battle tactics, no opposition party openly challenged the decision to defend the drachma. Nor was anyone willing to step up when Venizelos later offered to resign and form a coalition government (Dafnis, 1997 [1974]: 533). What opposition parties lacked in policy ideas, they made up in *schadenfreude*.

Ideas mattered. Many believed the crisis to have been caused by excess speculation which had to be purged before the economy could recover. Finlayson had dubbed his proposed method of credit restraint the 'castor oil method', because of the cathartic effects it would alleg-edly bring to the economy.[64] More importantly, memories of inflation were still fresh and added to the 'fear of floating' (Calvo and Reinhart, 2002). Asked by a senior British Treasury official why Greece was not devaluing the drachma to relieve the pressure on its economy, Venizelos explained that he 'was afraid it would cause general collapse and infla-tion'.[65] Such entrenched misgivings, informed by the traumatic experi-ence of past inflation, played a crucial role in delaying many countries' exit from gold (Wolf, 2008).

What is more, the country was sailing in unchartered waters. Despite their orthodox ideas, policymakers were well aware that present condi-tions defied orthodoxy. Uncertainty about the future added to their vacil-lations. In a hurriedly scribbled postscript to one of his letters to Venizelos, Tsouderos wondered whether there was any point in keeping up the fight: 'In the event of a global readjustment, won't everyone be in the same posi-tion anyway? Or might those who gave up sooner gain by arguing their

---

[64] For an early formulation, see Finlayson, *Report on the Proceedings of the meeting of the Financial Committee*, February 1930, in BOEA OV9-192/66. For a tour d' horizon of Greek economists' views on the Great Depression, see Psalidopoulos (1989); cf. De Long (1990) on what he calls the inter-war 'liquidationist' view.

[65] Leith-Ross, Note of an interview with Venizelos, 28 January 1932, in BOEA OV80-6/15.

burden had been intolerable? [...] Some moments are so challenging and extraordinary that one cannot know which road to take.'[66]

As it turned out, neither road was long. By early 1932, negotiations in London and Paris had led nowhere. Geneva was increasingly pessimistic about the prospects of the upcoming Lausanne conference and officials were bracing for turbulence. Things in Athens were no better. For the first time since the onset of the crisis, commercial banks were feeling the pinch: liquidity was down and the fall in bond prices had left a hole in their balance sheets. In February, the default of a small commercial bank caused a minor bank run, which galvanized the Bank of Greece into action. For the first time ever, the country's new bank of issue acted as the lender of last resort, promptly doubling its credits.[67] With import restrictions taking a toll on public revenue, the central bank also made its first advances to the state – thus resuming a practice that had been abandoned since the signing of the Geneva Protocol. By the end of March, central-bank lending had more than tripled since the sterling devaluation and circulation was up for the first time in months. Having thus abandoned all pretence of stringency, bank officials were already working out the details of the upcoming devaluation.[68]

The final act was played out in April, during an emergency session of the League of Nations Council devoted to Greece, Austria, Hungary, and Bulgaria. Debtor countries reiterated their proposals for a transfer moratorium and additional credits. The response was underwhelming, even by League standards: any moratorium or new loan had to be taken up directly with the bondholders. Venizelos promptly announced Greece had crossed the Rubicon. On 27 April the drachma formally abandoned the gold standard. A few days later, Greece missed the coupon payments on its foreign debt. The battle had been lost.[69]

---

[66] Tsouderos to Venizelos, 8 March 1932, in IATE A3-S1-Y2-F2/1; at the time Tsouderos was in Paris, trying to solicit French support for new credits. For an astute discussion of the interplay between uncertainty and ideational lock-in, see Blyth (2002).

[67] It is thus unclear why Chouliarakis and Lazaretou (2014: 26) believe the Bank did not undertake any rescue effort and 'continued to implement a strongly anti-inflationary policy'.

[68] As early as 10 February 1932, a Bank memo for Venizelos considers devaluation and default inevitable and proposes a dual exchange rate system. The decision to increase the discount rate (from 11 per cent) to 12 per cent in January 1932 was a statutory obligation inasmuch as the Bank's cover had just fallen below 40 per cent and should *not* be mistaken for a policy shift.

[69] Details in the lengthy memorandum by Finlayson, *Greece's departure from the Gold standard*, 9 May 1932 in BOEA OV80-6/167, which also contains translations of key legislation.

9.6 THE AFTERMATH, 1932–1939

The drachma's fall was precipitous; within days, it was trading at half its par value. Expectations of further depreciation, fuelled in part by the Bank of Greece's secret purchases of foreign exchange on the black market, led to overshooting. Early in 1933, the exchange rate turned a corner and by late March the dollar devaluation had caused substantial capital inflows. Instead of letting the exchange rate rebound, however, the central bank rushed to re-peg to gold (via the Swiss franc), thus 'locking in' a 58 per cent devaluation and siphoning off foreign exchange to rapidly rebuild its reserves (Figure 9.5).[70] Of course, convertibility was never restored, and exchange controls remained in place, as the state regulated trade and the Bank of Greece monopolized foreign exchange transactions. A multiple exchange rate system was introduced, with basic food imports being afforded more favourable rates, paid for by de facto export levies. The official parity was maintained until September 1936, when the collapse of the 'gold bloc' promoted a switch back to a sterling peg.

The Bank of Greece's policy after 1932 has often been described as 'conservative'; freed from the statutory shackles imposed by the gold exchange standard, the Bank is nevertheless said to have refrained from policy activism (Trapeza tis Ellados 1978: 142). The 1933 decision to re-peg the drachma has been described as 'surprisingly inflexible', revealing 'an obsession with orthodoxy' (Kostis 2003: 477; 2018: 256). Pushing the argument even further, Christodoulakis (2013) has recently argued that Greece constitutes an exception to the rule that countries released from their 'golden fetters' recover faster. In his view, devaluation ended up eroding domestic demand and prolonging the economy's malaise, which ultimately led to the collapse of democracy in 1936, when Prime Minister Ioannis Metaxas dismissed parliament and imposed a dictatorship of fascist overtones. Using a broad brush, this section sketches

---

[70] Another source of foreign exchange reserves was the so-called drachmification decree of 29 July 1932, which forced the conversion of all domestic liabilities expressed in foreign exchange into drachmas at a rate favouring the drachma. The government defended the measure on equity grounds, arguing that foreign exchange creditors – including holders of deposits in foreign exchange – should not profit from the devaluation. In fact, the measure was aimed to plug a hole in bank balance sheets, where foreign exchange liabilities outstripped assets. See Pyrris (1934: 228–239), Vouros (1938: 52) and Finlayson to Niemeyer, 6 August 1932, in BOEA OV80-7/61; cf. H. Finlayson, *The 'drachmification' decrees*, 25 September 1935 in BOEA OV80-13/66.

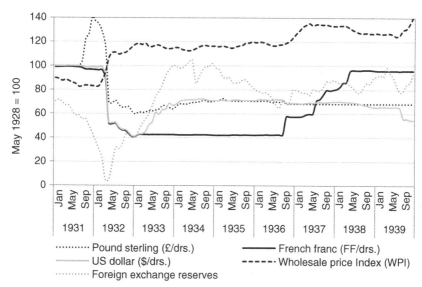

FIGURE 9.5 Drachma exchange rate, prices, and foreign exchange reserves, 1931–1939
Source: See Appendix.

post-1932 policy and performance, focusing on these arguments, both of which are found unconvincing.[71]

Economic recovery after 1932 was swift (Table 9.2). After previous crop failures, the 1932 harvest was exceptionally good and provided much needed relief to the trade balance. Ever since the first refugee loan, land reform and reclamations had been steadily increasing the area under cultivation. Finally, the results were becoming apparent; along with a belated recovery in yields, agriculture soared: by the end of the decade, production had doubled. Manufacturing rebounded strongly in 1933 and continued to rise steadily thereafter; thanks to a rapid build-up in energy, industrial production grew even faster. Much of the stimulus for this growth came from the country's inevitable shift to autarky. The effects of devaluation were compounded by import quotas that favoured incumbent merchants and encouraged import substitution. The return

---

[71] Greece's economic developments and policy in the 1930s are discussed more generally by Mazower (1991: part IV); for those able to read Greek, Kostis (2018: chapter 3) offers a modern tour d' horizon while Petmezas (2012) provides valuable insights into agricultural policy. Monetary developments are best chronicled in Pyrsos (1946); in what follows, references to these works are kept to a minimum.

TABLE 9.2 *Greece after 1932: economic activity, prices/wages, monetary, bank, and fiscal data, 1933–1939*

	1933	1934	1935	1936	1937	1938	1939
Economic activity (1928=100)							
GDP (real)	112.5	115.2	120.0	120.5	137.6	134.7	134.5
% change	*5.8*	*2.4*	*4.2*	*0.3*	*14.2*	*−2.1*	*−0.1*
Agriculture	145.6	140.8	142.3	140.0	200.9	180.6	:
% change	*24.0*	*−3.3*	*1.0*	*−1.6*	*43.4*	*−10.1*	:
Manufacturing	105.2	120.2	125.2	129.9	135.3	140.8	:
% change	*12.8*	*14.3*	*4.2*	*3.7*	*4.2*	*4.0*	:
Industry	114.4	133.0	141.3	152.2	159.5	168.8	:
% change	*11.3*	*16.2*	*6.2*	*7.7*	*4.8*	*5.8*	:
Prices and wages (1928=100)							
Wholesale prices	116.1	114.5	116.5	118.5	132.6	129.5	128.4
% change	*13.0*	*−1.4*	*1.8*	*1.7*	*12.0*	*−2.4*	*−0.8*
Consumer prices	106.5	109.6	111.9	114.7	127.6	128.6	127.3
% change	*9.2*	*2.9*	*2.1*	*2.5*	*11.3*	*0.7*	*−1.0*
Manuf. wages	96.8	97.6	102.4	:	:	:	:
% change	*8.3*	*0.8*	*4.9*	:	:	:	:
Monetary and bank data (end of year, 1928=100/bn. drs.)							
FX reserves (1928=100)	93.2	95.3	76.9	74.8	82.3	84.0	86.9
% change	*147.3*	*2.3*	*−19.3*	*−2.7*	*10.0*	*2.1*	*3.4*
Circulation (1928=100)	95.8	99.9	105.2	109.0	119.1	127.2	166.1
% change	*15.6*	*4.4*	*5.3*	*3.6*	*9.3*	*6.8*	*30.6*
M0 (1928=100)	108.8	119.8	107.4	117.6	120.7	127.7	158.5
% change	*34.7*	*10.1*	*−10.4*	*9.5*	*2.6*	*5.9*	*24.1*
M3 (bn. drs.)	23.3	24.5	24.7	25.7	29.2	31.4	34.1
% change	*12.5*	*5.2*	*0.8*	*4.0*	*13.6*	*7.6*	*8.5*
Deposits (bn. drs.)	18.3	19.4	19.2	20.0	23.0	24.7	25.2
% change	*11.6*	*5.6*	*−0.9*	*4.2*	*14.8*	*7.7*	*1.8*
Credits (bn. drs.)	14.8	16.1	17.0	18.2	21.7	21.1	20.8
% change	*0.4*	*9.3*	*5.6*	*6.7*	*19.4*	*−3.0*	*−1.1*
Fiscal data (% of GDP)							
Primary balance	5.3	4.9	4.5	1.5	1.7	:	:
Budget balance	1.7	0.9	1.0	−2.4	−1.3	:	:

: data not available. The table continues the data series presented in Table 9.1 above.
Sources: See Appendix.

of inflation caused real interest rates to plummet and liquidated hitherto 'frozen' credits. These results are hard to miss or decouple from the country's departure from gold.[72] Greece is no exception to the golden fetters rule; nor is there a simple correlation between economic and political crisis. Most historians pin the unravelling of Greece democratic institutions to the social cleavages that emerged after the country's expansion during the Balkan wars, as well as the failure of the political class to adapt to changing circumstances. If anything, the historian Mark Mazower argues, 'it was economic *growth*, which taxed the capacities of the existing system and pointed the way to an eventual realignment of political forces' (Mazower 1991: 285, emphasis in original).

Of course, one should not paint too rosy a picture of Greece's post-1932 economy. Shut off from global financial markets, the country was forced to rely on a much smaller pool of domestic resources. Imports fell from approximately 40 per cent of GDP in 1928 to an average of 20 per cent in the 1930s and balance of payments constraints remained binding (Figure 9.3). The shift to autarky led to de-specialization, eroding productivity. Impressive growth rates built upon meagre baseline figures. Manufacturing, which still accounted for a fraction of total output, was fragmented and uncompetitive. Conditions in the countryside remained precarious and debt continued to weigh heavily on farmers' shoulders. Export industries such as mining, metalworks, and tobacco suffered the most and cities that had once been export hubs became rife with discontent. Unable to mediate in labour disputes, authorities turned increasingly to repression, directed against the threat of communist agitation – more imagined rather than real. Exports stagnated, with tobacco proving the hardest to recover, at least until clearing arrangements gradually made Germany into Greece's main trading partner.[73]

Faced with these challenges, economic policy struggled to adjust. The People's Party government that came to power after 1932 was torn between the need for greater state intervention and its own conservative

[72] Christodoulakis (2013) places undue weight on notoriously unreliable data, not least unemployment figures 'estimated' by the federation of labor unions and used primarily as a bargaining chip (Charitakis et al., 1932: 355–358). He also draws on the Kostelenos et al. (2007) data which are less reliable as a source of *annual* growth rates; production volume indices are far more reliable for those years and far more consistent with the estimates of GDP growth used here (and adopted by Maddison (2003: 29), who also explains the limitations of alternative series).

[73] Greece's external trade policy and the role of clearings in particular is discussed at length in Kacarkova (1976) and Pelt (1998), with Kakridis (2017: 118–131) focusing on the role of the Bank of Greece in clearing arrangements.

predilections. Ambitious policy initiatives faltered on opposition from the party's own base (Mazower 1991: 236ff). Industrial investment was discouraged to minimize capital imports and promote 'rationalization'. It was only in agriculture that the institutional apparatus established over the previous decade was put to extensive use: minimum price guarantees, improved crop varieties, increased credit facilities and debt moratoria – courtesy of an increasingly activist Agricultural bank – became the norm. Public works continued, albeit at a diminished pace. The suspension of external debt amortization and the curtailment of interest payments provided much needed relief to the budget.[74] After 1932, servicing annual debt (interest *plus* amortization) dropped to around 4 per cent of GDP, down from almost 11 per cent in the 1927–31 period.[75] Along with a gradual rebound in tax revenue, this helped Greece avoid a severe retrenchment on primary spending. The Bank of Greece had to step in to provide sizeable advances to the government, with the amounts outstanding averaging 5 per cent of GDP at year's end. But these were largely offset by the drachma deposits held by the IFC, which continued to collect revenue pledged for debt service and refused to release it without foreign bondholder consent (Vouros 1938: 102–110). Such accounting squabbles aside, the overall budgetary position remained fairly satisfactory, with the first deficits appearing after 1936, when the Metaxas regime increased defence expenditure for rearmament (Table 9.2).

Turning to monetary policy more generally, there is little evidence of it being unduly restrictive. Inasmuch as exchange controls and trade restrictions remained in place, the decision to re-peg the drachma to gold in 1933 primarily served as an anchor to guide domestic inflation expectations. In practice, effective exchange rates were determined by a host of restrictions, import levies, and export subsidies – not to mention the special rates at which trade was carried out through clearing arrangements. Moreover, there was an obvious difference between re-pegging after a 58 per cent devaluation and trying to avoid a devaluation in the first place.

---

[74] Negotiations with foreign bondholders started in the summer of 1932. A stopgap agreement to suspend amortisation and transfer 30 per cent of interest due was reached on the eve of the September elections, but final settlement would be postponed for decades. Temporary agreements were renegotiated almost annually; by January 1940, interest transfers were up to 43 per cent. A summary of negotiations is found in Wynne (1951: 352–357); for the Bank of Greece's role, see Kakridis (2017: 85–91 and 115–118).

[75] Vouros (1938: 64) and Mazower (1991: 198–202) reach similar conclusions but provide more modest estimates; their calculations omit economies from the suspension of amortization or the curtailment of interest on internal debt.

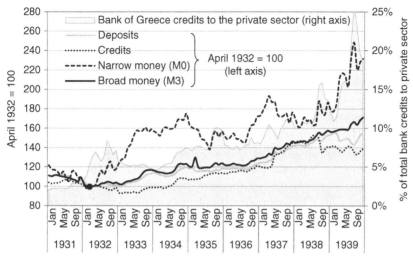

FIGURE 9.6 Key monetary and credit variables in Greece, 1931–1939
Source: See Appendix.

It thus comes as little surprise that, after Chile, Greece experienced the most rapid reflation of any of the countries tracked by the League of Nations after 1931. Still, inflation remained below the rate of depreciation, restoring the real exchange rate to its pre-crisis levels.

None of this seems consistent with monetary stringency. Of course the devaluation caused a temporary dip in total loans and deposits, not least since all foreign currency deposits were forcibly converted into drachmas at an unfavourable rate (Figure 9.6). Yet most monetary indices soon surpassed their pre-crisis levels and commercial discount rates drifted from their peak of 12 per cent on the eve of devaluation to 7 per cent by January 1934. The Bank of Greece stood by to inject liquidity whenever bank deposits were threatened by political instability and gradually increased its relative position within the banking system. Government advances notwithstanding, the bank's *private* loan portfolio increased from a trifling 2 per cent of total lending in early 1931 to 15 per cent by the end of 1938. The National Bank remained by far the largest institution and had privileged connections to government but the new central bank could no longer be ignored or intimidated as easily.

Relations with the government were harder to navigate. Once the political pendulum had swung back in conservative territory, the Bank of Greece was regarded as a hostile, Venizelist institution that had to be liquidated. The new People's Party government immediately revived plans to merge the Bank of Greece with the National Bank.[76] It was only after repeated protests by London and Geneva that senior government officials reaffirmed their commitment to the Geneva Protocol, in June 1933. But relations with the government remained prickly, for political rather than economic reasons. Following an abortive Venizelist coup, in March 1935, Tsouderos was publicly accused of having abused his position to bankroll the insurgency and had to step down for nine and a half months. The ensuing countercoup purged the upper echelons of the army and bureaucracy from Venizelos supporters and rekindled plans for a merger with the National Bank (Venezis 1955: 182; 1966: 126ff).

In this context, the bank's apparent 'conservatism' can also be cast in another light. In a hostile political milieu that questioned the bank's raison d' être, the decision to peg the exchange rate could be interpreted as an attempt to maintain a semblance of independence by adopting a visible, albeit largely symbolic, nominal anchor. A similar line of reasoning explains the considerable efforts made to maintain a direct line of communication with Geneva. Finlayson's services were retained until May 1937, several years after his initial contract had expired. Not that there was much reason to question the bank's allegiance to the government.[77] In practice, it was probably the shared memory of inflation more than anything else, that explains why Greek policy makers remained cautious not to inflate the economy after 1932. But to blame them for undue conservatism or a delayed recovery is hard to reconcile with the data.

The Metaxas dictatorship did not bring any radical change to the balance of financial power or the outlines of economic policy. Nor did political intrigue subside, as shown by Tsouderos's subsequent removal from office. After a failed attempt to overthrow the dictatorship in 1938, the underground dissenters agreed that the governor of the Bank of Greece was the most suitable candidate to lead the next coup against Metaxas. His liberal connections aside, Tsouderos was seen as a guarantor of monetary stability; apparently, even conspirators had to consider the

---

[76] Finlayson to Niemeyer, 14 and 26 November 1932 both in BOEA OV80-8/37 and 46.

[77] The handling of bilateral clearing balances is a case in point. Over time, tobacco exports to Germany led to the accumulation of substantial credits. By late 1935, the Bank of Greece held a net balance of 24.3 million Reichsmarks (or 984.2 million drachmas). Normally, such balances would be offset by opposite trade flows, but Greece was unable to procure sufficient imports from Germany. Meanwhile, exporters received the equivalent drachmas, thus boosting the money supply and saddling the bank with overvalued Reichsmarks. When the bank sought to reduce these credits in 1936, mass protests by tobacco workers broke out. The government and bank were forced to back down.

inflationary implications of their actions. Alas, in June 1939 the police intercepted some of the governor's private correspondence. Tsouderos was promptly dismissed and replaced by a member of Metaxas's inner circle, the governor of the National Bank, Ioannis Drossopoulos. Inasmuch as Drossopoulos was known for his hostility toward the central bank, this was probably as close as the Bank of Greece ever came to being amalgamated with its predecessor. Yet Drossopoulos died a few days into the job and was replaced by Varvaressos, an inside man with every intention of keeping the Geneva Protocol intact.[78]

On the eve of the Second World War, the Bank of Greece had come a long way from where it had started in May 1928. Its balance sheet had almost quadrupled, and its loan portfolio had grown from a modest 50 million to more than 4 billion drachmas – not to mention the extra 11 billion in state advances. Its original staff of 400 had grown to 2,200, scattered across 20 branches and a brand-new headquarters in downtown Athens. Several of its short-fallings persisted, but it was experiencing sustained growth. It would take the hyperinflation brought by foreign occupation and monetary anarchy in the 1940s to place the Bank of Greece in complete control of the commercial bank system.

APPENDIX: NOTES ON DATA SOURCES

Historical gross domestic product (GDP) estimates by Kostelenos et al. (2007) deflate values by a price index heavily reliant on agricultural prices, which fluctuate wildly and exaggerate overall output swings; Kostelenos et al.'s 2007 figures for 1920–1929 are thus spliced with growth estimates used by Maddison (2003: 29), which are more consistent with production volume indices.

Annual Statistics of Agricultural Production provide yearly volume and price data on production for twenty-two products; the agricultural production index used here is derived by chain-linking value estimates in terms of the previous year's prices. Similarly, Christodoulaki (2001) finds the oft-cited Supreme Economic Council (AOS) indices misleading and comes up with an improved manufacturing and industrial activity index, both of which are used here. Nominal average wage estimates are based on figures for male workers in Riginos (1987: 38), whose estimates are superior to those by Anotaton Oikonomikon Symvoulion (1935: 22).

---

[78] The best background source for the narrative in this paragraph is Dafnis (1997 [1974]: 874–879); on Varvaressos's ascent and policy, see Kakridis (2017: 140ff).

Banknote circulation, money supply, and foreign exchange reserve
data are taken from the Bank of Greece Monthly Bulletin, along with
monthly data on commercial and central bank deposits, loans, and cash
balances; reserve data between September 1931 and December 1933
are corrected for creative accounting practices used to mask the drain
in reserves, as discussed in Pyrsos (1946: 113). Money supply (Mo, M3)
data follow the definitions and methodology of Lazaretou (2014), which
is also the source of exchange rates and price indices. Official and commercial discount rates are derived from Kyrkilitsis (1934) and successive
issues of George Charitakis's *Greek Economic Yearbook* (*Oikonomiki
Epetiris tis Ellados*).

Balance of Payments data are reconstructed from annual Bank of
Greece Governor Reports, starting from table 32 in the Annex to the
Report for 1933. The public revenue and expenditure data cited in most
secondary sources are mutually inconsistent and misleading. Many of
the sources for this confusion are discussed in a short report published
by the League of Nations' Economic Intelligence Unit in 1936, titled
Public Finance, 1928–35. The data used here are compiled from primary
sources, with interest and amortization payments derived separately
from Dertilis (1936: 151).

REFERENCES

Unpublished (Archival) Sources

Istoriko Archeio Trapezas tis Ellados (IATE) [Bank of Greece Historical Archives],
    Athens (Greece).
    A3 Emmanouil Tsouderos Archive
    A5 Kyriakos Varvaressos Archive
Archeio Eleftheriou Venizelou (VA) [Eleftherios Venizelos Archive], Benaki
    Museum, Athens (Greece) [www.venizelosarchives.gr].
Bank of England Archive (BOEA), Bank of England, London (United Kingdom).
    OV80 Overseas Department – Greece
    OV9 Papers of Otto Ernst Niemeyer

Published Sources

Accominotti, Olivier and Eichengreen, Barry (2016). 'The Mother of All Sudden
    Stops: Capital Flows and Reversals in Europe, 1919–32'. *Economic History
    Review*, 69(2): 469–492.
Alogoskoufis, Georgios and Lazaretou, Sofia (1997). *I Drachmi: Nomismatika
    kathestota kai dimosionomikes diataraches sti neoteri Ellada* [The Drachma:

Monetary Regimes and Fiscal Disturbances in Modern Greece]. Athens: IMOP – Athinaïki Oikonomiki Publications.

Anotaton Oikonomikon Symvoulion (1935). *Oi deiktai oikonomikis drastiriotitos tis Ellados kata ta eti 1928–1934* [Economic Activity Indicators for Greece in the Years 1928–1934]. Athens: National Printing Office.

Bank of Greece (1929). *Report for the Year 1928 of the Governor of the Bank of Greece Alex. N. Diomede at the General Meeting of Shareholders on April 6, 1929*. Athens: Bank of Greece.

Bank of Greece (1934). *The Economic Situation in Greece and the Bank of Greece in 1933: Report read by Mr. E. J. Tsouderos, Governor of the Bank of Greece, before the General Meeting of Shareholders Held on February 14, 1934*. Athens: Bank of Greece.

Bloomfield, Arthur I. (1959). *Monetary Policy under the International Gold Standard: 1880–1915*. New York: Federal Reserve Bank of New York.

Blyth, Mark (2002). *Great Transformations: Economic Ideas and Institutional Change in the Twentieth Century*. Cambridge, UK: Cambridge University Press.

Bordo, Michael D. and Rockoff, Hugh (1996). 'The Gold Standard as a "Good Housekeeping Seal of Approval"'. *Journal of Economic History*, 56(2): 389–428.

Calvo, Guillermo A. and Reinhart, Carmen M. (2002). 'Fear of Floating'. *Quarterly Journal of Economics*, 117(2): 379–408.

Charitakis, Giorgos, Kalliavas, Aristomenis, and Mikelis, Nikolaos (eds.) (1932). *Oikonomiki Epetiris tis Ellados 1931* [Greek Economic Yearbook 1931]. Athens: Typografeion S. K. Vlastou.

Chouliarakis, George and Lazaretou, Sophia (2014). 'Déjà vu? The Greek Crisis Experience, the 2010s Versus the 1930s: Lessons from History'. Bank of Greece Working Paper 176.

Christodoulaki, Olga (2001). 'Industrial Growth in Greece between the Wars: A New Perspective'. *European Review of Economic History*, 5: 61–89.

Christodoulaki, Olga (2015). 'The Origins of Central Banking in Greece'. PhD Dissertation. London School of Economics and Political Science.

Christodoulakis, Nicos (2013). 'Currency Crisis and Collapse in Interwar Greece: Predicament or Policy Failure?' *European Review of Economic History*, 17(3): 272–293.

Dafnis, Georgios (1997 [1974]). *I Ellas metaxy dyo polemon, 1923–1940* [Greece between Two Wars, 1923–1940], 2nd. ed. Originally published in 1974. Athens: Kaktos Publications.

De Long, Bradford J. (1990). '"Liquidation" Cycles: Old-Fashioned Real Business Cycle Theory and the Great Depression'. *National Bureau of Economic Research Working Paper Series*, No. 3546.

Dertilis, George B. and Costis, Constantine (1995). 'Banking, Public Finance, and the Economy: Greece, 1919–1933', in Charles H. Feinstein (ed.), *Banking, Currency, and Finance in Europe Between the Wars*. Oxford: Oxford University Press, 458–471.

Dertilis, Panagiotis B. (1936). *Le problème de la dette publique des états balkaniques*. Athens: Éditions Flamma.

Dritsa, Margarita (2012). *Emmanouil Tsouderos, 1882–1956: kentrikos trapezitis kai politikos* [Emmanouil Tsouderos, 1882–1956: Central Banker and Politician]. Athens: Bank of Greece.

Eichengreen, Barry (1990). 'International Monetary Instability between the Wars: Structural Flaws or Misguided Policies', in Yoshio Suzuki, Junichi Miyake, and Okabe Mitsuaki (eds.), *The Evolution of the International Monetary System*. Tokyo: University of Tokyo Press, 71–116.

Eichengreen, Barry (1992). *Golden Fetters: The Gold Standard and the Great Depression, 1919–1939*. New York: Oxford University Press.

Eichengreen, Barry and Sachs, Jeffrey (1985). 'Exchange Rates and Economic Recovery in the 1930s'. *Journal of Economic History*, 45(4): 925–946.

Flores Zendejas, Juan H. and Decorzant, Yann (2016). 'Going Multilateral? Financial Markets' Access and the League of Nations Loans, 1923–8'. *Economic History Review*, 69(2): 653–678.

Kacarkova, Vera (1976). 'Handelsbeziehungen zwischen Deutschland und Griechenland in den 30er Jahren des XX. Jh.'. *Études Balkaniques*, 3: 43–60.

Kakridis, Andreas (2009). 'Deus Ex Machina? Truman/Marshall Aid, Engineers, and Greece's Post-war Development Discourse'. *Journal of Modern Greek Studies*, 27(2): 241–274.

Kakridis, Andreas (2017). *Kyriakos Varvaresos: I viografia os oikonomiki istoria* [Kyriakos Varvaressos: Biography as Economic History]. Athens: Bank of Greece.

Kakridis, Andreas (2018). 'I ptochefsi tou 1893 kai o Diethnis Oikonomikos Elegchos' [The 1893 Default and International Financial Control]. *Neoellinika Istorika*, 5: 195–240.

Kakridis, Andreas (2021). 'I Trapeza tis Ellados kai i "machi tis drachmis": apantontas se orismenes vasikes katigories' [The Bank of Greece and the "Battle for the Drachma": Responding to Some Basic Charges], in Andreas Kakridis and Sotiris Rizas (eds.), *I Krisi tou 1929 kai i Ellada: Oikonomikes, politikes kai thesmikes opseis* [Greece and the Crisis of 1929: Economic, Political and Institutional Aspects]. Athens: Bank of Greece, 71–101.

Kakridis, Andreas and Rizas, Sotiris (eds.) (2021). *I Krisi tou 1929 kai i Ellada: Oikonomikes, politikes kai thesmikes opseis* [Greece and the Crisis of 1929: Economic, Political and Institutional Aspects]. Athens: Bank of Greece.

Kontogiorgi, Elizabeth (2006). *Population Exchange in Greek Macedonia: The Rural Settlement of Refugees 1922–1930*. Oxford: Oxford University Press.

Kostelenos, Georgios, Vasileiou, Dimitrios, Kounaris, Emmanouil, Petmezas, Sokratis, and Sfakianakis, Michail (2007). *Piges oikonomikis istorias tis Neoteris Elladas: Posotika stoicheia kai statistikes. Akatharisto Egchorio Proion, 1830–1939* [Sources in Modern Greek Economic History: Quantitative Data and Statistics. Gross Domestic Product, 1830–1939]. Athens: National Bank of Greece Historical Archive & Center for Planning and Economic Research.

Kostis, Konstantinos P. (1986). *Oi trapezes kai i krisi, 1929–1932* [Banks and the Crisis, 1929–1932]. Athens: Commercial Bank of Greece Historical Archive.

Kostis, Konstantinos P. (1997). *Synergasia kai antagonismos: ta 70 chronia tis Enosis Ellinikon Trapezon* [Cooperation and Competition: 70 Years of the Hellenic Bank Association]. Athens: Alexandreia Publications.

Kostis, Konstantinos P. (2003). *Istoria tis Ethnikis Trapezas tis Ellados, 1914–1940* [History of the National Bank of Greece, 1914–1940]. Athens: National Bank of Greece.

Kostis, Konstantinos P. (2018). *O Ploutos tis Elladas: I Elliniki Oikonomia apo tous Valkanikous Polemous Mechri Simera* [The Wealth of Greece: Greece's Economy from the Balkan Wars until Today]. Athens: Pataki Publications.

Kostis, Konstantinos P. and Tsokopoulos, Vasias (1988). *Oi Trapezes stin Ellada, 1898–1928* [Banks in Greece, 1898–1928]. Athens: Hellenic Bank Association & Papazisis Publications.

Kyrkilitsis, Andreas D. (1934). *Ai trapezai en Elladi* [Banks in Greece]. Athens: n.p.

Kyrkilitsis, Andreas D. (1935). *I Ethniki Trapeza tis Ellados kai allai emporikai trapezai kata tin periodon 1928–34* [The National Bank of Greece and Other Commercial Banks During 1928–34]. Athens: Kyklos Publications.

Lazaretou, Sophia (1996). 'Macroeconomic Policies and Nominal Exchange Rate Regimes: Greece in the Inter-war Period'. *Journal of European Economic History*, 25: 647–670.

Lazaretou, Sophia (2005). 'The Drachma, Foreign Creditors, and the International Monetary System: Tales of a Currency during the 19th and the Early 20th Centuries'. *Explorations in Economic History*, 42: 202–236.

Lazaretou, Sophia (2014). 'Greece: From 1833 to 1949', in *South-Eastern European Monetary and Economic Statistics from the Nineteenth Century to World War II*. Athens, Sofia, Bucharest and Vienna: Bank of Greece, Bulgarian National Bank, National Bank of Romania and Oesterreichische Nationalbank, 101–170.

Lazaretou, Sophia (2015). 'The Evolution of Banking and Central Banking in Modern Greece: A Historical Retrospect'. *History of Economic Thought and Policy*, 1: 59–82.

Maddison, Angus (2003). *The World Economy: Historical Statistics*. Paris: Organisation for Economic Co-operation and Development.

Mazower, Mark (1991). *Greece and the Inter-war Economic Crisis*. Oxford: Oxford University Press.

Meyer, Richard Hemmig (1970). *Banker's Diplomacy: Monetary Stabilization in the Twenties*. New York and London: Columbia University Press.

Nurkse, Ragnar (1944). *International Currency Experience: Lessons of the Inter-war Period*. New York: Columbia University Press for the League of Nations Economic, Financial and Transit Department.

Pantelakis, Nikos S. (1988). *Symmachikes pistoseis: Kratos kai Ethniki Trapeza (1917–1928)* [Allied Credits: State and the National Bank of Greece (1917–1928)]. Athens: National Bank of Greece Cultural Foundation.

Pantelakis, Nikos S. (2018). *Alexandros N. Diomidis (1874–1950): Enas afthentikos ekprosopos tis astikis taxis* [Alexandros N. Diomidis (1874–1950): A Genuine Representative of the Bourgeoisie]. Athens: Metamesonykties Publications.

Pelt, Mogens (1998). *Tobacco, Arms and Politics: Greece and Germany from World Crisis to World War, 1929–41*. Copenhagen: Museum Tusculanum Press.

Pepelasis-Minoglou, Ioanna (1993). 'The Greek State and the International Financial Community, 1922–1932: Demystifying the Foreign Factor'. PhD Dissertation. London School of Economics and Political Science.

Petmezas, Sokratis (2012). *Prolegomena stin istoria tis ellinikis agrotikis oikonomias tou mesopolemou* [Prolegomena to the History of the Agricultural Economy in Interwar Greece]. Athens: Alexandreia Publications.

Petridis, Pavlos V. (ed.) (2000 [1932]). *To ergon tis Kyverniseos Venizelou kata tin tetraetian 1928–1932: Ti ypeschethi proeklogikos kai ti epragmatopoiise* [The Venizelos Government in Action between 1928 and 1932: Election Promises and Actions]. Originally published in 1932. Athens: University Studio Press.

Ploumidis, Spyridon (2013). '"Peasantist Nationalism" in Inter-war Greece (1927–41)'. *Byzantine and Modern Greek Studies*, 37(1): 111–129.

Psalidopoulos, Michalis (1989). *I krisi tou 1929 kai oi Ellines oikonomologoi – Symvoli stin istoria tis oikonomikis skepsis stin Ellada tou mesopolemou* [Greek Economists and the Crisis of 1929 – A Contribution to the History of Economic Thought of Interwar Greece]. Studies in Modern Greek History. Athens: Commercial Bank of Greece Foundation for Research and Education.

Psalidopoulos, Michalis (2019). *History of the Bank of Greece, 1928–2008: From Government's Banker to Guardian of Financial Stability*. Athens: Bank of Greece.

Pyrris, Nicolas (1934). *La crise monétaire en Grèce* [The Monetary Crisis in Greece]. Paris: Librairie L. Rodstein.

Pyrsos, Georgios A. (1936). *Symvoli eis tin istorian tis Trapezis tis Ellados. Tomos A' – Ta kata tin idrysin* [Contribution to the History of the Bank of Greece. Vol. A – Founding the Bank]. Athens: Kyklos Publications.

Pyrsos, Georgios A. (1946). *Symvoli eis tin istorian tis Trapezis tis Ellados. Tomos Defteros* [Contribution to the History of the Bank of Greece. Vol. 2]. Athens: Typoekdotiki.

Riginos, Michalis (1987). *Paragogikes domes kai ergatika imeromisthia stin Ellada, 1909–1936: Viomichania-Viotechnia* [Productive Structures and Labour Wages in Greece, 1909–1936: Industry and Small-scale Manufacture]. Athens: Commercial Bank of Greece Foundation for Research and Education.

Santaella, Julio A. (1993). 'Stabilization Programs and External Enforcement'. *Staff Papers – International Monetary Fund*, 40(3): 584–621.

Schuker, Stephen A. (2003). 'Money Doctors between the Wars: The Competition between Central Banks, Private Financial Advisers, and Multilateral Agencies, 1919–39', in Marc Flandreau (ed.), *Money Doctors: The Experience of International Financial Advising 1850–2000*. London and New York: Routledge, 49–77.

Thomadakis, Stavros B. (1985). 'Monetary Arrangements and Economic Power in Nineteenth-Century Greece: The National Bank in the Period of Convertibility, 1841–1877'. *Journal of the Hellenic Diaspora*, 12(4): 55–90.

Tooze, Adam and Ivanov, Martin (2011). 'Disciplining the "Black Sheep of the Balkans": Financial Supervision and Sovereignty in Bulgaria, 1902–38'. *Economic History Review*, 64(1): 30–51.

Tounta-Fergadi, Areti (1986). *To prosfygiko daneio tou 1924* [The 1924 Refugee Loan]. Thessaloniki: Paratiritis Publications.

Trapeza tis Ellados (1978). *Ta prota peninta chronia tis Trapezis tis Ellados* [The First Fifty Years of the Bank of Greece]. Athens: Bank of Greece.

Tunçer, Ali Coşkun (2015). *Sovereign Debt and International Financial Control: The Middle East and the Balkans, 1870–1914*. Basingstoke, UK; New York: Palgrave Macmillan.

Valaoritis, Ioannis A. (1902). *Istoria tis Ethnikis Trapezis tis Ellados, 1842–1902* [History of the National Bank of Greece, 1842–1902]. Athens: n.p.

Venezis, Ilias (1955). *Chronikon tis Trapezis tis Ellados* [Chronicle of the Bank of Greece]. Athens: Bank of Greece.

Venezis, Ilias (1966). *Emmanouil Tsouderos, o prothypourgos tis Machis tis Kritis* [Emmanouil Tsouderos, the Prime Minister of the Battle of Crete]. Athens: n.p.

Vouros, Georgios K. (1938). *Ta deka eti tis Trapezis tis Ellados* [Ten Years of the Bank of Greece]. Athens: n.p.

Wolf, Nikolaus (2008). 'Scylla and Charybdis. Explaining Europe's Exit from Gold, January 1928-December 1936'. *Explorations in Economic History*, 45(4): 383–401.

Wynne, William H. (1951). *State Insolvency and Foreign Bondholders*, Vol. II. New Haven: Yale University Press.

Zolotas, Xenofon E. (1936). *Katefthynseis tis oikonomikis mas politikis* [Directions of our Economic Policy]. Athens: Publications D. N. Tzaka – S. Delagrammatika & Co.

10

The Bulgarian National Bank, 1926–1935

Revamping the Institution, Addressing the Depression

Roumen Avramov

10.1 INTRODUCTION

The Bulgarian National Bank (BNB) played a pivotal role in the economic history of the country,[1] particularly during the institutional transformations that both preceded and accompanied the Great Depression. Yet the measures undertaken during 1926 to 1935 were intrinsically incoherent, and led to contradictory outcomes. While the banking reforms of 1926 and 1928 were conducted in a liberal spirit, and addressed the impact of the wartime economy on the bank of issue and its pre-war structural weaknesses, these newly adopted principles had to be hastily abandoned, or modified, with the onset of the Great Depression. The unintended ad hoc strategic or tactical decisions did help the economy overcome the immediate crisis but they also had long-term consequences. The BNB came to be placed at the core of the interventionist policies during the 1930s and the Second World War, thus paving the way for its future role in the communist planned economy.

After acceding to independence in 1879, Bulgaria boasted many archetypical features of the peripheral economies, including under-developed financial intermediation, frequent monetary regime switches, difficulties in maintaining a fixed exchange rate, and repeated fiscal disequilibria (Bordo and Kydland, 1995; Lazaretou, 2014). The country is part of

---

[1] I draw extensively on previous texts on the history of the Bulgarian National Bank where I discuss the issues in detail (see Avramov, 1999, 2003, 2006, 2007). Those sources are not specifically referred to. I would like to thank Andreas Kakridis for his insightful and pertinent comments, without in any way engaging his responsibility.

South-Eastern Europe, whose economic history has attracted considerable interest both nationally as well as from an international, comparative perspective. In particular, a coordinated research initiative conducted by eight central banks in the region, has led to the establishment of the South-Eastern European Monetary History Network (SEEMHN), which produced a meticulous compilation of parallel monetary and historical statistics. The project has been instrumental in highlighting numerous similarities, noteworthy differences, as well as examples of path dependence (Morys, 2014).

This chapter adds to the literature in three ways. First, I focus on BNB's frequently overlooked state ownership, which sparked fierce domestic opposition to the 1928 reforms initiated by the international financial community. No other country saw the privatization of the central bank figure as prominently at the heart of its reform agenda. The controversy this provoked reveals, in my view, important characteristics of Bulgaria's economic culture. My second point concerns foreign conditionality, as treated by Tooze and Ivanov (2011), who claim that Bulgaria paid the price for creditor concessions after the moratorium on 20 April 1932 through tighter external control. Here, I argue that both the overall framework and rigour of foreign economic supervision had already been embedded in the new style of conditionality attached to the 1926 and 1928 loans sponsored by the League of Nations. Finally, by contrasting the devaluation and default strategies adopted by Bulgaria and Greece during the Depression, I sustain that Eichengreen's hypothesis: namely that heavy defaulters and countries who left the gold exchange standard performed better relative to countries that sought to maintain their reputation as 'decent debtors', is not corroborated by the experience of these two countries (Eichengreen and Portes, 1989; Eichengreen, 1991).

The rest of the chapter proceeds as follows. Section 10.2 outlines the key milestones in the BNB's transformation. Section 10.3 summarizes and puts the main arguments of the debate on the Bank's privatization into perspective. Sections 10.4 and 10.5 comment on the institutional side-effects of the Great Depression, which developed due to the credit crunch, the problem of foreign exchange transfer, and the quest for price flexibility, and had impact on the recovery that ensued. The supporting statistical data are presented in Table 10.1, at the end of the chapter. References to the domestic political background are not covered, as this has already been discussed extensively in Bulgarian historiography.

10.2 THE ROAD TO THE GREAT
TRANSFORMATION: KEY MILESTONES

The BNB was established in January 1879 as a state-owned commercial and deposit bank.[2] In 1885 it was granted the monopoly of note issue, and over the following decades Bulgaria sought to adhere to the leading international monetary standards by pegging the lev to a specie-convertible currency. Successive target systems were the Latin Monetary Union, the classical gold standard, and the gold-exchange standard. Local economic conditions, however, were ill-suited to these systems. This resulted in a series of untimely decisions, inappropriate imitations, and recurrent rule suspensions.

The national currency, the lev, was introduced as legal tender in 1880. It was set on par with the French franc, and the coinage ratios of the Latin Union were adopted as well. A protracted period of monetary chaos ended in 1887, when foreign currencies (basically Russian roubles) where finally demonetized (Dimitrova and Ivanov, 2014). Subsequently, the BNB strove to eliminate the *agio* (the premium on gold vis-à-vis silver) and introduce the gold standard. Those attempts proved unsuccessful due to fiscal laxity and the severe economic crisis of 1897-8. Gold convertibility was suspended between 1899 and 1902. It was only after the floating of two foreign loans that opportunities for arbitrage between gold and silver finally disappeared. From 1906 to 1912, the BNB operated on a quasi-gold standard, linked to the French franc, with a 33.3 per cent cover ratio, and effective gold convertibility at the fixed parity. While silver backed banknotes remained legal until 1924, they were steadily displaced by gold banknotes. In 1912, the BNB's claims in convertible currencies were included in its gold reserves, thus prefiguring the future gold-exchange standard.

The system functioned smoothly until the onset of the first Balkan war, on 10 October 1912. At this point gold convertibility was suspended once again. After the end of hostilities, in July 1913, the external value of the lev was temporarily stabilized, while a deflationary reduction of government debt vis-à-vis the BNB was achieved. However, when Bulgaria entered the First World War on the side of the Triple Alliance, in October 1915,

---

[2] The BNB was established during the Russian occupation (after the Russo-Turkish war of 1877-8) and a couple of months before the modern Bulgarian state became an autonomous entity. Strictly speaking, from 1879 to 1908 (when the sovereign Kingdom of Bulgaria was proclaimed) the country was a principality, tributary to the Ottoman Empire, but enjoying large independence in its domestic and foreign policy.

the government relied heavily on the printing press to finance its soaring debt. From 1916, the Treasury ceded German war advances to the BNB, in exchange for state loans in paper leva. The domestic note issue was supposed to be backed by assets accumulated in Germany, but in reality war advances were a fictious warranty: the German currency itself was inconvertible, and its gold cover had declined to insignificant proportions. After the war, those assets were blocked, and, with German hyperinflation their value evaporated, imposing considerable losses on the BNB.

In 1920 the lev's gold cover had fallen to 1.56 per cent (excluding claims against Germany), the BNB's portfolio of commercial paper discounts was limited, and the monetization of government debt stood at an all-time high. Moreover, as a defeated country, Bulgaria faced exorbitant reparation payments (2.5 billion gold francs), which were imposed by the Treaty of Neuilly in November 1919. Between 1920 and 1923 the lev floated freely, though some unconvincing attempts to stabilize the currency were made. In this unstable economic environment, the need for a complete overhaul of the monetary system had become imperative. Reforms followed the blueprints drawn up at the Brussels (1920) and Genoa (1922) international conferences: both boiled down to a bold deflationary programme and the establishment of a genuine central bank.

The domestic political situation in the post-war years was just as turbulent as the country's exchange rate. After the populist government of the Bulgarian Agrarian Union (1919–23) was overthrown by the military in favour of a right-wing coalition, the following few years were tainted by the harsh repression of any signs of leftist agitation. In January 1926, a more moderate government was installed, heralding a period lasting several years when democratic constitutional order was observed and traditional parties alternated in power.

Two important milestones preceded the transformation of the BNB in 1926 and 1928. The first was a law enacted in July 1922, which limited the bank's advances to the government by capping the BNB notes in circulation to twelve times the value of the Bank's gold reserves. At the same time, a schedule for the amortization of the outstanding government debt to the bank was adopted.[3] The legislation left a window

---

[3] The law followed the logic of the legislation adopted in Greece with the establishment of international financial control in 1898, after the 1893 default. The Greek legislation banned 'the use of money creation as a financing instrument ... set a statutory limit [66 million drachmas] in notes ... specified that starting from 1900, the government should amortize its floating debt to the National Bank of Greece by 2 million drachmas annually' (Lazaretou, 2014: 115).

open for short-term state financing through the discounting of a limited amount of Treasury bills (T-bills) by the BNB.

The second milestone was granting the BNB full monopoly rights in foreign exchange trading and the anchoring of the lev to the dollar on 12 December 1923. Supported by the provisions of the 1922 law and improvements in country's fiscal position, the decision stabilized the currency de facto at one-twenty-sixth of its pre-war parity, a rate that correctly reflected the scale of wartime devaluation.[4] The frictionless operation of the foreign exchange market depended on the balance of payment equilibrium, and the availability of sufficient reserves. Over the next three years, the BNB was able to fill the gaps with short-term credits and thus eliminate previous fluctuations.

De jure stabilization under the gold-exchange standard was clearly the next monetary goal. The move required substantially greater reserves, which in turn implied returning to international capital markets for new loans. For a country in Bulgaria's condition at the time, this was impossible without the intermediation of the League of Nations. The League's support was granted in exchange for radical conditionality, which focused on revamping the bank of issue into a pillar of convertibility and a lender of last resort (a 'banks' bank'). These institutional reforms were laid down in the wake of two operations arranged under the aegis of the League: the Loan for the Settlement of Refugees in Bulgaria (1926) and the Stabilization Loan (1928).

10.3 TEMPLATE VS. IDIOSYNCRASY

Banks of issue are based upon a Faustian bargain: the sovereign's right to issue money is delegated to a special entity, but in return for this privilege the bank is assumed to render services and lend money to the state. The relationship is highly contentious and asymmetric. To the extent that the bank is within reach, the solidity of the pledge depends on the government's restraint. Confidence in the currency, a public good in itself, is at stake, and abuses can have catastrophic economic consequences. The equilibrium rests on delicate conventions and fragile rules.

Granting credible independence to the BNB was thus considered a necessary condition for the success of post-war monetary reform. Attaining this goal meant questioning the Bank's mission, track record, and

---

[4] The exchange rate against the dollar was fixed at 139 leva, corresponding to 92 leva per gram of pure gold.

structure. In a broader sense, it meant questioning the basics of economic life, as shaped by the institution over the previous fifty years. Prior to 1928, the inherent tensions with the state had been handled with mixed success; solutions were usually inspired by mainstream models, with the deviations reflecting local particularities. Various detailed regulations had sought to safeguard the personal and organizational autonomy of BNB management (Balgarska Narodna Banka 1929: 132). In reality, however, the BNB was strongly dependent upon the government. There was no doubt that, in many aspects of its day-to-day operations, quite apart from financial emergencies, politics prevailed over economic and institutional considerations. Only sporadically, did governors' personal touch manage to marginally enhance the Bank's autonomy.

The cash nexus was important here too. In its original form (1879–85), the BNB was not allowed to grant loans to the state. Subsequent amendments permitted direct credits, as long as they were short-term and did not surpass a certain fixed amount. In practice, legal provisions were repeatedly disregarded either due to temporary crises or to systematic policy bias. The most far-reaching example was the outright monetization of budget deficits which led to the wartime inflation (1916–18). The master plan of the BNB's transformation in the 1920s sought to eliminate the possibility that this could ever happen again.

Last but not least, the BNB's autonomy was put under strain by its own activities as a commercial bank. As the oldest and, for a long time, largest credit entity in Bulgaria, the BNB determined the terms of credit on the Bulgarian market. Thus, for all its self-proclaimed conservatism, the Bank propagated a culture of soft budget constraints. Indeed, its lenience towards debtors was considered a virtue by local elites, who believed it contributed to national development. The same logic drove credit relations with the state, whose ownership of the Bank fostered widespread insider-lending and conflicts of interest. Anecdotal intercessions in favour of particular individuals aside, governments were able to orient the BNB's resources towards their own political priorities, support of specific institutions, networks, or social strata, or for addressing emergencies. During the first quarter century of its existence, the Bank lavishly financed municipal, regional, and educational infrastructure as well as other public ventures. The board occasionally tried to resist such political interference, but its effective independence was too limited.

The frequency of state intrusion set up a difficult legacy that had to be tackled with the reforms of 1926 and 1928. A mass of accumulated non-performing debt had to be restructured out of the proceeds of the

League's loans, while a new institutional design had to be developed to forestall further abuses. The BNB was recapitalized as former advances extended – at the government's behest, and under state guarantees – to the two other state banks (the Bulgarian Agricultural Bank and the Bulgarian Central Cooperative Bank) were paid back. Furthermore, improper commercial banking activities were eliminated: the BNB's direct credit operations, including the rollover of arrears and the issuing of state-guaranteed loans were discontinued. Following the League's template, the new 'banks' bank' had to regulate the domestic credit market indirectly, through rediscounting and interest rate policies. The ultimate purpose was to clean up the BNB's balance sheet, that is, to ensure the liquidity needed for its transformation into a genuine central bank as well as unrestricted convertibility at a fixed exchange rate.

The long history of transgressions against the Bank's independence was the principal contention raised by the League of Nations to justify BNB privatization. Shareholders' private interests were held to offer the strongest protection vis-à-vis state interference. The governor of the Bank of England, Montagu Norman, had laid down the principles of this creed, which was accepted as a universal model during the interwar years. The idea, however, was not new. It had already been well established at the time when the BNB was founded and received its note-issuing privilege (Leroy-Beaulieu, 1879). In fact, during the liberal late nineteenth century, the Bank of England served as the archetypal bank of issue. It was a *private* bank, regulated by specific institutional rules and constraints, and by the subtle, informal interplay between the polity and private stakeholders. State owned banks were then an unpopular rarity (Pommier, 1904: 428).

Against this background, the BNB's state-run model constituted an exception, all the more since neighbouring countries like Greece, Serbia, and Romania already had private banks of issue. This exception, defended passionately over the next decades, was a national idiosyncrasy: more than elsewhere, the view of the state as the primary agent of social development enjoyed widespread public support.

The 1879 statute was a temporary arrangement put into place prior to the implementation of thorough legislation in 1885. During this interlude, three projects for a private (or mixed) bank of issue were put forward, only to be rejected. All of these proposals were drafted by foreigners (two by Russian businessmen and one by a French adviser). The 1885 version of the law was based on the understanding that private capital is speculative by nature and has no 'moral rights' over the 'state affair' of money issue and *seignorage*. It was taken for granted that private ownership of the national bank would lead straight to foreign control. Shareholding governance may have been convenient and rational in abstract terms, it was claimed, but it was not appropriate for the archaic socioeconomic conditions prevalent in Bulgaria at the time. Government ownership was assumed to be fully compatible with the Bank's autonomy and proper management.

Before the First World War, occasional domestic political or scholarly proposals for a private bank of issue had been unsuccessfully mooted from time to time. By and large the BNB was perceived to be an honest counterpart to the state, loyally providing its services in exchange for the generous privileges it had been granted. Only foreign creditors persistently advocated drastic changes to this status quo. Their point of view was summed up by Georges Bousquet, the bondholders' representative in Sofia, in a treatise on the BNB submitted to the French minister in Bulgaria in 1909. His overarching message was that the Bank was little more than a department of the Treasury and that the only effective way to guarantee future foreign loans to the country was to redesign it. As a connoisseur of the local milieu, he had no illusions as to the local élites' willingness to privatize the Bank. Thus, Bousquet proposed conditionality along the lines of 'foreign money against BNB reform'. His proposal anticipated, almost to the letter, what was to happen seventeen years later.

In the meantime, Bulgaria was defeated in the First World War and became subject to additional supervision. The Inter-Allied Commission instituted by the peace treaty was entrusted with monitoring the country's demilitarization and securing reparation payments. Those tasks required strong conditionality, encompassing monetary and fiscal policy, taxation, foreign debt management and, critically, institutional reform. In the eyes of the Inter-Allied Commission, the entire economy constituted a pledge against the reparations. Therefore, the Commission acted as the custodian of monetary orthodoxy and liberal economic principles, which were perceived to be threatened by post-war populism and nationalism. It was directly involved in the preparation of the budget and law making; and it constrained the money supply by imposing the currency-board-like law on nominal money issue in 1922. Without promoting the overhaul of the BNB, the Commission – along with the other actors with conditionality powers – supported every move to enhance the Bank's autonomy.

More radical institutional reform came in the mid-1920s, when the constellation of political, economic, and ideological factors related to the 1926 Refugees' Loan brought the questions of the independence and ownership of the BNB back to the fore. The country's international position was affected by the changing approach to the German reparation problem, negotiations with pre-war loan bondholders, and Franco-British rivalry for control of Bulgarian finance. This was important because the League loans created an influential nucleus of Anglo-Saxon creditors whose goals stood at odds with those of the country's pre-war French bondholders.[5]

Precedents of the new borrowing format required by the League of Nations' patronage had been set with the loans to Austria (1922), Hungary (1924), and Greece (1924). A common feature to these was the increasing importance of the League's Financial Committee, where the Bank of England exerted the dominant influence. The Financial Committee was the accepted mediator between the governments of creditor and debtor countries, as well as bondholders' communities. It arbitraged divergent evaluations of country risk in masterful technocratic reports; counterbalanced overdependence on a single creditor (in the case of pre-war Bulgaria, this was France); and it amalgamated the instruments of external control. Overall, the League of Nations had the leverage to exert unique moral/political suasion and provide additional guarantees.

BNB reform entered the League loans' conditionality package from the very beginning. The economic rationale for the transformation was linked to negative developments detailed in a series of alarmist reports by the governor, Assen Ivanov (Mollov, 1926–8). The decrease in the Bank's reserves between 1925 and 1926, he argued, threatened its monopoly of foreign exchange and questioned the country's capacity to meet reparation payments. These problems were explicitly attributed to the government's inconsistent attempts to achieve a reduction in the budget deficit.

The amendments to the BNB law enacted in November 1926 addressed the independence problem in several ways. Credit to the government was tightened further. The state's rights to the Bank's profits were curtailed, at the very time when its obligation to repay its debt to the BNB was being reaffirmed. The board's autonomy was enhanced and the liquidation of the Bank's long-term assets was accelerated. State ownership, however, remained in place. Moreover, economic trouble persisted to the extent that even the Dawson clause was evoked.[6] The proceeds from

---

[5] The Refugees' Loan was floated in pounds and dollars in London and New York respectively. This was the case for the 1928 Stabilization Loan as well, but it included an additional tranche in French francs, floated in Paris.

[6] The principle of the Dawson plan was that reparation payments should not endanger the monetary stability of the debtor in which case they could be suspended.

the Refugees' Loan proved insufficient to secure credible convertibility. The legal cover ratio was not attained and the bank resorted once again to expensive short-term foreign exchange credits (see Table 10.1). Additional external finance was required, fuelling renewed external demands for more stringent institutional reform. During the negotiations for the Stabilization Loan, the debate concerning the BNB's autonomy turned into a doctrinal controversy on the merits of privatization.

The talks began in late 1927. The new bylaws of the Bank of Greece (a private shareholding company), which had recently been approved by the League of Nations, were presented as the blueprint. In the words of the Committee, 'independence can be best secured by constituting the Bank as an independent corporation with shares ... This is the solution which has been adopted in the case of all recently founded central banks ...' (League of Nations, 1927: 378). Following a Financial Committee's mission to Sofia, headed by Sir Otto Niemeyer and including Jacques Rueff, the Memorandum adopted on 11 December 1927 detailed the financial situation in the country, calibrated the parameters of the loan, and formulated the principles for the final reform of the BNB. The British Foreign Office and the Bank of England considered the shareholding scheme to be a *conditio sine qua non* for the Financial Committee's approval of the loan and saw no reason to make an exception for Bulgaria (Mollov, 16 January 1928). The only tolerable compromise was to issue shares which would be temporarily retained by the state, before being offered to private investors.

The British side presented this as an apolitical decision. In their deliberately simplified account, the Financial Committee was portrayed as an impartial intermediary, merely relaying the proposals of European and American bankers. As a matter of fact, the Committee was directly involved in negotiations concerning borrowing terms. In their capacity of former and acting private, or central, bankers, its members were part of the international financial community, and the potential for conflicts of interest was acute. They were by no means unbiased brokers. In Bulgaria's case, the most influential figure was Otto Niemeyer. As a key player in the British financial establishment (the Treasury and the Bank of England), he was repeatedly approached by the Bulgarian authorities for economic, political, and diplomatic advice and intercession. During the most intense phase of the talks with the underwriting banks to secure the Stabilization Loan, letters and telegrams were exchanged between the negotiators and Niemeyer daily, at frantic speed (Mollov, October 1928).

The Protocol approved by the Council of the League of Nations and signed in Geneva by the Bulgarian government on 10 March 1928 paved the way for the Stabilization Loan. Two annexes detailed the amendments to the existing BNB law and the plan for transforming the Bank's statute and ownership into a shareholding entity (League of Nations, 1928). The Bank's capital was to be composed of shares of relatively small denomination, owned exclusively by Bulgarian nationals. A major innovation (recently introduced by the newly created Esti Pank in Estonia) consisted in the appointment of a League adviser to the BNB. This was considered the strongest form of direct external surveillance, and a warranty for the Bank's independence. The adviser was nominated by the League and appointed by the Bulgarian government. He worked 'through and in consultation with the Board ... [had] the right to attend all meetings of the Board ... in a consultative capacity ... to exercise a suspensive veto ... [to approve] any alteration of this Law proposed at a General Meeting' (League of Nations, 1927: 384). The adviser functioned like an informal member of the board who could veto decisions suspected of contradicting the terms of the Protocol. In line with the changing balance of financial power, his appointment generated an intense struggle for influence between France and Britain.[7]

The change in the Bank's ownership was set to follow a vague schedule equivalent to an adjournment *sine die*. The government's commitment was reduced to a simple declaration of intent and a verbal endorsement of the League's principles. The Memorandum stipulated that 'no immediate change has been made in the constitution of the BNB which is a State Bank. The Bulgarian Government has however, undertaken in the Protocol to protect the independence of the BNB from any political influence whatsoever ... Moreover, the Government has recognized that it is desirable to transform the BNB into an independent corporation with a private capital' (League of Nations, 1928: 7). This fuzzy formula was devised to accommodate the concerns of the Bulgarian authorities and placate public opinion. Privatization had been obstinately and successfully resisted both on the domestic and on the diplomatic front. The

---

[7] Between 1928 and 1931 the post of adviser was held by the commissioner of the League of Nations in Bulgaria, the Frenchman René Charron, who had been instated in 1926 according to the stipulations of the Refugees' Loan. In 1931–2 the adviser to the BNB was Jean Watteau, again a French citizen, who became commissioner of the League in 1932. A compromise on the next adviser was struck with the appointment of the 'neutral' Prof. Nicholas Koestner, a respected Estonian academic with British leanings, who exerted the function until 1940.

question of the Bank's ownership ran deep, going to the roots of Bulgarian economic culture, reviving old anxieties and concerns. When the Geneva Protocol was submitted for ratification to the National Assembly in April 1928, customary political intrigues were overshadowed by an ideologically charged discussion.[8]

Paradoxically, however, despite the division of opinion on the BNB's independence and on the priority of the private sector in the economy, both sides converged in defending the maintenance of the Bank's public ownership. Traditionalists opposed the Protocol altogether, bewailing the loss of the credit resources previously supplied by the Bank. The most liberal-minded supporters of the BNB's transformation and autonomy, in turn, resorted to *reductio ad absurdum*. Without rejecting privatization – which the government had, after all, subscribed to on paper – they sought to demonstrate that the League's model was impossible to implement under the current circumstances since such extravagant reform would defy common sense. Bowing to address Bulgarian appeals for a 'democratic' shareholding structure that would offer some protection against 'big finance', the Financial Committee had proposed a cooperative-like oxymoron with highly dispersed capital stock[9], where the most influential private interests would be still represented on the board by business associations. Just like in 1885, the very existence of a capitalist class capable of subscribing the stock offered was questioned in a country where 'there are no more than 1,000–2,000 people who own shares and merely 10,000 know what a share is' (National Assembly 13 April 1928: 1435–1436). In a candid note, the majority's MP Iossif Fadenheht concluded that:

when, one day, the League of Nations will remind us of the formally assumed obligations, the government in place will reiterate: there are not enough capitalists in the country; there is no Parliament able to vote ... the reform; there is no press which could prepare public opinion for this reform [...] The government is as free as if the [Leagues'] formula did not exist [...] We will not say that it is useless [...] We will vote the entire text [of the Protocol] which acknowledges the usefulness of the reorganization. The National Assembly is not willing to argue

[8] Still, reform of the Bank eventually caused a split in the parliamentary majority which provoked the resignation of the government and a cabinet reshuffling in September (Parvanova, 1999).
[9] The BNB was supposed to issue 500,000 shares of 1,000 leva with an agreed limit of 250 shares per person. For the sake of comparison, the capital of the Bank of Greece was divided into 80,000 shares and listed on the Athens Stock Exchange in June 1930. Presently it still has about 19,000 private stakeholders.

on this theoretical question with the Financial Committee. But the Parliament reserves for the government the right to decide when this useful thing will happen because there are many useful things that cannot be realized. (National Assembly 12 April 1928: 1373)

Ultimately, the BNB was never privatized, or indeed transformed into a shareholding company.[10] The political class maintained its cherished direct control of the Bank, while all other features introduced at the League's behest were adopted.

In hindsight, it seems that both sides overstressed the issue and that the importance of ownership was probably exaggerated. Examples of private ownership leading to monetary disruption and, conversely, state banks implementing cautious monetary management abound. Even the British financial press remarked that, while a privatized central bank might be preferable, in less-developed countries a government-controlled bank would be a lesser evil than one subject to foreign control. As a contemporary commentator acknowledged, questions of prestige and dogmatism were at play (Pasvolsky, 1930:112, 295–296). At any rate, the controversy remains indicative of the competing attitudes regarding the management of the economy that were prevalent at the time.

The re-evaluation continued in the 1930s and 1940s. The spirit of the age had become openly anti-liberal and dirigisme was accepted in both East and West. In the wake of the Second World War, a wave of nationalizations affected many central banks including – ironically, given that Montagu Norman was still alive – the Bank of England. In this environment, even Asen Christophoroff, one of the most prominent liberal Bulgarian economists, retrospectively justified the obstinate defence of the BNB's statist model. Without questioning the rationale for an independent central bank, he observed that by attaining one of the highest levels of financial statism in the period preceding the Second World War, the country had probably mitigated the shock of forced post-war nationalizations and accumulated precious know-how of the state-led initiatives to come. The excesses of the communist monobank, however, promptly demonstrated the far-reaching harmful consequences of this system.

---

[10] Strictly speaking, a segment of the BNB's activities was privatized. The functions of its former Mortgage department were taken over by the new Bulgarian Mortgage Bank. Twenty per cent of the capital was owned directly or indirectly by the state, and 70 per cent by foreign investors. After ten years the foreign stake was acquired at par value by the state. The creation of this private bank met similar opposition as the plans to privatize the BNB.

10.4 UNINTENDED TRANSFORMATIONS I: THE 1927–1929 EXPANSION AND ITS AFTERMATH

BNB reforms coincided with the peak of the business cycle that immediately preceded the Great Depression (see Table 10.1). The abrupt shift in economic outlook derailed the reforms: some measures were not implemented, while new changes were made to the Bank.

The capstone of the League's plan for Bulgaria was the lev's legal stabilization with respect to gold. This was expected to take place six months after floating the Stabilization Loan, along with the resumption of unrestricted convertibility. Unfavourable developments after the onset of the Great Depression halted those plans. With the consent of the League's adviser, the law on foreign-exchange transactions was not amended as foreseen and Bulgaria maintained the exchange regime it had introduced in December 1923.[11]

No less important, the BNB had to address the 1927–9 credit inflation, that is, the way the economy was responding to the inflow of the two foreign loans. This entailed managing affluence, which is often harder than dealing with shortages. During this period, private business and the state displayed all the well-known symptoms of irrational exuberance.

The initial wave came with the proceeds of the Refugees' Loan in 1927, the sizable inflow of short-term foreign credits and favourable export performance (see Table 10.1). The improvement in the BNB's foreign exchange balance, however, proved to be short-lived – and expensive. Contrary to its new mandate, the Bank refrained from raising the discount rate so as to avoid negative assessments of the economy's stability; besides, a higher discount rate would have increased the high interest rate differential with other countries.[12] The Governor's warnings about the palliative effects of the loan and the urgent need for structural consolidation in the government's finances were of little avail (Mollov, 28 October 1926, sheet 55). The incipient credit expansion continued to be fostered by this positive outlook and widespread optimism.

This fragile equilibrium was seemingly placed on firmer ground with the Stabilization Loan, but the deal came too late in what was, by then,

---

[11] The BNB did not fully liberalize access to foreign exchange, but discontinued the risk guarantee it provided. The argument was that, given the Stabilization Loan, the Bank did no longer need any short-term borrowing. Foreign business therefore requested that the Bank either resume risk coverage while preserving the forex monopoly, or fully abandon the latter and relegate risk insurance to the private sector (Mollov, 1929).

[12] BNB's discount rate (10 per cent) was the highest in Europe, only comparable to the Greek one.

a disruptive global economic environment. Loan proceeds compounded with the 1928 reform multiplied the BNB's capacity to support domestic credit. Before long, a wave of credit euphoria embraced all segments of the banking system. At its crest were the foreign banks that benefited from rising confidence abroad and access to external resources. The freshly recapitalized state-owned Bulgarian Agricultural Bank, not to mention the hypertrophied and privileged universe of the cooperative banks were also particularly active. The bonanza spread further amidst the myriad of illiquid, poorly capitalized, and often mismanaged small private houses. As might have been expected, these forces led to an import boom and a sharp deterioration of the balance of trade (Table 10.1).

The pace of expansion was unsustainable. The first setbacks were felt by mid-1929 and coincided with the peak of the business cycle in May. Negative indications began undermining the stability of the lev at a time when supporting the exchange rate was supposed to be the BNB's single priority. Once added to the clouds cast over global markets, those trends induced a rise of the discount rate in July, which further destabilized commercial banks. A general crisis of confidence was reached in September–October, when Baklov Brothers,[13] an important establishment, went bankrupt and several other Bulgarian banks started facing insolvency, or a run on their deposits. Some businesses were left to their creditors, but distressed systemic banks and cooperative structures were refinanced by the BNB. By the end of 1929, the Bank tightened its refinancing policy while claiming – a little disingenuously – to have exhibited caution all along, even during the credit boom. The economy entered a protracted contraction of credit which was reinforced by the BNB's statutory discontinuation of direct lending to business and the government. Inevitably, this generated widespread complaints among those who had previously overindulged in credits.

Credit deflation was nurtured by the depletion of the BNB foreign exchange reserves, the withdrawal of deposits from commercial banks, the spread of bankruptcies and insolvencies, the credit squeeze in trade and the accumulation of arrears. A sizeable shock came with the liquidation of the short-term external credits contracted during the boom by

---

[13] It is telling of the credit euphoria that, just three months prior to their bankruptcy, the BNB had inspected the company's books and concluded – by overlooking its negative net worth – that it was a perfectly managed and liquid enterprise. The Bank had decided to refinance the firm on the ground of its owners' reputation ('the past of the firm, their moral qualities, wide networks in the business community and social status'). One of the associates was … the BNB's board member designated by the Chambers of Commerce.

the foreign banks operating in the country. At the same time, the top Bulgarian private institutions curtailed their placements. Government expenditures fell, albeit at a much slower pace than revenues.

Yet the Bank's distress brought about important institutional reforms. The outbreak of the Great Depression and the tightening of monetary policy revealed the real condition of many financial institutions. The need to monitor and, if possible, seek to curb the ongoing decapitalization of the financial sector occasioned the initial move towards a policy of bank supervision. The Law for Deposit Protection (January 1931) laid down the basic standards for liquidity and capital to be enforced by a Banking Council, which would bring together representatives of the Ministry of Finance and the private banks under the leadership of the BNB. The new Council mapped the state of the banking system, orchestrated its restructuring, and removed the wreckage left behind by the unsustainable credit expansion of the late 1920s and the subsequent crisis.

According to its new prerogatives, the BNB functioned as a lender of last resort. Minor episodes of bank distress may not have provoked much turbulence, but the crisis of the 'Credit Bank', which was owned by Deutsche Bank (echoing the Creditanstalt's bankruptcy in Vienna, on 13 July 1931), generated genuine systemic risk in the Bulgarian market. However discretely, the incident was addressed according to the almost complete set of the Bagehot's rules, with implicit reference to the 'too big to fail' argument (Ryaskov, 2006).

In other instances, BNB's discretionary decisions boiled down to the liquidation of establishments that were no longer considered viable; the consolidation of decapitalized banks; and the formation, under state initiative, of some banking conglomerates. The number of private shareholding banks was drastically reduced (Table 10.1) and mergers led to two major new establishments, in 1934. The first was Balgarski Credit, officially a private company, which was de facto state managed, with the BNB in control of most senior positions as its principal shareholder. In the second half of the 1930s and during the Second World War, this mega-structure functioned as a favourite instrument of state intervention. The second major financial pillar was the product of the merger of the Bulgarian Agricultural Bank and the Bulgarian Central Cooperative Bank which formed the mighty Bulgarian Agricultural and Cooperative Bank, active in the influential cooperative world as well as in financing government initiatives. At the same time, as external short-term credits dried up, the 'big four' foreign banks lost their previous position in what was dubbed the 'nationalization' of foreign deposits, that is, their replacement by domestic resources (Christophoroff, 1939: 79). Finally, the conservative credit policy of leading Bulgarian private banks made room for public institutes to increase their market share. It is interesting to note that a significant proportion of savings were withdrawn from the banking system to finance the 1932–3 real estate boom.

As elsewhere, a core macroeconomic problem was the substantial increase in the debt burden brought about by global deflation and the deterioration of the terms of trade (Table 10.1). This translated into trouble with the commercial banks' balance-sheets and the government's budget. In another unintended change in its remit occasioned by the Great Depression, the BNB became involved in the search for solutions. At a time of growing popular resentment, demands for debt relief became widespread and increasingly vocal. Following a series of populist proposals at the National Assembly that would have led toward a would-be 'debtors' dictatorship' and widespread moral hazard, the matter was consistently addressed in August 1934, when a more balanced model was implemented. Its objective was to offset some of the impact of depressed export prices on the purchasing power of the agricultural sector (see Nier, 1934:74; Christophoroff, 1939: 11). The operation helped stabilize peasants' disposable income, although this had already benefited from numerous subsidies.[14] According to the scheme, the state would be involved in the repartition of the losses through a new 'amortization agency'. This 'hospital bank' would have a double function: to issue low-interest, long-term bonds to replace the non-performing loans in the banks' portfolios; and to collect claims from relieved debtors (mostly peasants), whose liabilities were reduced by a third on average. At the end of the day, the plan constituted a nationalization of private debt accumulated during the credit boom of the late 1920s. The agency was thus a peculiar state bank, comparable in size to the Bulgarian Agricultural Bank. The BNB was duly represented on its board, but also served as its creditor whenever necessary. The bail-out generated pre-programmed budget expenses which ultimately had to be partially covered by the central bank.

10.5 UNINTENDED TRANSFORMATIONS II: FROM DEPRESSION TO RECOVERY

Another kind of spontaneous transformation of the BNB occurred during the second phase of the Great Depression, after the 1931 banking

---

[14] The agricultural debt eligible for reduction represented 52 per cent of the total claims of the banking system in 1931. The approved demands for debt relief by 1939 equaled 20 per cent of the 1934 national income.

crisis in Central Europe and Britain's withdrawal from the gold standard. Bulgarian authorities were called upon to respond to the two principal dilemmas faced by peripheral economies in South-East Europe: how to default, and whether to manage the broken gold-exchange standard through devaluation.

10.5.1 Transfer and Moratorium

The scarcity and inaccessibility of foreign exchange (the 'transfer problem') became a paramount concern. Suddenly deprived of external financial and commercial credits, countries in the region depleted their reserves. Interest rate changes were no longer effective in steering capital inflows. In the case of the BNB, despite a temporary trade surplus (due to an excellent harvest), and the Hoover moratorium on reparations (15 April 1931), the net foreign reserve position deteriorated dramatically after May 1931 (Table 10.1).

At first, it seemed as though the problems could be tackled by conventional means. Early in 1931, the BNB had dismissed any idea of changing the exchange rate, expressing its confidence in the self-corrective capacity of markets, enhanced by export-promoting measures (BNB Annual Report, 1930: 105). Yet, what had once appeared unthinkable, was later introduced with urgency after the British pound left gold in September 1931. Like many other countries, Bulgaria rushed to introduce the recently decried import quotas and pre-authorizations, as well as drastic exchange and capital controls (Nenovsky and Dimitrova, 2007). According to the BNB's adage, 'our trade balance became an expression of our balance of payments' (BNB Annual Report, 1934: 3). Trade policies became the new face of monetary policy. At the same time, the widespread recurrence to clearing arrangements substituted for settlement in 'free' currencies. In 1932–4 Bulgaria signed ten bilateral agreements, the most important one being that with Germany (November 1932). The only other option for preserving the meagre stock of reserves was a partial moratorium on foreign debt payments. By the end of 1931 this was widely considered to be in the interest of both the debtors and creditors. The difficulty was to find the point of equilibrium in the loss-sharing formula, and to converge to mutually suitable solutions.

The sequence of defaults that began in Latin America and Hungary in 1931 soon reached the Balkans (Bulgaria, Greece, Yugoslavia in 1932, and Romania in 1933). As usual, the importance of default in small

economies was not related to the volume of debt at stake, but to the setting of precedents, potential contagion, or complaints of discrimination.
Creditors treat every incident with similar zeal, and – without being a fore-
runner – Bulgaria deserved the greatest attention. Although the Bulgarian
and the Greek default occurred simultaneously (April–May 1932) and
were closely interrelated in political terms, they were quite different. The
Greek case consisted in a unilateral 'heavy default', while the Bulgarian
one – though hardly frictionless – was much more akin to a 'cooperative moratorium'. The dichotomy is a test of Eichengreen's hypothesis
that heavy defaulters and countries who left the gold-exchange standard
performed better in the wake of the Depression than those that sought
to keep a reputation of 'decent debtors' (Eichengreen and Portes, 1989;
Eichengreen, 1991).

    Greece and Bulgaria entered the 1932 crisis with different credentials
(Nier, 1934; Wynne, 1951; Ivanov et al., 2009; Lazaretou, 2005, 2014;
Reinhart and Trebesch, 2015). Since 1877, Greece had experienced
three fiat money periods and the 1893 debt repudiation.[15] Importantly,
after the resolution of the default in 1898, the country never ceased
to serve its foreign debt in accordance with the schedule agreed with
the creditors. Bulgaria's financial reputation, in turn, had been tar-
nished by two episodes of suspended gold convertibility (1899–1902;
1912–29) and by a partial post-war moratorium on foreign debt, negotiated through *force majeure* with the creditors. Moreover, the country
was burdened with severe reparation payments. After 1919, successive
Bulgarian governments sought to keep a low profile. They sought to
conciliate the League of Nations and keep communications channels
with creditors open, meeting reparation obligations (but only after
maximal reductions), enhancing the country's foreign credit and establishing the reputation of an exemplary debtor by reaching stable agreements with the bondholders.

    When the interruption of payments became unavoidable, the two
countries behaved differently (Tooze and Ivanov, 2011). In the context
of the events leading up to April 1932 and following the default, Bulgaria
aimed at a civilized moratorium. Prime Minister Nikola Moushanoff was
convinced that 'we are too weak to solve the problems with provocations'

---

[15] I take 1877 as starting point in order to have comparable time spans for the two countries. The Bulgarian track record was shorter due to the more recent independent status
acquired in 1879. If we look further back, Greece has had two more sovereign defaults
(1827, 1843) and three additional fiat money episodes (1831, 1848, 1868).

(Ivanov, 2005: 61), whereas the Greek government rejected the recommendations that had been submitted by the Financial Committee in March 1932. After April 1932 Bulgaria kept paying a fraction of its obligations,[16] whereas Greece's chaotic relations with its creditors included full suspension of contact and/or intermittent instances of non-payment. Talks with bondholders' associations, the League, and foreign governments led to regular revisions of previously agreed terms.[17]

The BNB was actively involved in the debt negotiations where Bulgaria obtained cuts in the portion of coupons to be transferred in foreign exchange, suspensions of amortization payments, or buy-backs of the non-transferred interest in levs against effective cash payments in foreign currency. Compromises reflected market conditions: in 1932–9 holders of Bulgarian post-war bonds received, on average, one-third of the contractual coupon rate, whereas those of pre-war loans cashed between 13 per cent and 18 per cent (Wynne, 1951: 573), matching the depreciation of the bonds on the market. These differences reflected economic, as well as political factors. Animosity between the two groups of bondholders was strong and occasionally escalated into open clashes, but the League loans benefited from more refined political-cum-diplomatic protection. Given the recent insight that during the last two centuries, the returns on external sovereign bonds have been sufficiently high (on average) to compensate for the risks of default, major wars, and global crises (Meyer et al., 2019), the losses of the creditors from the aforementioned nominal haircuts should be treated with caution.

On the debtors' side, the reduced transfer during the Depression had tangible effects. According to the only comparative assessment, the resources spared between 1931 and 1935 amounted to around 19 per cent of exports and 11 per cent of cumulative government's expenditure in Bulgaria, compared to 18 per cent and 11 per cent respectively in Greece (Tooze and Ivanov, 2011: 44). The striking parity between the two countries is not in line with Eichengreen's hypothesis as the 'heavy' and the 'model' defaulter seemed to have obtained identical

---

[16] The moratorium reduced the transfer in foreign exchange to half of the amount due. The non-transferred part was deposited in a special fund in levs. During the following years, the transfer declined to 25 per cent before reaching 40 per cent in 1939 (Table 10.1).

[17] The definitive resolution of the 1932 defaults took decades. For Greece it ended in 1964, while in Bulgaria the last agreement concerning the bonds was signed with the United Kingdom in 1987. The deadline for the buy-back of the outstanding bonds by Bulgaria was October 1989. Five months later (March 1990) the country defaulted on foreign debt accumulated during the communist regime.

results.[18] Furthermore, the macroeconomic response (as suggested by real GDP changes) also runs in part contrary to the hypothesis. In 1932 GDP grew slightly in Bulgaria while it declined in Greece; in 1933 both countries registered positive rates (faster in Greece); during 1934–5 the trends diverged (noticeable acceleration in Greece and marked decline in Bulgaria); and throughout the recovery after the Depression (1935–8) Bulgaria posted on average higher growth rates compared to Greece (Table 10.1). To assess causality is obviously elusive, and the differences in GDP rates can hardly be attributed directly or exclusively to the divergent choices of 1932.[19]

It has been argued that the 1930s' debt deals were accompanied by the increased hardening of economic conditionality (Tooze and Ivanov, 2011: 44). The claim is mainly based on the establishment, in May 1933, of the 'Committee of the four', comprising the BNB's governor, the director of the Debt Directorate, the Leagues' commissioner in Bulgaria, and the League's adviser to the BNB. The Committee reached decisions unanimously, which meant that the League's representatives enjoyed the power of veto, and its responsibility covered all important issues on the economic agenda. Nevertheless, the Committee was not a new idea. Its framework dated back to the 1928 BNB's transformation, which definitively blurred the distinction between 'external' and 'domestic' decision-making. The Committee slightly reconfigured the well-known eminent players who had already been interacting for years. The old 'money against reforms' slogan was simply reformulated into 'debt servicing reduction against reforms'. Overall, the debt crisis provided the opportunity to reaffirm a well-established philosophy and to reactivate previously crafted tools of control.

The interrelated problems of debt and transfer shifted focus as the question of fiscal balances came to the fore. In the periphery, the classical gold standard's automaticity, which operated as a 'good housekeeping seal of approval' was replaced by the visible hand of external conditionality, which required deflationary adjustment.

Bulgaria's newly appointed minister of finance, Stefan Stefanov (whose initial inventory of the situation in December 1931 revealed, in plaintive

---

[18] The conjecture gains certain plausibility for this case only in a quite ambiguous reading: if the equivalence's interpretation is that Bulgaria's docility did not pay (a 'punishment'), while the Greek 'provocation' was not castigated (that is, somewhat 'rewarded').

[19] There are problems with the data as well. The two time-series with real GDP are far from strictly comparable. The figures for Greece, for instance, are at constant 1914 prices (SEEMHN); those for Bulgaria at constant 1939 prices (Chakalov, 1946: 117).

tones, that he had inherited off-budget liabilities, out of control expenses, biased data, and hidden deficits), emerged as the champion of austerity. The foreign debt burden was unsustainable and the need for structural reforms was urgent, he argued. By adopting a rhetoric close to that of the creditors and the Financial Committee, Stefanov became isolated within the cabinet and the target of local vested interests. Inevitably, he became the mediator in the intellectual no man's land separating the creditors from Bulgarian politics. Stefanov prepared the first relatively consistent policy agenda which, besides the conventional expense-squeezing and revenue-boosting measures, proposed to revise the pension system, restrain the autonomy of state enterprises, introduce stricter budgetary control, and reduce generous industrial subsidies. When goals were not met in 1932, a new draft, the 'Plan Stefanov', was reluctantly adopted by the government in February 1933. Critically, the plan addressed the lobbying power of the mighty cooperative and educational establishments. But the results were disappointing again. Despite huge short-term fiscal effort, the budget remained in deficit. On the other hand, the fundamental strata of the Bulgarian economic system remained intact.

Along with other reforms, the Depression induced changes to the spirit and the letter of relations between the BNB and public finance. Significant fiscal aspects of the 1928 provisions were disrupted. The government failed to liquidate its war and post-war debt to the BNB, and new techniques, approved by the League of Nations, were found to circumvent the constraints on the Bank's ability to finance the budget deficit via Treasury bill discounting (Table 10.1). Conventions were broken, proving once again the futility and the frailty of the securities designed to protect its resources from the state.

By this stage the reformist impetus of the 1920s had faded. The momentum slowed to a standstill as civic tolerance for deeper economic changes reached its limit. The political scene was changed by the bloodless military coup of 19 May 1934, which suspended the constitution and established an autocratic, non-party regime dominated by the King for the next decade. It undertook steps to discipline the administration, recording budget surpluses after 1936, while some important ongoing economic projects, such as the domestic debt-relief settlement, were completed. In March 1935, the government reached a stable agreement with foreign creditors and relations with League representatives gradually calmed down. But no fresh economic vision emerged. Throughout its existence, the regime merely perpetuated and accentuated the interventionist policies it had inherited. Whether this should be labelled 'progress in state-building' or growth in the state's 'managerial capacity' (Tooze and Ivanov, 2011: 44, 46) is less certain. Because, besides the huge waste of resources and inefficiency, those developments were obtained at the cost of lasting democratic and market deficits. In reality, the driving forces of the economic upturn after 1935 were chiefly related to the dynamism of Bulgaria's economic partners.

10.5.2 Devaluation

Sterling's devaluation in September 1931 prompted the amendment of the BNB law – with the League's consent – to 'exceptionally' permit the Bank to trade in 'unstabilized' currencies for the needs of current account transactions.[20] The last, assumedly stable, link of the lev to gold remained the French franc, and the Bulgarian currency integrated the 'Gold bloc' until its disappearance with the franc's exit from the gold-exchange standard in September 1936.

In early 1932, however, devaluation was on the table. Chosen by neighbouring Greece in April, this alternative was discussed in Bulgaria as well. Public proposals and cabinet rumours suggested various options: a 30 per cent to 50 per cent 'controlled' depreciation of the lev; narrowing the gold cover of the monetary base; or supplementary money issuing through credits of the BNB to the government (Ivanov, 2005). For different reasons, none of these ideas had any chance of prevailing. Devaluation would have had an immediate impact on savings and on the lev-denominated budget credits allocated to external debt servicing, just as the 66 per cent devaluation had done in the Greek case. The inflationary path would have favoured domestic debtors, but the overriding understanding was that their debt overload should be cleared by legislative relief. Widespread nationalist discourse strongly opposed a departure from the existing monetary regime, which was seen as a symbolic 'surrender'. In a country where iconoclastic economic thinking was marginal, the gold basis of the national currency was fetishized as an inviolable shield: this was both an ideological cliché and a reference to the bad memories of wartime and post-war inflation. Finally, Bulgaria was ruled by a heterogeneous coalition headed by Moushanoff – a mild and consensual politician, whose temperament was very different from that of the Greek prime minister at the time, Eleftherios Venizelos.

---

[20] The procedure was repeated when the US dollar was devaluated in March 1933.

In each of these scenarios, however, a certain depreciation of the lev was inevitable. The decision to remain on gold by keeping the sacrosanct cover ratio while avoiding outright devaluation meant that more discreet mechanisms to overcome deflation would be needed. In cereal markets, the solution was to subsidize crops through the established state procurement monopoly (Hranoiznos). A more sophisticated system was applied to tradable goods, whose international trade was suffocated by the generalized restrictions of payments in 'free' currencies. The scheme entailed an implicit devaluation without amending the lev's official gold value. The innovation introduced in the second half of 1933 was to cautiously liberalize the exchange regime through the introduction of 'private compensation deals'. In a system where imports were overwhelmingly subject to quotas, those deals allowed a portion of export revenues in 'free' currencies to be sold to domestic importers at a premium. Thus, a legal segment of free foreign exchange and gold trading developed, managed and monitored by the BNB. The premium had the effect of devaluation by stimulating exports, raising the prices (including the domestic) of tradable products, and temporarily reorienting, prior to 1937, part of the export to non-clearing partners (Table 10.1).

Despite the new techniques, clearing arrangements remained dominant throughout the decade. In 1937, Bulgaria was the champion among forty countries relying on the system with the greatest share for exports and the second largest for imports (Christophoroff, 1939: 45; see Table 12). The fetters imposed by the clearing arrangement, however, proved to be more flexible than expected. As demonstrated by Assen Christophoroff (1939), the smooth operation of the agreement with Germany was a crucial factor in accounting for Bulgaria's remarkable economic expansion after the Depression. The synchronization of business cycles in both countries allowed Bulgaria to skip the 1937–8 crisis that affected the liberal economies. German clearing accounted for over half of Bulgaria's foreign trade turnover and permitted a depreciation of the lev vis-à-vis the Reichsmark,[21] which favoured Bulgarian exports to Germany and supported a price increase for those producers at home (Table 10.1). The German economic upswing and the boom in German imports, agricultural in particular, during the second half of the 1930s thus provided a strong boost to the Bulgarian economy.

---

[21] The parity generated a clearing surplus in favour of Bulgaria which was partially offset by a slightly negative premium (around -2.0 per cent) for the Reichsmark in private compensation deals.

Tooze and Ivanov (2011: 47–48) are right to observe that relations with Germany were apparently conducted on an equal basis and avoided traditional debt conditionality. But their interpretation is overly politicized and reads long-term geopolitical goals into what was an ad hoc economic policy. They erroneously assert that the bilateral clearing agreement occurred in 1933, thus attributing it to the National Socialists, when the framework was in fact established in November 1932, that is, before Hitler seized power. The clearing instrument was inherited, not devised by the Nazis. The reasons for the mutual interest in it were economic, not political: at a time when international trade and payments were stifled, clearing was the only tool that worked. But behind its seemingly milder form, the arrangement would prove to entail just as many strings as old-style conditionality: it served to bind the Reich's future ally to itself.

The preservations of a formal tie with gold required the maintenance of several conventions, notably the cover ratio. The statutory limit was threatened on many occasions after 1935, but the BNB employed its talent for creative accounting to safeguard its reputation. After the collapse of the 'Gold bloc', the national statistical yearbook (not the BNB's annual reports) stopped reporting the foreign exchange reserves as 'authentic' (gold-backed, convertible) assets and put all holdings under the heading 'other currencies'. As a result, adherence to the gold-exchange standard disappeared even in statistical terms. Moreover, given the proxies adopted that allowed greater price flexibility in the domestic market, the very question of whether to stay on gold, or devalue, lost the existential relevance it had formerly enjoyed in 1932. Indeed, before the outbreak of the Second World War the loosening of the central bank's policy did not generate inflationary pressures. The legal breach of the monetary rule came soon after Bulgaria joined the Axis, in March 1941, and occupied extensive territories in Greece and Yugoslavia in April. In May, the entire monetary edifice was effectively overhauled when the cover was redefined from 'gold and foreign *gold* currencies' to 'gold and foreign currencies'.[22] The point was to include the Reichsmark in the ratio. In so doing, the BNB explicitly shifted to an 'inconvertible-backed' monetary regime. As in the First World War, the money supply was based on a hollow asset (the clearing mark), which lacked genuine monetary qualities.

---

[22] The difference between 'foreign gold' and 'foreign' currencies was that the former entered the cover at par while the latter at 1:4 ratio.

10.6 CONCLUDING REMARKS

The great transformations of the BNB between 1926 and 1935 were, in common with changes to central banks across the region, a period of contradictory swings in policy. Within the span of a single decade, the BNB was subject first to liberal reforms, only to become caught up in the anti-liberal tide that changed the course of economic policy. The 1920s witnessed a foreword-looking exercise conceived as the closing page of a turbulent period and the orderly launch of the next monetary regime. The innovations brought about by the Great Depression, in turn, were a response to wholly unpredicted circumstances that took the Bank into uncharted territory. What emerged from the Depression clearly contradicted the tidy reform model of 1928.

The most obvious consequence of the turmoil was the suspension of convertibility, the quintessence of the 1928 reform. With regard to foreign exchange and trade-related functions, the crisis reduced the Bank to the role of a rationing centre and petty comptroller.

Independence, the second main goal pursued in 1928, was also weakened. Faced with extraordinary circumstances, the BNB was forced to ever-closer interaction with the government, becoming involved in several new regulatory structures. This turned out to be both a source of strength, as well as vulnerability. While it did not necessarily imply that the Bank was blindly aligned with the executive's views, compromises and suboptimal monetary decisions were inevitable as the institutional and political weight of the two partners was unequal. Thus, the entire 1928 blueprint was altered. The BNB had initially been entrusted with the sole mission of safeguarding the stability of the nation's currency. But during and after the Depression, the Bank assumed a myriad of heterogeneous duties. Automatism (which reinforced independence) was supplanted by extreme discretion. Instead of fine-tuning the markets, the bank administered them, as it steadily expanded the range of its command tools. In the words of the minister of finance from 1933, 'the entire economic life [was] concentrated into the BNB' (Ministry of Finance, 31 March 1933).

The institution was conscious of this metamorphosis. 'We are in a transition from a free to managed economy', stated its 1934 Annual Report. 'This trend emerged a few years ago and no one knows how it will conclude. We know very well what the free economy is, but what would represent the managed one is still unknown. Its profile is not

clearly shaped. We can only guess that this development will end some-
where in the middle ground. Such is habitually the line of progress' (BNB
Annual Report, 1934: 2–3).

This transition sowed the seeds for the future role of the bank. The
autocratic political turn of May 1934, the widening scope of dirigiste
measures, and eventually the Second World War, consolidated the shift
from market forces. The BNB had already become a cornerstone of a
bold interventionist edifice. By the end of the 1930s, and all the more so
on the eve of the communist takeover in 1944, it presided over an overwhelmingly state-managed banking system. Given this economic background, any comprehensively statist utopia appeared to be consistent
with the past, politically palatable, and intellectually legitimate.

Several decades on, these two core issues resurfaced, albeit in a
completely new context. Viewed over the *longue durée*, the Bulgarian
currency board arrangement introduced in 1997 in the wake of a devastating financial crisis sought to address problems akin to those in 1928.
Still in place today, this pristine, minimalist mechanism is a rule-based
regime where the utmost simplification is attained by amputating the
central bank's functions and instruments that, if distorted or abused,
endanger monetary stability. In this sense, the board is the epilogue to
a long cycle in the BNB's institutional evolution: by re-erecting clear-
cut barriers between monetary and fiscal policy; assuring unimpeded
convertibility; transferring (more radically than in 1928) monetary sovereignty abroad; and transforming the BNB from a far from perfect
policy-setter into a transparent policy-taker. The erstwhile formulation
of the independence issue lost its raison d'être; the old debate seems
definitively closed.

The key differences are now the outlook and the landscape. In contrast with the situation at the end of the 1920s, the BNB has an unequivo-
cal exit strategy. The euro is a statutory target set in stone in the treaties.
Once a member of the Eurozone, Bulgaria will share the benefits in
real time, together with the responsibility for the potential drawbacks
of the common currency. On the other hand, the problem of central
bank independence has found its European solution. The emphasis of
the 1926–8 reforms anticipated the global trend initiated in the 1980s
that achieved completion with the establishment of the European Central
Bank. Nowadays, this institution seems to demonstrate that something
fairly close to a truly independent (implicitly) state-owned central bank
is feasible.

TABLE 10.1 *Basic economic indicators of Bulgaria, 1926–1938*
National accounts, prices, credit and banking, current account and
foreign trade data

	1926	1927	1928	1929	1930	1931	1932
National accounts							
GDP (current prices, mil. lev)	49,419	52,462	56,529	56,207	48,641	44,561	39,273
National income (1939 prices, mil. lev)	37,408	40,776	40,152	39,380	43,383	49,745	50,067
% change	:	9.0	–1.5	–1.9	10.2	14.7	0.6
Prices							
Wholesale price index (1934/35=100)	164.4	164.6	177.2	182.6	148.3	122.2	107.1
Export price index (1934/35 = 100)	161.8	175.7	219.1	243.8	176.1	150	114.6
Credit and banking							
Number of private shareholding banks				137	140	133	130
Bank credits outstanding (mil. lev)	:	10,611	13,182	15,634	14,250	13,904	13,569
BNB discount rate (%)	10.0	10.0	9.0	10.0	10.0	9.5	8.0
Treasury debt to BNB (mil. lev)	4,585	4,610	3,735	3,470	3,162	2,995	2,903
T-bills held by BNB (mil. lev)	385	238	256	256	157	279	293
T-bills discounted (% of budget revenues)	:	:	:	:	:	:	:
BNB gold assets (mil. lev)	1,188	1,277	1,323	1,388	1,455	1,511	1,519
BNB for. ex. reserves (mil. lev)	511	1,447	3,270	1,310	905	407	209
Cover ratio (%)	20.2	30.1	49.5	42.7	36.5	37.7	36.1
Current account and trade							
Current account receipts (mil. lev)	6,468	8,729	10,732	7,995	7,989	6,495	3,693
Current account payments (mil. lev)	7,199	8,023	8,327	9,662	8,404	7,068	3,956
Current account balance (mil. lev)	–731	706	2,405	–1,667	–415	–573	–263
Foreign exchange transfer for							50–40
debt's service (% of amount due)							
Compensation Premium in FF (%)							
Export value (mil. lev)	5,618	6,627	6,231	6,397	6,191	5,934	3,382
% share of clearing	–	–	–	–	–	–	:
% share of Germany	:	:	:	:	:	:	:
Import value (mil. lev)	5,631	6,197	7,109	8,325	4,590	4,660	3,471
% share of clearing	–	–	–	–	–	–	:
% share of Germany	:	:	:	:	:	:	:
Trade balance (mil. lev)	–13	430	–878	–1,928	1,601	1,274	–89
Export volume (1926 = 100)	100.0	110.7	96.5	81.0	111.6	150.8	117.8
Import volume (1926 =100)	100.0	102.3	111.6	131.9	81.4	97.9	92.5

: not available
– not applicable

TABLE 10.1 *Basic economic indicators of Bulgaria, 1926–1938*

(*continued*)

	1933	1934	1935	1936	1937	1938
National accounts						
GDP (current prices, mil. lev)	35,633	34,564	36,569	40,188	46,565	51,295
National income (1939 prices, mil. lev)	50,912	46,592	44,453	54,125	57,184	58,674
% *change*	1.7	–8.5	–4.6	21.8	5.7	2.6
Prices						
Wholesale price index (1934/35 = 100)	95.7	99.1	100.9	102.3	115.4	119.6
Export price index (1934/35 = 100)	95.5	93.2	106.8	116	135.6	161.2
Credit and banking						
Number of private shareholding banks	121	118	99	95	90	89
Bank credits outstanding (mil. lev)	13,534	13,277	13,218	14,348	15,504	16,467
BNB discount rate (%)	8.0	7.0	6.0	6.0	6.0	6.0
Treasury debt to BNB (mil. lev)	2,830	2,728	2,671	2,551	3,495	3,441
T-bills held by BNB (mil. lev)	318	345	860	936	385	400
T-bills discounted (as % of budget revenues)	10.6	16.6	9.9	10.7	0.9	0.3
BNB gold assets (mil. lev)	1,545	1,547	1,591	1,652	1,994	2,006
BNB for. ex. reserves (mil. lev)	201	200	583	772	696	1,279
Cover ratio (%)	35.4	35.7	33.4	34.2	31.6	31.2
Current account and trade						
Current account receipts (mil. lev)	2,809	2,889	4,293	4,526	5,826	:
Current account payments (mil. lev)	2,855	2,937	3,974	4,258	5,780	:
Current account balance (mil. lev)	–46	–48	319	268	46	:
Foreign exchange transfer for debt's service (% of amount due)	40–25	25–32.5	25.0	32.5	32.5	32.5
Compensation Premium in FF (%)			33.8	31.0	30.5	32.0
Export value (mil. lev)	2,846	2,534	3,253	3,910	5,019	5,578
% *share of clearing*	79.0	77.2	69.4	65.5	77.2	:
% *share of Germany*	48.0	49.5	50.5	47.1	58.9	:
Import value (mil. lev)	2,202	2,247	3,009	3,181	4,986	4,934
% *share of clearing*	78.3	80.2	81.7	79.9	74.0	:
% *share of Germany*	48.9	59.8	66.7	58.2	51.4	:
Trade balance (mil. lev)	644	287	244	729	33	644
Export volume (1926 = 100)	100.9	92.0	104.6	126.7	143.6	:
Import volume (1926 =100)	63.0	65.6	88.7	95.6	134.9	:

: not available
– not applicable

Sources: Nominal GDP from SEEMHN (2014); National income and current account data from Chakalov (1946); BNB data from BNB Annual Reports; data on export/import volumes, German and clearing trade shares and Treasury bills discounted by the BNB (as % of budget revenue) from Christophoroff (1939); figures on the exchange transfer for foreign debt derived from Avramov (2007) and based on consecutive agreements with creditors (from July 1934 to December 1936, part of the exchange goes for the buy-back of 10 per cent of the non-transferred amounts in levs); all other data from various issues of the Annuaire statistique du Royaume de Bulgarie.

REFERENCES

Unpublished (Archival) Sources

Mollov, Vladimir (Minister of Finance 1926–1931). Papers. National Library of Bulgaria. Bulgarian Historical Archive, Fund 361 (cited in the text as Mollov).
The Minister of Bulgaria in London to V. Mollov, 16 January 1928, File 325, sheets 7–9.
Telegrams to/from A. Lyapcheff and A. Buroff, October 1928, File 826, sheets 119–242.
Letter to V. Mollov, 'La situation des changes en Bulgarie', between December 1928 and July 1929, File 800, sheets 94, 95.
Reports of the Governor of the Bulgarian National Bank Assen Ivanov to V. Mollov, 1926–1928, File 800, sheets 32–92.
Report of the Governor of the Bulgarian National Bank Assen Ivanov to V. Mollov, 7 December 1929, File 799, sheets 87–105.
Ministry of Finance. Central State Archive, Fund 362K (cited in the text as Ministry of Finance).
Report of the Minister of Finance Stefan Stefanov to the Prime Minister, 31 March 1933, Inventory 1, File 93, sheet 46.

Published Sources

Annuaire statistique du Royaume de Bulgarie (1926–1938). Sofia: Direction Nationale de la Statistique.
Avramov, Roumen (ed.) (1999). *120 Years Bulgarian National Bank, 1879–1999 (An Annotated Chronology)*. Sofia: BNB.
Avramov, Roumen (2003). 'Advising, Conditionality, Culture: Money Doctors in Bulgaria, 1900–2000', in Marc Flandreau (ed.), *Money Doctors. The Experience of International Monetary Advising 1850–2000*. London: Routledge, 190–215.
Avramov, Roumen (2006). 'The Bulgarian National Bank in a Historical Perspective: Shaping an Institution, Searching for a Monetary Standard', in Roumen Avramov and Sevket Pamuk (eds.), *Monetary Fiscal Policies in South-East Europe: Historical and Comparative Perspective*. Sofia: BNB, 93–108.
Avramov, Roumen (2007). *Komunalniat kapitalizam. Iz balgarskoto stopansko minalo* [Communal Capitalism. Reflections on the Bulgarian Economic Past], Vols I–III. Sofia: Fondatzia balgarska nauka i kultura, Centre for Liberal Strategies.
Balgarska Narodna Banka (1929). *Yubileen Sbornik na Balgarskata Narodna Banka 1879–1929* [Jubilee Book of the Bulgarian National Bank 1879–1929]. Sofia: BNB.
Bordo, Michael D. and Kydland, Finn E. (1995). 'The Gold Standard as a Rule: An Essay in Exploration'. *Explorations in Economic History*, 32(4): 423–464.
Bulgarian National Bank (1929–1938). *Annual Reports*. Sofia: BNB.

Chakalov, Assen (1946). *Natsionalniat dohod I razhod na Balgaria 1924–1945* [The National Income and Outlay of Bulgaria 1924–1945]. Sofia: Pechatnitsa Knipegraf.

Christophoroff, Assen (1939). *Razvitie na koniunkturnia tzikal v Balgaria 1934–1939* [The Course of the Trade Cycle in Bulgaria, 1934–1939]. Publications of the Statistical Institute for Economic Research, Sofia University, Nos 1–2. Sofia: Statistical Institute for Economic Research.

Dimitrova, Kalina and Ivanov, Martin (2014). 'Bulgaria: from 1880 to 1947', in SEEMHN (ed.), *South-East European Monetary and Economic Statistics from the Nineteenth Century to World War II*. Bank of Greece, Bulgarian National Bank, National Bank of Romania, Oesterreichische Nationalbank.

Eichengreen, Bary (1991). 'Historical Research on International Lending and Debt'. *Journal of Economic Perspectives*, 5(2): 149–169.

Eichengreeen, Bary and Portes, Richard (1989). 'Dealing with Debt: the 1930s and the 1980s'. World Bank Policy, Planning and Research Working Papers, WPS No. 259. Washington, DC: World Bank.

Ivanov, Martin (2005). 'Mojehme li da devalvirame leva? Kakvo se krie zad ortodoksalnia Balgarski Otgovor na Goliamata Depresia?' [Could We Devalue? What's Behind the Orthodox Bulgarian Response to the Great Depression?]. *Istorichesku Pregled*, 61(3–4): 60–80.

Ivanov, Martin, Todorova, Tsvetana, and Vachkov, Daniel (2009). *Istoria na Vanshnia Dalg na Balgaria, 1878–1990* [History of the Foreign Debt of Bulgaria, 1878–1990], Vols I–III. Sofia: BNB.

Lazaretou, Sophia (2005). 'The Drachma, Foreign Creditors and the International Monetary System. Tales of a Currency during the 19th and the Early 20th Century'. *Explorations in Economic History*, 42(2): 202–236.

Lazaretou, Sophia (2014). 'Greece: from 1833 to 1949', in SEEMNH, *South-East European Monetary and Economic Statistics from the Nineteenth Century to World War II*. Bank of Greece, Bulgarian National Bank, National Bank of Romania, Oesterreichische Nationalbank: 101–170.

League of Nations (1927). *Memorandum of the Financial Committee*, 6 December 1927 Geneva: League of Nations.

League of Nations (1928). *Bulgarian Stabilization Loan. Protocol and Annexes approved by the Council of the League of Nations and Signed on Behalf of the Bulgarian Government on March 10, 1928. With the Relevant Public Documents*, C. 338. M. 96. 1928. II. [F. 547], 8 October 1928. Geneva: League of Nations.

Leroy-Beaulieu, Pierre Paul (1879). *Traité de de la Science des Finances*. Paris: Guillaumin et cie.

Meyer, Josefin, Reinhart, Carmen M., and Trebesch, Christoph (2019). 'Sovereign Bonds Since Waterloo'. NBER Working Papers no. 2543 (February). Cambridge, MA: NBER.

Morys, Matthias (2014). 'South-Eastern European Monetary History in a Pan-European Perspective. 1841–1939', in SEEMHN, *South-East European Monetary and Economic Statistics from the Nineteenth Century to World War II*. Bank of Greece, Bulgarian National Bank, National Bank of Romania, Oesterreichische Nationalbank: 25–53.

National Assembly of Bulgaria (1928). 'Minutes of the XXII National Assembly, I Regular Session'. Sofia: National Assembly of Bulgaria.

Nenovsky, Nikolai and Kalina, Dimitrova (2007). 'Exchange Rate Control in Bulgaria: History and Theoretical Reflections'. *Bulgarian National Bank Discussion Papers* no. 61.

Nier, Henri (1934). *La politique de moratoire en matière de fonds d'États dans les pays Balkaniques 1932–1934.* Paris: Les Éditions Domat–Montchrestien.

Parvanova, Rumjana (1999). 'The Stabilization Loan to Bulgaria of 1928'. *Bulgarian Historical Review* (1–2): 72–96.

Pasvolsky, Leo (1930). *Bulgaria's Economic Position. (With Special Reference to the Reparation Problem and the Work of the League of Nations).* Washington, DC: The Brookings Institution.

Pommier, Louis (1904). *La Banque de France et l'Etat.* Paris: A. Rousseau.

Reinhart, Carmen M. and Trebesch, Christoph (2015). 'The Pitfalls of External Dependence: Greece, 1829–2015'. *Brooking Papers on Economic Activity*, Fall: 307–328.

Ryaskov, Marko (2006). *Memoirs and Documents.* Sofia: BNB.

South-East European Monetary History Network (SEEMHN) (2014). *South-East European Monetary and Economic Statistics from the Nineteenth Century to World War II.* Bank of Greece, Bulgarian National Bank, National Bank of Romania, Oesterreichische Nationalbank.

Tooze, Adam and Ivanov, Martin (2011). 'Disciplining the "Black Sheep of the Balkans." Financial Supervision and Sovereignty in Bulgaria, 1902–38'. *Economic History Review*, 64(1): 30–51.

Wynne, William (1951). *State Insolvency and Foreign Bondholders. Vol. II. Selected Case Histories or Governmental Foreign Bond Defaults and Debt Readjustments.* New Haven: Yale University Press.

11

Macroeconomic Policies and the New Central Bank in Turkey, 1929–1939

Şevket Pamuk

11.1 INTRODUCTION

Many developing countries around the world experienced radical change during the 1930s. The contrast between 'before and after 1929' may often be exaggerated, but there is little doubt that in many parts of the developing world international trade and capital flows declined and import-substituting activities increased during this decade. The crisis changed the nature of political power, weakening large landowners and export-oriented interests, as well as the commitment to the liberal order that had prevailed until the First World War. This was a period when many countries' control fell into the hands of the populists, and nationalists began to favour autarky and import-substituting industrialization.

Not all countries experienced this to the same degree. For one thing, both the policy and the capacity for withstanding economic shocks differed substantially from country to country. On the whole, colonies connected to the European powers adhered more closely to orthodox regimes. Moreover, countries where the landed interests were powerful, or difficult to challenge, also tended to greater passivity, and stuck to the orthodox model. By contrast, the ability and willingness to manipulate exchange rates, tariffs, and domestic credit were strongest in the formally independent countries that were either large or had relatively autonomous public sectors.

In developing countries, the governments that did embrace interventionism during the 1930s deployed a range of policies. These included exchange-rate policies, import repression and import diversion, expansionary monetary and fiscal policies, as well as a long list of other measures ranging from wage repression and public works programmes to debt repudiation.

These should not be viewed as a comprehensive, theoretically informed set of measures, however; they were mostly implemented on an ad hoc basis by different governments in response to the specific conditions in each country. Moreover, the evidence shows that those developing economies that shifted towards protectionism and inward-looking policies generally fared better during the Great Depression than those that adhered to the earlier, export-led strategy (Diaz Alejandro, 1984: 17–39; Maddison, 1985).

This chapter examines the nature of macroeconomic policy in Turkey, the role played by the new central bank that was established in 1930, and the performance of the economy up until 1939. Turkey had emerged as one of the successor states after the disintegration of the Ottoman Empire following the First World War. In sum, during the nineteenth century, the Ottoman economy had remained open, and foreign trade and foreign investment had expanded steadily. With the outbreak of the First World War, the Ottoman economy turned inward due to the disruption of foreign trade. After the war of independence Turkey was established as a new republic in 1923. In this new political and economic environment, the fledgling nation state managed to acquire the necessary autonomy to shape its own political and economic institutions and pursue its own economic policies.

The Great Depression impacted Turkey primarily through the sharp decline in the prices of agricultural commodities. The policies the government, led by an urban-based elite, developed in response were somewhat eclectic. The strongly protectionist measures of the early years were superseded in 1932 by the adoption of etatism, or, to be more specific, import-substituting industrialization led by the state. Although exchange rate policies resulted in the appreciation of the currency, fiscal policy remained cautious and the national budgets were kept balanced until 1938.

In the 1920s, as governments and political and economic elites in the developed countries sought to construct a new international economic order in the hope of recovering the economic stability and prosperity of the pre-war era, a new emphasis was placed on the role of central banks. The adoption of the gold standard, central bank independence, fiscal restraint and international cooperation were promoted as pillars of a new international economic system (James, 2001: 31–100; Eichengreen, 2008: 41–90). Many less developed countries were influenced by the growing international approval for the role of central banks. Soon they would begin to establish central banks of their own. However, the structure and role of the central bank in less developed countries during the turbulent 1930s differed from the vision that had initially been put forward by its proponents. As international cooperation declined, and the global economy disintegrated, the actual status of the newly established central banks, and their role in macroeconomic policy, varied considerably in each of the less developed countries in accordance with differing pre-existing conditions.

Turkey set up a new state bank as its central bank with new legislation in 1930, and it began its operations the following year. Yet the Bank did not pursue an independent monetary policy but followed the government's lead. During the 1930s Turkey did not adopt the gold standard or gold convertibility and maintained strong controls over foreign-exchange transactions. The central bank kept the monetary base unchanged until the latter half of the 1930s. Indeed, Turkey was able to avoid the banking failures and monetary instability that hampered many less developed economies during this decade due to the cautious monetary policy that placed great emphasis on balancing the budget, strengthening the control of foreign trade, and the urban economy. In order to achieve greater self-sufficiency by the end of the decade, it also curtailed the economy's international linkages.

The economic performance of Turkey during the 1930s was stronger than that of most other countries around the Eastern Mediterranean. Severe import repression was an important factor behind the strong performance of the industrial sector during the 1930s. The protectionist measures adopted by the government, as well as the restrictive foreign-trade and foreign-exchange regimes (including bilateral trading arrangements), sharply reduced the volume of imports, creating attractive conditions for small and medium-sized domestic manufacturers. But there is another explanation for the overall performance of both the urban and the national economy. Agriculture, the largest sector of the economy, employing more than three-quarters of the labour force during the 1930s and accounting for close to half of GDP, registered a significant increase in output during the 1930s. This strong performance was due to the availability of uncultivated land, combined with the demographic and economic recovery of the countryside after a decade of war up until 1922 (Pamuk, 2018: 166–203).

11.2 TURKEY'S ECONOMY DURING THE INTERWAR PERIOD

The period between 1913 until 1945 was exceptionally difficult, both for Turkey's population and its economy. In addition to the Depression, the country suffered two world wars, and the radical redrawing of its borders which presaged the transition from the Ottoman Empire to the

Şevket Pamuk

TABLE 11.1 *Turkey's basic economic indicators, 1923–1946*

	1913	1923	1929	1939	1946	1950
Population in millions	16.5	13	14	17.5	19	21
Share of agriculture in the labour force (%)	n.a.	n.a.	80	77	77	77
GDP per capita in 1990 PPP dollars	1,150	720	1,150	1,425	1,180	1,600
Share of agriculture in GDP (%)	40	40	46	42	42	45
Share of manufacturing in GDP (%)	12	12	9	17	13	16
Share of industry (incl. construction) in GDP (%)	16	16	14	22	18	21

Sources: Calculations based on Turkey, State Institute of Statistics; Bulutay et. al. (1974).

TABLE 11.2 *Periodization of economic growth in Turkey, 1923–1950*

Average annual rates of growth (%)	1923–29	1930–39	1940–45	1946–50	1913–50
Population	2.0	2.0	1.1	2.2	0.7
GDP	8.8	5.2	−5.8	8.4	1.6
GDP per capita	6.8	3.2	−6.9	6.1	0.9
Agricultural output	11.1	4.4	−8.4	12.1	
Manufacturing output	6.9	7.2	−6.7	8.3	

Sources: Calculations based on Turkey, State Institute of Statistics; Bulutay et. al. (1974).

nation-state. There were sharp fluctuations in population, GDP, and GDP per capita. Periods of expansion (before 1914, 1923–9, 1929–39, and 1945–50) were disrupted by war (1914–22 and 1939–45). Tables 11.1 and 11.2 summarize these fluctuations. They also indicate that Turkey's GDP per capita in 1950 stood approximately 30 per cent higher than its level in 1913, an average annual rate of increase of 0.7 per cent.[1]

[1] Utilizing official statistics, (Bulutay et al., 1974) constructed national income accounts for the period 1923 to 1948. These series were then linked to the official production, tax collection, and foreign trade series of the Ottoman period and the reasonably detailed estimates for national income prepared by Vedat Eldem (1970) for the years before the First World War by Işık Özel (1997), producing comparable series for the area within the present-day borders of Turkey.

The leadership of the new nation state was keenly aware that Ottoman financial and economic dependence on Europe had created serious political problems. At the Lausanne Peace Conference of 1922–3, the new state fought hard for the right to determine the nature of the relationships between new institutions governing the economy and the rest of the world, and especially with the European powers. After lengthy negotiations, important changes were made on three fundamental issues. First, the commercial and legal privileges of European citizens and companies were abolished. Second, the free trade agreements that the Ottoman state had signed and was unable to change unilaterally during the nineteenth century were cancelled. In addition, the new state obtained the right to decide on its own customs tariffs after a transition period that ended in 1929. And, after several rounds of negotiations that lasted as late as 1928, the Ottoman external debt was restructured and divided between the successor states. According to the agreement, Turkey would take over 67 per cent of the total Ottoman debt and debt repayments would begin in 1929 (Tezel, 1986: 163–196).

Turkey did not have a central bank during the 1920s. In the Ottoman era during the nineteenth century, the Imperial Ottoman Bank owned by French and British investors, had been given special privileges and assumed many of the functions of a central bank. Most of these privileges were ended by the Ankara government after the First World War but the Ottoman Bank continued its operations as a commercial bank in the 1920s. At the same time, the Ankara government began to consider using public funds to set up a state bank that would function as the central bank. Having lived through the difficult Ottoman experience with paper money and inflation during the First World War, the new political leaders were firmly in favour of monetary and price stability. They followed closely the developments in central banking in Western as well as South-Eastern Europe. In the late 1920s, the government asked for, and received, a number of detailed studies from European and Turkish experts on the potential for establishing a central bank in Turkey.[2]

---

[2] Foreign experts who were consulted by the Turkish government between 1927 and the end of 1929, that is, before the new central bank was established, include a Mr. Friedleb of the Dutch Internationale Bemiddeling- en Handelmaatschappij (IBH), who visited in 1927; little is known about him, but US Consular correspondence identified him "as an Iranian citizen of Russian origin" (Consulate to Secretary of State, 4 January 1928, State Department Archives 567.519/3121, Roll 60). Next came Gerard Vissering, President of De Nederlandsche Bank, who visited and submitted a report in 1928, followed by two Germans (Karl Mueller and Hjalmar Schacht), who visited and submitted (short) reports in 1929, and the Italian Count Giuseppe Volpi, who visited and submitted a report in late 1929. Both Vissering and Schacht exerted considerable influence, but advocated the

They also consulted the Ottoman Bank which had its headquarters in France (Tekeli and İlkin, 1997: 242–317).

The 1920s was a period of rapid recovery for Turkey's economy. The extent of land under cultivation grew and agricultural production began to increase. With the growth in agricultural income, the urban economy began to recover as well. New investments started to replace the physical capital destroyed during the wars. As demand in world markets rose, exports expanded. Of course, recovery had a long way to go: population in the area within Turkey's current borders had declined by nearly 20 per cent during and after the First World War and output had almost halved. Thus, GDP per capita for the same area had declined by as much as 40 per cent prior to 1918. It is estimated that per capita incomes only returned to their 1914 levels in 1929. Pre-war levels in total population and total production were not reached until the mid-1930s. Before that, however, the onset of the Great Depression in 1929 would be a major turning point, for the world at large and for Turkey as well (Pamuk, 2018: 184–194).

11.3 THE GREAT DEPRESSION

The principal impact of the Great Depression on the Turkish economy was the sharp decline in the price of agricultural commodities. The price of wheat and other cereals declined by over 60 per cent between 1928–9 and 1932–3, and it remained at this level until the end of the decade. Prices of the leading export crops –tobacco, raisins, hazelnuts, and cotton– also declined by an average of 50 per cent, although they recovered somewhat later in the decade. Since these decreases were greater than the decline in the prices of non-agricultural goods, Turkey's external terms of trade deteriorated by over 25 per cent, while the domestic terms of trade shifted against agriculture by 31 per cent from 1928–9 to 1932–3. By contrast, the physical volume of exports continued to rise after 1929, perhaps reflecting the continued recovery in output levels. Nonetheless, the result was a sharp decline in the real income for most market-oriented agricultural producers. The adverse price movements produced an acute agricultural slump, especially in the more commercialized regions of the country. As of the summer of 1929, the economy experienced a foreign exchange shock, arising in part from the higher volume of imports before an expected increase in tariffs, as well as the anticipation of the first annual payment on the Ottoman

establishment of a private central bank, which the Turkish government opposed. Thus, Turkey turned to Volpi, who was more sympathetic to the idea of a state-owned bank.

debt (Tekeli and İlkin, 1977: 75–90; Tezel, 1986: 98–106). The difficulties in the foreign exchange markets, and the instability of the exchange rate of the lira that became manifest in the summer of 1929, helped to convince the government to establish the central bank the following year. The Central Bank of the Republic of Turkey was duly established with new legislation in June 1930 and formally began its operations in October 1931 (Tekeli and İlkin, 1997: 242–317).

The government was not free to change tariff policy until 1929, but as soon as the restrictions of the 1923 Lausanne Peace Treaty came to an end it began to move towards protectionism and exerting its control over foreign trade and foreign exchange. A new tariff structure was adopted in October 1929, before the collapse on Wall Street, reflecting the desire of the new state elites in Ankara to exercise greater control over the economy. Average tariffs on imports are estimated to have increased from 13 per cent to 46 per cent in 1929 and to more than 60 per cent by the second half of the 1930s. Equally important, tariffs on imported food and consumer manufactures were raised more than the tariffs for agricultural and industrial machinery and raw materials. For this reason, effective rates of protection on targeted final goods were substantially higher. In addition, quantity restrictions on imports for a long list of goods were introduced in November 1931. These lists were updated frequently, and some of the tariffs were raised again during the 1930s as import substitution spread to new sectors (Yücel, 1996: 74–84, 105–113). The immediate beneficiaries of this marked shift to protectionism were the small and medium-sized manufacturing enterprises in many parts of the country, consisting of textile mills, flour mills, glass works, brick factories, tanneries, and others which began to enjoy high rates of growth. One study has estimated the average rate of growth of the manufacturing sector at 6.3 per cent per annum between 1929 and 1933 (Zendisayek, 1997: 54–106; see also Kazgan, 1977, 231–273; Boratav, 1981, 170–176; Yücel, 1996, 113–130).

The crisis that began in 1929 had a number of other important repercussions. First, concern with trade deficits and balance-of-payments problems moved the government increasingly towards clearing and barter agreements and bilateral trade. In addition, strong controls were applied to foreign-exchange transactions. By the second half of the decade, more than 80 per cent of the country's foreign trade was being conducted under clearing and reciprocal quota systems. These bilateral arrangements also facilitated the expansion of trade with Nazi Germany, which offered more favourable prices for Turkey's exports as part of its well-known strategy towards south-eastern Europe. Germany's share

TABLE 11.3 *Turkey's foreign trade, 1924–1946*

	1924–25	1928–29	1938–39	1945–46
Exports (US dollars, millions)	92.5	81.5	107.5	192.0
Imports (US dollars, millions)	114.5	97.0	105.5	108.5
Exports/GNP (%)	12.8	11.4	6.9	5.2
Imports/GNP (%)	15.8	14.4	6.8	2.8
Trade balance/GNP (%)	−3.0	−3.0	+0.1	+2.4
External terms of trade (export/import prices, index)	129	100	79	68

Sources: Turkey State Institute of Statistics; calculations based on Bulutay et al. (1974).

in Turkey's exports rose from 13 per cent in 1931–3 to an average of 40 per cent for 1937–9. Similarly, its share of Turkey's imports increased from 23 per cent in 1931–3 to 48 per cent in 1937–9 (Tekeli and İlkin, 1982: 221–249; Tezel, 1986: 139–162).

It is significant that the government did not use exchange-rate policy to improve the balance of payments in order to soften the impact of the Depression. On the contrary, even though the government did not pursue gold convertibility, the existing parity of the Turkish lira vis-à-vis gold was kept unchanged while the leading international currencies were devalued. As a result of the actions of other governments, the lira was revalued by a total of 40 per cent against both sterling and the dollar between 1931 and 1934, and the new parities were maintained until the end of the decade (Tezel, 1986: 144–150). The real exchange rate against the leading trade partners thus appreciated sharply during this period (Hansen, 1991: 374–375). The impact of these exchange-rate movements on export volumes was limited, because the exports consisted mostly of agricultural commodities with low price elasticity of demand. Equally important, a growing part of Turkey's exports in the 1930s began to be covered by bilateral trade agreements and clearing arrangements.

Even though the export volume continued to rise in absolute terms, these far-reaching changes in the structure of foreign trade, combined with the adverse price movements and the increases in GDP later in the decade, led to a sharp decline in the share of exports in GDP from 11.4 per cent in 1928–9 to 6.9 per cent in 1938–9 (Table 11.3). It is thus clear that exports did not act as a source of recovery for the national economy during the 1930s and that the causes of recovery have to be found elsewhere.

Government concern with the balance of payments led to a cessation of payments on the external debt and a demand for a new settlement after the first annual payment in 1929. The subsequent negotiations, aided by the crisis of the world economy and demands for resettlement by other debtors, produced a favourable result, reducing the annual payments by more than half for the rest of the decade. At the same time the Ankara government sought foreign funds and expertise for its industrial projects. Due to the world economic crisis, however, inflows of foreign capital remained quite low (Tezel, 1986: 165–189).

In response to declining agricultural prices, the government founded the Soil Products Office and began to support purchases of wheat and tobacco from 1932. These purchases remained limited, however. Until the end of the 1930s, wheat purchases averaged 3 per cent of total production and around 15 per cent of the amount sold on the market (Özbek, 2003). Support purchases may have prevented wheat prices from falling further, but prices of agricultural crops did not recover and relative prices remained unfavourable for agriculture until 1939. In fact, the price movements in favour of manufacturing, along with protectionism, were seen by the government as an opportunity for rapid industrialization.

Manufacturing began to play a more important part in domestic consumption. In the absence of largescale industrial enterprises, the immediate beneficiaries were the small and medium-sized manufacturing enterprises in many parts of the country consisting of textile mills, flour mills, glass works, brick factories, tanneries, and others, all of whom began to experience high rates of growth. Industrialization through import substitution was under way (Yücel, 1996: 74–113).

11.4 ETATISM

The difficulties faced by the agricultural and export-oriented sectors quickly led to popular discontent with the single-party regime, especially in the more commercialized regions of the country: western Anatolia, along the eastern Black Sea coast, and in the cotton-growing Adana region in the South. The wheat producers of central Anatolia who were connected to urban markets by rail were also hit by the sharp fall in prices. In 1932, as the unfavourable world market conditions continued, the government announced the beginning of a new strategy called 'etatism', or state-led, import-substituting industrialization.

Etatism envisioned the state becoming a leading producer and investor in the urban sector. A first five-year industrial plan was adopted in 1934 with the assistance of Soviet advisors. This document provided a detailed list of investment projects to be undertaken by state enterprises, rather than an elaborate text of planning in the technical sense of the term. A second five-year plan was initiated in 1938, but its implementation was interrupted by the war. By the end of the decade, state economic enterprises had emerged as important, even leading, producers in a number of key sectors such as iron and steel, textiles, sugar, glass works, cement, utilities, and mining (Boratav, 1981: 172–189; Tekeli and Ilkin, 1982: 134–220; Tezel, 1986: 197–285; Hansen, 1991, 324–335; Gürsel, 2005).

Etatism involved the extension of state-sector activities and control to other parts of the urban economy. Railways were taken over from European ownership and nationalized and the newly constructed railway lines were transformed into state monopolies. Most of the state monopolies which had been handed over to private firms in the 1920s were taken back. In transportation, banking, and finance, state ownership of key enterprises was accompanied by increasing control over markets and prices. At the same time, the single-party regime maintained tight restrictions on labour organization and labour union activity. These measures paralleled the generally restrictive social policies of the government in other areas. It is significant that, despite considerable growth in the urban sector during the 1930s, real wages never increased beyond those of 1914 (Pamuk, 1995: 96–102).

Etatism has undoubtedly had a long-lasting impact on Turkey. For better or worse, this experiment would prove to be inspirational for other state-led industrialization attempts in the Middle East after the Second World War.[3] From a macroeconomic perspective, however, the contribution of the state to the industrialization of Turkey remained modest until the Second World War. For one thing, state enterprises in manufacturing and many other areas did not begin operations until the middle of the decade. The total number of active state enterprises in industry and mining on the eve of the Second World War did not exceed twenty. Official figures indicate that in 1938 total employment in manufacturing, utilities, and mining remained below 600,000, or about 10 per cent of the labour force. State enterprises accounted for only 11 per cent of this amount, or about 1 per cent of total employment in the country. Approximately 75 per cent of employment in manufacturing continued to be provided by small-scale private enterprises (Tezel, 1986: 233–237).

---

[3] For the influence of etatism on state-led industrialization strategies in other Middle Eastern countries after the Second World War, see Richards and Waterbury (1990: 174–201).

Yet it would be difficult to argue that the private sector was hurt by the expansion of the state sector during the 1930s. The strongly protectionist measures of the government helped the host of small and medium-sized enterprises producing for the domestic market. Some large private enterprises in the foreign trade sector were affected adversely by the contraction of foreign trade. This was, however, more due to the disintegration of international trade than to etatism itself. By investing in large expensive projects in intermediate goods and providing them as inputs, the state enterprises promoted the growth of private enterprises in the manufacturing of final goods for the consumer. Private investments continued to be supported and subsidized during the 1930s. Nonetheless, the private sector remained concerned that the state sector might expand at its own expense. Tensions between the two sides continued.

11.5 FISCAL AND MONETARY POLICIES

In response to the Depression and rising unemployment, many developed and developing countries adopted state interventionism. Many of these countries also adopted expansionary fiscal and monetary policies to stimulate their economies, basically running budget deficits and printing money to finance them. In 1936, Keynes published his *General Theory* but at the beginning of the 1930s these practices were not based on any theory and were a search for solutions in the dark, more than anything else.

One of the striking features of the macroeconomic policy in Turkey during the 1930s was that fiscal policy emphasized balanced budgets and monetary policy remained restrained in the wake of the Depression. While state interventionism expanded rapidly and state-led industrialization was accepted as the main strategy after 1929, the government's macroeconomic policy was cautious and stayed away from expansionary fiscal and monetary policies until the end of the decade. The price support programme for agricultural crops remained small despite the marked decline in prices. State expenditure on new industrial and other economic enterprises was limited in large part because the numbers of new state enterprises remained small, as discussed in the previous section. Railroad construction was the largest item of government economic spending during the interwar period. In fact, the basic principle guiding macroeconomic policy during this period was 'balanced budget-strong money'. Government revenues and expenditures increased only modestly, from about 13 per cent to 15 per cent of GDP in the late 1920s, to a new range of 17–19 per cent during the 1930s. National budgets remained mostly balanced until 1938 when

TABLE 11.4 *Rising share (%) of domestic banks in total deposits in Turkey, 1924–1939*

	1924	1928	1933	1939
Share of private domestic banks	12	20	27	34
Share of state banks	10	28	43	46
Share of foreign banks	78	52	30	20
Total	100	100	100	100

Source: Tezel (1986: 113).

deficits emerged due to increased military spending and preparations for war (Tezel, 1986: 368–388; Yücel, 1996: 62–73).

The approach to monetary policy was similarly restrained but accommodative during the 1930s and more generally during the interwar period. The new central bank began its operations towards the end of 1931. The basic principle that guided its policies until the end of the decade was to keep unchanged the amount of currency (banknotes plus coinage) inherited from the Ottoman era. Yet the money supply or M2 still increased, thanks to the activities of the new domestic banks and the strong decline in the price level after 1929.

One priority for the government during the early years of the new nation state was to increase the share of domestic banks. While the numbers of foreign banks and their deposits in nominal terms remained little changed, the numbers of domestic banks, both private and state-owned, national and local, increased rapidly, from eighteen in 1924, to thirty-nine in 1929, and to forty-seven in 1933. These new domestic banks were able to increase their deposits and credit. As a result, their shares in total deposits and total credits increased significantly while the shares of foreign banks declined until the end of the 1930s (Table 11.4). The numbers of depositors in the banking system also increased from about 10,000 in 1924, to 60,000 in 1929, and to 115,000 in 1939. Thanks to the expansion of the deposits and credits of the new domestic banks, M2 increased by 42 per cent from 1925 to 1929 (Table 11.5).

Currency in circulation did not increase until later in the decade but thanks to the expansion of bank deposits and credit, the nominal money supply increased by an additional 68 per cent from 1929 to 1938. There was an even larger increase in the real money supply after 1929 due to the decline in the price level. The aggregate price level as represented by the GDP deflator declined by more than 50 per cent between 1929 and 1934 (Table 11.5). As a result, the real M2 doubled during this period

TABLE 11.5 *Money supply and the price level in Turkey, 1925–1939*
in millions of liras, except the price level index,
where 1925=100

	Currency	Deposits	M2	Price Level
1925	156	46	212	100
1929	168	133	301	108
1934	155	145	300	52
1938	191	316	507	59
1939	256	272	528	65

Source: Tezel (1986: 111).

although the price level recovered somewhat after 1934. Monetary policy was relaxed after 1934. Currency in circulation increased by 25 per cent, as did M2 by 71 per cent from 1933 to 1938. The discount rate of the new central bank started at 8 per cent in 1931 and declined to 5 per cent in later years, despite the continuation of price deflation. In other words, real interest rates remained quite high, which may have created problems for the urban economy. Nonetheless, the increase in the money supply met the needs of a growing economy and helped support the ongoing monetization of the agricultural sector. However, the government did not adopt a policy to address the problems of indebted agricultural producers arising from deflation (Tezel, 1986: 110–114; Gürsel, 2005).

In many less developed economies during the 1930s, high external debt, falling export prices, budgetary difficulties, and governments' fiscal difficulties led to trouble with servicing external debt and spread over to the banking sector, resulting in bank failures and continued monetary instability. While Turkey did experience some problems with the banks, it was able to avoid the worst of these problems. This was in part due to the cautious fiscal and monetary policy pursued by the government and the central bank.

The government's strategy to reduce international linkages, and create a more self-sufficient economy in anticipation of yet another war, also reduced the risks of creating or importing banking and monetary instability. Turkey did not adopt the gold standard or gold convertibility during the 1930s. Payments on the outstanding international debt was suspended after 1930, international capital inflows remained low and the share of both exports and imports to GDP declined during the 1930s. With greater control of foreign trade, the government was able to maintain trade surpluses until the end of the decade.

It would be useful to explore the reasons for the cautious policy stance of the government at a time when many countries were following expansionary policies in response to the Great Depression. Most importantly, the strongly protectionist measures adopted in 1929 and in subsequent years led to significant increases in manufacturing output. In other words, thanks to strongly protectionist policies, a measure of industrialization and growth was being achieved without resorting to the measures later dubbed 'Keynesian'. In fact, as Tables 11.1 and 11.2 show, not only industry but agriculture and the economy as a whole did reasonably well and achieved moderately high rates of growth during the 1930s. Moreover, İsmet İnönü, who was prime minister between 1924 and 1937, and many of his associates in government had observed the financial and monetary policies during the Ottoman era very closely. Financing large budget deficits by external borrowing had created problems not just for the economy but also in foreign policy. In addition, the substantial quantity of paper money printed during the First World War had led to record levels of inflation. The government was thus reluctant to repeat those experiences. Finally, the Republican People's Party in power during the 1930s had eliminated all political opposition and did not face any competition during the 1930s. The party leadership and the government did not feel strong popular pressure to pursue more aggressive macroeconomic policies. The Republican People's Party governments were thus able to adopt and maintain a balanced budget–strong money stance during the 1930s.[4]

11.6 SOURCES OF ECONOMIC GROWTH

We have an apparent puzzle. There is evidence of strong performance by the industrial sector, the urban economy, and the national economy. At the same time, aggregate figures show that the contribution of the state sector to the urban economy, both as an investor and as a producer, did not begin until the middle of the decade and remained rather modest for the 1930s as a whole. How, then, can we explain these growth rates?

In the absence of the use of currency depreciation, fiscal policy, or monetary policy to expand aggregate demand, the strong protectionist measures adopted by the government beginning in 1929 emerge as one

---

[4] The government's reluctance to pursue expansionary policies was, of course, consistent with the orthodoxy of the period. For a survey of the restrictive fiscal and monetary policy that prevailed in the United States and Western Europe until 1933, see Temin (1989: chapter 2) and Eichengreen (1992).

of the key causes of the output increases (see Table 11.2; also Tezel, 1986: 102–103). The rising tariff rates combined with the increasingly restrictive foreign trade and exchange regimes sharply reduced imports from 15.4 per cent of GDP in 1928–9 to 8.7 per cent by 1932–3 and 6.8 per cent by 1938–9. Even more importantly, the composition of imports changed dramatically. The share of final goods declined from 51 per cent in 1929 to 21 per cent in 1940, while the share of intermediate goods rose from 26 per cent to 54 per cent and of machinery and equipment from 9 per cent to 22 per cent during the same period. Severe import repression thus created very attractive conditions for domestic manufacturers after 1929. These mostly small and medium-sized producers achieved relatively high rates of output growth for the entire decade until the Second World War. The available evidence indicates clearly that in textiles and several other manufactured goods such as sugar, domestic producers had replaced most, if not all of imports by the end of the 1930s (Yücel, 1996: 89–130; Zendisayek, 1997: 54–105).

There is yet another explanation for the overall performance of both the urban and the national economy, which has often been ignored by economists and economic historians. For that, we need to turn to agriculture, the largest sector of the economy, employing more than three-quarters of the labour force during the 1930s and accounting for close to half of the GDP. The collapse of commodity prices and the deterioration of the inter-sectoral terms of trade after 1929 had severe consequences for most agricultural producers. Not only did market-oriented producers, both small and large, in the more commercialized, export-oriented regions of the country experience a decline in their standard of living, but so did the more self-sufficient producers of cereals in the interior. The sharp decline in agricultural prices also increased the burden of the indebted peasantry, forcing many to give up their independent plots and accept sharecropping arrangements.

One of the responses of the government was to initiate, after 1932, direct and indirect price support programmes in wheat and tobacco. It began to purchase wheat from the producers, first through the Agricultural Bank, and later via an independent agency established for this purpose, called the Soil Products Office. Until the end of the decade, however, such purchases remained limited, averaging 3 per cent of the overall crop or about 15 per cent of the marketed wheat (based on Atasağun, 1939; Bulutay et al., 1974).

Nonetheless, evidence from a variety of sources, including official statistics, show that agricultural output increased by 50–70 per cent during the 1930s, after adjustments are made for fluctuations due to weather. This evidence points to an average rate of growth of more than 4 per cent per year for aggregate agricultural output during the decade. Similarly, foreign trade statistics indicate that Turkey turned from being a small net importer of cereals at the end of the 1920s into a small net exporter of wheat and other cereals on the eve of the Second World War, despite a population increase of 20 per cent during the 1930s.[5]

The next task would be to explain these substantial increases in output in the face of unfavourable price movements. Two different and not mutually exclusive explanations appear possible, although it may not be easy to assess the contributions of each without more detailed research. First, government policies may have played a role. Most importantly, the abolition of the tithe in 1924 may have contributed to the recovery of the family farm by improving the welfare of small and medium-sized producers through helping them to expand the area under cultivation or to raise yields. Another important contribution of government policy was the construction of railways, which helped integrate additional areas of central and eastern Anatolia into the national market. Railways may have encouraged the production of more cereals in these areas. The government was also involved in a number of other programmes in support of the agricultural sector, such as the expansion of credit to farmers through the state-owned Agricultural Bank, and the promotion of new agricultural techniques and higher-yielding varieties of crops. Despite the rhetoric from official circles, these programmes did not receive substantial resources, however, and their impact remained limited.

The second explanation focuses on the long-term demographic recovery of the family farms and their response to lower prices. In the interwar period, Anatolian agriculture continued to be characterized by peasant households that cultivated their own land with a pair of draft animals and extremely basic implements. Most of the large holdings were rented out to sharecropping families. Large-scale enterprises using imported machinery, implements, and wage labourers remained rare. Irrigation and the use of commercial inputs, such as fertilizers, also remained very limited. Due to the availability of land after the death and departure of more than three million peasants, both Muslim and non-Muslim, during the protracted war of 1912–22, increases in production in the interwar era were achieved primarily through the expansion of cultivated land.

---

[5] Turkey State Institute of Statistics, *Statistical Yearbooks* 1930–1 and 1940–1.

After the wars ended and the population began to increase at annual rates of around 2 per cent, the agricultural labour force followed suit, albeit with a time lag. While yields changed little, the area under cultivation expanded substantially during the 1930s. The area cultivated per person and per household for agriculture increased. The number of draft animals rose by about 40 per cent during this period, both confirming the material recovery of the peasant household and facilitating the expansion in cultivated area (Shorter, 1985). Comparisons of the late Ottoman and early Turkish statistics indicate that per capita agricultural output did not return to pre-First World War levels until 1929 and the early 1930s. Total agricultural output within the 1930s borders reached pre-war levels in the second half of the decade.

11.7 CONCLUSION

The case of Turkey during the Great Depression is exceptional in the eastern Mediterranean, not only because of the extent of government interventionism, but also the strength of economic recovery. Moreover, the policy mix in Turkey was unusual compared to the activist government initiatives in other developing countries in Latin America and Asia. Government interventionism in Turkey during the 1930s was not designed, in the Keynesian sense, to increase aggregate demand through the use of devaluations and expansionary fiscal and monetary policies. The preference of the government for balanced budgets and a strong currency was influenced by the unfavourable experiences of the Ottoman governments with external debt until 1914 and with a paper currency inflation during the First World War. Instead of expansionary macroeconomic policies, a closed, autarkic economy was developed. The increasing central control through the expansion of the public sector was directly related to the bureaucratic nature of the regime.

Like many other less developed countries, Turkey established a new central bank during the interwar period. As international cooperation declined and the global economy disintegrated during the 1930s, the new central bank contributed to the government's efforts for macroeconomic stability. Paralleling the cautious fiscal stance of the government, the central bank did not expand the monetary base until the end of the 1930s. While Turkey did experience some problems with its banks during this decade, it was able to avoid the worst. This was in part due to cautious fiscal and monetary policies. In addition, the government's strategy to reduce the external linkages of the economy and create a more self-sufficient economy reduced the risks of creating or importing banking and monetary instability. Payments on the outstanding international debt was suspended after 1930 and the share of both exports and imports to GDP declined during the 1930s. With greater control of foreign trade, the government was also able to maintain trade surpluses until the end of the decade.

REFERENCES

Atasağun, Yusuf S. (1939). *Türkiye Cumhuriyeti Ziraat Bankası* [The Agricultural Bank of the Republic of Turkey]. Istanbul: Kenan Basımevi.

Boratav, Korkut (1981). 'Kemalist economic policies and etatism', in Kazancıgil, A. and Özbudun, E. (eds.), *Atatürk: Founder of a Modern State*. London: C. Hurst, 165–190.

Bulutay, Tuncer, Tezel, Yahya S., and Yıldırım, Nuri (1974). *Türkiye Milli Geliri (1923–1948)* [Turkish National Income (1923–1948)], 2 vols. Ankara: Ankara Üniversitesi.

Diaz Alejandro, Carlos (1984). 'Latin America in the 1930s', in Thorp, R. (ed.), *Latin America in the 1930s: The Role of the Periphery in the World Crisis*. London: Macmillan, 17–49.

Eichengreen, Barry (1992). 'The Origins of the Great Slump Revisited'. *Economic History Review*, 45(2): 213–239.

Eichengreen, Barry (2008). *Globalizing Capital, A History of the International Monetary System*, 2nd ed. Princeton and Oxford: Princeton University Press.

Eldem, Vedat (1970). *Osmanlı İmparatorluğu'nun İktisadi Şartları Hakkında Bir Tetkik* [A Study on the Economic Conditions of the Ottoman Empire]. Istanbul: İş Bankasi Publications.

Gürsel, Seyfettin (2005). 'Growth Despite Deflation: Turkish Economy during the Great Depression'. Paper presented at the Sixth Congress of the European Historical Economics Society, Istanbul, September.

Hansen, Bent (1991). *Egypt and Turkey: The Political Economy of Poverty, Equity and Growth*. Oxford: Oxford University Press for the World Bank.

James, Harold (2001). *The End of Globalization, Lessons from the Great Depression*. Cambridge, MA and London: Harvard University Press.

Kazgan, Gülten (1977). 'Türk ekonomisinde 1927–35 depresyonu, kapital birikimi ve örgütleşmeler' [The Depression of 1927–35 in the Turkish Economy: Capital Accumulation and Organizations], in Aksoy, Atilla and Pirili, Mustafa (eds.), *Atatürk Döneminin Ekonomik ve Toplumsal Sorunları* [Economic and Social Problems in the Ataturk Era]. Istanbul: İktisadi ve Ticari İlimler Akademisi Derneği, 231–274.

Keynes, John Maynard (1936). *The General Theory of Employment, Interest, and Money*. New York: Harcourt, Brace and Company.

Maddison, Angus (1985). *Two Crises: Latin America and Asia, 1929–38 and 1973–83*. Paris: Organisation for Economic Co-operation and Development (OECD), Development Centre Studies.

Özbek, Nadir (2003). 'Kemalist Rejim ve Popülizmin Sınırları. Büyük Buhran ve Buğday Alım Politikaları, 1921–1937' [The Kemalist Regime and the Limits of Populism: The Great Depression and Wheat Purchase Policies, 1921–1937]. *Toplum ve Bilim*, 96: 219–38.

Özel, Işık (1997). 'The Economy of Turkey in the Late Ottoman and Republican Periods: A quantitative analysis'. MA thesis, Boğaziçi University, Istanbul.

Pamuk, Şevket (1995). 'Long Term Trends in Urban Wages in Turkey, 1850–1990', in Zamagni, Vera and Scholliers, Peter (eds.), *Labour's Reward: Real Wages and Economic Growth in 19th and 20th Century Europe*. Aldershot: Edward Elgar, 89–105.

Pamuk, Şevket (2018). *Uneven Centuries: Economic Development of Turkey since 1820*. Princeton and Oxford: Princeton University Press.

Richards, Alan and Waterbury, John (1990). *A Political Economy of the Middle East*. Boulder: Westview Press.

Shorter, Frederic C. (1985). 'The Population of Turkey after the War of Independence'. *International Journal of Middle East Studies*, 17(4): 417–441.

Tekeli, İlhan and İlkin, Selim (1977). *1929 Dünya Buhranında Türkiye'nin İktisadi Politika Arayışları* [Turkey's Search for Economic Policy in the 1929 World Depression]. Ankara: Orta Doğu Teknik Üniversitesi.

Tekeli, İlhan and İlkin, Selim (1982). *Uygulamaya Geçerken Türkiye'de Devletçiliğin Oluşumu* [The Formation of Etatism in Turkey in Practice]. Ankara: Orta Doğu Teknik Üniversitesi.

Tekeli, İlhan and İlkin, Selim (1997). *Türkiye Cumhuriyet Merkez Bankası: Para ve Kredi Sisteminin Oluşumunda bir Aşama* [The Central Bank of the Republic of Turkey: A Stage in the Formation of the Money and Credit System], 2nd, expanded ed. Ankara: Türkiye Cumhuriyet Merkez Bankası.

Temin, Peter (1989). *Lessons from the Great Depression*. Cambridge, MA: MIT Press.

Tezel, Yahya. S. (1986). *Cumhuriyet Döneminin İktisadi Tarihi (1923–1950)* [Economic History of the Republican Era (1923–1950)], 2nd, expanded ed. Ankara: Yurt Yayınları.

Turkey State Institute of Statistics (1994). *Statistical Indicators, 1923–1992*. Ankara: State Institute of Statistics.

Yücel, Yelda (1996). 'Macroeconomic policies in Turkey during the Great Depression, 1929–1940'. MA thesis, Boğaziçi University, Istanbul.

Zendisayek, Beril (1997). 'Large and Small Enterprises in Turkish Industrialization during the Great Depression'. MA thesis, Boğaziçi University, Istanbul.

12

Latin American Experiments in Central Banking at the Onset of the Great Depression

Juan Flores Zendejas and Gianandrea Nodari

12.1 INTRODUCTION

In an economic slowdown a major problem that affects currency stability is fiscal dominance. This refers to the situation where an expansionary fiscal policy constrains the implementation of monetary policy (Sargent and Wallace, 1981). Fiscal dominance typically develops in the context of high levels of public debt, as central banks must support a government's effort to reduce servicing costs. Since the 1980s Latin America has been seen as a region where fiscal dominance occurs during the periods when populist governments have been in power; expansionary fiscal policies, to finance large public investment projects and social welfare programmes while the central banks pursue accommodative monetary policies, are characteristic of their terms office (Edwards, 2019). This has generally resulted in the government defaulting on international debt agreements and in a substantial increase in the level of inflation.

This chapter considers the early years of the central banks in Latin America. We analyse how central banks made use of the monetary policy tools at their disposal in the aftermath of the Great Depression. We begin with an assessment of the motives underlying the creation of the first central banks in Latin America during the 1920s. By and large these new institutions were set up to solve the persistent problem of monetary instability, a condition that had led to conflict between those socio-economic groups who either benefited or lost out from exchange depreciation. The establishment of a central bank was typically followed by the adoption of the gold standard regime and, in many cases, monetary reform was accompanied by a set of banking and fiscal reforms, usually devised by foreign advisors, or 'money doctors'.[1] Governments expected central banks to provide monetary stability, to become a secure source of finance, to foster the capacity of the banking sector, to provide credit to the private sector through re-discount operations, and to act as lenders of last resort. But while the Depression led to the deterioration of central bank independence, it also triggered a set of institutional reforms that expanded the range of instruments needed to conduct the region's monetary policy. Furthermore, the onset of the Depression severely affected Latin America's economies, causing a sharp deterioration in the fiscal position of most countries. In certain cases, governments decided to abandon the gold standard, impose exchange controls and, ultimately, default on their external debt. Central banks pursued expansionary monetary policies partly as a response to the governments' financial needs, but also to support economic activity through the provision of credit.

The literature on Latin America's central banking in the interwar period has focused on the role of foreign advisors who supported Latin American governments to adopt the gold standard. Viewing this through the lens of US colonialism, historians have studied the role of foreign advisors in central America at the turn of the twentieth century, and two decades later in South America, when Edwin Kemmerer, Professor of Economics at Princeton University visited the Andean countries and designed the central banks that were established in the 1920s (Seidel, 1972; Rosenberg and Rosenberg, 1987; Drake, 1994; Rosenberg, 1999). Other works have looked at the missions led by Otto Niemeyer from the Bank of England, who advised Brazil and Argentina during the 1930s (Sayers, 1976; Fritsch, 1988; Sember, 2018). There is a consensus that the Depression marked a turning point in economic policy. In the 1930s, the money doctors became less influential, in part because they did not tailor their advice to the changing situation in Latin America.[2] Subsequently, governments seized their countries' monetary institutions, leading to a permanent situation of high inflation and exchange instability (Jácome, 2015).

This standard account oversimplifies the implementation of monetary policy by Latin American central banks at the beginning of the 1930s and underestimates the role of the money doctors during those years. While economic historians have emphasized the emergence of a new development model based on state-led industrialization, the role of central banks

---

[1] See Drake (1994), Eichengreen (1989 [1994]), and Flores Zendejas (2021).
[2] For a survey of this literature, see Flores Zendejas (2021).

in this later, transitionary period merits greater attention.[3] We know that on the eve of the Great Depression, national monetary authorities promoted a set of unspecified countercyclical policies that fostered central banks discretionary powers (Pérez Caldentey and Vernengo, 2020). However, several questions regarding the timing and the motivation for central banks' participation in this new development model remain unanswered. Furthermore, since we do not know what these 'countercyclical economic policies' were, it is hard to judge whether they were truly innovative.

In this chapter, we posit that while Edwin Walter Kemmerer favoured specific countercyclical policies, local policymakers opposed them for fear of jeopardizing the credibility of the gold standard. To a certain degree, the history of Latin American central banks in the 1930s is no different from that of central banks in other regions who similarly experienced a loss of autonomy.[4] Yet in several cases, following the initial phase of currency devaluation, Latin American central banks managed to maintain exchange rate targeting while adhering to the new development model that prioritized the support for industry. As we demonstrate, the role of central banks as providers of capital would be short-lived, but it was relevant during the transition to the new banking system that emerged in the 1940s, when development banks dominated the industrialization process in the region.

This chapter is structured as follows. In Section 12.2, we survey the economic and financial situation in Latin America during the 1920s. Section 12.3 traces the history of central banks and provides a general account of the decision to establish new banks. Section 12.4 focuses on the institutional autonomy of central banks, which allowed them to operate without government interference, a key feature of their design. We show the degree to which this design helped to shape the central banks established after the Kemmerer missions to Latin America, whose governments retained considerable influence, not least through the power to nominate a high proportion of board members. This, however, was not to be the case for the handful of Latin American central banks designed by British money doctors at the same time. In Section 12.5 we describe how the monetary and fiscal orthodoxy established by the Kemmerer

---

[3] On the economic history of Latin America during that period, see Bértola and Ocampo (2013), Bulmer-Thomas (2003), and Thorp (1984).

[4] During the 1930s, a great number of central banks all over the world acted as government agencies in charge of exchange-rate management, the implementation of clearing agreements, and commercial banks' supervision. For an overview see Toniolo (1988).

missions was abandoned after the onset of the 1929 crisis. Our historical analysis suggests that, after suspending convertibility and introducing exchange controls, the expansionary monetary policy implemented by central banks led to a short-lived economic recovery. After an initial devaluation, beginning in 1934 when inflation rates began to diminish accordingly, central banks did not completely disregard the relevance of exchange-rate targeting. Overall, we demonstrate how Kemmerer's advice in the aftermath of 1929 was instrumental in the first phase of central banks' countercyclical policies. The loss of autonomy and the increase in state lending by central banks that occurred in certain countries were a consequence, we argue, of political turmoil and conflict, not an explicit stimulus policy decision. Section 12.6 concludes.

12.2 LATIN AMERICA IN THE EARLY 1920S

The development model of the period between 1870 and the Great Depression has been described as a commodity export-led boom (Bértola and Ocampo, 2013). While tariffs were among the highest in the world, falling transport costs, capital inflows, and improved infrastructure led to a rapid integration of Latin America into the world economy.[5] Rates of economic growth had increased before the First World War but decelerated thereafter. In a few cases, GDP per capita had caught up to, and even surpassed, that of its European counterparts, and in part this explains the increase in immigration from southern European countries to Latin America, and to Argentina and Uruguay in particular. Nevertheless, Latin America remained largely agricultural and most of the labour force was still engaged in production for domestic markets. Thus the region's economic performance depended upon the behaviour of commodity prices – 'the commodity lottery', as it has been called by Díaz-Alejandro (1982) – and on the connection between the export sector and the rest of the economy.

This economic model produced a range of effects: living standards varied considerably, with per capita income in the richest countries such as Argentina, Chile, and Uruguay being about five times that of the poorest ones, such as Brazil, Colombia, and Peru (Bulmer-Thomas, 2003). What is more, inequality within countries remained stark during the same period (Prados de la Escosura, 2007). This disparity fuelled social conflict, although there was less political instability compared to the

---

[5] On tariffs levels, see Coatsworth and Williamson (2004).

decades after independence.[6] By the late nineteenth century, the region's institutional frameworks had achieved a certain level of stability but were still heavily conditioned by local social and geographical factors. Cuba and Brazil relied on cash-crop agriculture and had only recently abolished slavery in the 1880s, although by this point wage-labour was already widespread. Most countries' exports were concentrated in just a handful of commodities, and only a few countries, for example Argentina, Peru, and Mexico had achieved some level of diversification. In some cases cottage industries had started to develop, accompanied by growing urbanization and the development of the services sectors (Bértola and Ocampo, 2013: 129).

Economic historians have studied the pace of financial development in the region showing that, even during the 1920s, medium and short-term loans were still lacking in Latin America although commercial banks had already been established in most countries for some time (Díaz-Alejandro, 1985). Local politics and the late development of capitalism has been shown to account for the slow launch of financial markets in the region (Marichal, 2020). Although Argentina had the most developed financial sector, as indicated by the size and geographical expansion of its largest bank, the Banco de la Nación, different indicators of financial development suggest that it lagged behind countries in South-Eastern Europe. Our own estimates, based on data concerning commercial and saving bank deposits as reported by the League of Nations, show that deposits per capita were 255 US\$ in Argentina, the highest for Latin America, and several times greater than the figures for other countries such as Salvador (2.67) and Ecuador (2.85). For comparative purposes, the figure was 273 US\$ for the United States (Della Paolera and Taylor, 2007).[7]

The export-led model was characterized by strong macroeconomic volatility. Government revenues were heavily dependent on customs duties, which exposed them to fluctuations in foreign trade. This volatility had also an impact on the countries' money supply. Since exchange availability was dependent upon capital flows, downturns in the world economy could lead to abrupt cessations of capital inflows (Triffin, 1944). However, despite monetary instability being a persistent problem

---

[6] See Bates et al. (2007), Sicotte and Vizcarra (2009).

[7] These strong variations can also be observed for the deposits to note issue ratio, even if the highest figure is the one for Chile (4.31) followed by Argentina (2.37) and Brazil (1.50). Again, these outcomes lie largely behind their US counterpart, whose figure was 9.83 for the United States (our own computations based on the League of Nations Economic and Financial Section [1927]).

across the region, by the time the First World War broke out most South American countries had switched to the gold standard. Across South America, this shift had taken place at different times during the nineteenth century. In countries such as Chile, Brazil, and Colombia, the last decade of the nineteenth century saw national economic elites ideologically divided between the so-called *papeleros*, who supported fiat money credit expansion, and the *metalistas* or *oreros*, who wished to reduce the money supply in order to appreciate the value of the currency and stick to the gold standard (Martín Aceña and Reis, 2000). Mexico and other Central American countries, where the banking system was still underdeveloped, switched from bimetallic regimes to variants of a 'limping gold standard',[8] where silver remained an important component of circulation in the early 1920s (Kemmerer,1940). Despite these differences, most Latin American countries alternated between the gold standard and periods of fiat money, even if the gold standard remained the dominant monetary regime throughout the continent during the first decades of the twentieth century.[9]

When the First World War broke out, most Latin American countries suspended the formal requirements of the gold standard either by refusing to redeem paper money in gold or by prohibiting the free export of gold. Until 1919–20, however, these provisions meant little. The war caused a marked increase in the prices and physical volume of almost every major export, causing the gold value of practically every currency to rise above official parity with the dollar.[10] However, institutions in charge of money issuing and exchange management retained an eclectic approach until the latter part of the 1920s. In the decades preceding the First World War, countries such as Mexico, Brazil, Argentina, and Paraguay created public agencies called 'stabilization' or 'exchange offices' which, in tandem with public or semi-public banks, were in charge of managing convertibility.[11] As for the issue of paper money, in some cases the treasury retained the

---

[8] See Conant (1903).

[9] See for instance table 1 in Meissner (2005, p. 391).

[10] See Kemmerer (1916) and 'Problems of Reconstruction in South America. Second Meeting: Exchange and Currency Problems', by Frank Fetter, 14 February 1933, in the Archives of the Council of Foreign Relations (hereafter ACFR), Studies Department Series, Box 130, Folder 1.

[11] These institutions were set up by respective governments to issue and redeem local money in return for gold or bills of foreign exchange at fixed rates. This task was executed by the Caja de Conversión (Argentina); Caixa de Conversão (Brazil); Comisión de Cambios y Moneda (México); Caja de Conversión (Costa Rica), and Oficina de Cambios (Paraguay); see McQueen (1926).

capacity to issue notes (Brazil), while in others, private banks held this privilege (as was the case in Argentina, Chile, and in Mexico prior to the revolution in 1911).[12]

12.3 THE LANDSCAPE OF CENTRAL BANKS' FOUNDATIONS IN LATIN AMERICA

There is no single reason why some Latin American countries decided to establish a central bank during the interwar period. Scholars have largely focused on three non-exclusive factors. First, the role of external influence played a part, either in the form of outright coercion, as happened in Central America, or through the more subtle influence of a money doctor. Foreign advisors were seen to be necessary to attract foreign capital and to provide the expertise in central banking that was still lacking in the region. Second, the political economy could impede the establishment of a central bank, if groups with a vested interest in the national bank had blocked attempts to establish one (Calomiris and Haber, 2014). Later interwar economic challenges, particularly after 1929, weakened the capacity of these interest groups to resist reform and enhanced the capacity of Latin American states to establish new institutions, including central banks. Third, some scholars highlight the importance of institutional development, including the emergence of large national banks, which performed some of the functions of central banks, and the establishment of monetary agencies that met the needs of different monetary regimes; these changes eventually led to the creation of central banks, intended to meet the needs of the new monetary and banking systems (Marichal and Díaz Fuentes, 2016).

Here, we revisit these arguments and show why these factors do not entirely explain why so many central banks were established in the 1920s, or why the new institutions that came into existence were so diverse.[13] As we go on to demonstrate in the following section, some governments established central banks with little autonomy, while other institutions were set up to provide monetary stability and perform lending-of-last-resort functions. The differences between one country and the next led to diverse reactions as the crisis of 1929 began to impact the region.

---

[12] For an overview on financial development's differences amongst Latin American countries during the nineteenth and early twentieth century see Marichal and Gambi (2017).

[13] According to Triffin (1944, p. 96) during the interwar period, central banks of Latin America 'present the most diverse pattern from country to country'.

External influence and 'dollar diplomacy' never led directly to the establishment of a central bank, or even a sole issuing institution. The first money doctors to arrive in Central America had emphasized the need to introduce fiscal reforms to provide the necessary fiscal balance and secure external debt servicing. Exchange-rate stability was also perceived as a means to achieve this goal. But Central American countries were faced with an implicit conflict between exporting oligarchies, who benefited from exchange-rate depreciation, and governments, who favoured a fixed exchange rate to tackle 'original sin', that is, the problem that state revenues were collected in local currency, but debt was mostly serviced in foreign exchange.[14] Given the region's main creditors were European investors, it was the risk of foreign intervention in the event of a sovereign default on external debt which prompted the US government to assume a proactive role in the region.

The US government and the US money doctors designed many of the fiscal and monetary regimes in Central America, but neither foresaw the establishment of a central bank. In Nicaragua, the US government favoured the appointment of a collector general and set up the Banco Nacional de Nicaragua (a new state bank), in 1911. This new institution held the monopoly of money issue and maintained the currency on the gold standard until the 1930s, with a brief interruption in 1914. In 1920, Arthur Young acted as a foreign advisor in Honduras, where he proposed the adoption of the gold standard, albeit without a central bank. This effort was not entirely successful and silver, along with the US dollar, continued to circulate in the 1920s.[15] After signing a treaty with the US government in 1915, Haiti created the Banque Nationale de la Republique d' Haiti, an affiliate of the National City Bank of New York, which was granted the sole right of note issue. In Panama, where the US government held a particular interest due to the construction of the canal, no banks of issue were established. Early in 1909, the US dollar was declared the only legal tender in the country and became the principal medium of exchange.[16]

Other Central American countries implemented reforms designed to maintain the gold standard, even without being visited by a money

---

[14] See Bulmer-Thomas (1987); on the problem of 'original sin' see Eichengreen and Hausmann (1999).

[15] On the contrary, and without the presence of a money doctor, El Salvador managed to introduce a gold-standard regime in 1919 (from a silver standard) which remained until 1932.

[16] For an overview see Mc Queen (1926); even today, Panama has no central bank.

doctor. El Salvador managed to switch from a silver to a gold standard in 1919, and stayed on gold until 1932. In 1921, Costa Rica established the Banco International as the sole note-issuing authority, while the Caja de Conversión was in charge of holding foreign exchange reserves; the latter began to convert notes to gold in 1924, a regime that lasted until 1932 (Bulmer-Thomas, 1987: 32).

In the rest of Latin America, the new central banks established in the 1920s were a direct outcome of Kemmerer's missions, even if in some cases, the policies he recommended were only implemented several years after his visits. The first of his missions took place in Mexico (1917) followed by Guatemala in (1919). In Mexico, the government's decisions to adopt the gold standard, establish a central bank, and pursue fiscal reform in 1925, were all based on the policy blueprints provided by Kemmerer which were implemented despite high levels of political instability (Nodari, 2019). To a certain extent, this was similar to the situation in Guatemala, where the central bank was established in 1926 (Kemmerer and Dalgaard, 1983). From 1923 to 1930, Kemmerer's missions led to the creation of central banks in Colombia (1923), Chile (1925), Ecuador (1926), and Bolivia (1928).[17] In Peru, the government had already established a bank of re-discount and issue, the Banco de Reserva del Peru in 1922, but its statutes were overhauled by Kemmerer during his 1930 mission.

Argentina did not establish a central bank until 1935, indicating how financial development did not necessarily lead to the establishment of a central bank. However, it is worth noting that debates on the convenience of establishing a central bank may easily date back to 1899, when a project to convert Argentina's National Bank into a state bank (a central bank owned entirely by the state) was first presented. Subsequent schemes aimed at centralizing note-issuing functions with currency convertibility, as well as fostering long-term credit. After 1914, discussions on the advantages of having an autonomous central bank intensified, and largely focused on the benefits of strengthening re-discounting operations and providing price stability to maintain the value of wages (Lorenzutti, 1996). These schemes were unsuccessful in part because the National Bank functioned as a lender of last resort to private banks and did so under favourable conditions that encouraged excessive risk-taking (Della Paolera and Taylor, 2007:174). This arrangement, together with the fact that the Bank provided a secure supply of resources to the state through

---

[17] On the historical narrative of these visits, see Drake (1989).

its re-discounting of Treasury bills, implied that there was significant interest in maintaining the status quo.

There are other examples of domestic politics and state finance impeding the establishment of central banks in Brazil, Uruguay, and Venezuela. In Brazil, money was issued by the Banco do Brasil, a state-run bank where 52 per cent of the shares were publicly owned. The British mission of 1923, led by Edwin Montagu, recommended that Banco be transformed into a central bank, with the state selling its entire stake in the bank (Fritsch, 1988: 90). Once the reform had been implemented, the government of Brazil expected to raise a new foreign loan in return. But a British loan embargo imposed in 1924 delayed the establishment of the central bank and this prompted the Banco do Brasil to pursue an expansionary monetary policy, which was mainly used to finance the federal government.[18] In Uruguay, central bank functions were divided between a private bank, which had the sole right to issue paper money, and the Treasury, which supervised the banking system while managing the national monetary system as a whole. In Uruguay political and economic elites had been thwarting plans to establish a central bank since the 1930s (Baudean, 2017). Finally, in Venezuela, four private banks were in charge of issuing paper money redeemable in gold on demand (McQueen, 1926); as one might expect, they were also opposed to the creation of a central bank in the 1930s (Crazut, 1970).

12.4 MONEY DOCTORS, CENTRAL BANKS, AND THE QUESTION OF AUTONOMY

The central banks created in the 1920s were designed to maintain monetary and banking stability and to provide limited state finance. As with other monetary institutions designed during the 1920s, Kemmerer's central banks were expected to maintain currency convertibility into gold at a fixed price, respect the real bills doctrine (providing just as much credit as was required by the legitimate needs of business), and follow the so-called rules of the game, tightening monetary policy in response to gold outflows and loosening it when those were reversed (Jácome, 2015). Furthermore, the design of most central banks followed the principles that had been outlined at the International Conferences of Brussels and Genoa of 1920 and 1922. They were to be free from political pressure, while the government was expected to run sound

---

[18] See Fritsch (1988) and Villela (2017).

TABLE 12.1 *Monetary and fiscal variables in Latin America, 1917–1922*

Country	Inflation rate (%)	Exchange rate volatility[1]	Budget deficit (% of revenues)[2]	Loan in New York in 1921–1922
Central bank and foreign advisor				
Bolivia	NA	0.22	43.0	Yes
Chile	7.0	0.40	11.8	Yes
Ecuador	4.7	0.28	5.5	No
Colombia	6.9	0.09	6.5	No
Average	6.2	0.25	16.7	
Central Bank – no foreign advisor				
Guatemala[3]	NA	0.02	4.7	No
Mexico	4.8	0.05	−11.9	No
Peru	7.9	0.16	18.1	Yes
Average	6.4	0.08	3.6	
No central bank				
Argentina	4.4	0.14	23.6	Yes
Brazil	6.4	0.36	42.0	Yes
Uruguay	3.4	0.23	23.0	Yes
Venezuela	2.4	0.10	−1.5	No
Average	4.2	0.21	21.8	

Notes: 1. Measured as the ratio of the mean exchange rate to its standard deviation.
2. Deficits are measured as % of public revenues; negative figures represent budget surpluses.
3. While Kemmerer visited this country twice, in 1919 and 1924, the final outcome differed from Kemmerer's original proposals.
Sources: MOxLAD database with the exceptions of Uruguay (Bértola et al. 1999) and Venezuela (Carrillo Batalla 2002).

fiscal policies (League of Nations, 1923). The independence of the central bank was the price to secure exchange rate stability and lower inflation rates.

Nevertheless, macroeconomic imbalances did not always lead to the establishment of central banks. Table 12.1 presents basic fiscal and monetary data for a sample of countries in the five years preceding the foundation of Latin America's first central bank. Countries are divided into three groups: the first includes 'Kemmerer countries', that is, those that established central banks during the 1920s, based on Kemmerer's recommendations. The second group consists of countries that established a central bank without the direct intervention of a money doctor; this group includes Guatemala and Mexico, which had both been visited by Kemmerer some time before (see earlier). The third group comprises countries that did not establish a central bank at all in the 1920s.

Table 12.1 reveals no clear causal pattern between macroeconomic performance and the decision to set up a central bank. On average, the countries that established central banks were more exposed to inflation (with Peru and Chile facing the highest inflation rates). However, Argentina and Brazil had similar rates of inflation and yet did not create a central bank. These differences become more marked if we consider exchange rate volatility. Here we find that those countries that did not establish a central bank experienced greater volatility than those that did. Finally, many countries that did not establish a central bank had higher budget deficits (21.8 per cent of revenues); in fact, average deficits would be even higher if Venezuela, which ran persistent surpluses, were excluded. Kemmerer countries also suffered from large budget deficits, even though their figures were comparatively lower. By contrast, countries that set up a central bank without a foreign advisor had the lowest deficits, with Mexico even running surpluses.

Arguably the most important difference was access to foreign capital. Countries that had been able to access capital markets to raise state loans did not establish a central bank (Lewis, 1938). However we have good evidence that Bolivia, Ecuador, and Colombia were all countries that had struggled to float a loan in the New York capital market (Flores Zendejas et al., 2020). Mexico was also excluded from capital markets, and one reason for generating budget surpluses was to raise the capital necessary to establish a central bank. The suspension of Mexico's external debt service in 1924 – one year before the establishment of Mexico's central bank – also helped (Gomez-Galvarriato, 2019).

Previous studies have shown that governments appealed to money doctors so as to overcome domestic political resistance to policies that they intended to implement anyway.[19] The expectation that implementing Kemmerer's reforms would facilitate access to foreign capital markets also helped to justify this course of action.[20] However, as Table 12.1 shows, Bolivia and Chile had been able to secure loans in New York prior to Kemmerer's visit. But Kemmerer claimed that borrowing costs would decline once his reforms were implemented.[21] During a visit to

---

[19] See Drake (1989); cf. the claim made by Banco de la República [Colombia] (1990: 343), that the level of technical expertise in Kemmerer's second mission was impossible to find in the country.

[20] See for instance Drake (1989), Eichengreen (1989 [1994]) as well as Flores Zendejas et al., (2020).

[21] In a second visit to Guatemala in 1924, Kemmerer also urged Guatemala's government to accept a loan to support a set of economic and financial reforms. The government

Bolivia in 1928, Kemmerer expressed criticism of the 1922 loan with its high interest rate and underwriting fees, as well as the pledged revenues granted to creditors.[22] To improve the country's financial standing he recommended establishing a long-term relationship with a strong banking house in New York.[23] Finally, he recommended founding an independent central bank. In his eyes, Bolivia's Banco de la Nación Boliviana was using monetary policy to help finance the government and was therefore unable to provide exchange rate stability.[24]

How independent were Kemmerer banks compared to other central banks established in Latin America in the same period? Table 12.2 contains the relevant data. It shows that in most of Kemmerer's central banks concessions were extended from twenty to fifty years, except in Colombia, where the limit was set at twenty years. According to Kemmerer, a lengthy concession was necessary to guarantee a degree of autonomy from persistent political interference. However, setting the length of these concessions was preferable to an indefinite mandate, as each renewal required legislative approval, an official acknowledgement that central banks were protecting the nation's interest (Banco Central de la Reserva de Perú, 1997: 55). Table 12.2 also presents the initial proportion of state ownership envisioned in the legislation for setting up the central banks; this was higher in Kemmerer countries compared to other cases.[25] The exception was Mexico, a non-Kemmerer country where the state was initially expected to acquire at least 51 per cent of the shares. However, unlike Mexico, state-owned shares in Kemmerer banks did not secure the right to vote. And in central banks designed with the aid of British money doctors (Brazil and El Salvador), the state was prohibited from holding any shares.

---

refused the loan and established a central bank two years thereafter, to a large extent different to the original plan established by Kemmerer. See Rosenberg (1999) and Edwin Kemmerer Papers (hereafter EKP), 'Currency and Banking Reform', Box 168.

[22] This was a long-term loan for 25 million dollars with an underwriting fee of 9.2 per cent. Brazil issued two loans during the same year at slightly lower yields to maturity (7.3 and 7.8) but much lower underwriting fees (3 and 3.5 per cent, respectively). Data from Flandreau et al. (2010); original source is Young (1930).

[23] 'Report in support of a project of a General Banking Law, by the Commission of Financial Advisers', June 1927, in EKP, 'Kemmerer Commission of Financial Advisers', Box 79, folder 1.

[24] 'El Plan Kemmerer para la reorganización del Banco de la Nación Boliviana, 1927', in EKP, 'Banks and Banking, Banco de la Nación Boliviana, 1912–1927', Box 76, folder 4.

[25] In Kemmerer countries, governments were allowed to sell or buy shares according to the needs of the central bank and the capacity of commercial banks to furnish the necessary capital. However, the shares acquired by the government were not accompanied by the right to vote.

TABLE 12.2 *Latin American central bank's statutory characteristics: autonomy and limits on state lending (ordered chronologically, banks designed by Kemmerer marked with *)*

Country (date established)	Duration of concession (years)	% share of state-owned shares[1]	Board members appointed by the government[2]	Limits on lending to the state
Peru 9 March 1922	25	0	3/10	No limit
Colombia* 11 July 1923	20	50	3/9	30% of paid-in capital and reserves
Chile* 21 August 1925	50	13.3	3/10	30% of paid-in capital and reserves
Mexico 1 September 1925	30	51	5/9	10% of paid-in capital and reserves
Guatemala 11 December 1926	30	No provision	2/9	10% of paid-in capital and reserves
Ecuador* 4 March 1927	50	No provision	2/9	20% of paid-in capital and reserves
Bolivia* 20 July 1928	50	No provision	2/9	25% of paid-in capital and reserves (possibility to extend to 35% in case of emergency)
Argentina 28 March 1935	40	33.3	$1^{3}/12$	Only short-term loans up to 10% of tax revenues (averaged over the last three years)
Brazil [proposal][4] (Not established)	30	0	0/5	Up to one-eighth of state revenues (of the previous year)
El Salvador 26 July and 9 Sept. 1933	30	0	0/4	Temporary advances only (up to 10% of revenues from customs duties)
Venezuela 8 September 1939	50	50	$4^{5}/8$	Not allowed

Notes: 1. As foreseen in the enactment law establishing the bank (initial shares).
2. Board of directors members appointed by the government /the total number of members.
3. Excludes the president and vice-president, also elected by the executive, with Senate approval.
4. Proposal by Otto Niemeyer on the 4 July 1931.
5. Excludes the president, elected by the bank's shareholders from a list proposed by the government's president.
Source: Flores Zendejas (2021).

The newly established central banks differed in the government's capacity to influence the board of directors, the limits set on making loans to the state, and whether they could do business with the general public. Government involvement in the management of the central bank was greater in Kemmerer banks, compared to those set up with the help of British money doctors. Kemmerer insisted on providing central banks with a level of autonomy but foresaw that the government would play a role as a shareholder and would have the power to appoint the president and a certain number of board members (Table 12.2). Furthermore, limits on credits to the government were less stringent in Kemmerer countries. In Otto Niemeyer's view, the relatively high limits placed on state borrowing made Kemmerer banks less independent from national governments. This was true, as their statutes allowed governments to hold a 'substantial bulk' of shares as well as the 'nominative power for a proportion of members of the boards'.[26]

Of all the central banks established during the interwar period Mexico's was the least independent.[27] This can be partly explained by the Mexican government's constraint to provide the bulk of capital for the new institution, given the level of misgiving among commercial bankers. The civil war that had begun in 1914 had devastated the national banking system. Different revolutionary factions had forced banks to lend them money until Venustiano Carranza, elected president of Mexico by 1917, seized the banks to control their specie reserves. As a consequence, commercial banks viewed the operations of new central banks with suspicion. Suspicions were also raised when the central bank granted loans to firms and enterprises owned by government officials (Gomez-Galvarriato, 2019).

12.5 CENTRAL BANKS AND FISCAL DISTRESS

The Great Depression affected Latin America in various ways. Export revenues declined following the fall in commodity prices and with a general increase in protectionism (Díaz-Alejandro, 1983). Since most public revenue was trade-related by the end of 1929 Latin American countries were experiencing fiscal strain and balance-of-payment difficulties.

---

[26] 'Central Banks in Latin America', 25 May 1933, in BOEA OV188/1.
[27] As some contemporaries also underlined, the 'Mexican central bank would seem to be much more under the control of the Government than is common in central banks in other countries' (Sterrett and Davis 1928, p. 127).

By 1931, foreign banks had cancelled their lines of credit to Latin American governments and banks. To make matters worse, the many foreign banks operating branches in Latin America were squeezed of credit by the head offices in Europe and the United States.[28] As investment rates plummeted, governments were unable to issue new loans.

At the onset of the crisis, Latin American countries adopted an 'orthodox response' (Eichengreen 1992: 230–232). Most countries tried to limit imports and boost exports by raising import duties in order to preserve the foreign exchange needed to maintain convertibility and continue to service their foreign debt. Many central banks and monetary authorities introduced restrictive policies, raising re-discount rates to preserve their international reserves.[29] However, the deteriorating position of the balance of payments forced central banks to use their reserves to finance current account deficits and resort to deflationary policies.

As austerity policies and orthodox adjustments failed to strengthen trade balances, most Latin American governments were forced to suspend the payment of their external debt, abandon the gold standard, and/ or introduce some form of exchange control. Table 12.3 shows how each country resorted to one of these options, albeit at different times during the crisis. It is interesting that the first countries to devalue were those lacking a central bank. Argentina and Uruguay suspended the gold standard before the end of 1929; Brazil followed in November 1930, and by the beginning of 1933, only Venezuela and Central America's 'dollarized' countries maintained their peg to the US dollar, at least until Franklin Delano Roosevelt declared the gold embargo in April 1933.

In general, departure from the gold standard was presaged by the introduction of exchange controls. These sought to prevent fluctuations in the exchange rate, reduce foreign exchange speculation, and slow the pace of depleting international reserves (Díaz-Alejandro 1983: 11). By early 1932, only Mexico, Peru, and Venezuela had not resorted to foreign exchange

[28] According to a rough estimate presented by Guillermo Butler Sherwell, head of the Latin American Section of the Federal Reserve Board, the amount of foreign credit cancellation during 1931 in Latin America reached US$ 283,5 million. See 'The Latin America exchange problem', by Guillermo Butler Sherwell, in EKP, Box 170, Folder 8, 'Latin America, 1927–1940'. This amount was equivalent to 1.5 times the total amount of Latin American loans issued in New York in 1928 and 1929 (according to the figures presented in Lewis (1938).

[29] From 1929 to 1931 Chile increased the re-discount rate from 6 to 9 per cent; Colombia increase the rate from 7 to 8 per cent in 1929, Bolivia from 7 to 9 per cent and the Central Bank of Peru increased its rate six time between 1928 and 1929; see Jácome (2015).

TABLE 12.3 *Suspension of the gold standard, introduction of exchange controls, and suspension of debts payments in Latin America during the Great Depression*

Country	Monetary Unit	Gold standard suspended officially	Exchange controls introduced	Exchange rate first falls below parity	Debt amortization suspended[1]
Uruguay	Peso	1 December 1929	7 September 1931	April 1929	May 1933
Argentina	Paper peso	16 December 1929	13 October 1931	November 1929	–
Paraguay	Peso	–	20 June 1932	November 1929	June 1932
Brazil	Milreis	November 1930	18 May 1931	December 1929	October 1931
Bolivia	Boliviano	25 September 1931	3 October 1931	March 1930	January 1931
Venezuela	Bolivar	–	1 December 1936	September 1930	–
Mexico	Peso	25 July 1931	–	August 1931	January 1928
Salvador	Colon	7 October 1931	August 1933	October 1931	February 1932
Colombia	Peso	24 September 31[2]	24 September 1931	January 1932	February 1932
Costa-Rica	Colon	–	16 January 1932	January 1932	August 1932
Nicaragua	Cordoba	13 November 1931	13 November 1931	January 1932	January 1932
Chile	Peso	19 April 1932	30 July 1931	April 1932	July 1931
Peru	Sol	14 May 1932	–	May 1932	May 1931
Ecuador	Sucre	8 February 1932	2 May 1932	June 1932	July 1929
Cuba	Peso	21 November 1933	2 June 1934	April 1933	December 1933
Guatemala	Quetzal	–	–	April 1933	February 1933
Haiti	Gourde	–	–	April 1933	–
Honduras	Lempira	–	27 March 1934	April 1933	–
Panama	Balboa	–	–	April 1933	May 1933

Notes: 1. Only suspensions of sinking fund payments are recorded. Some of these countries continued to pay interest on their debt: Uruguay (until July 1933); Paraguay (until April 1933); Colombia (until April 1933); Salvador (until January 1935); Guatemala (until May 1939). Mexico temporarily deferred debt payment in 1928; by the end of 1930, the country had signed a new agreement with the International Committee of Bankers, before finally suspending debt payment in January 1932.
2. Despite having officially abandoned the gold standard, Colombia only suspended internal convertibility and maintained its pre-1931 peg to the dollar until March 1933; see (Ocampo 1984).

Sources: League of Nations (1936), table 122, p. 231); information in debt servicing drawn from various issues of the *Annual report of the Council of the Corporation of Foreign Bondholders.*

controls. Implemented differently in each country, they mostly functioned as a sort of exchange clearing, whereby drawings of foreign exchange were remitted according to their availability at the central bank's reserves. Argentina, Uruguay, and Mexico were the only countries that did not to restrict gold exports: all the other countries implemented some form of gold embargo.[30] Given the high proportion of public debt denominated in foreign currency, other governments attempted to remain on gold and only defaulted later (Bordo and Meissner, 2020).[31] For the most part, countries defaulted on foreign debt repayment after exchange controls had been introduced and the suspension of the gold standard (Table 12.3) (Jorgensen and Sachs, 1989). By 1934, Argentina, Haiti, and the Dominican Republic were the only countries still servicing their external debt normally.[32]

Figure 12.1 plots the evolution of real GDP, inflation, exchange rates against the US dollar, and budget deficits between 1928 and 1935 for a sample of Latin American countries. It shows that the range of Latin America's experiences has probably been underestimated. Chile saw the greatest drop in GDP, while Colombia's income never dipped below its pre-crisis level (1928). In terms of inflation, it is interesting to note that deflation was a common feature (the notable exception being Chile), and so it remained until 1932, precisely when Chile saw an upsurge. Chilean exceptionality, abetted by the short-lived socialist coup of June 1932, was noted by contemporary commentators. In early 1933, US economist Frank Fetter showed how budgetary deficits had forced the Chilean government to turn to the central bank for help. As a result, between 1932 and 1933 paper money issue 'more than doubled in the period of a year'.[33] Across the board, exchange rates witnessed high rates of depreciation in South America, particularly in Argentina and Chile, although all Latin American exchange rates remained stable throughout the decade.

---

[30] 'The Latin America exchange problem', by Guillermo Butler Sherwell, in EKP, Box 170, Folder 8, 'Latin America, 1927–1940'.

[31] Most governments held a ratio between 70 per cent to 95 per cent foreign to total debt (most foreign debt being denominated in foreign currencies); own estimates based on United Nations (1948).

[32] Certain Argentinean provinces and cities defaulted in the early 1930s on their external debts.

[33] According to Fetter, at the beginning of 1933 'over 80 per cent' of the total earning assets of the Chilean central bank represented government debt 'and a good part of the rest represented advances that do not belong in the portfolio of a central bank'. See 'Problems of Reconstruction in South America. Second Meeting: Exchange and Currency Problem. Session led by Professor Frank Fetter', 14 February 1931 in ACFR, Studies Department Series, Box 130, Folder 1.

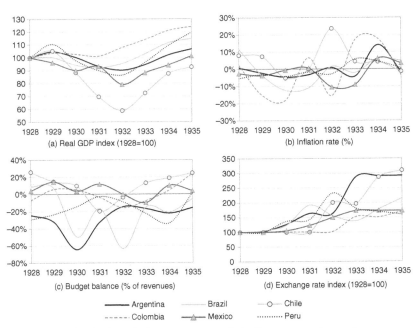

FIGURE 12.1 Latin America's macroeconomic indicators, 1928–1936.

Sources: Several issues of the League of Nations' Statistical Yearbook are used to derive inflation rates and budget deficits; real GDP is calculated from Bértola and Ocampo (2013), table A1, pp. 287–288. Exchange rates in terms of units of local currency per US$ are drawn from Global Financial Data. Mexico's inflation and deficit figures are drawn from the MOxLAD database. GDP figures and exchange rates are indexed at 1928=100; budget balances are defined as the percentage share of the budget balance to central government public revenue.

12.6 NEW FUNCTIONS OF CENTRAL
BANKS SINCE THE 1930S

Much of the historical literature has focused on the new monetary policy tools and institutional innovations introduced by central banks. The major institutional changes taking place in the early 1930s have been described as the starting point of modern central banking in Latin America. New re-discounting policies and the open-market operations implemented by central banks are seen to have marked the beginning of a 'more proactive, and in some cases explicitly countercyclical policy' which put an end to the orthodox measures that had been advocated by the money doctors in the past (Pérez Caldentey and Vernengo, 2020: 960). Institutional change did foster the first phase of Latin American economic recovery. Nevertheless, it was not local policymakers, but Kemmerer who initially proposed these reforms and encouraged their implementation.

Latin American governments and central bankers had sought external support since 1930. Nevertheless, the advice proffered by Kemmerer and British money doctors differed substantially regarding the monetary policies to be implemented (Flores Zendejas, 2021). Kemmerer visited Colombia in 1930 and Peru in 1931 and attended two multilateral conferences in Washington and Lima. According to a Bank of England report on the bank's missions to Latin America, Niemeyer only visited Brazil in 1931 and Argentina in 1933, while Powell, who had previously advised El Salvador, went to Argentina in August 1935, to serve as a technical adviser to the new central bank.[34] Kemmerer's visit to Colombia took place in August 1930. Contrary to popular belief, his advice was to increase, rather than restrict overall lending. The mission proposed raising the total amount of credit provided to local governments and the general public, as well as giving coffee growers a stronger voice in the determination of monetary policy. They had complained about insufficient credit from the time the central bank was founded. To meet their demands the government was tasked to appoint three new members to the Bank's board of directors, representing the chamber of trade, industry, and the coffee growers. Assistance was provided to the growers by widening the sort of financial assets (short-term commercial paper) that could be presented to the central bank for re-discounting.[35] Kemmerer tried to tailor other reforms to local circumstances. Since paper eligible for re-discount was scarce, he encouraged national and municipal authorities to increase lending to the private sector in order to tackle the shortfall of credit following the 1929 crisis.[36]

---

[34] Niemeyer was also invited to Paraguay when he was visiting Brazil, in 1931; the invitation was declined and the Governor of the Bank of England referred them to the Bank for International Settlements (BIS). Memorandum on 'Bank of England Missions to Latin America', 25 October 1935 in BOEA OV16/2.

[35] This advice resembled the content of US Banking Act of 1932 which expanded Federal Reserve discount and re-discount policy; see Meltzer (2003, 358).

[36] See article titled 'El Banco de la Republica ha principiado a otrogar prestamos a particulares', *El Tiempo*, 22 October 1930. According to Kemmerer, with the exception of the Federal Reserve Bank of the United States, the central banks of France, Germany, Greece, Hungary, Italy, Japan, Latvia, Netherlands, Poland, Russia, Sweden, and Switzerland were allowed to embark on regular banking business with the public. The Bank of England, despite being chiefly a 'banks' Bank' had no limitation on dealing with public; see 'Provisions of Status of Leading Central Banks', EKP Box 236, Folder 8 (Central Banks).

These expansionary recommendations – lowering re-discount rates, extending the maturity of eligible commercial paper, lowering commercial banks' reserves with the central bank – were criticized by local policymakers. But Kemmerer had noticed that the ratio of central bank reserves to notes and deposits stood above 80 per cent – well-above the statutory requirement of 60 per cent – and he encouraged authorities to reduce it.[37] He also proposed raising the central bank's upper limit on state loans to 30 per cent of its capital and surplus. This would be accomplished indirectly, through the acceptance of short-term government securities to serve as collateral against loans to commercial banks and the general public. Furthermore, Kemmerer defended the role of government representatives on the board of directors and, despite some initial reluctance, proved to favour the idea of raising the limit on state loans to a 'modest extension', in emergencies.[38] Finally, the mission recommended the conduct of open-market operations to develop an active market for short-term government securities, and the design of a new scheme for agrarian bank credit.[39]

During his visit to Peru in early 1931, Kemmerer proposed reforms to the central bank statutes that were largely in line with his previous suggestions to Colombia. In a more orthodox vein, he recommended fiscal reforms to signal a commitment to balanced budgets, which would help Peru to secure a new foreign loan (Banco Central de la Reserva de Perú, 1997: xxxv). He proposed shifting tax revenues away from custom duties and toward direct taxation. However, in the midst of the political turmoil that followed the military revolt of August 1930, Kemmerer's advice was largely disregarded (Quiroz, 1993).

Between 5 and 13 October 1931, Kemmerer attended the Fourth Pan-American Commercial Conference in Washington and expressed his new views on monetary and banking policy reforms. While still a strong proponent of the gold-exchange standard, he introduced new ideas about the role of central banking in response to the crisis. According to him, Latin American central banks had to be re-organized to operate as 'quasi-public

---

[37] 'Reforma de la Ley Bancaria', *El Diario Nacional*, 22 September 1930. Other sectors also demanded that the level of reserves be lowered; see for instance 'A Trascendentales reformas a la legislación bancaria vigente en la República', *Relator*, 8 May 1930.

[38] 'Exposition of Motives of the Law amending Law 25 of 1923, The Organic Law of the Bank of the Republic' in EKP, Box 132, Folder 5 (Banks and Banking – Banco de la República, 1930–1933), 18.

[39] 'Kemmerer Bill-Banking Policy', 3 October 1930, in EKP, Box 132, Folder 2 (Banks and Banking – General, 1926–1931).

institutions'. On the one hand, this would protect them from becoming 'tools of politics', exploited by national governments; on the other, it would spare them from the 'equally great danger' of being controlled by bankers who operated primarily for financial profit. In order to avoid this danger, Kemmerer proposed reforming the Bank's board of directors, so that no more than ten members would be chosen equitably by representatives of the government, the commercial banks, and a select group representing the interest of agriculture, industry, commerce, and organized labour. He also strongly recommended that central banks share their profits with their national governments and open the door to a future increase in the amounts central banks were allowed to advance to the state.[40]

Kemmerer attended the South American Conference of Central Banks, which was held in Lima in December 1931. The meeting was convened by Bolivia's central bank and included representatives from Kemmerer banks and the Federal Reserve. One goal was to set up a reform agenda and promote international credit to the real economy. After a review of the state of leading central banks in the world, Kemmerer argued that central banks needed to abandon the real bills doctrine and increase the discount and re-discount of paper generated by agricultural, industrial and commercial transactions. Central bankers agreed to reform their statutes in order to develop re-discount and credit operations, thorough the creation of a system of bankers' acceptances. Kemmerer recommended making use of open-market operations, easing monetary policy, and extending lender-of-last-resort facilities in cases where there was 'urgent need of assistance'.[41]

As the crisis deepened, political instability grew, increasing the pressure on central banks to advance funds to the state. War broke out between Bolivia and Paraguay between 1932 and 1935 (the Chaco War), as well as between Colombia and Peru, between September 1932 and May 1933. Chile experienced a coup in June 1932. When the Chaco War broke out in 1932, Bolivia initially met the expenses by raising taxes on the mining sector, but before long the country had resorted to monetary finance (Peres-Cajías, 2014).[42] The League of Nations (1935:159) reported that, between 1931 and 1933, Bolivia's central bank increased the level of

---

[40] 'Currency Stabilization in Latin America. Address of Edwin Walter Kemmerer', in EKP, Box 259, Folder 2 (Fourth Pan American Commercial Conference, 1931).

[41] See EKP, Box 236, Folder 8 (Conference of South American Central Banks, Lima, Peru, 1–12 December 1931).

[42] Peres-Cajías (2014, p. 94) further posits that exchange controls were used as an income tax, as mining companies were obliged to sell their foreign exchange gains at an overvalued exchange rate, while the government sold them at market rates.

credit to the government by a factor of thirteen, representing almost 75 per cent of the bank's total assets by the end of the year. Comparable figures for Chile's central bank show that its public loans accounted for 67 per cent of assets in 1933, up from 15 per cent, in 1931.

Central bank lending to the state could be facilitated through a set of reforms that benefited other sectors as well. To give a typical example, in July 1931, Chile's central bank was allowed to extend its discount and lending operations in foreign currency enabling it to buy bonds denominated in foreign currency from the state. Furthermore, in September 1931, the legal minimum of gold reserves (the cover ratio) was reduced from 50 to 30 per cent, only to be cut to 25 per cent in January 1932. At the same time, limits on advances to the state were raised from 20 to 80 per cent of the Bank's capital and reserves. In Ecuador, the legal minimum of gold reserves was reduced to 25 per cent of deposits and 50 per cent of banknotes (down from 50 per cent of notes and deposits combined) after a new Banking Law was passed in December 1931. In Peru, despite Kemmerer's recommendations, the reserve cover ratio was cut to 50 per cent of notes (rather than 50 per cent of notes and deposits) in May 1932. What is more, banking acceptances were allowed to constitute up to 50 per cent of the total reserve, instead of 40 per cent. Finally, the government was permitted to increase its credit limit at the central bank from two to three months' revenue.[43]

The increased amount of credit available ended up benefiting other sectors as well. In Chile, under pressure from the socialist coalition that took power in June 1932, the central bank used its reserves to pay for imports and finance other public-sector bodies. Credits were channelled to programmes for unemployment relief and industrial development.[44] In Colombia, the central bank was allowed to make loans according to the following rules: up to 15 per cent to banks and the general public, and no more than 30 per cent of its paid-up capital and surplus to the state. As for the legal reserve minimum against notes and deposits, this was reduced from 50 to 40 per cent in November 1931. The bank also participated in various public programmes aimed at providing relief to debtors and coffee exporters; in 1933, it also bought shares from the newly created central mortgage bank.[45] Lastly, Kemmerer's proposal to

---

[43] 'Central Banks in Latin America', 25 May 1933 in BOEA, OV188/1.
[44] 'Central Banks in Latin America', 25 May 1933 in BOEA, OV188/1, pp. 3–4 (on Chile).
[45] 'Central Banks in Latin America', 25 May 1933 in BOEA, OV188/1, p. 2 (on Colombia); the mortgage bank was created by the government in 1932 to revive mortgage credit in Colombia.

establish a state-owned agricultural bank was realized in 1932, when the Caja de Credito Agraria was founded (Drake, 1989: 71).

How did these experiences compare to those of countries where central banks were absent? In these cases, credits to the government were provided by the main commercial banks. In Argentina, where advances on government securities increased more than 30 per cent between 1929 and 1931, most of the increase came from the Banco de la Nación (League of Nations, 1935: 155). However, this bank also increased its re-discounting operations to commercial banks against government securities. Argentina's Caja de Conversión began to issue domestic currency in exchange for commercial bills and, in 1932, also against treasury bonds (Díaz-Alejandro, 1983; Della Paolera and Taylor, 2007). In Brazil, circulation was reduced in 1930 as the Banco de Brasil and the Stabilization Office cut their notes (the latter was abolished at the end of 1930). However, the Federal Treasury increased its issues to finance the budget deficit and also through large issues of Treasury notes. In Central America, Guatemala, Nicaragua, and Honduras struggled to defend their dollar peg, while Costa Rica and El Salvador allowed their rates to float before re-pegging to the dollar after Roosevelt's devaluation (Bulmer-Thomas, 1984).

Unlike Kemmerer, Niemeyer did not favour any measures intended to ease the economic effects of the crisis. In Brazil, Niemeyer defended the idea that a central bank's mandate was solely to maintain monetary stability and not to 'take wider commercial risks or to provide capital for long term investment', as this could create conflict with the bank's main goal (Niemeyer, 1931). He maintained that foreign investment had to be encouraged, for which sound public finances and a stable currency were necessary (Niemeyer, 1931: 19). In the case of Argentina, Niemeyer was opposed to open-market operations and exchange controls, or any other countercyclical measure (Sember, 2018: 170).

While governments across Latin America were attempting to gain control of their central banks, the opposite was happening in Mexico where, in the 1930s, a mix of orthodox and heterodox reforms was implemented to make the Bank more autonomous. Despite being legally built as a central bank, until 1931 the Bank of Mexico functioned more as an instrument for the direct promotion of investments, rather than a proper central bank (Nodari, 2019). After 1931, the legally mandated minimum gold reserve remained intact at 50 per cent, but the bank was allowed to issue paper money backed by silver reserves (100 per cent). Even though the bank could not engage in direct loan and discount operations with the public, the Organic Law approved in April 1932 introduced a new re-discount policy in line with Kemmerer countries' reforms (Diario Oficial, 1932). While members of the Board of the New York Federal Reserve welcomed these reforms as a step towards greater central bank autonomy,[46] their British counterparts were more cautious. In fact, according to the Bank of England, the Bank of Mexico needed to be classified as a Kemmerer-style central bank, although its 'great evil still lies in the political control', a fact described as 'probably unavoidable' in the Latin American context.[47]

Mexico's experience converged with those of Kemmerer countries to the extent that they all began to establish a system of national banks that were capitalized entirely by the state and whose principal aim was to encourage agricultural development (Bank of Agricultural Credit and National Ejidal Bank) and finance public works (National Mortgage Bank of Public Works). Last but not least, in 1934, the Nacional Financiera was founded with the primary goal of developing the national capital market and promoting industrialization. Similar institutions were created in Colombia, where, following Kemmerer's advice, the government established the Caja Colombian de Credito Agrario, in 1932. In Peru, an agrarian bank was set up in August 1931, using funds obtained by the reduction of the central bank's capital (Seidel, 1972). These new public institutions were all associated with their respective central banks. Their operation was of paramount importance to the promotion of national agriculture and industrial growth in the late 1930s. They contributed to a revival of commercial bank credit and fostered a new economic model where the state took on a leading role in guiding economic development (Moreno-Brid and Ros, 2009; Patiño Rosselli 1981).

12.7 CONCLUSIONS

In 1944, having recently completed his mission as a money doctor in Paraguay, Robert Triffin published a study on the recent evolution of central banks in Latin America. He criticized the League of Nations' central banking advice, pointing out that 'however good in general', it was primarily derived from the experience of industrialized nations and could 'often be rightly regarded by less developed countries as impracticable or even irrelevant to their problems' (Triffin, 1944: 101).

---

[46] 'Strictly Confidential. Conditions in Mexico', 1 June 1932 in AFRB, Correspondence Files Division, Misc.4.1.
[47] 'Bank of Mexico', Exp. 1/2 in BOEA, OV166/1.

As we have shown in this chapter, a proper assessment of the fragilities in the design of the original central banks in Latin America requires identifying the strategies and tools which they used to tackle the consequences of the Great Depression. In this chapter we followed their evolution from the 1920s until the middle of the 1930s. We underscored how, in the 1920s, governments with substantial budget deficits that faced difficulties in accessing capital markets introduced various measures to pursue monetary stability, secure additional sources of finance, and help their banks provide credit to the private sector. The establishment of central banks was followed by the adoption of the gold standard and, in many cases, these monetary reforms were accompanied by a set of banking and fiscal reforms, generally designed by foreign advisors or money doctors. Kemmerer central banks, despite minor differences between them, were designed to follow the rules of the game, while maintaining a certain level of autonomy (although the state was still expected to participate as a shareholder). Presumably more alert to national economic constraints, Kemmerer recommended higher limits on central bank loans to the state, compared to the advice offered by Otto Niemeyer.

During the 1920s and until the Great Depression, central banks operated smoothly. Once the orthodox responses to the crisis failed to produce a turnaround, most Latin American countries suspended the gold standard and introduced exchange controls, before eventually defaulting on their external debt. Contrary to Triffin's comments and the conventional narrative about Latin American money doctors, Kemmerer's advice played an important role in promoting some of the institutional reforms which allowed central banks to react proactively to the Great Depression. While exchange rate targeting persisted as the prevalent monetary anchor, Latin American central banks used a broad range of instruments to reflate their economies and promote domestic credit expansion.

New legislation introduced in the early 1930s expanded both the scope of action and the discretionary powers of central banks. Banks were allowed to undertake open-market operations, pursue more flexible and extensive discount and re-discount policies, extend loans directly to the public, and advance more funds to their governments. Not all reforms performed as expected. For example, the effectiveness of open-market operations was hampered by the lack of a well-developed financial market in most Latin American countries. Thus, credit expansion mainly took the form of a direct increase in central bank loans and investments. After an upsurge in re-discounts to increase liquidity, central banks extended credit to the general public as well as to official and semi-official development institutions. Such reforms went hand in hand with the reduction in the banknotes' legal cover ratio and a more tolerant attitude toward government borrowing. Wartime exigencies led some governments to seize control of the printing press, thus heralding long periods of high inflation and exchange rate instability. Nevertheless, in other countries such as Colombia, Mexico, and Argentina, the post-1929 reforms played a key role in supporting countercyclical policy and fostering economic recovery. Overall, this process of re-organization paved the way for the emergence of modern central banking on the Latin American continent.

REFERENCES

Unpublished (Archival) Sources

Archive of the Federal Reserve Bank of New York (AFRB), New York (United States).
Archives of the Council of Foreign Relations (ACFR), Princeton (United States). Studies Department Series
Bank of England Archive (BOEA), London (United Kingdom).
  OV188 Overseas & Foreign Department; Latin America – General
Edwin Kemmerer Papers (EKP), Princeton (United States).

Published Sources

Banco Central de Reserva del Perú (1997). *La Misión Kemmerer en el Perú: informes y propuestas.* 1st ed. Lima. Perú: Banco Central de Reserva del Perú.
Banco de la República (Colombia) (ed.) (1990). *El Banco de La República: Antecedentes, Evolución y Estructura.* Bogotá, Colombia: El Banco.
Bates, Robert H., Coatsworth, John H., and Williamson, Jeffrey G. (2007). 'Lost Decades: Postindependence Performance in Latin America and Africa'. *Journal of Economic History*, 67(4): 917–943.
Baudean, Marcos (2017). 'El problema de la creación del Banco Central como organización autónoma en Uruguay', in Carlos Marichal and Thiago Gambi (eds.), *Historia bancaria y monetaria de América Latina (siglos XIX y XX): Nuevas perspectivas.* Santander: Editorial Universidad de Cantabria; Alfenas (Brasil): Universidade Federal de Alfenas, 339–396.
Bértola, Luis, Calicchio, Leonardo, Camou, María, and Porcile, Gabriel (1999). 'Southern Cone Real Wages Compared: A Purchasing Power Parity Approach to Convergente and Divergente Trenes, 1870–1996', UR. FCS-UM. www.colibri.udelar.edu.uy/jspui/handle/20.500.12008/4664.
Bértola, Luis and Ocampo, José Antonio (2013). *The Economic Development of Latin America since Independence.* Repr. Initiative for Policy Dialogue Series. Oxford: Oxford University Press.

Bordo, Michael D. and Meissner, Christopher M. (2020). 'Original Sin and the Great Depression', National Bureau of Economic Research, Working Paper 27067, https://doi.org/10.3386/w27067.

Bulmer-Thomas, Victor (1984). 'Central America in the Inter-War Period', in Rosemary Thorp (ed.), *Latin America in the 1930s: The Role of the Periphery in World Crisis*. St Antony's Series. London: Palgrave Macmillan UK, 279–314.

Bulmer-Thomas, Victor (1987). *The Political Economy of Central America Since 1920*. Cambridge: Cambridge University Press.

Bulmer-Thomas, Victor (2003). *The Economic History of Latin America since Independence*. Cambridge: Cambridge University Press.

Calomiris, Charles W. and Haber, Stephen H. (2014). *Fragile by Design: The Political Origins of Banking Crises and Scarce Credit*. Princeton Economic History of the Western World. Princeton: Princeton University Press.

Carrillo Batalla, Tomás Enrique (2002). *Cuentas nacionales de Venezuela,1874–1914*. Caracas: Banco Central de Venezuela.

Coatsworth, John and Williamson, Jeffrey (2004). 'Always Protectionist? Latin American Tariffs from Independence to Great Depression'. *Journal of Latin American Studies*, 36(2): 205–232.

Conant, Charles A. (1903). 'The Future of the Limping Standard'. *Political Science Quarterly*, 18(2): 216–37.

Crazut, Rafael J. (1970). *El Banco Central de Venezuela: notas sobre la historia y evolución del Instituto, 1940–1970*, Banco Central de Venezuela Colección XXX Aniversario. Caracas: Banco Central de Venezuela.

Della Paolera, Gerardo and Taylor, Alan M. (2007). *Straining at the Anchor: The Argentine Currency Board and the Search for Macroeconomic Stability, 1880–1935*. Chicago: University of Chicago Press.

Diario Oficial, Gobierno de los Estados Unidos Mexicanos (1932). *Ley Que Reforma La de 25 de Agosto de 1925, Constitutiva Del Banco de México*. Vol. 29. http://dof.gob.mx/nota_to_imagen_fs.php?codnota=4423128&fecha=12/04/1932&cod_diario=185920.

Díaz-Alejandro, Carlos (1982). *Latin America in the 1930s*. New Haven, CT: Economic Growth Center, Yale University.

Díaz-Alejandro, Carlos F. (1983). 'Stories of the 1930s for the 1980s', in Pedro Aspe Armella, Rudiger Dornbusch, and Maurice Obstfeld (eds.), *Financial Policies and the World Capital Market: The Problem of Latin American Countries*. Chicago: University of Chicago Press, 5–40.

Díaz-Alejandro, Carlos (1985). 'Argentina, Australia and Brazil Before 1929', in D. C. M. Platt and Guido di Tella (eds.), *Argentina, Australia and Canada: Studies in Comparative Development 1870–1965*. St Antony's Macmillan Series. London: Palgrave Macmillan, 95–109.

Drake, Paul W. (1989). *The Money Doctor in the Andes: The Kemmerer Missions, 1923–1933*. Durham: Duke University Press.

Drake, Paul W. (1994). *Money Doctors, Foreign Debts, and Economic Reforms in Latin America from the 1890s to the Present*. Jaguar Books on Latin America; No. 3. Wilmington, DE: SR Books.

Edwards, Sebastian (2019). 'Monetary Policy, Fiscal Dominance, Contracts, and Populism'. *Cato Journal*, 39(1): 33–50.

Eichengreen, Barry (1989 [1994]). 'House Calls of the Money Doctor: The Kem-
merer Missions to Latin America, 1917–1931', in Guillermo. A. Calvo, Ronald
Findlay, Pentti J. K. Kouri, and Jorge Braga de Macedo (eds.), *Debt, Stabiliza-
tion and Development: Essays in Memory of Carlos Díaz-Alejandro*, Oxford,
Blackwell; reprinted in Paul W. Drake (ed.) (1994), *Money Doctors, Foreign
Debts, and Economic Reforms in Latin America from the 1980s to the Present.*
Wilmington, DE: Scholarly Resources, 110–132.

Eichengreen, Barry (1992). *Golden Fetters: The Gold Standard and the Great
Depression, 1919–1939*. New York: Oxford University Press.

Eichengreen, Barry and Hausmann, Ricardo (1999). 'Exchange Rates and Financial Fragility', in *New Challenges for Monetary Policy: A Symposium*. Kansas
City: Federal Reserve of Kansas City, 329–368.

Flandreau, Marc, Gaillard, Norbert, and Panizza, Ugo (2010). 'Conflicts of Interest, Reputation and the Interwar Debt Crisis: Banksters or Bad Luck?' *IHEID
Working Papers* 02–2010. Economics Section, The Graduate Institute of International Studies.

Flores Zendejas, Juan (2021). 'Money Doctors and Latin American Central Banks
at the Onset of the Great Depression'. *Journal of Latin American Studies*, 53(3):
429–463.

Flores Zendejas, Juan, Soto, David Lopez, and Amador, David Sanchez (2020).
'New Paradigms and Old Promises: Central Banks and the Market for Sovereign Debt in the Interwar Period'. Working Papers of the Paul Bairoch Institute
of Economic History; 1/2020 https://archive-ouverte.unige.ch/unige:129346.

Fritsch, Winston (1988). *External Constraints on Economic Policy in Brazil,
1889–1930*. Basingstoke, UK: Macmillan.

Gomez-Galvarriato, Aurora (2019). 'La Etapa Inicial Del Banco Central: Creación, Consolidación y Crisis, 1925–1932', in Leonor Ludlow and María Euge-
nia Romero Sotelo (eds.), *El Banco de México a Través de Sus Constructores
1917–2017*. UNAM, Mexico: Ciudad de México, 223–254.

Jácome, Luis Ignacio (2015). 'Central Banking in Latin America'. IMF Working
Papers. Washington: International Monetary Fund.

Jorgensen, Erika and Sachs, Jeffrey (1989). 'Default and Renegotiation of Latin
American Foreign Bonds in the Interwar Period', in Barry Eichengreen and
Peter H. Lindert (eds.), *The International Debt Crisis in Historical Perspective.*
Cambridge, MA: MIT Press, 48–85.

Kemmerer, Donald L. and Dalgaard, Bruce R. (1983). 'Inflation, Intrigue, and
Monetary Reform in Guatemala, 1919–1926'. *The Historian*, 46(1): 21–38.

Kemmerer, Edwin Walter (1916). *Modern Currency Reforms; a History and Dis-
cussion of Recent Currency Reforms in India, Porto Rico, Philippine Islands,
Straits Settlements and Mexico*. Harvard Pre-1920 Social History/Business
Preservation Microfilm Project 2038. New York: The Macmillan Company.

Kemmerer, Edwin Walter (1940). *Inflation and Revolution; Mexico's Experience
of 1912–1917*. Princeton and London: Princeton University Press and Oxford
University Press.

League of Nations (1923). *Brussels Financial Conference, 1920: The Recommendations and Their Application; a Review after Two Years*. Geneva: League of
Nations.

League of Nations, Department of Economic and Social Affairs Fiscal and Financial Branch (1935). *Commercial Banks, 1929–1934*. League of Nations. Publications. II Economic and Financial. 1935.II.A.2, Geneva: League of Nations.

League of Nations. Economic and Financial Section (1927). *International Statistical Yearbook*. Publications of the League of Nations. II, Economic and Financial. Geneva: League of Nations, Economic and Financial Section.

League of Nations, Economic Intelligence Service (1936). *Statistical Year Book of the League of Nations, 1935/1936*. Geneva: League of Nations.

Lewis, Cleona (1938). *America's Stake in International Investments*. Institute of Economics of the Brookings Institution. Publication No. 75. Washington, DC: The Brookings Institution.

Lorenzutti, Jorge A. (1996). *Dinero, política y bancos. Historia del Banco Central de la República Argentina 1935–1995*. Buenos Aires: Dunken, Universidad Abierta Interamericana.

Marichal, Carlos (2020). *El Nacimiento de La Banca En América Latina, Finanzas y Política En El Siglo XIX*. Mexico, Ciudad de México: El Colegio de Mexico AC.

Marichal, Carlos and Díaz Fuentes, Daniel (2016). 'The Emergence of Central Banking in Latin America in the Early 20th Century', in Carl-L. Holtfrerich and Jaime Reis (eds.), *The Emergence of Central Banking from 1918 to the Present*, Studies in Banking and Financial History. London: Taylor & Francis.

Marichal, Carlos and Gambi, Thiago (eds.) (2017), *Historia bancaria y monetaria de América Latina (siglos XIX y XX): Nuevas perspectivas*. Santander: Editorial Universidad de Cantabria; Alfenas (Brasil): Universidade Federal de Alfenas.

Martín Aceña, Pablo and Reis, Jaime (2000). *Monetary Standards in the Periphery: Paper, Silver, and Gold, 1854–1933*. Basingstoke: Macmillan; New York: St Martin's Press.

McQueen, Charles Alfred (1926). *Latin American Monetary and Exchange Conditions*. U.S. Bureau of Foreign and Domestic Commerce. Trade Information Bulletin, No. 430. Washington: Government Print Office.

Meissner, Christopher M. (2005). 'A New World Order: Explaining the International Diffusion of the Gold Standard, 1870–1913'. *Journal of International Economics*, 66(2): 385–406.

Meltzer, Allan (2003). *A History of the Federal Reserve. Volume I: 1913-1951*. Chicago: University of Chicago Press.

Moreno-Brid, Juan Carlos and Ros, Jaime (2009) *Development and Growth in the Mexican Economy: An Historical Perspective*. Oxford: Oxford University Press.

Niemeyer, Otto Ernst (1931). 'Informe presentado al gobierno del Brasil sobre las finanzas de ese país', Río de Janeiro.

Nodari, Gianandrea (2019) '"Putting Mexico on Its Feet Again": The Kemmerer Mission in Mexico, 1917–1931'. *Financial History Review*, 26(2): 223–246.

Ocampo, Jose Antonio (1984). 'The Colombian Economy in the 1930s', in Rosemary Thorp (ed.), *Latin America in the 1930s: The Role of the Periphery in World Crisis*. St Antony's Series. London: Palgrave Macmillan, 117–143.

Patiño Rosselli, Alfonso (1981). *La prosperidad a debe y la gran crisis, 1925–1935: capítulos de historia económica de Colombia.* Bogota, Colombia: Banco de la República.

Peres-Cajías, José Alejandro (2014). 'Bolivian Public Finances, 1882–2010. The Challenge to Make Social Spending Sustainable'. *Revista de Historia Economica – Journal of Iberian and Latin American Economic History*, 32(1): 77–117.

Pérez Caldentey, Esteban and Vernengo, Matías (2020). 'Heterodox Central Banking in the Periphery', in Stefano Battilossi, Youssef Cassis, and Yago Kazuhiko (eds.), *Research in the History of Economic Thought and Methodology.* Singapore: Springer, 953–80.

Prados de la Escosura, Leandro (2007). 'Inequality and Poverty in Latin America: A Long-Run Exploration', in Timothy J. Hatton, Kevin H. O'Rourke, and Alan M. Taylor (eds.), *The New Comparative Economic History : Essays in Honor of Jeffrey G. Williamson.* Cambridge, MA: MIT Press, 291–315.

Quiroz, Alfonso W. (1993). *Domestic and Foreign Finance in Modern Peru, 1850–1950: Financing Visions of Development.* St Antony's/Macmillan Series. Basingstoke: Macmillan in association with St Antony's College.

Rosenberg, Emily S. (1999). *Financial Missionaries to the World: The Politics and Culture of Dollar Diplomacy, 1900–1930.* Cambridge, MA: Harvard University Press.

Rosenberg, Emily S. and Rosenberg, Norman L. (1987). 'From Colonialism to Professionalism: The Public-Private Dynamic in United States Foreign Financial Advising, 1898–1929'. *The Journal of American History*, 74(1): 59–82.

Sargent, Thomas J. and Wallace, Neil (1981). 'Some Unpleasant Monetarist Arithmetic'. *Quarterly Review*, 5(3): 1–19.

Sayers, Richard Sidney (1976). *The Bank of England: 1891–1944.* Cambridge and London: Cambridge University Press.

Seidel, Robert N. (1972). 'American Reformers Abroad: The Kemmerer Missions in South America, 1923-1931'. *The Journal of Economic History*, 32(2): 520–545.

Sember, Florencia (2018). 'Challenging a Money Doctor: Raúl Prebisch vs Sir Otto Niemeyer on the Creation of the Argentine Central Bank', in Luca Fiorito, Scott Scheall, and Carlos Eduardo Suprinyak (eds.), *Including a Symposium on Latin American Monetary Thought: Two Centuries in Search of Originality*, Research in the History of Economic Thought and Methodology, Vol. 36C. Emerald Publishing Limited, 55–79.

Sicotte, Richard and Vizcarra, Catalina (2009). 'War and Foreign Debt Settlement in Early Republican Spanish America'. *Revista de Historia Económica (Second Series)*, 27(2): 247–289.

Sterrett, Joseph Edmund and Davis, Joseph Stancliffe (1928). *The Fiscal and Economic Condition of Mexico: Report Submitted to the Internatioanl Committee of Bankers on Mexico.* New York: International Committee of Bankers on Mexico.

Thorp, Rosemary (ed.) (1984). *Latin America in the 1930s: The Role of the Periphery in World Crisis*, St Antony's Series. London: Palgrave Macmillan.

Toniolo, Gianni (1988). *Central Banks' Independence in Historical Perspective.* Berlin and New York: De Gruyter.

Triffin, Robert (1944). 'Central Banking and Monetary Management in Latin America', in Seymour E. Harris (ed.), *Economic Problems of Latin America*. New York: McGraw-Hill Book Company, Inc.

United Nations, Department of Economic and Social Affairs Fiscal and Financial Branch (1948). *Public Debt, 1914–1946*. United Nations Publication Sales No. 1948 XVI. 1. New York: United Nations.

Villela, André (2017). 'Las funciones de banca central antes del banco central: el caso del Banco de Brasil', in Daniel Díaz Fuentes, Andrés Hoyo Aparicio, and Carlos Marichal (eds.), *Orígenes de la globalización bancaria: experiencias de España y América Latina*. Santander: Genueve Ediciones, 437–457.

Young, Ralph Aubrey (1930). *Handbook of American Underwriting of Foreign Securities*. Washington: Government Printing Office.

13

Central Banks in the British Dominions in the Interwar Period

John Singleton

13.1 INTRODUCTION

As in Central and Eastern Europe and Latin America, a mix of external and domestic pressures resulted in the establishment of central banks in the British dominions between the wars. Central banks were created from scratch in South Africa in 1921, in New Zealand in 1934, and in Canada in 1935, and a central bank evolved inside an existing state-owned commercial bank in Australia (Singleton, 2011: 57–68).[1] Although the dominions to some extent shared the financial underdevelopment of countries in Central and Eastern Europe, they were not afflicted by the economic crisis and extreme instability that affected those parts of Europe in the aftermath of the First World War.

The Bank of England held influence in the dominions, but it had to tread cautiously when dealing with countries that were members of the extended British family, albeit sometimes wayward ones. The United Kingdom could not interfere in the dominions' monetary arrangements in the way that it did in India.[2] Nor could it impose personnel on dominion

* I'd like to thank the editors of this volume for feedback, and Bernard Attard, Catherine Schenk, and Grietjie Verhoef for advice and/or copies of sources that were hard to obtain during the COVID-19 lockdown.

[1] The dominions were the self-governing parts of the empire, namely Australia, Canada, New Zealand, South Africa, the Irish Free State, and Newfoundland. The Irish Free State did not acquire a central bank until 1943 (Drea, 2013) and Newfoundland never had one. Whilst not a dominion, India acquired a central bank in 1935. Currency boards were the norm elsewhere in the British Empire. Note that Australia, Canada, India (that is the British Raj), New Zealand, South Africa, and the United Kingdom all signed the Treaty of Versailles individually and not as a bloc.

[2] See Chapter 14, this volume.

central banks, unlike the League of Nations which appointed advisers or watchdogs to several Eastern and Central European central banks in return for arranging loans (Santaella, 1993: 597–598).[3] To quote the leading historians of financial relationships within the British Empire, the 'appearance of central banking in the Dominions registered both the beginning of the Dominions' attempts to further their own [financial] autonomy and Britain's determination to keep financial control in changing circumstances' (Cain and Hopkins, 2016: 550). This intra-imperial dance was conducted in one corner of the global stage; Central and Eastern Europe and Latin America occupied other corners. The main central banks – the Federal Reserve System, the Bank of England, the Bank of France, and the Reichsbank, and their respective governments – performed centre stage.

The chapter begins with some background on the economic and political situation in the dominions between the wars. The next section examines what contemporary experts had (or had not) to say about how central banks should operate in the dominions and other countries with relatively unsophisticated financial sectors. The development and achievements of central banks in Australia, South Africa, New Zealand, and Canada are then examined in turn. They formed links in the international chain of central banks that Montagu Norman and his allies set out to foster after 1918. Yet, to anticipate our conclusion, they did not achieve a great deal before 1939. Not only was their purpose far from clear, but they lacked most of the tools required to implement monetary policy. The extent of de jure and de facto independence acquired by the new central banks varied from case to case and was often contested. Nevertheless, the extension of central banking to the dominions laid the foundations for important contributions to economic management during and after the Second World War, as was foreseen by the Canadian economist, A. F. W. Plumptre (1940), in his contemporary survey *Central Banking in the British Dominions*.

13.2 THE DOMINIONS IN THE 1920S AND 1930S

British control over the dominions was secured between the eighteenth and early twentieth centuries. Australia, Canada, New Zealand, and South Africa were lands of British (and Irish) settlement. Canada also had a substantial French-speaking population in Quebec, and South Africa

---

[3] See Chapters 5, 6, and 10, this volume.

a large contingent of Afrikaners, the latter only partially reconciled to British dominance. All four countries had important non-white populations. But it was mainly the whites who were 'self-governing'; only the Maori in New Zealand enjoyed full citizenship. The dominions attracted British capital as well as migrants. All four – if only white South Africa is included – were high-income countries by the standards of the early twentieth century (Belich, 2009; Magee and Thompson, 2010; Cain and Hopkins, 2016).

The dominions were key suppliers of food and raw materials to the United Kingdom. Commercial and financial ties between the United Kingdom and the southern dominions were strong. Some of the largest banks operating in Australia, New Zealand, and South Africa were British owned and controlled. The southern dominions possessed currencies called pounds, though they were formally distinct from the British pound sterling and not always at par. Some gold reserves were kept locally, but the banks relied heavily on sterling reserves kept in London; in this sense there was a sterling area decades before the United Kingdom's final departure from the gold standard in 1931. When sterling was on gold, Australia, New Zealand, and South Africa were effectively on a gold exchange standard. When the British pound was floating, however, the southern dominions were on a sterling standard (Tocker, 1924; Eichengreen, 1992: 61–63). Canada was different: even before the First World War its economy was passing into the American orbit, a process that alarmed Canadian and British leaders. Canada's currency was called the dollar and not the pound. Imports from the United States overtook those from Britain, and the United States was catching up as an export destination. Although London remained Canada's main external source of capital, New York held the international reserves, comprising gold and US dollars, of the Canadian banks (Dick and Floyd, 1992: 19). Canada would never join the sterling area, despite being encouraged to do so by the British.

The dominions recorded strong population growth between the wars (Table 13.1). Commodity production and exports grew too, but prices were unstable and often depressed. Real GDP per capita (Figure 13.1) dropped sharply during the global depression of the early 1930s. The experiences of the dominions were not identical. Australia was consistently the most prosperous; Canada suffered the bumpiest ride; New Zealand was relatively stagnant before taking off in the mid-1930s; figures for South Africa are incomplete and probably the least reliable. Except in Australia, the early 1920s saw a fall in money supply; all four dominions

TABLE 13.1 *Population in the British Dominions (in thousands),*
1920 and 1939

	1920	1939
Australia	5,358	6,971
Canada	8,789	11,570
New Zealand	1,241	1,627
South Africa	6,153 (1913)	13,596 (1950)

Source: Bolt et al. (2018).

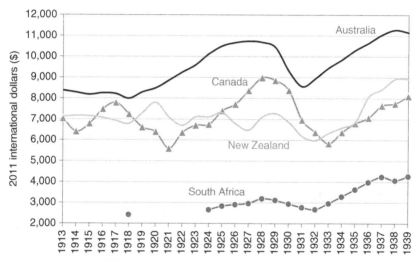

FIGURE 13.1 Real GDP per capita in the British Dominions, 1913–1939
Source: Bolt et al. (2018).

experienced substantial reductions in money supply in the late 1920s and
early 1930s, followed by recoveries of varying strength (Figure 13.2). The
South African and Australian central banks responded passively to the
global slump. To a greater or lesser extent, the dominion central banks
accommodated economic recovery in the mid- to late 1930s.

Before the First World War the dominions borrowed substantially in
London, and in the 1920s, when British savings were scarce, they enjoyed
preferential access to the London capital market (Cain and Hopkins,
2016: 473–475). Dominion governments at both federal and state levels were regarded as safe harbours for British capital. However, the
slump in commodity markets in the late 1920s brought into question the

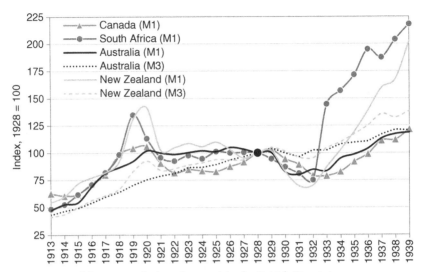

FIGURE 13.2 Money supply (1928 = 100) in the British Dominions, 1913–1939
Sources: Data on Australia from Butlin (1977: 101–102, Table IV.14); data
on Canada from Metcalf et al. (1996: Table A1); data on New Zealand from
Sheppard (1990) and Sheppard et al. (1990), and data on South Africa from
Bureau of Census and Statistics (1960: R12).

willingness of some governments, most notably in Australia, to service
London debt. Policymakers in the sterling dominions had the potential
to destabilize the financial nexus radiating from London, and this was an
important factor in the Bank of England's efforts to promote orthodox
central banking.

Politically and economically, the dominions became more assertive in
their relations with the United Kingdom after 1918. South Africa, which
featured a strong Afrikaner nationalist bloc, was a somewhat grudging
member of the British Empire. Pessimism about the outlook for primary
exports, balance of payments difficulties, incipient nationalism, and the
need for job creation led to the pursuit of import substitution policies in
the dominions. Tariffs were raised against both British and foreign goods,
though British goods retained a tariff preference. The United Kingdom was
prepared to absorb some commercial damage in order to bolster dominion
finances and reduce the risk of default (Cain and Hopkins, 2016: 529–559).

Managing relationships with the dominions was tricky. They were
important customers for British goods and capital and major suppliers of
food and raw materials. They were net assets rather than net liabilities,
but they could not be taken for granted. Canada was outside the sterling

area and at risk of being lost economically to the United States. South Africa was divided over the value of the British connection and the link to sterling. Australia and New Zealand showed signs of financial vulnerability and interest in unorthodox economic ideas. One way of keeping the dominions within the fold was to promote the formation of independent central banks with close ties to Threadneedle Street.

13.3 VIEWS OF THE CENTRAL BANKING EXPERTS

Interwar central banking experts, including those well-versed in the affairs of the dominions, thought that central banks on the periphery of the international economy, whether in Eastern Europe, Latin America, or the British Empire should emulate the behaviour of the Bank of England or the Federal Reserve System. Nothing could have been more unrealistic given the differences in their environments. The British, like the Americans, possessed 'money doctors' who advised and sometimes visited countries on the periphery to spread the gospel of central banking and financial orthodoxy: they included Sir Ernest Harvey and Sir Otto Niemeyer, both senior officials of the Bank of England, Sir Henry Strakosch, a confidant of Montagu Norman, and Sir Cecil Kisch, the Financial Secretary to the India Office in London.

Visiting Australia in 1927, Harvey stated that 'certain fundamental principles' of central banking were applicable everywhere (Harvey, 1927: 1). The 'primary function' of a central bank was 'the custody, regulation and protection of the central banking and currency reserves of the country' (Harvey, 1927: 3). It was desirable that the reserves of the banking system should be centralized in one institution (Harvey, 1927: 5–6). Monetary policy should aim to maintain 'the stability of the purchasing power of the national monetary unit as measured internally by the general level of commodity prices and by the relation of the unit to gold' (Harvey, 1927: 6). Although Harvey did not say whether central banks should be privately owned, he insisted that they be free from 'political and governmental control of policy and management' (Harvey, 1927: 7). The important question of *how* monetary policy could be implemented in underdeveloped financial markets was not addressed.

Kisch was co-author of a comparative textbook on central banking which received the imprimatur of Montagu Norman.[4] According to

---

[4] Norman wrote in the foreword: 'I commend [this book] not only to bankers and students but to all who are interested in financial reconstruction' (Norman 1932: vi).

Kisch and Elkin (1932: 110) the 'cardinal duty of a Central Bank is to safeguard the currency standard and to maintain sound conditions in the money market.'[5] Private ownership of the central bank was preferable, but there was room for compromise depending on the 'state of economic development and the sense of responsibility inherent in ... public and ... commercial life', provided that operational independence was not threatened (Kisch and Elkin, 1932: 28).[6] Strict controls must be placed on the amount the government could borrow from the central bank. The central bank should not try to compete for business with the commercial banks, whose cooperation was needed in the conduct of monetary policy (Kisch and Elkin, 1932: 111–112). Assuming that monetary policy was based on rediscounting and open-market operations (OMOs), the central bank required 'a portfolio of bills continuously maturing into cash, which in its turn may be converted into bills in unceasing process' (Kisch and Elkin, 1932: 129). Where liquid bill and bond markets were absent, the establishment of a central bank would encourage their development (Kisch and Elkin, 1932: 12). Kisch and Elkin were coy about the role of the central bank in a banking crisis, the term 'lender of last resort' not appearing in the index. They were content to leave the formulation of strategy at the global level to the Bank of England, the Federal Reserve Bank of New York, and other top central banks. Countries on the periphery had a responsibility not to weaken the reserve position of global financial centres. The framework for international cooperation would be provided by the Bank for International Settlements (BIS) and the League of Nations,[7] and no separate role for the sterling area group was contemplated (Kisch and Elkin, 1932: 153–177).

Central banking expertise in the British Empire was not confined to London. M. H. de Kock, deputy governor of the South African Reserve Bank (SARB), published the first edition of his text *Central Banking* in 1939. A solemn foreword by Johannes Postmus, governor of the SARB, decried the prevailing climate of innovation and extolled the virtues of old-time central banking (M. H. de Kock, 1939: vii–ix). Despite including some material on central banks on the periphery, and the SARB especially, de Kock discussed the principles and practice of central banking largely from the perspective of the core European countries and the United States. Recent developments were described, including the erosion

---

[5] In 1932 the suspension of the gold standard was still assumed (or hoped) to be temporary.
[6] These caveats were not explained.
[7] The dominion central banks were not yet members of the BIS.

of central bank independence, and the use of monetary policy to smooth the economic cycle, but such departures from orthodoxy were said to reflect a loss of discipline in economic policymaking following collapse of the gold standard (M. H. de Kock, 1939: 325).

Insofar as primitive financial markets hindered monetary policy on the periphery, de Kock argued that the central bank should foster a Treasury bill market, and in the meantime use the rediscount rate to signal its views on economic conditions and prospects (M. H. de Kock, 1939: 208, 245–249). The lender-of-last-resort function was approached by means of a historical survey of developments in the United Kingdom (M. H. de Kock, 1939: 101–104). Little was said about central bank cooperation, or indeed the imperial dimension of central banking, topics about which de Kock cannot have been ignorant (M. H. de Kock, 1939: 339–343). The tone was relentlessly conservative, clinging to the orthodoxy of the 1920s.

A substantially different approach was taken by Wynne Plumptre, a Canadian economist and political scientist. As a postgraduate in Cambridge, Plumptre was inspired by Keynes. He became assistant secretary to the Canadian Royal Commission on Banking and Currency which in 1933 recommended the establishment of a central bank (MacGregor, 1978). In *Central Banking in the British Dominions*, Plumptre (1940: 152–155) contended that the dominion central banks, as originally created, were ill-suited to their environment. Their advocates and designers, both locally and at Threadneedle Street, had not grasped that an off-the-peg model would cause 'incongruities and anachronisms' (Plumptre, 1940: 42). The effectiveness of central banking depended on 'the condition of the capital market in which it is practised' (Plumptre, 1940: 4). Without well-developed domestic capital markets, monetary policy would be difficult to implement. Only Canada came close to meeting the minimum requirements. Banking practices in the southern dominions had certain peculiarities that could further hinder monetary policy. Commercial banks in Australia, New Zealand, and South Africa did not aim for a constant cash ratio (Plumptre, 1940: 248–257), and they adjusted the supply of credit in response to changes in their sterling balances in London (Tocker, 1924). Overcoming the obstacles to effective monetary policy would take time, and central banks should encourage the development of financial markets. Plumptre was no more forthcoming than Kisch and Elkin were on the role of the central bank in dealing with stress in the banking system. His focus lay elsewhere, primarily in the arena of monetary policy.

The predicament of dominion central banks owed much to the motives of their promoters. Plumptre (1940: 193) believed that British enthusiasm for setting them up was tainted by 'financial imperialism'. From the perspective of the Bank of England, the mission of the dominion central banks was to ensure that governments followed orthodox financial policies,[8] that a pegged exchange rate was maintained against sterling, that external reserves were held in London, and last but not least that London debt was serviced without interruption.[9] Consequently, the dominion central banks should be independent of local political control, and privately owned if possible. After the suspension of the gold standard in 1931, the Bank of England placed even greater emphasis on cooperation with actual and projected dominion central banks. Although there was some support in the dominions for the Bank of England's vision, there was also opposition from those who wished central banks to promote reflation and economic development. Plumptre was critical of both sides in this debate: 'neither nationalism nor imperialism spoke with the still small voice of logic. Instead they spoke with many tongues, often babbling and contradictory.' (Plumptre, 1940: 201).

Central banks required 'emancipation' from the straitjacket of orthodoxy if they were to maximize their contribution to society (Plumptre, 1940: 153). The alternative framework offered by Plumptre was essentially Keynesian. Along with Keynes himself (Bibow, 2002), Plumptre did not believe that the ownership of the central bank was a matter of principle. Whether privately or publicly owned, what mattered most was that the government treated the central bank as a genuine partner in the areas of its expertise. The aim of domestic monetary policy should be to dampen fluctuations in economic activity. Central banks should also be permitted to adjust the exchange rate in support of counter-cyclical monetary policy (Plumptre, 1940: 345–393). He fervently hoped that governments would permit monetary policy to be conducted through the market mechanism rather than by means of direct controls (Plumptre, 1940: 426).

---

[8] Cain and Hopkins (2016: 529–559) concur with Plumptre.

[9] The sterling area of the 1930s was a loosely structured group of countries that used sterling as a reserve currency and pegged exchange rates to the British pound. Membership was voluntary for the dominions, but compulsory for the rest of the British Empire including India. Canada opted out, but several foreign countries, including Sweden and Portugal, joined (Cain and Hopkins, 2016: 501–525).

13.4 AUSTRALIA

Under legislation passed in 1911, the Commonwealth Bank of Australia (CBA) opened its doors in 1912. The CBA was initially a state-owned commercial and savings bank.[10] Central banking functions were acquired gradually between the wars (Table 13.2). It is difficult to put a precise date on when the CBA became a proper central bank. Kisch and Elkin (1932: 16) were adamant that it could not be a 'true' central bank whilst competing for business with the commercial banks, but that criterion seems rather brutal. Not until 1960 was the central bank spun off as the Reserve Bank of Australia.

Australia suffered a serious banking crisis in the 1890s. Public confidence in banks was slow to recover. American populist rhetoric filtered into Australia, and the commercial banks were condemned, especially on the political left, as bastions of 'money power' (Love, 1984). The level of service offered to customers was also deemed inadequate. After vigorous debate, a Labor government secured legislation to create a state-owned commercial and savings bank to offer an alternative to existing banks. It hardly needs saying that this initiative was deprecated by incumbent banks. As Giblin (1951: vii) put it, the CBA was 'in the hurly-burly' of politics from the outset, 'subject to violent dispute in Parliament and press' at every stage of its later development. The question of whether the CBA should also be a central bank was discussed and rejected in 1911, but the government anticipated that a central bank might emerge over time. The only central banking function performed by the CBA in 1912 was that of banker to the government as part of 'general banking business' (Cornish, 2008). Denison Miller, the first governor, was recruited from the Bank of New South Wales. He avoided aggressive competition with the commercial banks on the grounds that a future central bank would need their cooperation (Giblin, 1951: 3). In 1920, the Treasury's responsibility for issuing Australia's bank notes was transferred to a Note Issue Board, which although based at the CBA and chaired by Miller was in practice a strongly independent agency (Coleman, 2001).

M. H. de Kock (1939: 21) picked 1924 as the year in which the CBA became a fully fledged central bank. Plumptre (1940: 88, 94) felt that the CBA became a central bank 'in law' in 1924, but that it did not start to behave like one until 1929 or later. Dissatisfaction with the inflexible policy of the Note Issue Board, combined with a slow economic recovery from

---

[10] Commercial banks in Australia and New Zealand were known as trading banks.

TABLE 13.2 *Commonwealth Bank of Australia (CBA) legislation*

Commonwealth Bank Act 1911

Ownership	Central (Commonwealth) government.
Governance	Governor appointed by the government.
Primary function	'To carry on the general business of banking', especially commercial banking.
Note issue	Not permitted. Treasury has monopoly of note issue.
Government banker	Not mentioned, but carried on as 'general business of banking'.
Bankers' bank	No.
Market operations permitted	Discounting; making advances in connection with general banking business.
Other activities	Savings banking.

Commonwealth Bank Act 1920 (key changes only)

Note issue	Yes – exclusive. Note Issue Department set up within the Bank but 'distinct' from it. Partial gold backing. Follows strict rules.

Commonwealth Bank Act 1924 (key changes only)

Governance	Board comprising eight directors. Governor and seven other directors including the Secretary to the Treasury. All appointed by government.
Note issue	Note Issue Department fully absorbed into Commonwealth Bank. More flexibility in note issue.
Government banker	Amount of lending to government was restricted.
Bankers' bank	Interbank settlement must be through accounts at the Commonwealth Bank. Banks not specifically instructed to maintain reserves at the Commonwealth Bank.

Commonwealth Bank (Rural Credits) Act 1925 (key changes only)

Agricultural Finance	Distinct Rural Credits Department established within Commonwealth Bank.

Commonwealth Bank (Savings Bank) Act 1927 (key changes only)

Savings banking	Commonwealth Savings Bank established to take over the savings bank business, but still under control of the Commonwealth Bank.

Commonwealth Bank Act 1929 (key changes only)

Gold	Government could require holders of gold to sell it to the Commonwealth Bank. Government could restrict or ban gold exports.

Commonwealth Bank Act 1931 (key changes only)

Note issue	Permitted a reduction in gold reserve held against the note issue.

Commonwealth Bank Act 1932 (key changes only)

Note issue	Sterling could substitute for gold as backing for the note issue.

Source: All acts available online via www.legislation.gov.au

the slump of the early 1920s, prompted the Commonwealth Bank Act of 1924. Passed by the Bruce Page government, a coalition of the Nationalist and Country parties, the 1924 Act abolished the Note Issue Board and assigned its duties to the CBA. Commercial banks were now required to conduct interbank settlement through the CBA, and by implication maintain reserves there (Giblin, 1951: 30). Still feeling resentful, the commercial banks deposited as little of their local reserves as they could at the CBA.

Although appointed by government, the directors of the CBA enjoyed considerable autonomy. The dominant personality at the CBA was Sir Robert Gibson, the chairman from 1926 to 1934. Gibson was an expatriate Scot and Melbourne businessman of rigidly orthodox financial views (Schedvin, 1981). The deteriorating external situation in the late 1920s led to further extension of the CBA's powers. Under legislation passed in 1929 the commercial banks were coerced into selling the bulk of their gold to the CBA. In 1930, the CBA and the commercial banks agreed to pool receipts of overseas funds to help the government with London debt servicing (Giblin, 1951: 66–70). The Scullin Labor government, elected in 1929, introduced a bill to extract the central banking functions from the CBA and give them to a new reserve bank, but was unable to push the measure through Parliament (Schedvin, 1970: 172–176). In 1930, Sir Otto Niemeyer was despatched to Australia by the Bank of England, no doubt with the complicity of Gibson, to assess the financial position and tender stern advice. Niemeyer urged the Commonwealth (national) and state governments to pursue retrenchment and shun unorthodox measures (Attard, 1989; Millmow, 2010: 66–75). Nonetheless, the Commonwealth Treasurer, E. G. Theodore, later devised a programme of monetary expansion, whilst the Labor Premier of New South Wales, Jack Lang, suspended his state's contribution to the servicing of Australia's London debt. Canberra had to pick up the bill temporarily (Schedvin, 1970: 228–234). Facing government demands for more accommodation, Gibson asserted his independence and refused. Gibson essentially 'refused to cash any more government cheques' (cited in Cornish, 1993: 442), and the government, hopelessly divided over economic policy, accepted the rebuff. London must have been relieved when, in 1932, Labor was superseded by a broadly conservative government.

Lacking the capacity to conduct OMOs, and disapproving of large advances to the government, the CBA's remaining monetary tools were advances and rediscounting. Monetary conditions remained tight until recovery was already under way in 1933–4. Tentative efforts by the Commonwealth Savings Bank to engage in OMOs in 1936 proved discouraging (Plumptre, 1940: 96). The CBA asserted control over the exchange rate in 1931. Until then, the rate between the Australian and British pounds was managed by the commercial banks and there was no formal peg. In January 1931 market pressure led to a sharp depreciation of 30 per cent against sterling. The CBA followed the lead of the other banks in settling on a new rate. Towards the end of the 1931, however, the CBA announced that it would support a new, slightly stronger exchange rate, and from then onwards the other banks followed its leadership. The government tacitly acknowledged the CBA's responsibility for the exchange rate, and the new rate was held for the rest of the decade (Plumptre, 1940: 95; Millmow, 2010: 124). Several rescue operations were mounted to avoid the collapse of ailing state savings banks in 1931: the Commonwealth Savings Bank, a CBA subsidiary, took over the Government Savings Bank of New South Wales and the State Savings Bank of Western Australia (Fitz-Gibbon and Gizycki, 2001). The CBA also established price leadership in the setting of interest rates in the 1930s, demonstrating that its status vis-à-vis the commercial banks was improving.

A largely Keynesian alternative to Gibson's policies was proposed in 1936 by a royal commission on the banking system. It was recommended that the primary objective of the CBA should be to dampen fluctuations in the economic cycle. Although the conservative-leaning Lyons government, which had set up the royal commission for tactical reasons, did not act on its findings, they prefigured post-war developments (Millmow, 2010: 193–223). Between the wars the CBA evolved from a state-owned commercial bank and savings bank into something approaching a central bank, albeit without losing its commercial activities. Despite state-ownership, the CBA was assertive in its dealings with government, especially during the depression. During and after the Second World War, the CBA became a vital economic policy agency. The post-war Labor government, however, ensured that its independence was curtailed (Schedvin, 1992).

13.5 SOUTH AFRICA

Until the close of the First World War, the establishment of a central bank in South Africa was not a burning issue (Rossouw, 2011: S3–S5). Britain's suspension of the gold standard in March 1919 created difficulties for the South African banking system. It was now profitable for people living in South Africa to withdraw gold from the banks and send it overseas where its purchasing power was greater. Since South Africa had no mint, the banks would eventually run out of gold coins, and mining companies would be unable to pay workers in the gold coins that they demanded (Ally, 1994: 112–113).[11] In July 1919, the South African gold miners reached an agreement with the Bank of England to despatch their entire output for sale on the London gold market. The miners soon regretted being locked in by this agreement (Balachandran, 2008: 325–326), and Afrikaner nationalists saw it as an outrage.

The government resolved to seek advice on monetary problems in London, contacting Sir Henry Strakosch and John Maynard Keynes. Keynes declined the invitation to visit South Africa as a money doctor, but Strakosch, a financier and friend of Montagu Norman, accepted (Padayachee and Bordiss, 2015: 184). The main question was whether South Africa should remain on the gold standard or float with sterling. Staying on gold would in principle not be difficult for a major gold producer; it would also be an assertion of financial independence from the United Kingdom, a strategy with wide appeal among Afrikaners. By contrast, British interests would be served by South Africa following sterling and remaining within London's orbit.

Strakosch played an important role in persuading the South African Party government, led by Jan Smuts,[12] to follow sterling rather than gold, with the proviso that the South African currency return to the gold standard by 1 July 1925 (Ally, 1994: 114–119). The Strakosch mission also floated a proposal for a central bank. The central bank, it was argued, would help to modernize South Africa's financial infrastructure. Strakosch and Norman also hoped that it would give the Bank of England greater influence over South African economic policy. The central bank proposal was accepted, and the SARB, established by legislation in 1920, and came into operation in 1921 (G. de Kock, 1954: 13–22) (See Table 13.3 for a synopsis of subsequent legislation.).

Strakosch (1921: 174) described the mission of the SARB, rather blandly, as 'upholding the credit of the country, and … preparing for helpful intervention in an emergency'. His design was heavily influenced by the examples of the Federal Reserve Banks and the Bank of Java, partly to avoid the accusation that he was trying to impose a mini Bank of England. Strakosch is even said to have had a copy of Edwin Kemmerer's *A.B.C of the Federal Reserve System* beside him when revising the draft legislation (G. de Kock, 1954: 34).

---

[11] The South Africa mint opened in 1923.
[12] The SAP attempted to rally white British and Afrikaner citizens behind the British Empire.

TABLE 13.3 *South African Reserve Bank (SARB) legislation*

Currency and Banking Act 1920	
Ownership	Commercial banks and private shareholders.
Governance	Board comprising eleven directors: (a) governor, deputy governor and three others appointed by government, (b) three directors appointed by commercial banks and (c) three directors elected by other shareholders.
Primary function	Central banking was only one concern of the Act, the overall purpose of which was to 'secure greater stability in the monetary system'.
Note issue	Yes – exclusive. Partial gold backing.
Government banker	Permitted to act as banker to the government, but this not acted upon until late 1920s. Strict limits on purchase and rediscounting of government securities.
Bankers' bank	Commercial banks required to maintain minimum reserves at SARB.
Market operations permitted	Rediscounting, advances, OMOs.
General banking business	Not prohibited.
Exchange rate	No mention of responsibility for exchange rate.
Currency and Banking Amendment Act 1923 (key changes only)	
Governance	The three commercial bank directors replaced by three additional private shareholders' directors.
Bankers' Bank	Reduced the minimum reserves to be held at SARB.
Currency and Banking (Further Amendment) Act 1930 (key changes only)	
Market operations permitted	SARB permitted to hold securities of longer duration, enabling more assistance to the banks.
Finance Emergency Act 1931 (key changes only)	
UK's departure from gold	SARB granted emergency powers.
Legal Tender, Currency, Exchanges, and Banking Act 1933 (key changes only)	
Exchange rate	SARB permitted to buy and sell foreign exchange to prevent undue fluctuations in the exchange rate against sterling.

Sources: G. de Kock (1954: 23–42); Plumptre (1940: 58–64); Kisch and Elkin (1932: 404–410).

The SARB's authority and capacity for action were limited. US practice was followed in requiring commercial banks to hold minimum reserves at the reserve bank. The government, however, continued to bank with the commercial banks for several years before shifting its custom to the SARB. An agreement was reached with the gold producers in 1925 whereby the SARB became the sole buyer of their output. With a view to gaining traction over credit conditions and interest rates the SARB competed on a limited basis with the commercial banks. Assistance was provided to the troubled National Bank of South Africa in 1926. W. H. Clegg, the South African born chief accountant of the Bank of England, was chosen as the first governor. The British trusted that Clegg would exercise his influence in their favour, but his room for manoeuvre was limited. Gerhard de Kock (1954: 37) commented that the 1920 Act seemed to assume that 'the Bank was going to operate in an environment very similar to that of London or New York'. In practice, however, the thinness of South African financial markets reduced the scope for managing monetary and credit conditions. According to Plumptre (1940: 60), the young SARB was confined by a 'strait jacket of accepted tradition', to which we might add South African political divisions.

As the deadline for the resumption of convertibility drew nearer, the monetary policy debate was reopened. South Africa lobbied the British to return sterling to gold without delay, warning that they could not wait beyond July 1925 (Pressnell, 1978: 79–80). The Smuts government was followed in 1924 by the less amenable National-led government with Barry Hertzog as prime minister.[13] Hertzog set up a further inquiry into monetary arrangements, including whether South Africa should return to the gold standard independently of sterling. Shunning British expertise, the government chose the US money doctor, Edwin Kemmerer, and the Dutch central banker, Gerard Vissering, to make the investigation.[14] Kemmerer was well-connected in US banking and policymaking circles. The 1920s saw intense Anglo-American rivalry. Weaning the South Africans away from their dependence on London would benefit US financial and business interests. Norman underestimated the threat to the British position. Clegg and the SARB were unable to influence the outcome of the inquiry (Ally, 1994: 120–121). The Kemmerer–Vissering mission reported in favour of restoring gold convertibility regardless of any British decision. A split was avoided when sterling returned to gold in April 1925, before South Africa had taken action (Richards, 1925; Padayachee and Bordiss, 2015).

The gold versus sterling question re-emerged in September 1931 when sterling was forced off the gold standard. The initial reaction of the Hertzog

---

[13] Hertzog and his supporters were unsympathetic to the United Kingdom. Labour was National's junior partner.

[14] Kemmerer was Professor of Economics at Princeton, Vissering the president of the Netherlands Bank. Owing to illness, Vissering played a minor role.

government was to remain on gold. South Africa appeared to be in a solid financial position and the government did not wish to appear subservient to London. Clegg and the SARB supported the government's decision, as did the bulk of the South African elite (G. de Kock, 1954: 140–141). Within a few months, however, dissenting voices could be heard, not least in the opposition South African Party (SAP). Staying on the gold standard damaged important export industries, including wool and diamonds, and depressed incomes. The new SARB governor, Johannes Postmus, who replaced Clegg at the start of 1932, was even more committed to gold. Yet by December 1932, the deepening economic crisis, combined with withdrawals of gold from the banks in expectation of devaluation, compelled Postmus and the commercial banks to recommend the suspension of convertibility. The government acted on this advice and South Africa reverted to the sterling fold (G. de Kock, 1954: 161–163; Drummond 1981: 90–97). Between 1932 and 1933 South African M1 almost doubled, illustrating the stringency required by adherence to gold during 1931–2, and the relief brought by inconvertibility. The SARB pursued a largely passive monetary policy after 1932. Given the lack of policy tools they had little option, but passivity was consistent with a strong recovery.

Norman succeeded in Australia not because of manipulation but because the chairman of the CBA was equally committed to monetary orthodoxy, as were most political leaders except Theodore and Lang. Despite providing the SARB's first governor, however, the Bank of England had less actual influence of South Africa because of the strong Afrikaner hostility to British designs. Only the failure of Hertzog's gold policy in 1931–2 pulled South Africa back into the sterling area. Whilst privately owned, the SARB was less autonomous in practice than the government-owned CBA.

13.6 NEW ZEALAND

Although New Zealand, like Australia, was at the mercy of international commodity markets, it survived the initial onset of depression with less strain to its financial position. Some New Zealanders started to feel that their standing with creditors was tainted by association with Australia. Several banks operated in both countries, and they did not distinguish between the Australian and New Zealand portions of their sterling reserves. Was Australia spending New Zealand's sterling?

As 1930 wore on, the financially orthodox United government began to grasp that the crisis might not be short-lived (Singleton, 2003: 177).

Niemeyer was invited to add New Zealand to his travel itinerary, and tender advice on the exchange rate and how to separate the New Zealand and Australian monetary systems (Wright, 2006). Niemeyer was happy to oblige. He produced a report which recommended the formation of a central bank. In addition, he endorsed the government's policy of retrenchment, and the New Zealand pound's link through sterling to the gold standard. The 'reserve bank', as Niemeyer termed it, 'would be charged with the duty of [exclusively] managing the note-issue, accepting responsibility for the ultimate stability of the exchange [rate], holding reserve balances of the trading banks, and carrying the Government account' (Niemeyer, 1931: 3). An orthodox central bank would enhance New Zealand's reputation and signal separation from Australia. Niemeyer admitted that the local money market was only 'slightly developed', but he believed that a reserve bank could help remedy this deficiency (Niemeyer, 1931:4).

The reserve bank proposals provoked opposition from the commercial banks who feared the undermining of their own privileges (Hawke, 1973: 44). Some critics, including the economist Horace Belshaw, argued that Niemeyer's scheme should be brought up to date by adding responsibility for managing credit (and thus potentially for boosting the economy) and allowing for some flexibility in exchange rate policy (Brooke et al., 2019: 29–31). The reserve bank proposal was pushed temporarily into the background by more pressing matters, including a heated debate over devaluation. New Zealand's commercial banks still managed the exchange rate, presiding over a depreciation against sterling in 1931. As the depression continued, the need for further adjustment was discussed. Facing overwhelming government pressure, the commercial banks agreed to devalue the New Zealand pound against sterling in 1933 (Singleton, 2003: 179–182). The motivation for devaluation was largely redistributive: farmers had borne the brunt of the slump in world markets and their incomes should be raised. Nonetheless, devaluation helped to hasten recovery by loosening monetary conditions (Greasley and Oxley, 2002: 706–708).

Devaluation, which coincided with the start of the recovery, created space for the revival of the reserve bank scheme. The government, now a coalition of United Party and Reform Party, saw the reserve bank bill through in 1934. Only in the opposition Labour Party was it envisaged that the reserve bank could become a tool for stimulating the economy. The Reserve Bank of New Zealand (RBNZ) was born in 1934 (Table 13.4) and modelled in its essentials on Niemeyer's draft (Wright,

TABLE 13.4 *Reserve Bank of New Zealand (RBNZ) legislation*

Reserve Bank of New Zealand Act 1933	
Ownership	One third shareholders and two thirds government.
Governance	Board comprising nine directors: (a) governor, deputy governor appointed by government; (b) three directors appointed by government, and (c) four directors appointed by shareholders; plus Secretary to Treasury (non-voting).
Primary function	'to exercise control ... over monetary circulation and credit in New Zealand, to the end that the economic welfare of the Dominion may be promoted and maintained'.
Note issue	Yes – exclusive. Partial backing in gold or certain other assets including UK treasury bills and short-term sterling commercial bills.
Government banker	Yes. Strict limits on amount and duration of lending to government. Management of public debt.
Bankers' bank	Commercial banks must maintain reserves at RBNZ. Central bank to organize the clearing system.
Market operations permitted	Rediscounting, advances, OMOs.
General banking business	Not permitted, except some involvement in provision of agricultural credit.
Exchange rate	Permitted to buy and sell overseas currencies. No mention of responsibility for exchange rate.
Reserve Bank of New Zealand Amendment Act 1936 (key changes only)	
Ownership	Government.
Governance	All directors to be appointed by government. Secretary to the Treasury to become a voting member of board.
Primary function	'to give effect ... to the monetary policy of the Government, as communicated to it from time to time by the Minister of Finance', and to promote 'the economic and social welfare of New Zealand'.
Government banker	May grant an overdraft to the government (no limit specified) and underwrite government loans.
Primary industries	May grant credit to statutory marketing boards for primary products, e.g. dairy board.

Source: All Acts available online via www.nzlii.org/nz/legis/hist_act/

2006). Commercial banks lost the right to issue notes and were required to hold minimum reserves at the RBNZ. Government banking business was transferred to the reserve bank. Ownership was shared by the government and private shareholders. Exchange-rate policy had already been set in 1933, and the peg to sterling persisted. The government asked the Bank of England for help with finding a governor, and they recommended Leslie Lefeaux, a former chief cashier. Nothing radical was expected from the RBNZ. Given that there was no money market, the RBNZ could 'do little [so far] but act as the government's banker' (Hawke, 1973: 58).

Towards the end of 1935, a Labour government with socialist leanings was elected. One of Labour's first measures was to nationalize the RBNZ. More radically, the direction of monetary policy was placed unambiguously in the hands of the minister of finance. Lefeaux objected to this wanton rejection of central banking orthodoxy. Whilst sympathetic to this complaint, Sir Ernest Harvey, now deputy governor of the Bank of England, warned Lefeaux not to antagonize the new regime and thereby lose any remaining influence. 'I need not remind you', chided Harvey, 'that ultimate authority regarding credit and currency must rest with governments and that a central bank in any country is obliged to frame its own policies within the limits set by government decisions' (cited in Singleton, 2010: 27). British financial imperialism was tempered by discretion in New Zealand, in marked contrast to the case in India.

The Labour government instructed the RBNZ to reduce interest rates, subsidize farmers, and provide funding for a state housebuilding programme. The RBNZ became one of the first central banks authorized to vary the minimum reserve ratio of commercial banks, though this power remained dormant until after the Second World War (Hawke, 1973: 152–154).[15] A balance of payments crisis in 1938–9, exacerbated by Labour's expansionary policies, prompted the imposition of exchange controls, the administration of which was delegated to the RBNZ. British anger was tempered somewhat by the desire for unity as war approached (Greasley and Oxley, 2002: 717–718; McAloon, 2013: 42–46).

The policy regime in Wellington swung dramatically from orthodoxy to radicalism between 1935 and 1939 (Copland, 1939: 22). The RBNZ had been established on orthodox lines to oversee the banking system, defend the exchange rate, and strengthen the dominion's credit. But the election of a socialist government showed how easily a central bank could be taken over and bent to other ends, much to the dismay of the Bank of England.

---

[15] This technique was pioneered by the Federal Reserve System.

13.7 CANADA

Bordo and Redish (1987: 407–408) argue that in Canada in the 1920s most central banking functions were performed by the Treasury or the commercial banks.[16] The Bank of Montreal enjoyed a close relationship with the Canadian government. Under the Finance Act of 1914 the Treasury offered rediscounting and lender-of-last-resort facilities. Although the Canadian economy was particularly depressed in the early 1930s, there were no bank failures, and this suggests that current arrangements were adequate to ensure banking stability. After leaving the gold standard, at first informally, in the late 1920s, the Canadian dollar floated but tended to shadow the US dollar, except for a relatively short period between 1931 and 1933.

The early 1930s saw the emergence of a debate on central banking in Canada. Several issues were aired. Some Canadians, especially groups on the left, argued that a central bank could alleviate the depression. Others regarded a central bank as an essential component of national sovereignty, and a precondition for Canada to play a role in global monetary cooperation. According to Bordo and Redish (1987: 414–416), the desire to create an institution that would facilitate Canadian participation in a reconstructed gold standard – a forlorn hope in retrospect – was a strong motive for advocates of central banking in Canada. A central bank might also prove less vulnerable to political interference than the Treasury (Cain, 1996: 344). There was also an imperial dimension to the debate. The Bank of England and the UK government were eager to strengthen ties with Canada and persuade it to join the sterling area. An orthodox central bank in Ottawa would enhance British influence over Canadian policy, or so it was believed (Drummond, 1981: 54–64).

In 1933, R. B. Bennett's Conservative government set up a royal commission to review monetary policy and arrangements, and to consider whether a central bank should be established to promote the revival of prosperity at home and abroad. Lord Macmillan, a Scottish judge, was invited to chair the royal commission. Charles Addis, formerly of HSBC and a Bank of England director, was also appointed to the royal commission. The British hoped that their dreams for Canada were coming true. Despite the objections of two Canadian commissioners, who evinced suspicion of British intentions and scepticism of central banking in general, the royal commission reported in favour of setting up a central bank

---

[16] Known as chartered banks.

TABLE 13.5 *Bank of Canada legislation*

Bank of Canada Act 1934	
Ownership	Private shareholders
Governance	Board comprising nine directors: (a) governor, deputy governor (initially appointed by the government; replacements to be elected by directors with government approval); (b) seven other directors elected by shareholders; plus deputy minister of finance (non-voting; this was a civil servant, not a politician).
Primary function	'to regulate credit and currency in the best interests of the economic life of the nation, to control and protect the external value of the national monetary unit and to mitigate by its influence fluctuations in the general level of production, trade, prices and employment … [using] monetary action, and generally to promote the economic and financial welfare of the Dominion'.
Note issue	Yes – exclusive, but rights of chartered banks allowed to taper. Partial gold backing.
Government banker	Permitted, but the government continued to use the facilities of the commercial banks as well as those of the Bank of Canada; strict limits on amount and duration of lending to central and provincial governments.
Bankers' bank	Chartered banks must maintain minimum reserves at central bank.
	Chartered banks must relinquish domestically held gold reserves to central bank.
Market operations permitted	Rediscounting, advances, OMOs.
Exchange rate	No mention of responsibility for exchange rate.
Bank of Canada Amendment Act 1936 (key changes only)	
Ownership	New shares issued to give government majority ownership.
Governance	Additional directors appointed to give government majority control.
Bank of Canada Amendment Act 1938 (key changes only)	
Ownership	Government. Private shareholders were expropriated with compensation.
Governance	Board comprising 11 directors, all appointed by the government.

Sources: Dominion of Canada (1934: Part 1, 493–516); Dominion of Canada (1936: Part 1, 123–131) and Dominion of Canada (1938: Part 1, 147–153).

of orthodox design. The Canadian policy elite welcomed these findings, and the Bank of Canada came into being in 1935, with Graham Towers, an Anglophile Canadian banker, as the first governor. Even so, British hopes that Canada would join the sterling area were dashed. Neither the Canadian government nor the Bank of Canada was seriously interested in following that path which would have complicated economic relations with the United States (Fullerton, 1986; Cain, 1996).

The Bank of Canada was at first owned by private investors. Although the Liberal government that came to power in 1935 nationalized the central bank in two steps in 1936 and 1938, it was permitted to retain de facto autonomy (Plumptre, 1940: 139). Canadian Liberals were a far cry from New Zealand socialists (Table 13.5).

Whilst less sophisticated than capital markets in the United Kingdom or the United States, Canadian capital markets were more highly developed than those in the southern dominions, and this gave the Bank of Canada some modest scope for conducting market operations. The central government bond market became the main venue for the Bank of Canada's OMOs. No regular short-term money market existed until the 1950s, but Treasury bills were traded bilaterally between the central bank and the commercial banks. An unusual feature of the Canadian monetary framework was that the central government continued to hold accounts at the commercial banks as well as at the central bank. The cash reserves of the commercial banks could be altered by moving government funds to and from the central bank (Neufeld, 1958: 47–111; Watts, 1993).

There is little evidence of a change of monetary regime in Canada after 1935 (Bordo and Redish, 1987: 410–414). As a monetary policy agency, the Bank of Canada remained largely dormant in the late 1930s. Unlike the case of New Zealand, Canadian experience does not support the hypothesis that central banks created after the depression pursued a less orthodox path than those set up in the 1920s.[17]

13.8 DISCUSSION

The dominion central banks certainly looked like central banks. They were bankers' banks and provided banking services to their governments. Although banking systems in the British Empire were relatively stable, the Australian and South African central banks stepped in occasionally to prevent the disorderly collapse of ailing institutions. In so

---

[17] See Chapter 12, this volume.

far as commercial banks were compelled by law to maintain minimum reserves at the dominion central banks, Federal Reserve rather than Bank of England practice was followed. Dominion central banks were responsible for note issue. Either explicitly or implicitly, they were tasked with exchange-rate management. Arrangements for their ownership and governance varied, but there was a shift towards greater government influence or control in the 1930s, mirroring an international trend (Singleton, 2011: 104–108). Dominion central banks collected statistical data from their counterparties and offered advice to governments.[18] All were involved in the provision of credit to farmers. Agricultural finance was not an accepted function of central banks, but farmers in the settler economies were pummelled by the depression. Central banks could not evade such commitments. Perhaps the most idiosyncratic central bank was the CBA, a state-owned commercial bank onto which central banking functions were grafted.

Dominion central banks were empowered to engage in rediscounting and OMOs, once more making them resemble standard central banks (Table 13.6). It was perhaps in relation to OMOs that appearances were most deceptive. Commercial banks in the sterling dominions did not attempt to maintain constant cash ratios, focusing instead on liquid assets which included sterling balances in London. Markets for commercial and government securities of any duration were thin or non-existent, except to an extent in Canada. Australia started to issue Treasury bills, which could be rediscounted at the CBA, on a regular basis in 1929. However, the CBA viewed the government's resort to short-term finance with disquiet and sought to moderate the issue of bills. Conditions in New Zealand and South Africa were even more primitive. Overall, the capacity of central banks to influence market interest rates and credit conditions using the standard techniques of monetary policy was limited. In other words, it was difficult for them to make the commercial banks short of cash, though that was by no means a priority by the mid-1930s (Plumptre, 1940: 230–261).

Monetary coordination within the British Empire was largely informal. The British could still give directions to India but not the dominions. Until 1934–5, the only dominions with central banks were Australia and South Africa. Norman kept in touch through his 'empire letters' and encouraged the exchange of personnel. The British also convened an imperial central banking conference in 1937 (Sayers, 1976, Vol. 1: 209–210;

---

[18] These functions are not mentioned in the tables because they can be taken for granted.

TABLE 13.6 *Money markets in the British Dominions between the wars*

	Australia	South Africa	New Zealand	Canada
Short-term	No active commercial bill market. Regular Treasury bill issues from 1929 but no active market. CBA ambivalent towards government borrowing in this way.	No active commercial bill market. Treasury bills issued but held to maturity.	No active commercial bill market. Treasury bills issued but held to maturity.	Some use of commercial bills. Treasury bill tenders from 1934, eventually fortnightly. No active market: bilateral dealings between BoC and individual banks
Long-term	Market for long-term securities developing. Occasional discouraging attempts at OMOs. Uncertainty over whether market is ready for regular OMOs.	Narrow market for long-term securities.	No active market in long-term securities.	Fairly well developed commercial and government bond market but no central exchanges. OMOs conducted mainly in bonds.

Source: Plumptre (1940).

Vol. 2: 515–519). When the dominions pressed for a common reflationary strategy in the sterling area in the early 1930s, the United Kingdom made sympathetic noises but drew the line at sharing the management of interest rates and sterling. The Chancellor of the Exchequer, Neville Chamberlain, told his sister that the dominions should keep out of 'subjects they don't understand and on which they can be embarrassing to us' (cited in Drummond, 1981: 179–180). Niemeyer could be even blunter about his dealings with the 'colonial savages' (quoted in Cain, 1996: 342).

Nevertheless, a degree of coordination was achieved. Empire currencies (excepting the Canadian dollar) were linked to sterling and depreciated against the gold bloc in the 1930s. No efforts were made to hinder the accompanying monetary expansion. Summing up developments in South Africa between 1933 and 1939, Gerhard de Kock (1954: 232), concluded that the '[Reserve] Bank's credit policy was passive rather than active, involuntary rather than deliberate; it was a *symptom* of the new [and more liquid] monetary conditions, rather than the *cause* thereof.' The same was true elsewhere except in New Zealand after 1935 where reflation was deliberate.

13.9 CONCLUSION

The central banks established between the wars in the British dominions of Australia, Canada, New Zealand, and South Africa were, in many respects, central banks in waiting. Their ability to conduct monetary policy was, for the most part, limited by legislation that enshrined monetary orthodoxy, and by the underdevelopment of local financial markets. New central banks in peripheral European states and Latin America faced similar difficulties which would take time to overcome.

It is questionable whether the designers of central banks within the dominions understood their functions or their limitations. Although the Bank of England and its money doctors should have been better equipped to grasp local conditions, they showed little inclination to adapt their prescription of orthodox central banking to the circumstances. Perhaps this was because they regarded dominion central banks less as entities providing services to the host economy than as a means of lashing the dominions to the gold (or gold exchange) standards and holding local politicians in check. The League of Nations and assorted money doctors in other peripheral regions had a similar perspective.

Central banks from the core nations of the international monetary system and their envoys and collaborators did not get their own way all the time. Politicians and central bankers on the periphery had ambitions of their own. After the collapse of the gold standard the scope for experimentation widened. The Bank of England was forced to compromise when dealing with the dominions throughout the 1920s and 1930s. The Australian central bank proved the most amenable to the Bank of England's perspective. This was not a matter of Australian subservience. Rather the Commonwealth Bank of Australia happened, between 1926 and 1934, to be led by a chairman, Gibson, whose faith in monetary orthodoxy was unwavering. When some Labor ministers advocated reflation and default in the early 1930s, Gibson was able to defy them because Labor was weak and divided. Afrikaners regarded the South African Reserve Bank with suspicion. In the mid-1920s, South Africa contemplated returning to gold independently of the United Kingdom, and advice was sought from the American money doctor Edwin Kemmerer rather than Threadneedle Street or the SARB. By the early 1930s, however, the SARB had been tamed, and it supported the government's policy to stay on gold after September 1931. Only when that policy failed did South Africa return fully to the sterling area. Canada and New Zealand disappointed the Bank of England. Both countries were financially and politically stable and the establishment of central banks was not urgent. When Ottawa accepted a British-inspired plan for an orthodox central bank in 1933, the British were hopeful that it would draw Canada into the sterling area, but the Canadians refused to play that game. Canada regarded a peg against sterling as unattractive in view of its close economic ties to the United States. New Zealand's central bank was less than two years old when it was nationalized by a radical Labour government and transformed into a fiefdom of the minister of finance, to the horror of the governor and the Bank of England. Not altogether surprisingly, each case was different.

The experience of the dominions shows that central banking was contested terrain in the 1920s and 1930s. Governments in the dominions occasionally shocked and embarrassed the United Kingdom and the Bank of England when they pushed their central banks in directions that jarred with orthodoxy. Central bank independence depended less on legislation than on the demeanour of the government; central bank independence was strongest when governments were conservative, anxious to cooperate with the United Kingdom, or weak. The central banking blueprints handed down by UK experts were not tailored to conditions in the dominions. The same was true elsewhere on the periphery including in Central and Eastern Europe. Dominion central banks were part of a fragile global network in the 1920s and 1930s. The groundwork had been laid for central banks to make larger contributions during the Second World War and the ensuing decades of regulation and broadly Keynesian economic management. Nothing could have been further from Norman's intentions.

REFERENCES

Ally, Russell (1994). 'The South African Pound Comes of Age: Sterling, the Bank of England and South Africa's Monetary Policy, 1914–25'. *Journal of Imperial and Commonwealth History*, 22(1): 109–126.

Attard, Bernard (1989). 'The Bank of England and the Origins of the Niemeyer Mission, 1921–1930'. *Australian Economic History Review*, 32(1): 66–83.

Balachandran, Gopalan (2008). 'Power and Markets in Global Finance: The Gold Standard, 1890–1926'. *Journal of Global History*, 3(3): 313–335.

Belich, James (2009). *Replenishing the Earth: The Settler Revolution and the Rise of the Anglo-World, 1783–1939*. Oxford: Oxford University Press.

Bibow, Jörg (2002). 'Keynes on Central Banking and the Structure of Monetary Policy'. *History of Political Economy*, 34(4): 749–787.

Bolt, Jutta, Inklaar, Robert, de Jong, Herman, and van Zanden, Jan Luiten (2018). 'Rebasing "Maddison": New Income Comparisons and the Shape of Long-Run Economic Development'. www.rug.nl/ggdc/historicaldevelopment/maddison/releases/maddison-project-database-2018.

Bordo, Michael D. and Redish, Angela (1987). 'Why did the Bank of Canada Emerge in 1935?' *Journal of Economic History*, 47(2): 405–17.

Brooke, Geoffrey T., Endres, Anthony M., and Rogers, Alan J. (2019). 'The Economists and Monetary Thought in Interwar New Zealand: The Gradual Emergence of Monetary Policy Activism'. *History of Economics Review*, 73(1): 14–46.

Bureau of Census and Statistics (1960). *Union Statistics for Fifty Years 1910–1960*. Pretoria: Bureau of Census and Statistics.

Butlin, Matthew W. W. (1977). 'A Preliminary Annual Database 1900/01 to 1973/74'. Reserve Bank of Australia Research Discussion Paper No. 7701.

Cain, Peter J. (1996). 'Gentlemanly Imperialism at Work: The Bank of England, Canada, and the Sterling Area, 1932–1936'. *Economic History Review*, 46(2): 336–57.

Cain, Peter J. and Hopkins, Anthony G. (2016). *British Imperialism 1688–2015*, 3rd ed., London: Routledge.

Coleman, William (2001). 'Is it Possible That an Independent Central Bank is Impossible? The Case of the Australian Notes Board, 1920–1924'. *Journal of Money, Credit and Banking*, 33(3): 729–748.

Copland, D.B. (1939). 'The Commonwealth Bank – Co-operation or Compulsion?' *Economic Record*, 15(3): 21–39.

Cornish, Selwyn (1993). 'Sir Leslie Melville: An Interview'. *Economic Record*, 69(4): 437–57.

Cornish, Selwyn (2008). 'History and Development of Central Banking in Australia 1920–1970'. ANU Global Dynamic Systems Centre, Working Paper No. 3.

de Kock, Gerhard (1954). *A History of the South African Reserve Bank (1920–52)*. Pretoria: J. L. Van Schaik.

de Kock, Michiel H. (1939). *Central Banking*. London: P.S. King & Son.

Dick, Trevor J. O. and Floyd, John E. (1992). *Canada and the Gold Standard: Balance-of-Payments Adjustment, 1871–1913*. Cambridge: Cambridge University Press.

Dominion of Canada (1934). *Acts of the Parliament of the Dominion of Canada: Fifth Session of the Seventeenth Parliament*. Ottawa: Joseph Oscar Patenaude.

Dominion of Canada (1936). *Acts of the Parliament of the Dominion of Canada: First Session of the Eighteenth Parliament*. Ottawa: Joseph Oscar Patenaude.

Dominion of Canada (1938). *Acts of the Parliament of the Dominion of Canada: Third Session of the Eighteenth Parliament*. Ottawa: Joseph Oscar Patenaude.

Drea, Eion (2013). 'The Bank of England, Montagu Norman and the Internationalisation of Anglo-Irish Monetary Relations, 1922–1943'. *Financial History Review*, 21(1): 59–76.

Drummond, Ian M. (1981). *The Floating Pound and the Sterling Area*. Cambridge: Cambridge University Press.

Eichengreen, Barry (1992). *Golden Fetters: The Gold Standard and the Great Depression 1919–1939*. New York: Oxford University Press.

Fitz-Gibbon, Bryan and Gizycki, Marianne (2001). 'A History of Last-Resort Lending and Other Support for Troubled Financial Institutions in Australia,' System Stability Department, Reserve Bank of Australia, Research Discussion Paper 2001–07, Sydney.

Fullerton, Douglas H. (1986). *Graham Towers and His Times*. Toronto: McClelland and Stewart.

Giblin, L. F. (1951). *The Growth of a Central Bank: The Development of the Commonwealth Bank of Australia 1924–1945*. Melbourne: Melbourne University Press.

Greasley, David and Oxley, Les (2002). 'Regime Shift and Fast Recovery on the Periphery: New Zealand in the 1930s'. *Economic History Review*, 55(4): 697–720.

Harvey, Ernest (1927). 'Central Banking'. *Economic Record*, 3(1): 1–14.

Hawke, Gary R. (1973). *Between Governments and Banks: A History of the Reserve Bank of New Zealand*. Wellington: Government Printer.

Kisch, Sir Cecil H. and Elkin, Winifred A. (1932). *Central Banks*, 4th ed. London: Macmillan.

Love, Peter (1984). *Labour and the Money Power*. Melbourne: Melbourne University Press.

MacGregor, Donald (1978). 'In Memoriam: Arthur Fitzwalter Wynne Plumptre, 1907–1977'. *Canadian Journal of Economics*, 11(4): 714–718.

Magee, Gary B. and Thomson, Andrew S. (2010). *Empire and Globalisation: Networks of People, Goods and Capital in the British World, c. 1850–1914*. Cambridge: Cambridge University Press.

McAloon, Jim (2013). *Judgements of All Kinds: Economic Policy-Making in New Zealand 1945–1984*. Wellington: Victoria University Press.

Metcalf, Cherie, Redish, Angela, and Shearer, Ronald (1996). 'New Estimates of the Canadian Money Stock: 1871–1967'. University of British Columbia, Department of Economics, Discussion Paper No. 96–17.

Millmow, Alex (2010). *The Power of Economic Ideas: The Origins of Keynesian Macroeconomic Management in Interwar Australia 1929–39*. Canberra: Australian National University Press.

Neufeld, Edward P. (1958). *Bank of Canada Operations and Policy*. Toronto: University of Toronto Press.

Niemeyer, Sir Otto (1931). *Banking and Currency in New Zealand*. Wellington: Government Printer. www.rbnz.govt.nz/research-and-publications/fact-sheets-and-guides/otto-niemeyers-1931-report-on-banking-and-currency-in-new-zealand [last accessed 27 February 2023].

Norman, Montagu (1932). 'Foreword', in Sir Cecil H. Kisch and W.A. Elkin, *Central Banks*, 4th edition. London: Macmillan, v–vi.

Padayachee, Vishnu and Bordiss, Bradley (2015). 'How Global Geo-Politics Shaped South Africa's Post-World War I Monetary Policy: the Case of Gerhard Vissering and Edwin Kemmerer in South Africa, 1924–25'. *Economic History of Developing Regions*, 30(2): 182–209.

Plumptre, Arthur Fitzwalter Wynne (1940). *Central Banking in the British Dominions*. Toronto: University of Toronto Press.

Pressnell, L. S. (1978). '1925: The Burden of Sterling'. *Economic History Review*, 31(1): 67–88.

Richards, C. S. (1925). 'The Kemmerer-Vissering Report and the Position of the Reserve Bank of the Union of South Africa'. *Economic Journal*, 35(140): 558–567.

Rossouw, Jannie (2011). 'A Selective Refection on the Institutional Development of the South African Reserve Bank since 1921'. *Economic History of Developing Regions*, 26(Supp. 1): S3–S20.

Santaella, Julio A. (1993). 'Stabilization Programs and External Enforcement: Experience from the 1920s'. *Staff Papers (International Monetary Fund)*, 40(3): 584–621.

Sayers, Richard S. (1976). *The Bank of England 1891–1944*, Vols 1 and 2. Cambridge: Cambridge University Press.

Schedvin, C. Boris (1970). *Australia and the Great Depression*. Sydney: Sydney University Press.

Schedvin, C. Boris (1981). 'Gibson, Sir Robert (1863–1934)', in *Australian Dictionary of Biography*. National Centre for Biography, Australian National University, http://adb.anu.edu.au/biography/gibson-sir-robert-6310 [last accessed 27 February 2023].

Schedvin, C. Boris (1992). *In Reserve: Central Banking in Australia, 1945–75*. St. Leonards, Australia: Allen & Unwin.

Sheppard, David K. (1990). 'Annual Estimates of M1 and M3: 1862–1982'. *Reserve Bank of New Zealand Bulletin*, 53(4): 407–411.

Sheppard, David K., Guerin, K., and Lee S. (1990). 'New Zealand Monetary Aggregates and the Total Assets of Leading Groups of Financial Institutions, 1862–1982'. Money and Finance Group, Victoria University of Wellington, Discussion Paper No. 11, Wellington, New Zealand.

Singleton, John (2003). 'New Zealand: Devaluation without a Balance of Payments Crisis', in Theo Balderston (ed.), *The World Economy and National Economies in the Interwar Slump*. Basingstoke: Palgrave: 172–190.

Singleton, John (2010). 'The Winds of Change for Central Banks?' *Central Banking*, 20(3): 23–28.

Singleton, John (2011). *Central Banking in the Twentieth Century*. Cambridge: Cambridge University Press.

Strakosch, Henry (1921). 'The South African Reserve Bank'. *Economic Journal*, 31(122): 172–178.

Tocker, Albert H. (1924). 'The Monetary Standards of Australia and New Zealand'. *Economic Journal*, 34(136): 556–575.

Watts, George S. (1993). *The Bank of Canada: Origins and Early History*, ed. Thomas Kenneth Rymes. Ottawa: Carleton University Press.

Wright, Matthew (2006). 'The Policy Origins of the Reserve Bank of New Zealand'. *Reserve Bank of New Zealand Bulletin*, 69(3): 5–22.

14

Central Banking and Colonial Control

India, 1914–1939

G. Balachandran

14.1 INTRODUCTION

When the Reserve Bank of India (RBI) opened its doors to business on 1 April 1935, India became the only colony with a central bank. The story of how India acquired this curious distinction offers useful insights both into the history of central banking after the First World War, and the institutional and intellectual apparatuses for managing money at arm's length from representative governments, that central banking aimed to foster. Money emerged as an early domain of technical 'expertise', though much of this expertise was in fact quite parochial and mainly represented the views of bankers at least until the Bank of England began to promote and amplify it as the basis of sound monetary policy. Colonial central banking was even more overtly political; hence the prehistory and early history of the RBI help place the interwar spread of central banking in its wider context.

Proposals to establish a central bank in India date back to the late nineteenth century. Briefly revived in 1913, the idea gained currency in the mid-1920s mainly as a means to preserve London's overall control over Indian monetary policies that, for reasons explained in the next section, became vital to British economic and political interests in the colony. The history of central banking in India thus belongs to the history of late colonialism and metropolitan efforts to preserve colonial forms of control through less overt means, and with respect to currency, exchange rates, and monetary management, to hide behind a façade of technical expertise and institutional independence. Colonial India was governed for the most part by a bureaucracy one part of which was represented by the Government of India, and the other by a Whitehall department called the India Office, headed by a Secretary of State responsible to the British parliament. In 1919, too soon after the war to second-guess Britain's victory or India's contribution, Whitehall handed the prerogative for the colony's external tariffs to its outpost in Delhi, functioning partly under the scrutiny of a new colonial legislature that, though toothless and only partially elected on the basis of a limited franchise, became nevertheless a focus of public interest. Both ends of the colonial bureaucracy thereafter spent the next two decades resisting tariff pressures from India. Currency and exchange policies meanwhile remained the prerogative of the India Office, advised by a finance committee comprising a small group of City bankers and a loyal clique of former colonial civil servants.

India Office currency management had long been controversial and an object of criticism in both India and Britain; as is well known, John Maynard Keynes wrote his 1913 book on Indian currency and finance (Keynes, 1971) partly in response to such criticism. Reignited during the First World War, when Britain's financial problems brought India's currency system to the brink of collapse, this controversy was further inflamed by the deflationary squeeze India suffered in the 1920s and 1930s because of exchange-rate policies regarded in the colony as being mainly in Britain's interest (Balachandran, 2013). As the rupee exchange rate became a hot political issue, embittering Indian opinion and damaging public trust, an alarmed Bank of England drew up schemes to refine London's financial control of the colony through a central bank under its tutelage. While the India Office was loath to give up its powers, an independent, privately owned central bank under the Bank of England's wing was the City of London's price for granting India any semblance of representative government. However, vesting exchange and monetary policies in the newly formed RBI proved unnecessary, after the 1935 Government of India Act made 'finance' a 'reserved' subject, entrusted to an unelected white civil servant. What is more, the RBI's independence quickly turned into an irksome burden, after native business interests gained a dominant position on the Bank's central board, and the Bank's first governor, an Australian protégé of the Bank of England governor, Montagu Norman, was suspected to favour devaluation.

This chapter recounts this history in five sections. The next section sets out the imperial and global context in which monetary policies became a source of conflict in interwar India. Section 14.3 then describes attempts to transform the Imperial Bank of India, formed in 1921, by amalgamating the three Presidency Banks of Bombay, Calcutta, and Madras, into a quasi-central bank aligned with the Bank of England. Section 14.4 relates the failure of efforts to create a central bank in 1927–8; the RBI's actual creation in 1935 is the subject of the Section 14.5. Section 14.6 tells the extraordinary story of how, within a few years, the colonial government and the Bank of England brought an inconveniently independent institution to heel. The final section offers some conclusions.

14.2 INDIA, BRITAIN, AND WORLD MONEY, C. 1914–1937

For centuries, a view of India as a sink for gold and silver shaped attitudes in Europe towards precious metal flows to the subcontinent. The British East India Company went a step further to regulate them to serve its own ends or to assuage anxieties in Britain (Siddiqi, 1981). Despite advances in credit money and techniques for managing it, bankers never ceased to fret about gold outflows; the same outflows frequently preoccupied sovereign governments, particularly when they were large or occurred during periods of crisis. The anxieties and bullionist continuities suppressed in liberal doctrine also preyed heavily on bankers and public officials in their darker moments, as they appear to have done for Basil Blackett, a senior British Treasury official, in December 1919:

> if India demands payment [for its imports] in precious metals to an extent that is unreasonable, the British Government will be doing a doubtful service to the world in protecting India against the marauding invaders whose raids in olden times served the purpose of relieving her of superficial hoards of gold.[1]

Following the crash in silver prices and the closure of local silver mints in 1893, India's taste for precious metals increasingly turned towards gold. Its social and ritual uses expanded, the metal became a more reliable store of value, and imports surged on the back of rising commodity exports and incomes after the turn of the century (Keynes, 1971: 76). Exchange intervention in London, that is, sales of rupee drafts on India against sterling deposited with the Secretary of State, generically referred to as 'council bill sales', may have checked but failed to eliminate gold flows toward the colony. According to some trade estimates, on the eve of the First World War, India imported a quarter of the world's gold output (Balachandran, 2013: 39). While these flows caused recurring anxiety in London, Keynes took the more sanguine view that they were

---

[1] 'Indian exchange and currency committee', Blackett's undated note, December 1919; Blackett to Lucas, 9 January 1920, T160 18/F. 571, UK National Archives (UKNA).

merely a reflection of India's global counter-cyclical role. Hence, while Indian gold imports could trigger short-term strains in London, particularly during an 'inconvenient week', Keynes felt a 'creditor nation' like Britain ought overall to welcome their contribution to keeping inflation in check. India, he declared, was a 'true friend to the City' and an 'enemy' of inflation (Keynes, 1971: 70–71).

Keynes's understanding of India's counter-cyclical role reflected a simple but powerful model of production, consumption, and saving by Indian households. In 1913, India was a small, open economy whose prices and incomes broadly tracked world trends. An overwhelming proportion of income and employment was accounted for by peasant agriculture. Farmers spent their incomes on cloth or other consumer manufactures, or saved them in the form of precious metals, with those who could afford gold increasingly preferring it to silver, as a hedge against inflation. Savings were a function of incomes that rose or fell with agricultural commodity prices, hence a global boom increased gold flows to India. These flows, in turn, helped temper the boom.

Wartime and early post-war developments confirmed these relationships, particularly between world prices and the pressure of Indian demand on Western gold stocks. While Keynes thought India's appetite for gold would decline as its banking system developed, his analysis also implied that its gold imports would decline or reverse direction in the event of a slump in its exports and incomes. Thus, as interwar Britain struggled with monetary instability amid stubbornly high unemployment, Keynes's insights were deployed as a framework for managing the Indian economy. Hopes for a long-term decline in gold flows through developing the Indian banking system now gave way to the more pressing, short-term imperative of checking monetary gold flows to India by any means justifiable.

Since 1898, India was externally on a gold exchange standard with the rupee pegged to sterling at 16d. (or 16 old pence, that is, £1 = 15 rupees). Domestically the Indian currency system comprised token silver rupee coins – 'notes printed on silver', according to Keynes – and paper currency that the government was obliged to redeem in silver rupees on demand. The government maintained a 'paper currency reserve' (PCR) whose explicit purpose was to meet this demand and forestall a panic run on the paper currency. Hence, despite the latter's rising popularity, a substantial proportion of the PCR continued to be held in the form of silver rupees. In addition to silver rupees, PCR holdings included gold, mainly sovereigns, and UK treasury bills (Figure 14.1).

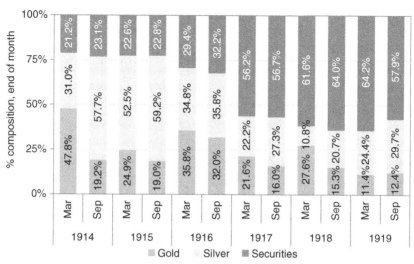

FIGURE 14.1 Composition of the Indian Paper Currency Reserve (PCR), 1914–1919
Source: Balachandran (2013: 57).

For nearly two decades leading up to the war, India functioned under a de facto currency board system in which the net external trade balance (or, more generally, the state of its current account) determined currency issue. India's external trade was highly seasonal, with a busy season from about October to April, when there was also a net expansion of currency circulation, and a slack season comprising the other months when there was a net contraction. Currency contraction, whether seasonal or resulting from an adverse turn in the current account, led to the return of silver rupees from circulation and augmented silver holdings in the PCR. This mechanism worked reasonably well so long as silver prices were low and silver rupees functioned as tokens that were worth more as currency than as bullion. The silver rupee's token character could be at risk, however, from a rise in silver prices. Should this rise be large enough for the coin to be worth more as bullion, there could be a flight from currency notes to silver rupees, in other words, a run on the PCR's silver rupee holdings. Revaluing the rupee in line with silver prices might prevent a run, but in that case the rupee would cease to be a gold currency and revert to the silver standard. This is precisely what happened during the First World War.

As Britain's wartime trade deficit increased, its trade with India, ordinarily in surplus, also went into deficit. India's own surplus during the war (Table 14.1) was lower on average than in the five years preceding

G. Balachandran

TABLE 14.1 *India's trade balance and currency circulation*
(in millions of rupees), 1914–1925

Financial Year (April–March)	Trade balance	Gross coin and note circulation	
		September	March
1914–15	437	605	616
1915–16	654	638	677
1916–17	955	715	864
1917–18	921	1,084	998
1918–19	848	1,344	1,535
1919–20	1,260	1,719	1,745*
1920–21	−775	1,576	1,661
1921–22	−209	1,794	1,748
1922–23	900	1,808	1,747
1923–24	1,449	1,792	1,858
1924–25	1,551	1,792	1,842

* Rs. 1,851 million in January 1920.
Source: Balachandran (2013: 114).

the war because of controls on exports unrelated to the imperial war effort. Nevertheless, with Britain commandeering the empire's gold resources to pay for its imports from the United States, India was obliged to settle its exports in British government securities. These IOUs piled up in the PCR, providing the backing for over 60 per cent of the note issue in March 1918 compared to about a fifth in March 1914; reserve holdings in gold and silver declined correspondingly (Figure 14.1).

A steady flight from paper currency, that is, a run on the PCR's holdings of silver rupees, was aggravated by wartime inflation that, together with a worldwide liquidity shortage, drove up the price of silver from 68 cents per ounce before the war to 90 cents by late 1917. This necessitated a rupee revaluation to 17d., to preserve the token character of the silver rupee coin and prevent it from being melted for bullion. With no relief in sight and the PCR running out of silver rupees by March 1918 (Figure 14.1), Britain struck an emergency deal with the United States to supply 200 million ounces of silver to India. This deal, which was legislated by the US Congress as the Pittman Act, after the Nevada senator and silver champion Key Pittman, fixed the price of silver at one dollar per ounce for the duration of the war and necessitated a further revaluation of the rupee to 18d. The rupee was successively revalued after silver prices resumed their rise after the war, following the lifting of US controls, to reach 22d. by the end of 1919. With the pound going off the gold standard in March 1919 and depreciating against gold, the rupee rose to nearly three shillings against the imperial currency in January 1920 (Balachandran, 2013: 96).

Restrictions on private gold imports to India continued after the war. The resulting premium on gold in India widened with each rupee revaluation, triggering Western fears of a gold drain to the colony and prolonging the restrictions. The rise in India's trade surplus after the war (Table 14.1) deepened such fears. This was the context for Blackett's dark forebodings and fantasies cited earlier. They would not have come as a surprise to informed observers in India, as they merely confirmed the suspicion that liberal principles were really a veneer for the colonial relationship and that Britain would not hesitate to abandon liberalism, should it cease to serve its own interests. With Britain's motives and its capacity to manage India's currency both in doubt, Indian demands for a gold standard that would be less susceptible to British manipulation grew.

An India Office committee appointed in 1919 to recommend the stabilization of the Indian currency system (the fourth such inquiry in less than three decades) seemingly responded to such concerns by formally recommending the adoption of a gold standard. Though Blackett viewed this prospect with particular alarm, the committee's immediate and most portentous recommendation was for a sharp revaluation of the rupee to two shillings (24d.) gold. This was nearly 50 per cent above the pre-war rate of 16d. (Table 14.2), and ten per cent above the prevailing rate fixed with reference to the price of silver. The India Office expected this overvalued rate to trigger capital flight from the colony; the resulting currency contraction would arrest the run on the PCR's silver holdings. In other words, the revaluation was designed not to stabilize India's currency and economy, but to stave off the threat to global gold supplies and stem the run on the PCR's silver holdings (Balachandran, 1993: 587).

In this respect, results exceeded expectations when the new rate was introduced in February 1920, in the midst of a gathering slump. India's trade balance immediately swung into negative territory, going from a surplus of Rs 1,260 million in 1919–20 to a deficit of Rs 775 million in 1920–1 (Table 14.1). As capital took flight, the government refused to abandon the two shillings peg until September 1920. The rupee dropped to 15d. after the peg was removed; by March 1921, it had slipped to 11d. (Table 14.2). Exchange losses over this period totalled £60 billion and India is estimated to have suffered a 6 to 10 per cent drop in real national income between 1919–20 and 1920–1 (Heston, 1983: 397–399).

G. Balachandran

TABLE 14.2 *Rupee–sterling and rupee–dollar exchange rates*
(1913 = 100), 1920–1925

Year	March Rs/£	March Rs/$	September Rs/£	September Rs/$	Ann. average Rs/£	Ann. average Rs/$
1920	203	145	139	102	154	116
1921	96	77	104	80	100	79
1922	95	86	97	89	97	88
1923	101	98	100	94	101	96
1924	103	91	108	99	108	97
1925	112	110	115	114	113	112

Source: Balachandran (2013: 136).

The 1920 stabilization package was, in blunt terms, an imperial debt default disguised as a colonial currency crisis. It liquidated India's accumulated wartime and post-war export surplus in exchange interventions to defend an overvalued and unsustainable parity, because Britain proved unwilling to redeem its wartime debts to the colony.[2]

This stabilization disaster presaged India's relentless monetary squeeze over the next two decades. Its main intent, given Britain's dependence on expansionary global conditions to restore its own external finances, was to disengage India from global expansionary pressures during the 1920s and intensify the impact of the slump in the 1930s. Thus, Keynes's diagnosis of India's counter-cyclical role became a guide to interwar policy in the colony. In the early 1920s, this meant raising the rupee beyond the pre-war rate of 16d. by keeping a tight rein on currency expansion and borrowing in London to finance India's sterling obligations. Hence despite large and unprecedented trade surpluses, currency in circulation remained practically unchanged between 1920 and 1925 (Table 14.1), and discount rates regularly touched 8 or 9 per cent. With sterling purchases restricted to force the rupee up, loans from London ended up financing nearly half of India's sterling obligations over 1922–5 (Table 14.3). Ignoring vocal Indian demands to restore the pre-war 16d. rate, the rupee was stabilized at 18d. in 1926, following the majority recommendation of yet another currency inquiry – this time by a royal commission. The rupee thus became perhaps the only currency to have been revalued after the First World War.

---

[2] See Balachandran (1993) for a more detailed account.

TABLE 14.3 *Financing of Government of India's liabilities in the United Kingdom (in millions of pounds sterling), 1921–1925*

Financial Year (April-March)	Total sterling expenditure	Net sterling purchases	Reduction in reserve	War office receipts	Sterling loans
1921–2	42.8		2.5	27.1	14.8
1922–3	40.9	4.8		3.3	31.3
1923–4	39.9	23.1		5.6	17.5
1924–5	61.9	41.5		1.7	18.5

Note: Figures may not add up because of accounting leads and lags.
Source: Balachandran (2013: 113).

As its critics had warned, the 18d. rate proved untenable from the start. The rupee hovered around the gold export point through much of the next five years, despite enduring a severe monetary contraction, which – together with foreign borrowing – financed a third of its sterling obligations between 1927 and 1930. Thanks to its overvalued currency, India found itself in Britain's rut when the depression began, and like Britain, hoped for a global expansion to set its economy afloat again.

The Depression took a heavy toll on India's foreign trade. In 1932–3, exports slumped to less than 40 per cent of their 1929 level; imports bottomed out at a similar level a year later (Table 14.4). The trade surplus, which averaged Rs 571 million over 1927–30, fell by over a third, to Rs 371 million, in 1930–1. The terms of trade turned predictably adverse and did not return to pre-Depression levels until the Second World War. Unit export prices fell more than domestic wholesale prices; by 1933, the country's Wholesale Price Index (WPI) stood at about two-thirds of its 1928 level (Table 14.4). India's current account deficit, which had been declining since 1927–8, largely due to falling gold imports, increased sharply in 1930–1; still, it remained below its level in the mid-1920s. Most remarkably, India ran a current account surplus in all but one year of the depression.

Pro-cyclical monetary and fiscal policies intensified the effects of the slump, particularly in rural India. As agricultural prices and incomes declined, distressed households began liquidating holdings of gold and silver in 1929. By early 1931, India began to export small amounts of gold. Gold exports surged after sterling's depreciation in September 1931 (Table 14.4); in the next seven months alone, outflows totalled over one-eighth of India's gold imports during the preceding seven

TABLE 14.4 *Balance of payments, terms of trade, and wholesale prices (WPI) in India, 1928–1937*

Fin. Year (April-March)	Exports	Imports	Net services	Gold Exports	Current account	Export prices	Import prices	Terms of trade	WPI
	in Rs million, (-) signifies net payments					(1928–9 = 100)			
1927–28	3,529	3,016	-495	-347	-329	102.6	103.7	98.9	141
1928–29	3,663	2,998	-627	-221	-183	100.0	100.0	100.0	100
1929–30	3,404	2,867	-496	-142	-100	92.5	96.7	95.7	82
1930–31	2,442	2,071	-495	-128	-251	73.3	83.0	88.4	69
1931–32	1,740	1,518	-527	580	275	60.7	74.4	81.6	65
1932–33	1,460	1,515	-506	655	95	56.7	67.6	83.9	62
1933–34	1,635	1,364	-461	571	380	54.9	65.9	83.3	63
1934–35	1,707	1,594	-464	525	174	55.5	65.4	84.9	65
1935–36	1,821	1,628	-480	374	88	58.2	64.4	90.3	65
1936–37	2,175	1,608	-507	278	338	58.7	65.1	90.1	72

Sources: Balance of payments from Balachandran (2013: 171); prices and terms of trade from Chaudhuri (1983: 840).

decades. Britain, gushed its finance minister, Austen Chamberlain '[had] discovered an astonishing gold mine' in India. It has 'put us in a clover. The French can take their balances ... without our flinching. We can accumulate credits for ... [repaying our loans] and safely lower the bank rate. So there is great rejoicing in the City' (Bridge, 1986: 73–74).

Between 1931 and 1937, Indian gold exports totalled £225 million, transforming the country's current account and turning a poverty-stricken colony into a major capital exporter (Table 14.4). India was now feted as the 'single most powerful force' for a 'general rise in world prices'; drawing gold out of the country became a major determinant of sterling policy.[3] Inasmuch as dissaving helped consumption remain buoyant, gold exports cushioned some of the income effects of the slump and national income estimates suggest a relatively small 3 per cent peak-to-trough decline in per capita real GDP between 1930 and 1935 (Maddison, 1971: 167; Heston 1983: 401–402). However, the depression was much deeper in the countryside, where despite enormous dissaving and asset liquidation, the nominal value of agricultural debt rose by over half, to reach Rs 18,000 million in the 1930s. The rural debt to income ratio also doubled. By 1939, a quarter of agricultural incomes was directed toward debt servicing, up from one-eighth back in 1929 (Goldsmith, 1983: 126–128).

14.3 MANAGING THE BLOWBACK: THE BANK OF ENGLAND AND THE IMPERIAL BANK OF INDIA

Colonial monetary and exchange-rate policies provoked widespread outrage in India. Business criticism in particular, grew more vocal, much of it directed at the monetary squeeze applied to raise the rupee above its pre-war rate. The Bombay-based Indian Currency League spearheaded a vigorous campaign against the 18d. rate, favouring the 1926 Commission's minority recommendation of 16d. Senior officials believed the trail of bitterness left by wartime and post-war currency controversies had damaged government's relations with business and driven it closer to the Congress party. Opposition to colonial financial policies intensified during the Depression, galvanizing a nationalist opposition frustrated by the government's refusal to relieve agrarian distress or utilize gold sales to support expansionary domestic policies. Thus, while money in colonial India had always been political, opinions grew sharply more

---

[3] Memorandum on exchange rates, 29 February 1932, T175/57; Note, 5 March 1932, T160/474 F. 12471/06/2; Memorandum on Prices, June 1932, T177/8, UKNA.

polarized in the 1920s and 1930s. The colonial government, seen as acting in London's interests and at its behest, was distrusted and isolated.

Sensing the darkening mood, Basil Blackett, who went to India in 1923 to serve as its finance minister, attempted to lighten the India Office's control, notably over foreign-exchange interventions, which he now began to conduct in Bombay rather than exclusively through London. Naturally, the India Office was not pleased, and nor were the London-based exchange banks nervous about where this might lead. As monetary controversies in India aggravated institutional tensions within the empire, and cast a cloud over London's authority, the Bank of England governor, Montagu Norman, began casting about for other arrangements to preserve it.[4] Alarmed by the prospect of greater democracy, he recognized that 'something important' was going on in India that London did not altogether understand.[5] Unlike the India Office, Norman did not believe Blackett was 'marching ... several paces ahead' of local opinion; rather he was merely 'being carried along by the new democracy'.[6] Thus, while Blackett had to be moderated, it was also essential to bridge the 'gulf' between London and India.[7]

Norman found the prospect of 'Indianization', as he described these changes, unappealing, and drew the line at the prospect of Indians – a 'race notorious for gossip and leakiness'– holding important positions in the colonial financial system. However, believing the movement to be irreversible, he turned his attention to 'forg[ing] such bonds' as to keep Indian monetary policy firmly within the Bank of England's orbit. To this end, in 'matters of form, and also ... in agency business', he was 'willing ... to make ... concessions, so long as he [knew] that the B[ank] of E[ngland] [would] be the power behind.'[8]

To this end, Norman sought to dress up the Imperial Bank of India in the robes of a quasi-central bank. Ever since its foundation, the Imperial Bank had been trying – rather ineffectually – to expand its discount operations; it had also taken tentative steps toward relieving the monetary stringency caused by the government's exchange-rate policies, by issuing

---

[4] Norman to Viscount Peel, 26 October 1922, G30/9, Bank of England Archives (BOEA).

[5] Norman to Siepmann, 12 September 1923; Siepmann to Norman, 31 January 1924, ADM 25/14, BOEA; Harry Siepmann was a friend to Blackett and adviser to Norman.

[6] Norman to Siepmann, 12 September 1923, ADM 25/14, BOEA.

[7] Norman to Siepmann, 14 November 1923; Siepmann to Norman, 31 January 1924, ADM 25/14, BOEA.

[8] Norman to Siepmann, 12 September 1923, ADM 25/14, BOEA; Cook to Blackett, 7 June and 13 June 1923, Mss. Eur. E397/22, British Library, Oriental and India Office Collection (OIOC).

small amounts of temporary, seasonal currency against rupee Treasury bills. Norman's priority, however, was to bring the Imperial Bank under his superintendence. He thus set out to reform the Bank, to reduce the influence of its Bombay-based shareholders and 'internationalize' its outlook. The relationship Norman sought between the two institutions was soon formalized as a 'permanent' agreement for the Imperial Bank to '"marry" the Bank of England lock, stock and barrel' and submit to the supervision of a London-based 'advisory committee'. In return, the Imperial Bank would gain future recognition as the Government of India's financial agent in London; such recognition would be accompanied by the transfer of Indian rupee loans and some government accounts with the Bank of England – possibly even control over foreign exchange operations.[9]

Despite pressure from the Bank of England and support from the Indian government, Imperial Bank reform was not easy. The India Office was a powerful obstacle, keen to preserve its power and ensure that the Imperial Bank was not granted any responsibility in matters of 'high finance'. The 'main fruits of the "marriage"', the Office insisted, ought to await the 'devolution of financial responsibility from the Secretary of State to the Government of India'.[10]

Norman's reform of the Bank involved appointing a 'Managing Governor from Europe'. After some delay, when Norman grumbled that Imperial Bank officials were not 'playing their parts', the Australian banker Osborne Smith was hired for the job. Smith, Norman affirmed, was 'willing to do anything we ask him to do in the cause of central banking'. The London advisory committee began its meetings in 1925, despite the India Office's continued reluctance.[11] Norman kept a close watch over the Bank, not least when he backed plans to buy up its shares to increase 'European control' and avert a possible Indian takeover; the plan had been concocted by a British business house in Calcutta, various City individuals and the editor of the *Economist* newspaper, Walter Layton. As Norman would explain to Osborne Smith, 'the object ... naturally

---

[9] Norman to Blackett, 21 May 1924, G3/180, BoE; Cook to Blackett, 24 May and 13 June 1923, Mss. Eur. E397/22, OIOC; 'Final Edition' of 'Confidential Suggestions', 19 March 1923, G14/96, BOEA.

[10] Secretary of State's financial dispatch, 3 May A&F/Nov. 1923-565-71-B, Finance Department, National Archives of India (FD/NAI); Cook's note, 7 December 1922,. May 1923-60-126-A, FD/NAI.

[11] Norman to Blackett, 8 December 1925, G3/182; Norman to Siepmann, 26 May 1924, ADM 25/14, BOEA.

recommends itself to us …' if only to 'retard … [and] postpone the inevitable as long as possible'.[12]

<h2>14.4 THE RESERVE BANK OF INDIA CONTROVERSY OF 1927–1928</h2>

Against this backdrop, the Royal Commission established in 1926 recommended setting up a privately owned central bank in India that would be independent of the government. This proposal was not to the liking of the India Office, its main witness, Financial Secretary Cecil Kisch, arguing that while the Brussels and Genoa resolutions were the 'guiding source of up-to-date currency theory and practice', they were not relevant to India where the central bank had to be closely associated with, if not directly controlled by the government. Only then would the Bank be in a position of strength and independence with respect to 'outside parties'.[13] Kisch even recommended close links between the central bank and the legislature, since the government was accountable to the latter for its exchange rate policy.[14] By 'government', of course, Kisch really meant the India Office. He also wanted the bank's board to be located in London, where – given his vital interest in managing Indian gold flows – the Secretary of State would be a strong voice.[15]

For reasons already discussed, the Bank of England had no interest in a government-owned central bank. The leading British member of the 1926 Commission (and, as such, its leading member) was Henry Strakosch, a City-based South African-born financier and close associate of Montagu Norman. Arguing for a 'non-political' and 'independent' bank of issue, Strakosch followed Norman's view that Whitehall control over Indian monetary policies would soon prove impossible to sustain, and that an 'independent' central bank was indispensable to plans for devolving more powers to the colony.[16] Knowing something of the history of the proposal, Keynes objected to a private central bank, but his views had little effect (Chandavarkar, 1989: 82, 106–107).

---

[12] Norman's note, 8 October and 30 November 1928; Norman to Osborne Smith, 31 December 1928, G1/317, BOEA; Edward Benthall, diary entry, 13 February 1929, Box 7, Benthall Papers, Archive of the Centre of South Asian Studies (CSAS), Cambridge.

[13] Hilton-Young Commission (HYC), *Evidence*, Q. 11000, 11141–11147, 11623–11625.

[14] HYC, *Evidence*, Q. 11140.

[15] HYC, *Evidence*, Q. 11179, 11627, 11181–11183, 11439–11449.

[16] Strakosch to Blackett, 17 October 1925, Hawtrey Papers, Htry 1/3/2, Churchill Archives Centre (CCA), Cambridge; Strakosch's note 'Imperial Bank of India', 28 February 1926, T176/25B, UKNA.

The task of overseeing the creation of the central bank fell to the India Office, thus giving it ample room for mischief. Shortly after the Commission submitted its report, its chairman, Edward Hilton-Young deplored the India Office's 'obstructive' attitude adopted 'in the hope that something may turn up to scotch the idea of a Bank of Issue and so preserve the influence of the Secretary of State'. British Treasury officials recognized the proposal would 'stick in the gullet of the India Office', and mobilized the Chancellor to apply pressure.[17] Receiving a flurry of enquiries about the India Office's progress with the Reserve Bank plan, Kisch took to circulating a scrapbook of adverse press comments about it.[18]

In the event, matters turned out rather well for the India Office. While unable to maintain its earlier attitude of complete opposition to the creation of a new central bank, the Office proved to be excellent at dragging its feet. What is more, recognizing that Indian business and political opinion sought to forge close links between the government and the proposed bank, the India Office made a complete about-turn and began championing 'independence' as a 'universally accepted central banking principle'. The harder Indian politicians pressed for government presence, the firmer the India Office insisted that only an 'independent central bank' could eliminate government and political intervention in 'affairs of currency and credit' whose 'risks have been abundantly proved by past experience'. Kisch recanted his earlier views by writing a book on central banks (Kisch and Elkin, 1932: 20–36). Arguing that no legislation was preferable to an 'unsound' one, the India Office managed to defeat all efforts at negotiation both in India as well as between Delhi and London.[19]

The India Office spotted its opportunity to derail plans for the new central bank in September 1927 when, in the course of informal discussions on the central bank bill, Blackett gestured toward a role for the legislature in the constitution of the new bank's board. Demanding that the Viceroy restrain Blackett, the India Office began mobilizing the City which it claimed received his ideas with 'mingled consternation and ridicule'. Blackett had 'smirched his financial reputation very badly'; he was a 'laughing stock' in the City and his judgement was in serious doubt. Norman agreed that Blackett's plan 'departed seriously' from the Commission's proposals, and the Secretary of State decided to place the

[17] Hilton-Young to Niemeyer and reply, 19/20 October 1926, T176/25B, UKNA; Treasury to India Office and reply, 21/22 October 1926, L/PO/2/3(i), OIOC.

[18] Note, 22 October 1926; Kisch to Carter, 20 October 1926, L/PO/2/3(i), OIOC.

[19] Memorandum on the Reserve Bank Bill, undated, L/PO/2/7(i), OIOC; Secretary of State to Viceroy and reply, 7 and 10 September 1927, L/F/7/2292, Colln 375, F. 19, OIOC.

bill in 'cold storage' until Blackett's departure from India, saying he was 'too hopelessly *brute*'. According to Kisch, Blackett's wish for a 'Bank Bill in my time at all costs' had gone too far. Still, even if the final bill had been to its complete satisfaction, the India Office had other plans to delay or abort the plan.[20]

What of the Bank of England? By 1928 Norman's enthusiasm for an Indian central bank began to wane, as he grew concerned about the 'dangers' that even the Reserve Bank's independence might hold for the London market. Writing to Osborne Smith, who was expected to take over as the first head of the new institution, he underlined the need for a 'close understanding and working arrangement' between the two central banks, similar to existing relations with the Imperial Bank of India.[21] According to Siepmann, the operational part of the deal would be an 'understanding' with the future Reserve Bank governor involving:

no agreement, no document, nothing that could be quoted or enquired into but complete freedom in form ... [for the Governor] to do as he likes with his money and simply a voluntary arrangement by which he tells us of his actions and intentions, and we tell him whether or not they would suit our book.[22]

Norman opposed a role for the government in the Reserve Bank of India because it would have come in the way of such clubby arrangements. Nor could he have accepted a role for the legislature and thus run the risk of the Bank's reserve and investment practices becoming matters of public debate. Norman's reaction to Blackett's ideas was hence one of 'consternation' that a bank holding 'an almost predominant position in the London Money Market ... should be in the hands of a directorate so constituted.'[23]

Thus, given Britain's dire external prospects, the bitterness surrounding money and exchange in the colony, and growing dominion distrust of sterling, the Bank of England could not risk weakening London's control over India's monetary affairs. If creating a potentially troublesome institution in such an important country were the only alternative, then the establishment

---

[20] India Office telegram, 14 September 1927; Birkenhead to Reading, 19 September 1927, Mss. Eur. D703/27, OIOC, italics in original; Kisch to Kershaw, 2 February 1928; Kershaw's note, 25 October 1927; Secretary of State to Viceroy, 27 October 1927, L/PO/2/7/ (i), OIOC; Secretary of State to Viceroy, 22 September 1927, L/PO/2/7(ii), OIOC; Norman to Strakosch, 26 September 1927, OV 56/1, BOEA; Norman's diary, 4 November 1927, ADM 20/16, BoE; Kisch to Norman, 13 February 1928, G1/312, BOEA.

[21] Norman to Birkenhead, 24 February; Norman to Smith, 9 March; reply, 22 April 1927, G1/312, BOEA.

[22] Siepmann to Blackett, 4 February 1927, Mss. Eur. E397/31, OIOC.

[23] Hirtzel's note, 16 September 1927, L/PO/2/7(ii), OIOC; Viceroy to Secretary of State 9 and 14 September 1927, Mss. Eur. D703/27, OIOC.

of a new central bank would have to wait. Meanwhile, it would be politics as usual. For all its failures, the India Office would be a more reliable intermediary for the Bank of England than a central bank acceptable to Indian public opinion and would thus have to remain in control.

14.5 THE RESERVE BANK AND POLITICAL REFORM

With negotiations over its constitutional future gaining momentum, power-sharing proposals between India's colonial rulers and elected representatives in the colony began taking shape in the early 1930s. Two imperial concerns that London tended to view as intertwined – Indian debts to Britain and the exchange rate – underpinned the British position that Indian representatives would not be allowed to exercise much control over financial matters. External borrowing had financed the rupee's rise from 13d. in March 1921 and its stabilization at 18d., five years later (Tables 14.2 and 14.3). Despite relentless Indian opposition to this rate, London insisted – even in the face of a collapse in trade and income during the slump – that a rupee devaluation would trigger a default on Indian debt. Given the incalculable consequences of such a default for British finances, the 18d. rupee became something of a totem for imperial financial and political stability.

Initial proposals envisaged entrusting financial matters to an Indian legislature whose powers would be hedged in by 'safeguards', including a central bank, to protect British financial interests. Whitehall and the Bank of England, however, would have none of it. Treasury officials echoed Norman's view that it was a 'fallacy to suppose that you can give democratic government and guard against its consequences … if finance passes, no Central Bank will be allowed to function … contrary to Indian aspirations'.[24] In the end, therefore, finance became a 'reserved' subject, controlled by a British civil servant as Finance Minister, who owed no responsibility to the legislature, but was accountable to the Viceroy and thereby to London. As for the new Reserve Bank, this would be a private shareholders' bank whose board, in the words of a UK Treasury official, would be 'white and sensible and not black and political.' Its officers would also 'for a long time to come, [be] men other than Indians.'[25]

---

[24] Norman to Schuster, 3 September 1930, G1/411, BOEA; 'Indian Constitutional Programme: Some Financial Aspects', 12 September 1930, T160/F.12471/05/2, UKNA.

[25] Waley's minute, 3 April 1933; T175/45, Hopkins's note, 29 October 1932, T177/16, UKNA.

In a move probably without historical parallel, the 18d. exchange rate was enshrined in the Reserve Bank of India Act, thus obliging the central bank to defend the rate and ensuring, ironically enough, that it could not be changed without a legislative amendment. Norman may have wanted the Reserve Bank to be able to stand up to a government dominated by Indians, but not to the Bank of England. Hence, he sought close relations or, as he now alluded, a '*Hindoo* marriage' between the two banks. In practice this was to mean 'general cooperation' with the Bank of England in 'matters affecting the ... management of sterling', with the Bank refraining from independent investment decisions.[26]

Norman was also keen for his new bride not to be seen in public. He opposed the opening of a Reserve Bank branch office in London, which he feared would be the 'thin end of the wedge' for weakening his bank's influence over the new central bank, particularly when it came to reserve investment decisions. Successive finance ministers were instructed to kill the idea.[27] The India Office also joined the campaign against a London office, which it claimed was contrary to the 'guiding principles established by experience'.[28] When the legislature insisted on a clause requiring the Bank to open an office in London, Norman deprecated it as likely to have adverse 'effects on the London market', and focused on ensuring it would not become 'a source of trouble' and that the functions of the London office were 'as unimportant as possible'.[29]

14.6 EPILOGUE

The Reserve Bank of India opened its doors to business on 1 April 1935. Its first governor was Osborne Smith, the Imperial Bank's managing governor, whom Norman had been grooming for this role since 1926. With the Bank holding no immediate value in the new constitutional

---

[26] Notes of meeting with Indian representatives to the Round Table Conference, July 1931; Norman to Strakosch, 7 July 1931, G1/310, BOEA; 'General Principles upon which Relations between the Bank of England and the Reserve Bank of India will be based', 3 October 1934, G1/314, BOEA.

[27] Norman to Kisch, 20 February 1934, G1/314; Norman's note, 30 November 1935, OV 56/47, BOEA; Grigg to Norman, 17 January 1934, G1/316, BOEA; Harvey's 'very secret' note, 6 March 1934, G1/313, BOEA.

[28] Report of the India Office 'Committee on Indian Reserve Bank legislation', 14 March 1933 and subsequent correspondence, notes and memoranda, March–May 1933, F. no. 7 (52)-F-1933, FD/NAI.

[29] Norman to Kisch, and reply, 20/26 February 1934, G1/314; 'Reserve Bank of India', 16 September 1935, C40/177, BOEA.

scheme and 'finance' now being a 'reserved' subject, efforts began to cut the new institution to size. Within a year, the India Office's top civil servant was complaining that the Reserve Bank of India Act gave too much power to the governor and not enough to the colonial government, to which he should play 'second fiddle'.[30] Similar concerns were voiced after the first elections to the Bank's central board, which gave seats to Bombay industrialists and others with a reputation for supporting independence from the government. The time had come to put the new institution in its place.

India's new finance minister, P. J. Grigg (1934–9), took to this task with relish. From London's standpoint in 1934, no one was more suited to this position than Grigg. Impending constitutional changes made it 'more important than ever' for Norman that the job should go to someone whose 'vertebrae' were not 'loose'.[31] Impenitently orthodox, and convinced – much like Norman – that sterling's departure from gold in September 1931 had marked the end of civilization, Grigg was a fervent imperialist in the mould of Winston Churchill, one of four British finance ministers he had served as private secretary. Redundant in London after September 1931, Grigg proved of enormous value in India where he channelled his deep feelings of 'exile' into virulent opposition to constitutional changes. Tellingly, 'ratio and protection' (that is, the exchange rate and tariffs) were his main tests for determining someone's political beliefs – whether they were pro-British or anti-British.[32]

Grigg was angered by the results of the first elections to the Reserve Bank's central board, which were different from what 'its promoters intended' and had let the board be 'dominated' by businessmen he believed were sympathetic to the Congress party and 'contributed largely to its funds' (Grigg, 1947: 290). Grigg believed independence was the 'Ark of the Covenant' of central banking and would later accuse 'governments of the Left' of converting the Bank of England into a branch of the Treasury (Boyle, 1967: 206). However, such views neither restrained Grigg's distrust of the Reserve Bank nor his confrontation with Osborne Smith, which ended with the latter's unceremonious removal from office.[33]

---

[30] Stewart to Grigg, 25 January 1936, Grigg Papers 2/3, CCA.

[31] Hoare to Niemeyer, 21 November 1933, G2/10; 'Finance Member', 23 October 1933, G1/411, BOEA.

[32] Grigg 1947; Grigg's letters to: Stewart, 23 July 1934, 2/20; Chamberlain, 17 August 1934 and 30 March 1936, 2/2; Floud, 22 February 1936, 2/7; his father, 6 July 1937, 2/9, Grigg Papers, CCA; Grigg to Snowden, 11 October 1929, T160, 426/F.11548, UKNA.

[33] Smith to Grigg and reply, 13/20 May; note, 16 May 1936, 3/4, Grigg Papers, CCA.

Monetary policy was a major source of disagreement, though ironically Grigg overruled the Reserve Bank's desire to lower interest rates, causing Smith to complain that he was 'sick to death' of Grigg trying to convert the central bank into a government department.[34] Grigg doubted Smith's commitment to the 18d. rate, and as their relations frayed, began to suspect that he was in league with 'devaluationists and currency speculators'. Hence, in an act with few known parallels in central banking history, he demanded and obtained intelligence intercepts of Smith's telephone calls and letters, as well as letters of his alleged mistress.[35] After finding nothing damaging to Smith, Grigg provoked a violent quarrel and threatened his own resignation if Smith was not removed. In the end, a reluctant Norman persuaded Smith to resign in return for generous retirement benefits and honours. Norman also made sure Smith was not succeeded by either of his Indian deputies.[36]

Relations between the Reserve Bank and the government touched another low in November 1938, when the Bank's central board overruled the new governor, a British-Indian civil servant named James Taylor, and recommended the rupee's devaluation. In response, the government – with Bank of England support – armed itself with powers to supersede the board and issued directives to the central bank, while leaning on exchange banks to refrain from booking forward transactions. Taylor and Norman discussed the rupee exchange rate in the same breath as the Reserve Bank's gold purchases in Bombay; these were conducted on behalf of the Bank of England, which at the time was attempting to build a war chest without weakening sterling too much. Such gold purchases necessitated dampening devaluation expectations that would have otherwise reduced gold arrivals in Bombay. Thus, as the governor turned against the Bank's central board and took instructions from the government and the Bank of England, a notionally 'independent' central bank had become, three years after its founding, a government department and an agent and subsidiary of the Bank of England.[37]

---

[34] Grigg to Smith, 8 March 1935; 14 November 1935; and reply, 18 November 1935, Grigg Papers, 3/2, CCA; Smith to Purshottamdas Thakurdas, 27 June, 21 July, 10 August and 10 September 1936, Box 105, Purshotamdas Thakurdas Papers, Nehru Memorial Museum and Library (NMML), New Delhi.

[35] Kershaw to Norman, 6 February 1934, G1/316, BOEA; Grigg to Stewart, 14 May 1934, Mss. Eur. D714/31, OIOC; the intercepted mail and Grigg's unfounded charges are in 3/10, Grigg Papers, CCA.

[36] Secretary of State to Viceroy, 20 August 1936, 3/5, Grigg Papers, CCA; for papers dealing with the resignation, see 3/2, 3/3, 3/4 and 3/10, Grigg Papers, CCA, and L/PO/3/2(i), OIOC.

[37] Taylor to Norman and reply, 15/22 November 1938; Norman to Baxter, 25 November 1938, G1/318, BoE; 'India Confidential', 31 May 1938, OV 56/3, BOEA.

14.7 CONCLUSION

The prehistory and early history of the Reserve Bank of India underline the importance of studying central banks as political projects rather than, or merely as, institutions to be examined through the lens of economic or monetary history. As a political project emblematic of metropolitan efforts to maintain colonial forms of control beyond direct colonial rule, the Reserve Bank of India belongs to the larger history of late colonialism, rather than just the history of central banking. In general, too, central banks may be of greater historical interest, or of historical interest for different reasons, than we might suppose.

The proliferation of central banks in the 1920s can be traced back to efforts to 'depoliticize' monetary policy in the wake of expanding democracy in Europe. Their story unfolded somewhat differently with settler colonial interests in the British dominions (cf. Chapter 13 in this volume). As the history of the US Federal Reserve underscores (Lowenstein, 2015), depoliticizing monetary policy was an intensely political and contested affair. While the story of the Reserve Bank bears out its political gestation and birth, it is equally worth noting that Indians had no say in its constitution. Nor could they hold its highest office until the political cataclysm unleashed by the Second World War forced a reconsideration of racial staffing polices for some colonial offices.

The Reserve Bank was so largely under the shadow of other institutions because of the political intrigues surrounding its birth and early functioning, that it was something of a make-believe central bank for its first two decades. There was no doubt who was the dependent spouse in its 'marriage' to the Bank of England. In addition to closer superintendence following the exit of its first governor and his replacement by a career civil servant, wartime exigencies deepened the government's shadow over the Bank. A third shadow was the Imperial Bank of India, which – until the 1950s – exercised much greater influence on lending rates than the Reserve Bank. Ironically, it was not until the 1950s, when the onset of planning prompted the Bank to repurpose itself for the monetary challenges of mobilizing investment resources for India's five-year plans, that India's central bank began to emerge as an organic part of the country's financial system (Balachandran, 1998). Thus, tempting as it may be to fit the Reserve Bank of India into the mould of other central bank histories, its late-colonial role and (in)significance can serve as a useful vantage point for (re-)considering central banking in a broader historical frame.

REFERENCES

Unpublished (archival) Sources

Archive of the Centre of South Asian Studies (CSAS), Cambridge (United Kingdom).
Papers of Sir Edward Charles Benthall
Bank of England Archive (BOEA), Bank of England, London (United Kingdom).
ADM Administration Department records
G1 Governor's Files, 1922–1967
G14 Committee of Treasury Files, 1919–1967
G30 Governor's Miscellaneous Correspondence
OV56 India – Country file
Churchill Archives Centre (CCA), Churchill College, Cambridge (United Kingdom)
Papers of Sir Percy James Grigg
Papers of Sir Ralph Hawtrey
National Archives (UKNA), Kew, Richmond (United Kingdom).
T Treasury
National Archives of India (NAI), New Delhi (India).
FD Finance Department
Nehru Memorial Museum and Library (NMML), New Delhi (India).
Papers of Purshotamdas Thakurdas
Oriental and India Office Collection (OIOC), British Library, London (United Kingdom).
L/F Finance Department
L/PO Private Office
Mss. Eur. European Manuscripts

Published Sources

Balachandran, G. (1993). 'Britain's Liquidity Crisis and India, 1919–1920'. *Economic History Review*, 46(3): 575–591.
Balachandran, G. (1998). *The Reserve Bank of India, 1951–1969*. Delhi: Oxford University Press.
Balachandran, G. (2013). *John Bullion's Empire: Britain's Gold Problem and India between the Wars*. London: Routledge.
Boyle, Andrew (1967). *Montagu Norman: A Biography*. New York: Weybright and Talley.
Bridge, Carl (1986). *Holding India to the Empire: The British Conservative Party and the 1935 Constitution*. New Delhi: Sterling Publishers.
Chandavarkar, Anand (1989). *Keynes and India: A study in Economics and Biography*. London: Macmillan.
Chaudhuri, K. N. (1983). 'Foreign Trade and Balance of Payments (1757–1947)', in Kumar, Dharma and Desai, Meghnad (eds.), *The Cambridge Economic History of India. Vol. 2, c. 1757–1970*. Cambridge: Cambridge University Press, 804–877.

Goldsmith, Raymond (1983). *The Financial Development of India, 1860–1977.* Delhi: Oxford University Press.

Grigg, Percy James (1947). *Prejudice and Judgement.* London: Jonathan Cape.

Heston, Alan (1983). 'National Income', in Kumar, Dharma and Desai, Meghnad (eds.), *The Cambridge Economic History of India. Vol. 2, c. 1757–1970.* Cambridge: Cambridge University Press, 376–462.

Keynes, John Maynard (1971). *Indian Currency and Finance,* Vol. 1 in Johnson, Elizabeth and Moggridge, Donald (eds.), *The Collected Writings of John Maynard Keynes.* Cambridge: Cambridge University Press.

Kisch, Cecil H. and Elkin, Winifred A. (1932). *Central Banks: A Study of the Constitutions of Banks of Issue (with an analysis of representative charters).* London: Macmillan.

Lowenstein, Roger (2015). *America's Bank: The Epic Struggle to Create the Federal Reserve.* New York: Penguin.

Maddison, Angus (1971). *Class Structure and Economic Growth: India and Pakistan since the Moghuls.* London: George Allen & Unwin.

Siddiqi, Asiya (1981). 'Money and Prices in the Earlier Stages of Empire: India and Britain 1760–1840'. *Indian Economic and Social History Review,* 18(3–4): 231–262.

Index